The Economic Potential of Islamic Countries, Part A

EMERALD STUDIES IN ISLAMIC ECONOMY AND FINANCE

Series Editors:

Muhammad Ismail
Iqra National University, Pakistan

Ahmet Faruk Aysan
Hamad Bin Khalifa University, College of Islamic Studies, Qatar

Forthcoming titles:

The Economic Potential of Islamic Countries Part B: Sustainability, Governance, Energy & Digital Transformation *Edited by Vusal Gasimli*

Modern Trends in Islamic Economy: Philanthropy, Finance and Marketing Innovations *Edited by Baker Ahmad Abdullah Alserhan and Torniker Khoshtaria*

Innovative Case Studies in Islamic Finance and Ethical Entrepreneurship *Edited by Omer Rafique*

Islamic Finance, Sustainability and Innovation: Shaping the Future *Edited by Ahmet Faruk Aysan, Syed Nazim Ali, Abdurahman Jemal Yesuf and Muhammad Fazlurrahman Syarif*

Human Capital and the Economics of Talent in Islamic Finance: Theory, Ethics and Practice *Edited by Muhammad Bilal Zafar, Hussain Mohi and Hassinan Ali*

The Economic Potential of Islamic Countries, Part A: Economics, Demographics and Financial Services

EDITED BY

VUSAL GASIMLI

Center for Analysis of Economic Reforms and Communication of the Republic of Azerbaijan, Azerbaijan

emerald PUBLISHING

United Kingdom – North America – Japan – India – Malaysia – China

Emerald Publishing Limited
Emerald Publishing, Floor 5, Northspring, 21-23 Wellington Street, Leeds LS1 4DL.

First edition 2026

British Library Cataloguing in Publication Data
A catalogue record for this book is available from the British Library

ISBN: 978-1-83708-001-4 (Print)
ISBN: 978-1-83708-000-7 (Online)
ISBN: 978-1-83708-002-1 (Epub)

Printed and bound by CPI Group (UK) Ltd, Croydon, CR0 4YY

INVESTOR IN PEOPLE

This book is dedicated to the tireless pursuit of progress and prosperity within the Islamic countries. It is a testament to the collective efforts of individuals, organizations, and nations committed to enhancing economic development, fostering cooperation, and empowering communities across the Islamic world.

To the visionaries and leaders who have championed economic growth and innovation within the Islamic world, your unwavering dedication inspires us all.

To the researchers, economists, and policymakers whose insights and expertise have shaped the discourse on Islamic economics and finance, your contributions are invaluable.

To the countless individuals and communities whose resilience and ingenuity fuel the engine of progress, this book is a tribute to your strength and spirit.

And to my colleagues whose support and encouragement have sustained me throughout this endeavor, I offer my deepest gratitude. Your belief in the importance of this work has been a constant source of motivation and inspiration.

May this book serve as a beacon of knowledge and understanding, illuminating the path toward a more prosperous and equitable future for all within the Islamic world and beyond.

With heartfelt appreciation,
Vusal Gasimli
Executive Director
Center for Analysis of Economic Reforms
and Communication of the Republic of Azerbaijan

Contents

List of Figures and Tables

Figures

Tables

Appendix

About the Editor

Prof. Dr. Vusal Gasimli heads the Center for Analysis of Economic Reforms and Communication of Azerbaijan, the Government's Delivery Unit. As a member of the Government Commission on Business Environment, he helped position Azerbaijan as a top reformer in the Doing Business rankings. He completed executive education at Harvard Kennedy School and holds a Master's-level degree from the University of Oxford. Prof. Gasimli engages in global policy forums, including the G20's T20, and consults for the ADB, EU, WB, and JICA.

About the Contributors

Hüseyin Akkaya graduated from Istanbul University, Faculty of Economics, Department of Finance in 2013. In 2015, he completed his master's degree at Sivas Cumhuriyet University, SBE, Department of Finance and in 2023, he completed his doctorate degree at Bursa Uludağ University, SBE, Department of Financial Law. Since January 4, 2016, he has been working as a Lecturer at Tokat Gaziosmanpaşa University, Artova Vocational School of Finance, Banking and Insurance, Department Finance Program. Between October 20, 2022, and May 20, 2023, he worked as a Guest Lecturer at Kyrgyzstan University of Economics and Entrepreneurship with temporary assignment. He has studies on finance and tax law. He also has a book titled *Model Proposal for Turkey in Combating Financial Crimes* (ORCID: 0000-0002-9886-6552).

Alshaymaa Alsadek holds master's degree of Planning and Economic Development, from the National Institute of Planning, Egypt. And now she works as a Developmental Planning Expert in Climate Change Risk Studies Unit of IDSC, the Egyptian Cabinet. She was a former Planning, Monitoring and Evaluation (P,M&E) Senior Researcher in the Ministry of Environmental Affairs for eight years. She was also a member of the editorial board of *Climate Policies* journal, and was responsible for editing the study of "Sea Level Rise Impact on The Food Security in Egypt." She participated in writing and editing several policy papers and reports such as, "The Productivity of Albrulus Lake," "International Experiences and Lessons Learnt for State Ownership Policy Document," "Monitoring Egypt's Score in The Indicator of Climate Change Performance 2020," "The 5 Years Achievements of Egypt, Indicators, Recommendations, Messages," "Establishment of a Monitoring and Evaluation Center Specialized in Assessing the Impact of Government Policies," "The Status of the Egyptian Lakes and Fisheries," and "the Renewable Energy in Egypt – Challenges and Opportunities."

Mehmet Fatih Aslantaş was born in 1983. He completed his doctorate in public finance at Bursa Uludağ University. He is currently working as an Assistant Professor at Kafkas University. He researches on budget and financial planning, economic crises, local governments, public expenditures, taxation. The author has many studies in these fields. He also lectures on public finance and local governments (ORCID: 0000-0002-5987-2976).

Tsegaye Assayew is an economist and development practitioner with over a decade of experience in public debt management, fiscal risk analysis, financial sector development, and operations management and strategies. His work spans multilateral institutions—including the World Bank and the African Development Bank—as well as national governments and private sector actors. He has delivered hands-on technical assistance across diverse settings, from fragile states like South Sudan and small island economies in the Pacific to large emerging markets such as Bangladesh and South Africa.

Dr. Assayew holds a PhD in Economics, Applied Mathematics, and Operations Research from the University of Bergamo, and was a research scholar at Washington University in St. Louis. His research sits at the intersection of firm-level productivity and macroeconomic stability, with a focus on twin deficits, the finance–growth nexus, fiscal risks, corporate financial fragility, and development operations. He works fluently in English and Amharic, with basic proficiency in French and Italian, and brings global expertise to both research and policy engagements.

Ahmet Faruk Aysan is a Professor at HBKU and the Associate Dean for Research. He has been the Board Member and Monetary Policy Committee Member of the Central Bank of the Republic of Turkey and has served as a consultant at various institutions such as the World Bank, the Central Bank of the Republic of Turkiye, and Oxford Analytica. He, who has many articles published in academic journals, is a recipient of the Bogaziçi University Awards and the MEEA Ibn Khaldun Prize. He is also a Research Associate at the University College London Centre for Blockchain Technologies and Non-Resident Fellow Middle East Council on Global Affairs.

Kenan Bağcı is a Research Assistant Professor at Qatar University. He received his MSc degree in Economics and Finance in Germany and his PhD in Economic and Finance in Switzerland. He has published in scholarly journals and magazines and contributed to numerous books, reports, and strategic documents across various fields of socio-economic development. Having worked at Statistical, Economic and Social Research and Training Centre for Islamic Countries for more than a decade, he led and contributed to numerous research studies and projects owned by various international organizations. His main areas of interest include international trade and trade policies, regional integration, industrial development, private sector development, labor markets, and digital transformation.

Esat Bakımlı is an Economist, received his PhD in Economics from Muğla Sıtkı Koçman University in 2011 on top of MA and BA in Economics. Primarily engaged in socio-economic development studies, he currently works as Senior Researcher at the Statistical, Economic and Social Research and Training Centre for Islamic Countries (SESRIC), a subsidiary organ of the Organization of Islamic Cooperation. Before joining SESRIC, he worked as Statistics Expert, in the field of economic statistics, at the General Authority for Statistics, Saudi

Arabia, between 2012 and 2020. With about two decades of experience in data analysis and research, he has several articles in refereed journals in addition to some other publications including reports, book chapters, and working papers.

Ouiam Chafik is a Strategic Foresight Officer at the Center of Foresight and AI (CFAI) of The Islamic World Educational, Scientific and Cultural Organization (ICESCO), where she leads research and strategic initiatives focused on integrating foresight and artificial intelligence into decision-making processes. She is a PhD candidate in Public Law and International Relations, with her research centered on "Foresight-driven Decision-making in a Thriving Artificial Intelligence Global Landscape." She has played a key role in developing the Islamic World Artificial Intelligence Charter and coordinating high-level international workshops across ICESCO's member states. Her portfolio includes extensive work on foresight studies, scenario planning, horizon scanning, and strategic analysis, as well as authoring and co-authoring numerous publications of the CFAI. Beyond this, she has played a leading role in planning and organizing strategic foresight training programs for decision-makers, promoting future literacy and anticipatory governance within ICESCO member states. She has represented the CFAI and ICESCO at international forums, workshops, and conferences, amplifying the voice of the Islamic world in global discussions on AI, youth empowerment, and sustainable development.

Gehad Omar Elkhateeb is a Political Researcher of Climate Change Risk Studies Department at the Egyptian Cabinet Information and Decision Support Center (IDSC) and Former Political Researcher in Al-Ahram Center for Political & Strategic Studies. She is editorial board member of *Climate Policies* journal published by IDSC. She was editorial board member of *Strategic Perspectives* and *Future Perspectives* journals. She was a member of the team that prepared the Egyptian government's report of political governance (2018–2019) presented to African Peer Review Mechanism. She was also a member of "Irregular Immigration Project"; Joint Research Project between Al-Ahram Center and Embassy of Denmark in Cairo. She was a member of "The Main Factors of Religious Radicalization and Violence" Joint Study between Al-Ahram Center in cooperation with Taba Foundation in UAE. She graduated from Cairo University, Faculty of Economics and Political Science. Now, she is a master's Researcher in Political Science. She wrote many articles and methodological papers specialized in international relations and traditional and non-traditional security threats as well.

Mohammad Omar Farooq is a Professor, Department of Economics at United International University, Bangladesh. He earned PhD in Economics from the University of Tennessee, Knoxville, USA and was a Ciriacy-Wantrup Postdoctoral Fellow at the University of California, Berkeley. He taught at a number of US universities for almost 20 years. Then, he taught/served in Bahrain for 15 years, including serving as the Head of Centre for Islamic Finance (Bahrain Institute of Banking and Finance). His primary research interests are economic development, financial institutions, history of economic thought, fintech, and Islamic economics/finance/banking/law/history. He has a keen interest in gender economics and genocide studies and contributed to these areas as well. His works have been published in *Journal of Economic Issues*, *International Journal of Islamic and Middle Eastern Finance and Management*, *International Journal of Social Economics*, *Review of Islamic Economy*, *Arab Law Quarterly*, *History of Economic Ideas*, *International Journal of Ethics and Systems*, *Journal of Islamic and Muslim Studies*, and more. He also serves as an editorial board member of a number of journals. Beyond his academic interests, he has been a prolific contributor to a broad range of Islamic issues through various Islamic media outlets. Inspired by Islam, he consistently writes from a self-critical, common-ground-seeking, bridge-building, and humanity-oriented perspective.

Benuka Ferdousi is a Senior Research Fellow at Bangladesh Institute of International and Strategic Studies. She has more than 15 years of academic and policy research experience in the fields of energy, migration, and related climate change/environment issues. She is particularly interested in renewable energy and its challenges, green energy politics and cooperation, and human security and developmental challenges posed by climate change. International migration and refugee issues are her secondary area of research, where she focuses on issues like vulnerabilities and human rights of migrants, human trafficking, migrant smuggling, feminization of migration, and governance issues. As a researcher with economics background, she has also worked on various economic and developmental issues of Bangladesh. She obtained her PhD from Economics Department of Jahangirnagar University. She obtained her MSS and BSS from Economics Department of University of Dhaka.

Kais Hammami is a leading expert in strategic foresight, scenario planning, and artificial intelligence (AI) governance. He made history as the first Arab to earn a PhD in Foresight, Organization, and Strategy from the Conservatoire National des Arts et Métiers (CNAM) in Paris (2003–2008), where his research received the highest honors. His second thesis explored foresight in Arab-Muslim culture, connecting the field to its cultural and philosophical dimensions. With 20 years of experience across Africa, Europe, Asia, and Latin America, he has expertise in strategic planning, strategic foresight, AI strategy and governance, change management, and more. He held the UNESCO Chair in Foresight, Anticipation, and Strategic Decision, focusing on advancing foresight knowledge in Africa and the Arab world. He has led over 250 international studies, providing strategic insights for national planning and development, including Tunisia's National Strategy by 2025 and Decentralization by 2039. He has been a member of editorial boards and scientific committees, including the Lipsor Papers at CNAM. He has taught foresight and strategic decision-making at esteemed institutions, such as the Sorbonne and Carthage University, and organized global events like the Future Forum and PISA Conference. His leadership at The Islamic World Educational, Scientific and Cultural Organization (ICESCO) led to impactful studies on the future of the Islamic World, African demographics, and future job skills.

Hammami has also facilitated training for over 6,000 participants globally, promoting foresight and strategic thinking.

Vusala Jafarova is the Head of Turkic World Research Center at the Center for Analysis of Economic Reforms and Communication of Azerbaijan Republic. She is IMF-certified professional on macroeconometric analysis and forecasting skilled in applied macroeconometrics, forecasting and analysis with International Monetary Fund (IMF) models, and monetary and fiscal analysis. She was appointed by Azerbaijan Government as Director's Advisor at the Board of Directors of Asian Development Bank in Manila Philippines during 2005–2008 after her service as Advisor at International Economic Coop Department at the Ministry of Economy working with International Financial Institutions on financing of infrastructure projects in Azerbaijan and drafting Country Partnership Strategies. She also worked at the International Economic Cooperation Department of the Foreign Ministry of Azerbaijan. Before that, she studied Business Administration at Manchester University and worked as Manager in energy division at Minale Tattersfield Co, in London, UK, and later as Head of Moscow office on CIS markets. She has publications on equilibrium real exchange rate, internal and external balances, trade liberalization, investment multiplier, and other model-based regression analysis. She holds MBA degree from Ateneo de-Manila University (2008), PhD in Econometrics from Economic Research Institute of Azerbaijan (2023), Energy Studies from Baku Energy School from ADA University of Azerbaijan (2023). and Executive Education on Public Finance Management from Harvard University (2009) (ORCID: 0000-0002-4711-4609).

Shabeer Khan is an accomplished academic currently serving as an Assistant Professor at the College of Business Administration, Al-Yamamah University, Saudi Arabia. Prior to this, he held the position of Assistant Professor and Head of International Relations at the Department of Islamic Economics and Finance, Sakarya University, Turkey, and also served as an Assistant Professor at the Department of Business Administration at Sukkur IBA University, Pakistan. He began his career as a Lecturer at Kohat University, Pakistan, and subsequently gained valuable research experience as a Research Assistant at INCEIF University, Malaysia. His impressive academic journey includes attaining a PhD in Islamic Finance from INCEIF, Malaysia, as well as a master's degree in Economics, a Postgraduate degree in Shariah (Islamic Jurisprudence), and an MS degree in Social Science from Pakistan. He is highly regarded in the field of Islamic finance and economics and contributes actively to the industry. He serves as a Shariah board member for Tayyib Advisory, UAE, and is a sought-after Shariah consultant for KalPay Financial Services, Pakistan, and Muawin, Pakistan. Additionally, he plays a pivotal role as a trainer and consultant with ifintel, Malaysia, where he imparts expertise in advanced econometric models, data analytics, and Islamic banking and finance. His dedication to research is evident through his publications in esteemed journals and his participation in national and international conferences. His research areas span Islamic banking, Islamic capital markets, Islamic social finance, and the informal economy, showcasing his commitment to advancing knowledge and innovation in these domains.

Youssef Lazaare has a multidisciplinary academic background encompassing linguistics, communication and media studies, social sciences, and international relations, earned through a bachelor's degree and two master's degrees, He has consistently placed academic research at the forefront of his professional journey. During his tenure at ICESCO's Center for Foresight and Artificial Intelligence, he has played a pivotal role in contributing to the Center's research initiatives and strategic projects. His efforts have supported the advancement of foresight methodologies, the exploration of emerging global trends, and the development of forward-thinking insights.

Hager Mahmoud Sayed is an Economic Researcher at Information and Decision Support Center of the Egyptian Cabinet, she serves as Young Climate Negotiator as a member of National Advisory Committee on Climate change. She has a Political Economy master's degree from Cairo University. She served as a member of COP27 Youth Taskforce, and was selected as a 2023 Max Thabiso Edkins Climate Ambassador under auspices of World Bank to represent Egypt. Further, she was a co-author in prize-winning research titled "The Effect of Climate Change on International Migration Movement" at IOM Research Competition; her research had been selected to be published by the Egyptian Scientific Institute within COP'27 special edition publication.

Muhammad Fazlurrahman Syarif is a PhD student in Islamic Finance and Economy at Hamad Bin Khalifa University (HBKU), receiving a full Qatar Foundation scholarship. He has won and received grants from multiple start-up competitions in Qatar and, including those organized by HBKU Innovation Center, the Digital Incubation Center, the Ministry of Communication and Information Technology-Qatar, Qatar University, and Qatar Development Bank. His start-up has been incubated by the prestigious Qatar Science & Technology Park, Member of Qatar Foundation. His research interests include fintech, sentiment analysis, social media credit scoring, chatbots, crowdfunding, Central Bank Digital Currency (CBDCs), blockchain, halal economy, sukuk, and e-learning. He began his career in Islamic Banking and Finance after completing his MBA in Islamic Banking and Finance at the Bangor University and attending Durham Islamic Finance Summer School at the Durham University in the United Kingdom.

Mehmet Yüce was born in Ağrı in 1973 and moved to Bursa in 1987 to study in university. After graduating from Uludağ University Finance Department in 1991, he started his master's degree in Uludağ University, Institute of Social Sciences, Department of Finance in the same year and was appointed as a Research Assistant in 1994. In 2001, he was assigned to Kyrgyzstan University of Economics and Entrepreneurship, Faculty of Business of the Turkish World. He was deemed worthy of many awards by the Kyrgyz State for his services in Kyrgyzstan.

After receiving the title of Associate Professor in 2005, he returned to Turkey in 2006. He became the Head of the Financial Law Department in 2008 and became a Professor in 2010. He served as the Dean of Uludağ University Faculty of Economics and Administrative Sciences, Dean of the Faculty of Law, and Vice-Rector. He served as the Dean of the Faculty of Turkic World Economics at the Azerbaijan University of Economics. In addition to his academic duties, he has been a Project Researcher at Center for Economic and Social Research (CETA), a think tank in Turkiye and a columnist for different newspapers in Turkey and Azerbaijan (Sabah Perspective). Currently, he is the Vice President of the Türkiye Environment Agency. He has 25 books and numerous articles on tax law, finance, Islamic economics, and the Turkic world (ORCID: 0000-0001-6398-5589).

Preface

This book is a dedicated exploration of the diverse opportunities and challenges inherent in the economies of more than 50 Islamic nations, spanning four continents and representing a quarter of the world's population and land surface. In an era marked by globalization and interconnectedness, the economic potential of the Islamic countries is a significant force in shaping the future of global prosperity. Prepared within the framework of the declaration of Shusha as the "Cultural Capital of the Islamic World" for 2024, this book reflects the collaborative efforts initiated at the 12th Conference of Ministers of Culture of the Islamic World held in Doha. The book was prepared as envisaged in the action plan approved by the Order of the Prime Minister of Azerbaijan for realization of the Declaration.

With the invaluable support and dedication of the Organization of Islamic Cooperation, Statistical, Economic and Social Research and Training Centre for Islamic Countries, Islamic World Educational, Scientific and Cultural Organization (ICESCO), Islamic Development Bank Institute (ISDBI), and other key organizations, this project showcases the concerted efforts to highlight and harness the economic potential of the Islamic world.

Foreword

In the name of Allah, the Most Gracious, the Most Merciful.

It is both a privilege and an honor to present this foreword for the book *The Economic Potential of Islamic Countries, Part A: Economics, Demographics and Financial Services*. This important publication has been prepared as part of the action plan for the declaration of Shusha as the "Cultural Capital of the Islamic World 2024," in alignment with the Presidential Decree of Azerbaijan. Shusha, with its rich historical and cultural significance, is an emblem of unity and cooperation, providing the perfect backdrop for this important initiative.

This book represents a collective effort to explore and highlight the vast economic potential within the Islamic world. Compiled with contributions from over 60 scholars from nearly 20 think tanks and research institutions, it provides a comprehensive analysis of the economic landscapes across the Organization of Islamic Cooperation member states. It aims to identify avenues for enhanced cooperation, mutual prosperity, and sustainable growth.

I would like to especially commend Prof. Dr Vusal Gasimli, the Executive Director of the Center for Analysis of Economic Reforms and Communication, for his dedicated leadership and invaluable contributions to the development of this publication. His efforts, alongside the collaboration of numerous experts and institutions, have ensured that this work will serve as a valuable resource in advancing economic cooperation across our member countries.

In today's interconnected world, economic diplomacy plays a crucial role in fostering stronger relationships between nations. *The Economic Potential of Islamic Countries, Part A: Economics, Demographics and Financial Services* seeks to provide a strategic framework for unlocking new opportunities for trade and collaboration, which is in line with Statistical, Economic and Social Research and Training Centre for Islamic Countries' mission to support the socio-economic development of Organization of Islamic Cooperation member states.

I express my sincere gratitude to all contributors whose research and expertise have made this publication possible.

As this book is presented on international platforms, I trust it will inspire constructive dialogue and cooperation, encouraging policymakers, business leaders, and scholars to work together for the greater economic integration of our nations. It is my hope that the insights and recommendations shared within these pages will help our countries realize their full economic potential.

May this book serve as a guiding light for deeper cooperation and a brighter, more prosperous future for the Islamic world.

H.E. Ms. Zehra Zümrüt Selçuk
Director General
Statistical, Economic and Social Research and
Training Centre for Islamic Countries

Acknowledgments

I would like to thank Vusala Jafarova, Project Coordinator for the book.

Introduction

Vusal Gasimli

Center for Analysis of Economic Reforms and Communication, Republic of Azerbaijan

This book presents a dedicated exploration of the diverse opportunities and challenges inherent in the economies of Islamic countries, spanning four continents and representing approximately a quarter of the world's population and land area. In an era defined by deglobalization, the economic potential of Islamic countries emerges as a significant force shaping the future of global prosperity.

The development of this book coincides with the declaration of Shusha, Azerbaijan's cultural capital, as the "Cultural Capital of the Islamic World" for 2024, which was announced at the 12th Conference of Ministers of Culture of the Islamic World held in Doha, Qatar, on September 25, 2023. The genesis of this work was further solidified through discussions with H. E. Ms. Zehra Zümrüt Selçuk, Director General of SESRIC (Statistical, Economic and Social Research and Training Centre for Islamic Countries), during which we reflected on the concept of ambidexterity – a blending of routine tasks and innovation.

This book was created in collaboration with SESRIC, Islamic World Educational, Scientific and Cultural Organization (ICESCO), the Center for Analysis of Economic Reforms and Communication, and a host of organizations. The support and dedication from these institutions, along with contributions from research institutes in Malaysia, Indonesia, Saudi Arabia, Morocco, Egypt, Pakistan, Turkey, and many other Islamic countries, were crucial in bringing this work to fruition. I am also deeply grateful to the co-authors, whose scholarly input has been indispensable in the development of this book.

Recent economic advancements in Islamic nations reveal a varied landscape of development. According to SESRIC, the average growth rate among Organization of Islamic Cooperation (OIC) countries slowed to 3.3% in 2023, down from 5.5% in 2022 – the highest level recorded since 2011. Nevertheless, it is projected to recover to 3.6% in 2024 and rise further to 4.2% in 2025.The collective gross domestic product (GDP) of OIC member countries gradually rebounded, reaching US$ 8.9 trillion in 2023, which accounts for 8.5% of global GDP. In Purchasing Power Parity (PPP) terms, the growth in GDP per capita within OIC economies – averaging 6.7% in 2023 – slightly above the global mean, signaling

The Economic Potential of Islamic Countries, Part A:
Economics, Demographics and Financial Services, 1–3

doi:10.1108/978-1-83708-000-720251001

a positive trend of economic convergence. The OIC Economic Outlook 2024 further highlights that agricultural activities account for a significant 10.1% of total value added in OIC countries, exceeding the 8.6% share observed in non-OIC developing nations, and a growing services sector are becoming increasingly important in shaping the composition of GDP, contributing an average of 48.5% to total value added. However, this share remains relatively low compared to 76.2% in developed countries and 55.4% in non-OIC developing nations, with the global average standing at 66.6%. In expenditure terms, final consumption remains dominant, with international trade continuing to play a pivotal role in the economies of these nations.

Intra-OIC trade, though growing, has not yet matched the pace of global trade. Additionally, the labor market shows modest improvements, with a slight increase in the employment-to-population ratio reaching the pre-pandemic level by 2023 (52.8%), though it still remains below the global average.

This book delves into the socio-economic potential of Islamic countries, offering valuable insights into the strengths, challenges, and opportunities across diverse nations. By examining various economic and social indicators, such as GDP growth, employment rates, education levels, and infrastructure development, it provides a comprehensive understanding of the region's economic landscape. Such knowledge is instrumental in crafting effective policies and strategies aimed at promoting sustainable economic development.

Understanding these dynamics allows policymakers, investors, and development agencies to identify key areas for intervention and investment. For example, the analysis underscores significant gaps in infrastructure development, presenting an opportunity to prioritize projects that enhance connectivity, productivity, and economic growth. The book also highlights disparities in access to education and healthcare, encouraging targeted interventions to foster human capital development and reduce socio-economic inequalities.

Furthermore, by exploring the unique challenges faced by Islamic countries – such as structural impediments and vulnerabilities to climate change – this work lays the foundation for tailored solutions that take into account the specific contexts of each nation. This personalized approach is crucial for ensuring that development efforts are effective, sustainable, and inclusive.

The book serves as an essential resource for policymakers, researchers, and practitioners dedicated to advancing sustainable economic development in the Islamic world. By offering evidence-based insights and actionable recommendations, it contributes to the formulation of policies and initiatives that promote economic growth, social progress, and environmental sustainability across Islamic countries.

In conclusion, while Islamic nations have shown resilience and progress in various economic domains, the ongoing challenges and disparities highlight the importance of continued policymaking and international collaboration. Strengthening both intra-Islamic cooperation and global partnerships is essential to bridging gaps and unlocking the full potential of these countries on the world stage. This book aims to support Islamic countries in fostering collective action and cooperation to address the challenges of the Anthropocene and the digital revolution through policy coordination, knowledge sharing, resource mobilization, cross-border initiatives, digital inclusion, and global representation. Through these roles, Islamic countries can contribute to a more coordinated and effective response to global challenges, emphasizing the need for collaboration and collective action.

Section 1

Economic and Trade Cooperation

Chapter 1

Economic Cooperation and Integration Among OIC Member Countries

Kenan Bağcı[a] *and Esat Bakımlı*[b]

[a]*Qatar University, Qatar*
[b]*SESRIC, Turkey*

1. Importance of Regional Economic Integration Amidst the Fears of Geoeconomic Fragmentation

Regional economic integration aims to promote economic cooperation and integration among participating countries, ultimately leading to benefits such as increased trade, investment, and economic growth within the region. The attempts to benefit from the economic opportunities of regional integration have a long history, dating back to the late 1950s. The successful example of the European Economic Community (EEC), which later evolved into the European Union, inspired hopes of achieving comparable economic advancement through regional integration. The success of the EEC served as a model for other regions and sparked interest among developing countries seeking to replicate its achievements (Wagner, 1983). These countries recognized the potential benefits of economic integration, including enhanced trade opportunities, industrial development, and economic diversification. Subsequently, many developing countries embarked on their own regional integration initiatives, forming free trade areas, customs unions, and other forms of economic cooperation. Examples include the Association of Southeast Asian Nations, the Southern African Development Community, and the Mercado Común del Sur (Mercosur) in South America.

Regional cooperation or integration is also crucial due to the inherent regional dimensions of phenomena requiring political action, such as migration and trade flows, necessitating regional governance responses; this is reinforced by the ability of regional frameworks to solve collective action problems and prevent races to the bottom in various policy areas like taxes, investment, and environmental protection, resulting in more efficient market processes and positive dynamic

The Economic Potential of Islamic Countries, Part A:
Economics, Demographics and Financial Services, 7–24

doi:10.1108/978-1-83708-000-720251002

effects. Moreover, specific economic theories, such as neo-classical trade theory and optimum currency area theory, elucidate the benefits of regional policies, while the absence of a global regime or the need for increased policy autonomy and negotiation power also justify regional cooperation initiatives. Evaluations of proposals for regional integration underscore the importance of considering both the net benefits and potential costs of non-cooperation across various sectors, emphasizing the spillover effects and multiplier impacts of regional cooperation on broader societal challenges (De Lombaerde, 2023).

In particular, regional trade liberalization has shown significant positive impacts on intra-regional trade worldwide, with a meta-analysis showing an average increase over 50% (Head & Mayer, 2014). Similarly, it is found that European monetary integration has raised trade (+50%) and investment (+30%) in the Eurozone, while fixed exchange rate regimes in Africa and the Caribbean ensure price stability but have uncertain growth effects (De Lombaerde, 2023).

Over the recent period, there has been a notable slowdown and even reversal in some aspects of global economic integration, driven by a combination of factors including economic challenges, geopolitical tensions, and the COVID-19 pandemic. The aftermath of the Global Financial Crisis (GFC) left many economies grappling with slow growth and rising inequality, fuelling skepticism about the benefits of globalization. This sentiment has been further exacerbated by the uneven distribution of gains from globalization, leading to a rise in populism and protectionism in some parts of the world. Events like Brexit and the trade war between the United States and China have highlighted the tensions surrounding globalization, with countries increasingly prioritizing their own interests over global cooperation. The COVID-19 pandemic has further strained international relations, disrupting global supply chains and exacerbating economic disparities. Geopolitical conflicts, such as the war in Ukraine, have added another layer of complexity to the global landscape, deepening divisions and increasing uncertainty about the future direction of globalization.

The term "geoeconomic fragmentation," as coined by Aiyar et al. (2023), aptly captures the phenomenon of a policy-driven reversal of global economic integration, often influenced by strategic considerations. This concept encapsulates the idea that geopolitical tensions and strategic interests are increasingly shaping economic policies, leading to a fragmentation of the global economic landscape. While fragmentation may entail strategic advantages for some countries in certain settings, it is very likely to involve significant economic costs in the aggregate. The fast-growing literature on the economic costs of global fragmentation has generated a wide range of quantitative estimates, reflecting the consideration of different channels as well as different assumed fragmentation scenarios (see, e.g., Bolhuis et al., 2023; IMF, 2022; Javorcik et al., 2022). For example, technological fragmentation can lead to losses in the order of 5% of GDP for many economies (Cerdeiro et al., 2021).

The benefits of globalization, disseminated through various channels, have historically catalyzed income convergence and poverty reduction globally, particularly benefiting low-income consumers and facilitating technological diffusion; however, the adverse consequences of geoeconomic fragmentation, such as trade unraveling, migration restrictions, reduced capital flows, and diminished international cooperation, would disproportionately impact low-income countries, less affluent consumers in advanced economies, hinder financial deepening, deprive host economies of valuable skills, reduce remittances, and jeopardize the provision of vital global public goods (Aiyar et al., 2023).

Against this background, this chapter aims to provide an overview of the progress made by the Organization of Islamic Cooperation (OIC) countries toward enhancing economic cooperation. The OIC, comprising 57 Member States with significant Muslim populations, stands as the second largest intergovernmental organization globally, following the United Nations. Founded with the mission to foster peace, stability, and cooperation among its members, the OIC has evolved to prioritize global development efforts and address the diverse needs of its constituents with a focus on promoting socio-economic development across four continents and impacting over two billion people. In an era of heightened globalization and multifaceted challenges such as security threats, environmental concerns, and economic fluctuations, the importance of multilateral cooperation cannot be overstated. By facilitating intergovernmental dialogue and fostering increased political and economic cooperation, OIC countries are increasingly engaged in seeking common interests and supporting cooperation as a means of overcoming shared obstacles. Expectations among OIC member states include political gains through strengthened partnerships, economic benefits from expanded opportunities and enhanced connectivity, and geopolitical advantages from greater stability and security (SESRIC, 2019).

The rest of this chapter is organized as follows. The next section briefly reviews the relative significance of OIC countries within the global economy, examining their roles and contributions. It then evaluates the dynamics of economic relations among OIC member states, considering factors such as trade, investment, and economic cooperation initiatives. Moving forward, it highlights major policies and initiatives aimed at enhancing economic collaboration within the OIC framework. By analyzing these aspects, the chapter offers insights into the current state of economic cooperation within the OIC and concludes by providing policy recommendations to further strengthen economic cooperation among member states.

2. OIC Countries as an Important Actor in the World Economy

The OIC countries, encompassing diverse economies across different regions, play a crucial role in shaping the global economy. Their collective impact spans various sectors, including energy, finance, trade, and tourism. The economic policies and market activities of OIC countries have a ripple effect on international markets, shaping global trade patterns and investment flows.

Understanding the diversity of OIC economies is vital not only in developing effective policies and strategies that can accommodate the unique needs and challenges of each economy but also in comprehending the broader dynamics of their role in the global economic landscape. The diversity of these economies is evident in their reliance on different sectors, such as oil and gas, agriculture, manufacturing, and services. Additionally, the OIC economies vary greatly in income levels, development stages, and economic structures. Indeed, it is important to note that 19 out of the 57 OIC countries are classified as fuel-exporting countries, 12 as non-fuel primary product exporters, and 21 as heavily indebted poor countries by the International Monetary Fund (IMF, 2024, pp. 119–121), 24 as low-income food-deficit countries by the Food and Agriculture Organization (FAO, n.d), and 21 as least developed countries by the United Nations (UN, n.d), while 8 countries are classified as high-income countries, 34 as middle-income countries, and 15 as low-income countries by the World Bank for the current 2024 fiscal year (World Bank, n.d).

In terms of reserves of crude oil and natural gas alone, the OIC countries possess a significant share of the global resources. As of 2021, it is estimated that the OIC countries collectively hold approximately 66% of the world's proven oil reserves and nearly 60% of the world's proven natural gas reserves. In particular, more than half of the crude oil reserves and more than two-fifths of the natural gas reserves are found in five OIC countries (Fig. 1.1). These huge natural energy resources grant these OIC countries a strong position to utilize significant gains for sustainable growth and development, as well as an array of economic and strategic advantages in trade, industrial competitiveness, and environmental protection (SESRIC, 2023). Overall, having the lion's share of these resources gives them considerable leverage in the global energy market and allows them to influence prices and production levels.

While the OIC countries represent a significant economic force on the world stage with their rich resources, their combined contribution to global GDP remains modest. Their collective GDP has increased more than threefold since the early 2000s, from about US$2 trillion to almost US$9 trillion in 2023. Their share in world GDP, which was around 5–6% at that time, has remained in the 8–9% range in recent years, after peaking at 9.3% in 2013–2014 (Fig. 1.2).

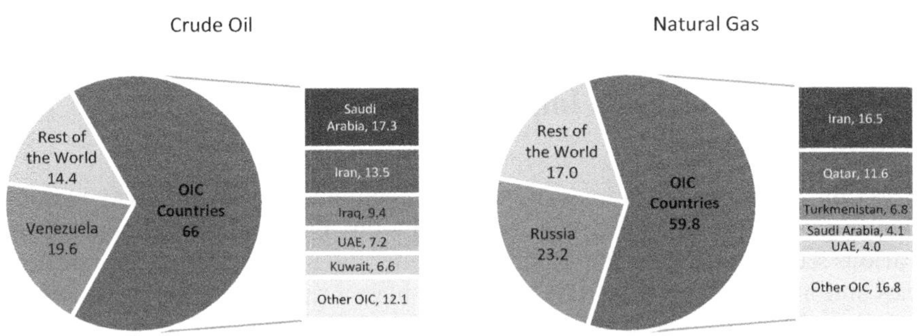

Fig. 1.1. Global Proven Crude Oil and Natural Gas Reserves, 2021 (%). *Source*: Adapted from SESRIC (2023). Prospects and Challenges of OIC Member Countries: SWOT Outlook 2023. Statistical, Economic and Social Research and Training Centre for Islamic Countries. Ankara.

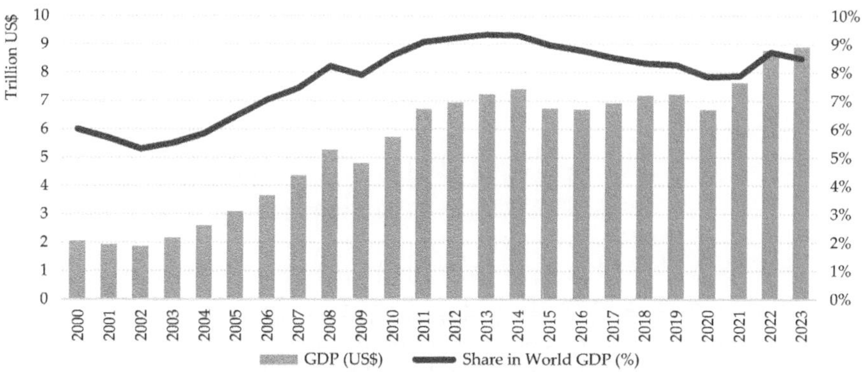

Fig. 1.2. Aggregate GDP of OIC Countries. *Source*: Author's compilation based on data from IMF, World Economic Outlook Database, April 2024, and UNSTATS, National Accounts – Analysis of Main Aggregates (AMA), December 2023.

Considering that the OIC countries account for a quarter of the world population, this indicates untapped potential for further economic growth and development and deeper integration within the block but also reflects the need for diversification beyond resource-rich economies to ensure long-term stability.

Relevant to the seemingly modest share of world GDP, it is worth noting the significant disparity in economic size among the OIC countries. As of 2023, Indonesia, Türkiye, and Saudi Arabia, each with an economy worth over a trillion dollars, are among the world's largest 20 economies, collectively account for about 40% of the OIC GDP, and make significant contributions to the world economy. However, despite the presence of several large economies, the OIC group also encompasses numerous smaller members. Notably, Comoros, Guinea-Bissau, and The Gambia represent the smallest economies within the group, with GDPs ranging between US$1 billion and US$3 billion. This heterogeneity highlights the need to foster economic cooperation and development initiatives within the OIC to ensure inclusive growth and prosperity for all member states.

Concerning international merchandise trade, the OIC countries play a crucial role as both exporters and importers in the global market. Their combined exports surged from approximately US$500 billion in 2000–2002 to a record high of US$3.1 trillion in 2022, followed by a modest projected decline to US$2.7 trillion in 2023. In parallel, their imports increased from around US$400 billion to more than US$2.5 trillion over the same period. It is noteworthy that the OIC countries enjoyed a trade surplus throughout the whole period under consideration, except in 2015–2016 (Fig. 1.3).

The increase in trade values resulted in a greater share of OIC countries in the global market. Their share in world exports rapidly increased from about 8% in the early 2000s to a peak of 13.3% in 2012, and has fluctuated in the range

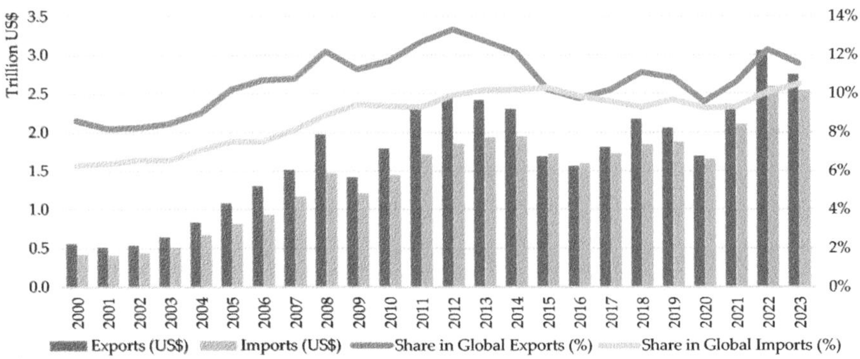

Fig. 1.3. Share of OIC Countries in Global Merchandise Trade.
Source: Author's compilation based on data from WTO STATS Database of World Trade Organization.

of 10–12% since then.[1] Reflecting their dependence on foreign markets to meet domestic consumption and development needs, their share in global imports, which was only above 6% in the early 2000s, exceeded 10% during 2013–2015 and consistently remained over 9% in the following years before rebounding to over 10% in the last two years (Fig. 1.3). Overall, the increasing market share, on the one hand, reflects the OIC countries' increasing integration into global trade networks and their ability to leverage their natural resources. On the other hand, it emphasizes the rising importance of international trade in driving their economic growth.

Beyond traditional trade, foreign direct investment (FDI) is another key driver of economic growth for OIC countries. FDI inflows serve as a vital source of capital, technology, and expertise, and stimulate GDP expansion, job creation, and industrial diversification, thereby fostering sustainable economic development. Nevertheless, it could be argued that the OIC countries' participation in the global FDI landscape remains below potential. The 2000s witnessed a surge in FDI inflows to OIC countries, from a mere US$12 billion in 2000 to US$131 billion in 2008, while the inflows remained at or below this level during the period from the 2009 GFC to the 2020 COVID-19 pandemic. Their share in global inflows, which sharply rose from below 1% to over 9% in the early 2000s, stagnated and averaged at 8.0% during one and a half decades (2005–2021). This could be attributed to several disadvantageous factors like perceived political instability, bureaucratic hurdles, and a limited focus on sectors attractive to foreign investors.

However, the recent rise in FDI inflows indicates a shift in perception and growing investor confidence. With a record-breaking US$156 billion inflow in 2022, the share of OIC countries in global FDI peaked at 11.8% (Fig. 1.4), reflecting the rising attractiveness of these economies to foreign investors. To sustain

[1]It should be noted that the global economic conditions contributed significantly to this fluctuation in the OIC countries' trade performance over the years, given their weight in global fuel exports that averaged at about 40% during that period.

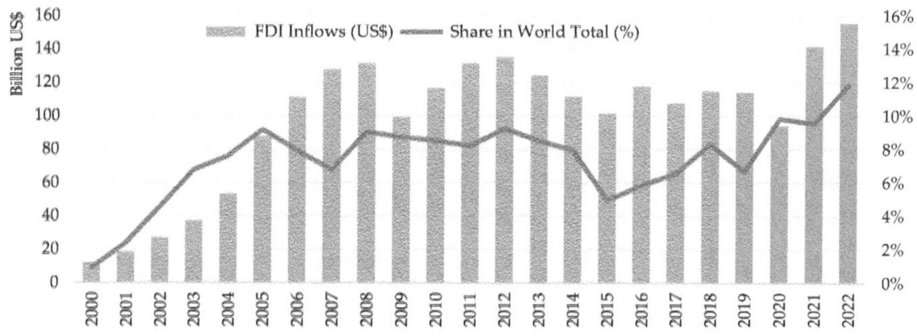

Fig. 1.4. FDI Inflows to OIC Countries. *Source*: Author's compilation based on data from UNCTAD Data Centre.

and augment their share in global FDI inflows, OIC nations need to not only further utilize their abundant natural resources and demographic dividends, but also create conducive investment climates cultivated through policy reforms and infrastructure development initiatives. Moreover, amidst evolving investment trends, the growing emphasis on sustainable investment practices[2] requires OIC countries to strategically position themselves to leverage their substantial renewable energy potential and spearhead initiatives aimed at promoting environmentally sustainable, green investment practices.

3. Intra-OIC Economic Relations

The OIC, with its 57 member states spanning continents and representing a diverse economic landscape, holds immense potential for fostering robust intra-OIC economic relations. By leveraging their collective strengths, sharing best practices, and promoting key areas of cooperation like trade, investment, tourism, and transport connectivity, the OIC countries can create a conducive environment for inclusive economic growth and development within their region. This can lead to enhanced regional integration, increased trade volumes, and a stronger position in the global market for OIC countries.

The trajectory of intra-OIC trade has witnessed a notable upward trend over the past decades, indicating a strengthening of economic interdependence among member states. From comprising merely 9.2% of total OIC trade in 1980, the proportion of intra-OIC trade surged to 20% by 2023 (Fig. 1.5), underscoring

[2]The 2023 edition of the *World Investment Report*, published by the United Nations Conference on Trade and Development (UNCTAD), is devoted to investing in sustainable energy. The report reveals that international investment in renewable energy has nearly tripled since the adoption of the Paris Agreement in 2015, though much of this growth has been concentrated in developed countries, with more than 30 developing countries not registering a single large international investment project in renewables. Nevertheless, it is noteworthy that four OIC countries, namely Kazakhstan, Egypt, Indonesia, and Morocco, were among the top 10 developing economies by international investment in renewable energy during 2015–2022 (UNCTAD, 2023).

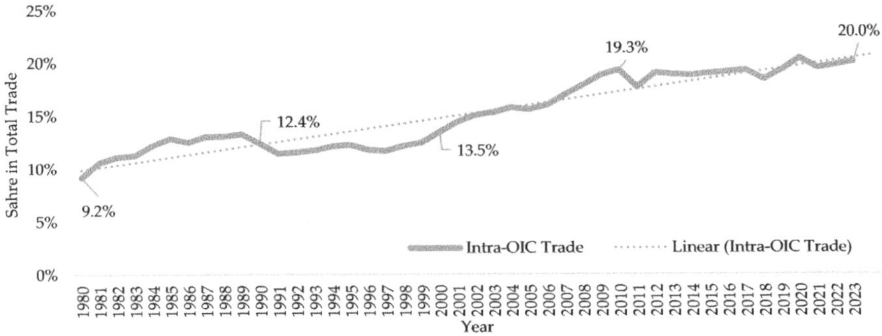

Fig. 1.5. Share of Intra-OIC Trade in Total Trade of OIC Countries (1980–2023). *Source*: Author's compilation based on data from IMF, Direction of Trade Statistics.

a growing recognition of the economic potential within the group. This surge can be attributed to factors like increasing market diversification, improved infrastructure, and most importantly, concerted efforts toward enhancing economic cooperation among member states. Nevertheless, there is still significant room for further growth and deepening of economic relations within the OIC to achieve the 25% target implied by the OIC-2025: Programme of Action[3] (OIC, 2016).

Reflecting the growing recognition of the benefits of economic cooperation and integration, the proliferation of regional trade agreements (RTAs) within the OIC region has provided member countries with preferential market access and tariff reductions, further stimulating trade flows and making it more attractive for OIC countries to do business with each other. As of today, all but one OIC member, Mauritania, participate in at least one RTA that has been notified to the GATT/WTO and is in force (Fig. 1.6). Türkiye stands out as a leader in this area, having signed a remarkable 26 RTAs, followed by Malaysia (17), Indonesia (16), and Kazakhstan (14). While the agreements an OIC member is party to are not necessarily limited to OIC members, many of them do involve a significant number of OIC members. For instance, Egypt, Sudan, Morocco, Tunisia, Iraq, Libya, Benin, Guinea, and Nigeria each are parties to RTAs that collectively involve more than 25 other OIC members, offering potential in the quest for deeper economic integration and collaboration among them.

The expansion of intra-OIC investment flows constitutes another pivotal aspect of fostering economic integration and cooperation within the region. The increase in these flows has the potential to strengthen economic ties, promote industrial development, and foster technology transfer among the member states. While some OIC countries have shown positive trends in attracting FDI from

[3]The Programme, adopted by the 13th Islamic Summit (Istanbul, 14–15 April 2016), identified 107 goals under 18 priority areas, with an implementation period covering 2016–2025. One of the nine goals under the priority area of "Trade, Investment and Finance" was to "Further increase intra-OIC trade by 6% up from the current percentage in 2015."

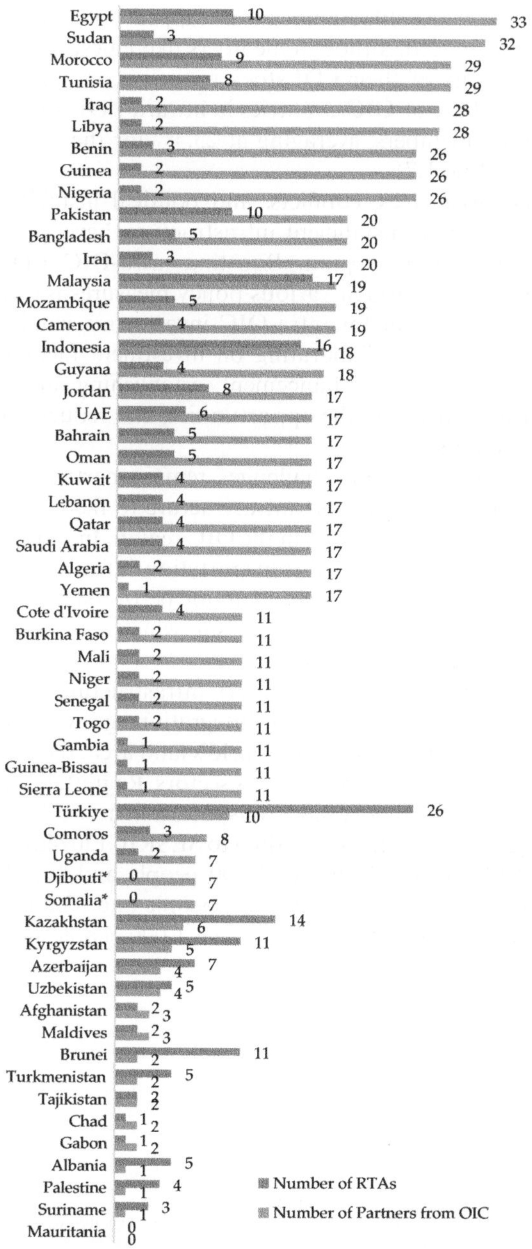

Fig. 1.6. Status of OIC Countries in Regional Trade Agreements (RTAs). *Source*: WTO. Regional trade agreements notified to the GATT/WTO and in force by country/territory. Regional Trade Agreements Database. Accessed on 7 May 2024. *Notes*: * Djibouti and Somalia currently do not appear to be signatories to any RTA, but are considered members of COMESA. Mauritania is not party to any RTA.

within the region, there is still significant untapped potential for deeper intra-regional investment. Indeed, although members like Palestine and Bahrain stand out with a vast majority of their FDI stock in their economies originating from the OIC region, the share of OIC countries in inward FDI stock is comparatively lower in many other members, averaging at 23.4% for the 23 member countries with available data (Fig. 1.7).

Regulatory inconsistencies, conflicts, and political instability in some OIC member states, along with insufficient infrastructure, have all hampered robust investment flows within the region. Boosting intra-OIC FDI flows requires addressing these barriers through various policy measures is essential, yet creating a conducive environment for intra-OIC investments would require actions in multiple fronts, such as collaborating on investment facilitation, regulatory coherence, and infrastructure enhancement, establishing an online investment database to inform the firms on the opportunities, and reducing trade barriers to enhance competitiveness.

On another front, significant challenges remain particularly in developing robust and well-connected transport infrastructure to facilitate trade, economic growth, and regional integration within the OIC region. In today's interconnected global economy, the significance of transportation infrastructure in facilitating connectivity, accessibility, and mobility cannot be overstated. This holds especially true for international trade and tourism, which serve as pivotal pillars of many economies within the OIC region.

In this connection, improving transport infrastructure stands as a crucial policy objective for fostering economic integration, growth, and prosperity in OIC nations. Spanning one-sixth of the world's land area, these countries possess immense economic potential across various sectors. Regrettably, many OIC countries currently grapple with inadequate transportation network density and capacity across all modes of transport. According to SESRIC (2024a), in OIC countries, the average road length is 2.5 km per 1,000 people and 16.5 km per 100 km^2 land area, compared with 4.6 km per 1,000 people and 33.2 km per 100 km^2 in non-OIC developing countries and 13.8 km per 1,000 people and 48.7 km per 100

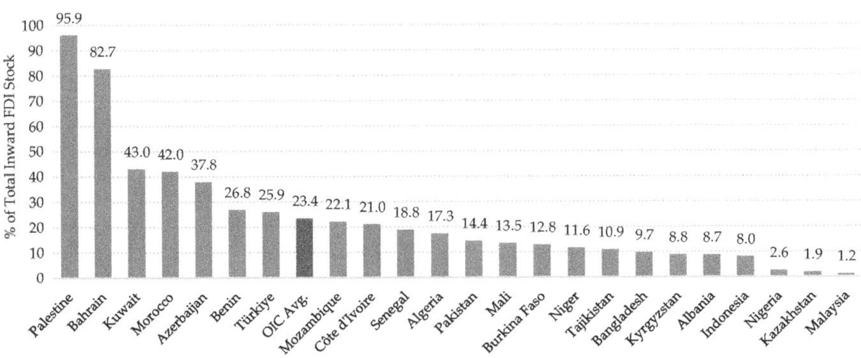

Fig. 1.7. Proportion of Inward FDI Stock Originating from OIC Countries, 2020 (%). *Source*: SESRIC and ICD (2022).

km^2 land area in developed countries. A similar situation exists in railway, air, and sea transportation, highlighting the lack of connectivity in this vital sector as a serious challenge for OIC countries.

Transportation networks serve as a critical pathway for countries to overcome various challenges and unlock opportunities within the tourism sector, which is seen by regional economic groups as a key driver of regional integration. Given their wealth of natural, geographical, historical, and cultural attractions, OIC countries hold substantial potential in tourism. However, underdeveloped transportation infrastructure, coupled with several other factors, poses significant barriers to realizing this potential, hindering the development of a sustainable international tourism sector within the OIC region. While the OIC countries have received an increasing share of global tourist arrivals in recent years, from 10.7% in 2016 to 14.8% in 2022, the share of intra-OIC arrivals is estimated to have stagnated and actually declined slightly, from 37.5% to 35.2% over the same period (SESRIC, 2024b, pp. 22–27).

A comprehensive indicator recently developed by the Islamic Development Bank (IsDB) provides insight into the overall situation of economic and regional integration within the OIC group. The IsDB Integration Index, constructed as a composite index, represents the five main dimensions of economic integration, namely, Trade and Investment Integration, Financial Markets Integration, Production Networks, Connectivity and Logistics, and Human Mobility and Institutional Integration (IsDB, 2022). The overall index scores showed a declining trend from 2010 to 2020, indicating a deterioration in economic integration over this period. In 2010, the most robust aspects of intra-OIC integration were trade and investment, followed by production networks. However, these two dimensions became the primary contributors to the decline in the overall scores during the period. Conversely, financial market integration remained the weakest dimension in terms of economic and regional integration among OIC countries (Fig. 1.8).

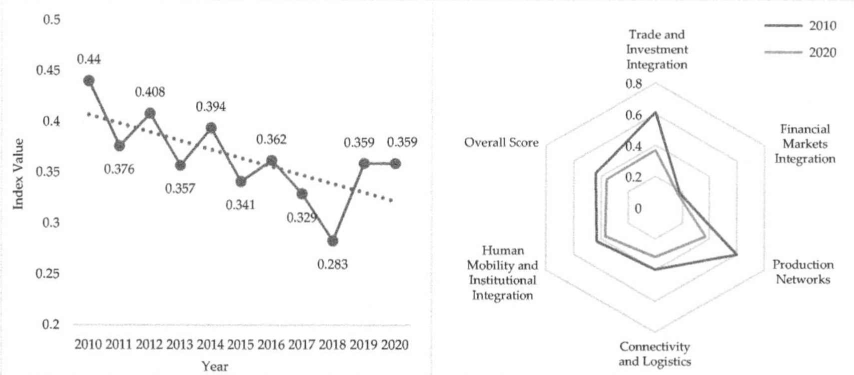

Fig. 1.8. Regional Economic Integration among OIC Countries: The IsDB Integration Index. *Source*: IsDB (2022).

Overall, there is significant progress and potential for economic cooperation and integration among the OIC member states. The upward trajectory of intra-OIC trade, the proliferation of regional trade agreements, and the expansion of investment and tourism flows underscore the growing recognition of the economic benefits of collaboration. Despite the positive trends, there are also challenges that prevent stronger economic cooperation, such as regulatory inconsistencies, inadequate infrastructure, and geopolitical instability. With collaborative actions and programs, OIC countries can create a conducive environment for inclusive economic growth, enhanced regional integration, and a stronger position in the global market.

4. Initiatives Toward Enhancing Intra-OIC Economic Cooperation

Regional integration can take various forms, such as free trade agreements, customs unions, common markets, and economic and monetary unions. The OIC, initially focused primarily on political issues such as the Palestinian conflict, has evolved into a platform increasingly dedicated to socio-economic concerns. It has envisioned the establishment of an Islamic Common Market (ICM) among its member states, driven by spiritual and cultural connections, where the objective of fostering intra-Islamic economic and trade cooperation toward the establishment of an ICM is explicitly outlined in the Charter of the OIC.

The idea of establishing an ICM among OIC countries was first proposed at the 1974 Lahore Islamic Summit. Since then, efforts were made to enhance economic and trade relations while addressing institutional challenges to cooperation. However, the slow implementation of the cooperation agreements has been a persistent challenge (Dabour, 2004). The 2003 Islamic Summit in Malaysia renewed focus on the ICM, adopting a resolution that underscored the importance of implementing existing agreements, coordinating economic cooperation, and creating free trade zones as steps toward the ICM. However, progress has been limited, largely due to the diverse economic structures and development levels of OIC countries (Hassan & Sanchez, 2016; Jafarli, 2017).

Today, socio-economic cooperation is at the forefront of the OIC's agenda, reflecting a broader shift toward addressing the developmental needs of member states. Regular high-level engagements, technical meetings, and the establishment of OIC institutions have driven significant progress in various sectors. Notably, the OIC has seen continuous progress in functional and sectoral cooperation among its member states (SESRIC, 2019). Furthermore, the development of strategic plans and working programs by different OIC organs and institutions has led to improved planning of activities. The adoption of joint documents outlining sector-specific action plans has further enhanced the framework, advancing OIC cooperation into a new and more effective phase.

At the 2016 Istanbul Islamic Summit, the OIC adopted the program of action for the years 2016–2025, emphasizing the significance of trade for development and acknowledging the inadequacy of intra-trade among member countries (OIC, 2016). One key aspect of the plan is its focus on trade facilitation, which involves streamlining customs procedures, reducing tariffs, and harmonizing regulations to facilitate the flow of goods and services across borders. It also prioritizes investment promotion, seeking to attract foreign investment, stimulate domestic entrepreneurship, and encourage innovation. Sectoral cooperation was an important dimension of partnership to encourage collaboration in areas such as agriculture, energy, tourism, and technology, to harness the comparative advantages of member countries (OIC, 2016).

In addition to broader OIC initiatives, many OIC institutions have undertaken efforts to enhance economic integration and increase intra-regional trade. A prominent initiative in this regard is the Trade Preferential System among the Member States of the OIC (TPS-OIC), developed by the Standing Committee for Economic and Commercial Cooperation (COMCEC). The TPS-OIC is based on three core agreements: the Framework Agreement, the Protocol on Preferential Tariff Scheme (PRETAS), and the Rules of Origin (RO). The legal foundation of the TPS-OIC has been completed in 2011, and by the end of 2014, the required number of member states had completed ratification, paving the way for its operationalization. Participating countries currently include Bangladesh, Iran, Jordan, Malaysia, Morocco, Pakistan, Turkey, Bahrain, Saudi Arabia, the United Arab Emirates, Kuwait, Qatar, and Oman. With these requirements met, the TPS-OIC became fully operational on July 1, 2022 (COMCEC Coordination Office, 2024). As of May 2022, however, 15 OIC countries had yet to ratify or sign the Framework Agreement, while 32 had ratified it but only 18 had endorsed both the PRETAS and RO agreements (Fig. 1.9). This limited engagement meant that the TPS-OIC was operational in only 14 member countries, which had ratified all three agreements and submitted their concession lists to the Trade Negotiating Committee (TNC) Secretariat. The slow pace of ratification and low participation by member states in the TPS-OIC agreements result in persistent trade barriers and limited economic cooperation across the OIC.

In addition to the TPS-OIC, the OIC Arbitration Centre was established in Istanbul in November 2021 as a recent initiative in response to the need for effective dispute resolution mechanisms in international trade upon the recommendation

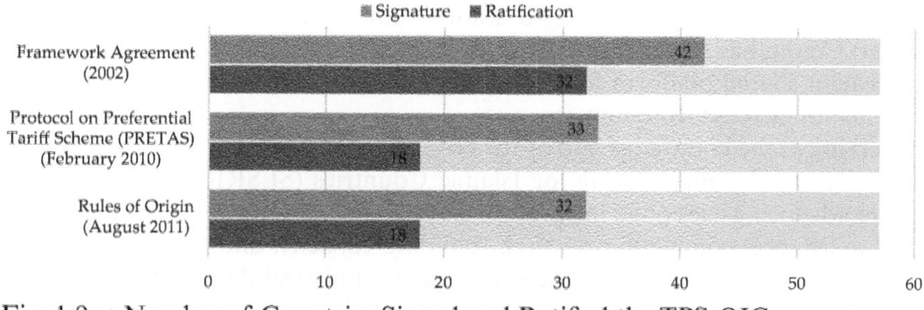

Fig. 1.9. Number of Countries Signed and Ratified the TPS-OIC.
Source: COMCEC. *Note*: The dates in brackets are the date of entry into force. As of May 15, 2022. Accessed on 22 April 2024. https://www.comcec.org/trade/tps-oic/trade-preferential-system-among-the-member-states-of-the-oic/

of the COMCEC ministerial meetings. The centre aims to resolve commercial and investment disputes among OIC countries and between OIC countries and non-members using traditional arbitration rules and alternative dispute resolution mechanisms.

Overall, the OIC has acted as a catalyst for establishing new organizations to address gaps in areas without pre-existing cooperative frameworks. Over time, this role has helped shape the OIC into a diverse institution with multiple bodies dedicated to advancing its objectives across various sectors. The COMCEC is the main multilateral economic and commercial cooperation platform of the OIC. COMCEC, the main platform for economic and commercial collaboration within the OIC, is celebrating its 40th year, serving as a key venue for tackling shared development challenges and fostering practical solutions. By mid-2023, the OIC encompassed 37 institutions (subsidiary, specialized, or affiliated), with 19 focusing on economic development, highlighting the enduring centrality of economic cooperation within the organization.

Several OIC institutions play a significant role in promoting regional integration among member countries, notably the IsDB and its affiliated entities. For instance, the IsDB's *Technical Assistance Programme for Regional and Global Integration in Trade* supports member states in advancing both intra-OIC and global integration through training, policy guidance, and technical assistance. The program's initiatives focus on facilitating integration and improving connectivity to unlock global economic opportunities for OIC members as they strengthen their ties to the international market. A key player within the IsDB Group is the International Islamic Trade Finance Corporation (ITFC), established in 2008 to boost trade among OIC nations through trade finance and development programs. By the end of June 2024, ITFC had approved a cumulative trade finance volume of US$81 billion, with disbursements amounting to US$66 billion (ITFC, 2024). ITFC also implements initiatives combining trade finance with development, such as the *Arab Africa Trade Bridge Programme*, which seeks to expand economic opportunities and support sustainable growth in Arab and sub-Saharan OIC countries. More recently, the *Trade Connect Central Asia+ (TCCA+)* program was launched to foster regional cooperation and inclusive growth among Central Asian OIC nations and Azerbaijan. (ITFC, 2024). Moreover, the IsDB Group, through the Islamic Corporation for the Insurance of Investment and Export Credit, has spearheaded the *OIC Business Intelligence Centre*, which aims to create a shared platform for accessible and cost-effective business and credit information across OIC countries.

Serving as the knowledge hub of the OIC, the Statistical, Economic and Social Research and Training Centre for Islamic Countries (SESRIC) plays a pivotal role in advancing economic integration among OIC countries by providing technical assistance, conducting research, building capacity, and fostering collaboration. Acting as a bridge for the exchange of statistical data and information among member states, it creates a solid foundation for evidence-based policy and decision-making. SESRIC's research reports and publications offer valuable insights that guide policy dialogue and the development of regional cooperation strategies. Additionally, SESRIC builds partnerships to encourage knowledge sharing, innovation, and best practices aligned with economic integration goals. Among other key institutions, the Islamic Centre for Development of Trade supports trade and investment growth within the OIC through capacity-building programs, trade promotion, and policy advocacy. It works to improve market access, exchange trade information, and provide business matchmaking services, enhancing economic linkages among member states. Representing the private sector representatives, the Islamic Chamber of Commerce and Development organizes business forums, trade exhibitions, and networking events, and advocates for policies that support economic cooperation and integration among OIC countries.

On another front, enhancing connectivity is vital to fostering economic cooperation among neighboring countries. A number of large scale initiatives have already been taken by OIC countries, supported by regional and international development agencies to improve connectivity and create new trade corridors between OIC countries. Among them are the OIC Dakar-Port Sudan Railway Project aiming to connect Senegal, Mali, Niger, Chad and Sudan through a 4,000-km-long railway corridor; Trans-Sahara Road Corridor aiming to connect five OIC countries between Tunisia, Algeria, Chad, Mali and Nigeria through a 4,500-km-long road corridor; and the recently initiated Türkiye-Iraq Development Road Project initiated by Türkiye, Iraq, Qatar, and the United Arab Emirates to connect the Asia and Gulf with Europe through 1,200 km of railways and highways. Türkiye is also aiming to develop the Zangezur Corridor to connect with Central Asian countries to promote trade and development in the region.

All these ambitious attempts reflect the willingness of OIC countries to engage in greater economic partnership with other OIC countries and harness the untapped potential of economic opportunities in the region. However, the lack of effective institutions and proper follow-up mechanisms lead to extremely sluggish progress in achieving economic integration. In the wake of developing a new program of action for the next decade starting in 2025, OIC countries need to focus on establishing effective modalities and frameworks for implementation of agreed actions and their management to realize the full benefits of these endeavors and preventing them from becoming wasted investments.

5. Concluding Remarks and the Way Forward

As highlighted in previous sections, fostering economic cooperation among its member states has been an integral part of the OIC's agenda for development, and over the years, the OIC has made some efforts to design the necessary framework required to initiate and implement collective Islamic actions aimed at fostering prosperity among its member states. Through strategic guidance on developmental challenges, promoting knowledge sharing and mutual learning, offering financial assistance, and supporting reforms aligned with the global development agenda, the OIC and its institutions aim to play a pivotal role in enhancing economic governance and the efficiency of state institutions among its members. In addition to the comprehensive strategic partnership documents, the adoption of various strategic documents on joint sectoral initiatives has significantly enhanced the potential for deeper OIC cooperation. These strategic frameworks and programs have marked a new phase in consolidating and increasing the effectiveness of collaboration among OIC member states.

The steady growth in intra-OIC trade can be seen as a success in the domain of economic cooperation, with the TPS-OIC offering significant potential for fostering closer economic ties. However, despite its importance, the TPS-OIC has received limited attention, and its capacity to drive economic collaboration among member states remains underutilized. In this context, envisioning the establishment of a common market for OIC countries appears unrealistic, particularly when the preferential trade agreement itself struggles to gain full participation and commitment from member states. Given the current level of economic cooperation and partnership, efforts to establish an ICM have likely been premature and overly ambitious. Nevertheless, the long-term feasibility of an ICM and enhanced economic policy coordination – both articulated as goals in various Islamic Summits – remains an open question. Existing studies, while limited, tend to support the idea of gradual economic integration among OIC members (e.g., Amin & Hamid, 2009; Dabour, 2004).

A critical aspect for the effective development of multilateral cooperation is political commitment, as it significantly influences the engagement of national administrations. Without strong governmental and institutional support, the chances for success remain low. Unfortunately, existing bilateral disputes within the OIC often fall within the political sphere, shaped by divergent views on historical events and ongoing conflicts. These issues include a range of challenges, from territorial disputes to refugee crises, and their slow resolution – or occasional escalation – impedes the stabilization of political relations, creating barriers to smooth cooperation within the OIC (SESRIC, 2019).

Nevertheless, there are emerging trends and opportunities that could support economic integration among OIC countries. The global economy is undergoing a profound transformation, driven primarily by increasing digitalization, automation, and artificial intelligence. In particular, the integration of digital technologies and advanced robotics is revolutionizing the manufacturing process and reshaping the workforce. These technologies are crucial for OIC economies as they significantly enhance productivity, efficiency, and innovation across various sectors. By capitalizing on these technological advances, OIC countries can stimulate growth, generate new job opportunities, and strengthen their competitiveness on the global stage. OIC countries have the chance to leapfrog traditional development stages by embracing cutting-edge technologies such as automation and robotics, thus accelerating their progress. However, realizing these opportunities requires strategic planning, substantial investment in infrastructure and human capital, and supportive policies to mitigate potential challenges.

On another front, the expansion of global value chains (GVCs) has played a crucial role in expanding the economic participation of developing countries. However, alongside growing regionalist sentiments, the economic impact of the pandemic has sparked discussions on the need to reconfigure GVCs. One potential strategy is to strengthen regional operations by relocating supply chains to closer, more accessible locations. In order to capitalize on the reorientation of supply chains, OIC countries must focus on reducing trade costs, enhancing technological capabilities, and improving their preparedness to handle supply chain risks. Investment in transport and communication infrastructure is particularly crucial to create an environment conducive to businesses seeking alternative value chain networks. OIC countries should also prioritize investments in human capital, expand research and development spending, and ensure strong protection for intellectual property rights. Additionally, measures should be taken to improve preparedness for various supply chain risks – such as disruptions in transportation and communication, financial market volatility, epidemic and pandemic threats, and cybersecurity vulnerabilities – by strengthening risk management frameworks.

In a regional context, OIC countries can focus on the establishment of sector-specific regional clusters to attract firms operating in those industries, enhance cost efficiency and achieve competitiveness. Establishing such clusters would again require strong political will and a deeper level of economic integration at the regional level. To complement such initiatives, OIC countries can establish regional logistic clusters to ensure the timely and cost-effective delivery of intermediate products. The interchangeability of transportation and logistics assets within such clusters would further enhance the efficiency of supply chains and further augment the competitiveness of the countries involved.

Overall, there are a wide range of opportunities for OIC countries to strengthen their economic ties and achieve greater welfare through intra-regional partnerships. In the light of rising geoeconomic fragmentation and increasing prominence of regionalism, it is becoming increasingly urgent for OIC countries to facilitate the regional movement of goods and people, and strengthen capacities to attract and enable the flow of investment in creating regional production networks, enhancing economic cooperation, and achieving stronger intra-OIC partnerships. This requires strong political commitment and a solid plan of action.

References

Aiyar, S., Chen, J., Ebeke, C., Garcia-Saltos, R., Gudmundsson, T., Ilyina, A., Kangur, A., Kunaratskul, T., Rodriguez, S. L., Ruta, M., Schulze, T., Soderberg, G., & Trevino, J. P. (2023). *Geoeconomic fragmentation and the future of multilateralism* [IMF Staff Discussion Note No. SDN/2023/01]. International Monetary Fund.

Amin, R., & Hamid, Z. (2009). Towards an Islamic common market: Are OIC countries heading the right direction? *IIUM Journal of Economics and Management*, *17*(1), 133–176.

Bolhuis, A. M., Chen, J., & Kett, B. (2023). *Fragmentation in global trade: Accounting for commodities* [IMF Working Paper No. WP 23/73]. International Monetary Fund.

Cerdeiro, D. A., Mano, R., Eugster, J., Muir, M. D. V., & Peiris, M. S. J. (2021). *Sizing up the effects of technological decoupling*. International Monetary Fund.

COMCEC Coordination Office. (2024). *CCO brief on trade*. https://www.comcec.org/wp-content/uploads/2024/10/Brief-on-Trade_2024.pdf

Dabour, N. M. (2004). Implications of establishing an Islamic common market: Gradual integration & possible consequences. *Journal of Economic Cooperation*, *25*(1), 71–98.

De Lombaerde, P. (2023). *Regional cooperation and integration: Why? Where? and so what?* [Working Paper No. 04/2023]. United Nations University, Institute on Comparative Regional Integration Studies.

Food and Agriculture Organization (FAO). (n.d.). *Low-income food-deficit countries (LIFDCs) – List updated June 2023*. https://www.fao.org/countryprofiles/lifdc/en/

Hassan, M. K., & Sanchez, B. A. (2016). The prospect of an Islamic common market. *Journal of Islamic Economics and Finance*, *1*(2), 69–114.

Head, K., & Mayer, T. (2014). *Gravity Equations: Workhorse, Toolkit, and Cookbook*. Handbook of International Economics. Elsevier.

IMF. (2022, October). *Regional economic outlook: Asia and Pacific*. International Monetary Fund.

IMF. (2024, April). *World economic outlook2024—Steady but slow: Resilience amid divergence*. International Monetary Fund.

IsDB. (2022). *IsDB Group technical report on the construction of the IsDB integration index*. Islamic Development Bank Group.

ITFC. (2024). *Report to the 40th Ministerial Session of the COMCEC*. International Islamic Trade Finance Corporation. https://www.comcec.org/wp-content/uploads/2024/10/ITFC-Report-comcec24-002.pdf

Jafarli, S. (2017). Moves towards an Islamic common market: An evaluation of potentials. *Journal of Economic Cooperation and Development*, *38*(3), 169–198.

Javorcik, B., Kitzmueller, L., Schweiger, H., & Yıldırım, M. (2022). *Economic costs of friend-shoring*. European Bank for Reconstruction and Development.

OIC. (2016). *The OIC-2025: Programme of action* (OIC/SUM-13/2016/POA-Final). Organization of Islamic Cooperation. https://www.oic-oci.org/docdown/?docID=16&refID=5

SESRIC. (2019). *50 years of OIC cooperation: Taking a future perspective by learning from the past* (OIC Outlook Report 2019/2). Authored by Erhan Türbedar. Statistical, Economic and Social Research and Training Centre for Islamic Countries.

SESRIC. (2023). *Prospects and challenges of OIC member countries: SWOT outlook 2023*. Statistical, Economic and Social Research and Training Centre for Islamic Countries.

SESRIC. (2024a). *Transportation for development in OIC member countries: Implications for trade and tourism & challenges for landlocked countries*. Statistical, Economic and Social Research and Training Centre for Islamic Countries.

SESRIC. (2024b). *International tourism in OIC countries: Empowering smart and sustainable tourism for development*. Statistical, Economic and Social Research and Training Centre for Islamic Countries.

SESRIC & ICD. (2022). *Investment outlook in the OIC countries*. Statistical, Economic and Social Research and Training Centre for Islamic Countries and Islamic Corporation for the Development of the Private Sector. https://sesricdiag.blob.core.windows.net/sesric-site-blob/files/article/826.pdf

UNCTAD. (2023). *World investment report 2023: Investing in sustainable energy for all*. United Nations Conference on Trade and Development.

United Nations. (n.d.). *LDCs at a glance: LDC list (updated December 2023)*. https://www.un.org/development/desa/dpad/least-developed-country-category/ldcs-at-a-glance.html

Wagner, N. (1983). Regional economic integration between developing countries: The example of South and South-East Asia. *Intereconomics*, *18*(6), 270–277. https://doi.org/10.1007/BF02928230

World Bank. (n.d.). *World Bank country and lending groups*. https://datahelpdesk.worldbank.org/knowledgebase/articles/906519-world-bank-country-and-lending-groups

Chapter 2

The Structure and Functioning of the Organization of Islamic Cooperation (OIC)

Mehmet Yüce[a], Hüseyin Akkaya[b] and Mehmet Fatih Aslantaş[c]

[a]*UNEC, Azerbaijan*
[b]*Tokat Gaziosmanpasa University, Turkey*
[c]*Kafkas University, Turkey*

1. Historical Development of the Organization of Islamic Cooperation

The Organization of Islamic Cooperation (OIC) (formerly known as the Organization of the Islamic Conference) was established in response to the outcry in the Islamic world following the arson attack on the Al-Aqsa Mosque in Jerusalem, Islam's third holiest site, by an Australian radical Jew on August 21, 1969. In the wake of these reactions, the first Islamic Summit Conference was held in Rabat, Morocco, on September 22–25, 1969. The conference aimed to strengthen cooperation and solidarity among member countries and protect the Islamic world's rights and interests. The organization's name was changed to the OIC at the 38th Council of Foreign Ministers (CFM) Meeting held in Astana, Kazakhstan, on June 28–30, 2011. During the First CFM Meeting held in Jeddah in March 1970, it was decided to establish a General Secretariat and for the Secretariat to operate in Jeddah until the liberation of Jerusalem. A Secretary General was also appointed (Republic of Türkiye Ministry of Foreign Affairs, 2022).

At the Third CFM Meeting held in Rabat in 1972, the Charter of the Islamic Development Bank (IDB) was adopted. This Charter was replaced by a new Charter adopted at the 11th IDB Summit in Dakar on March 13–14, 2008. The new Charter constitutes the fundamental founding document of the Organization, outlining its objectives, principles, membership, observer status, organs, peaceful settlement of disputes, budget and financial rules, and operational procedures. It is considered a significant milestone in the Organization's reform efforts, adapting to contemporary needs and fostering cooperation and activities among Islamic countries in the new global context shaped by profound international changes since 1972 (Ministry of Foreign Affairs of the Republic of Turkey, 2022).

The Economic Potential of Islamic Countries, Part A:
Economics, Demographics and Financial Services, 25–37

doi:10.1108/978-1-83708-000-720251003

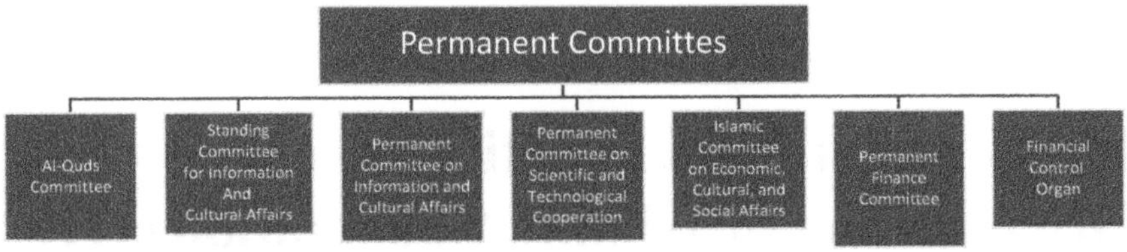

Fig. 2.1. Permanent Committees of the OIC. *Source*: OIC (2024d).

The Organization has the honor of uniting Muslims as a single body and embracing all causes close to the hearts of over 1.5 billion Muslims worldwide. It actively represents Muslims by protecting their vital interests and resolving conflicts and disputes involving member states through consultation and cooperation with the United Nations (UN) and other intergovernmental organizations. In order to safeguard the actual values of Islam and Muslims, the Organization has taken various steps to dispel misconceptions and vigorously advocates for the elimination of all forms of discrimination against Muslims (OIC, 2024a).

Under the OIC umbrella, there are numerous organs. Critical organs of the OIC include the Islamic Summit, the CFM, the General Secretariat, the Al-Quds Committee, and three Permanent Committees responsible for science and technology, economy and trade, as well as information and culture. Additionally, the OIC houses specialized agencies such as the IDB and the Islamic Educational, Scientific and Cultural Organization, alongside subsidiary and affiliated organizations crucial in enhancing cooperation among OIC member states in various fields. Fig. 2.1 depicts the permanent committees and Fig. 2.2 shows auxiliary organs (OIC, 2024b).

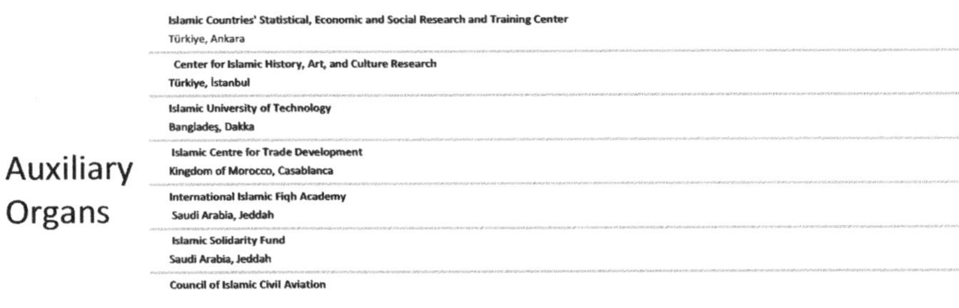

Fig. 2.2. Auxiliary Organs of the OIC. *Source*: OIC (2024b).

The literature emphasizes that despite the OIC potential, it has yet to make sufficient progress. Akgül (2013), within the framework of the Gravity Model, evaluated the trade relations among OIC countries and concluded that cultural and institutional differences among member countries hinder cooperation. Arslan (2014) emphasized the longstanding efforts towards enhancing cooperation among Islamic countries, highlighting the significance of the D-8 (Developing-8) Organization for Economic Cooperation. However, Arslan also underscored that these efforts have not been adequate, emphasizing the potential for future collaboration opportunities. Jeffery (2018) assessed the current challenges of the OIC in the 21st century, noting that globalization has significantly altered institutional structures while highlighting the organization's moderate success in medium-sized projects despite its overall lack of desired progress. Öztürk (2018) evaluated the position of OIC countries within global trade, emphasizing the low share of OIC countries in global trade and noting the inadequacy of commercial activities among these countries. Uslu (2018) concluded in his study on the problems of the OIC that despite its potential, the organization has not made significant progress since its establishment. Dağ (2018) argues for increasing trade among member states, enhancing the capacities of economic and trade institutions within member countries, supporting the private sector and investments, and promoting production and growth through knowledge and technology transfer, thereby contributing to the organization's goal of spreading prosperity. Mustafa and Bano (2020) concluded that there are significant challenges in the Islamic world. They advocated for strengthening the OIC through collective efforts, suggesting that the organization should play a constructive role through dialogue in controlling the rise of Islamophobia.

2. Member Countries of the OIC and Their Economic Situation

The OIC, comprising 57 member countries spanning four continents, is the largest international organization globally after the UN. The OIC aims to address issues related to Muslims across a wide geographical area, from Mindanao Island in the East to North America and South Africa to Siberia's interior. Despite showing a solid impression regarding capacity and potential, criticisms exist regarding its inability to mobilize its full potential due to varying levels of economic development, cultural and racial differences, regime conflicts, and sectarian disparities. Additionally, it has been criticized for remaining indifferent to global developments (Ataman & Gökşen, 2014, p. 8).

Before delving into an economic analysis of the OIC, it is worth mentioning the Standing Committee for Economic and Commercial Cooperation (COMCEC), the foremost multilateral economic and commercial cooperation platform in the Islamic world. Established during the Third Islamic Summit Conference held in Mecca/Taif in 1981 and operationalized during the Fourth Islamic Summit Conference in Casablanca, Morocco, in 1984, COMCEC serves as a central forum to address common development issues of the Islamic community (COMCEC, 2024).

In December 2005, during the Third Extraordinary Session of the Islamic Summit held in Mecca, OIC member states faced numerous challenges. They established a framework known as the Ten-Year Action Program to overcome them. This program was completed by the end of 2015. Since then, a new program for the next decade (2016–2025) has been adopted, named OIC-2025, based on the provisions of the OIC Charter, focusing on 107 targets across 18 priority areas. Key focus areas include Peace and Security, Poverty Alleviation, Counter-Terrorism, Climate Change and Sustainability, Investment and Finance, Palestine and Jerusalem, Food Security, Science and Technology, Moderation, and Interfaith Harmony (OIC, 2024a). Table 2.1 presents member countries and various parameters in light of these explanations.

Table 2.1. Member Countries of the OIC.

Countries	Date of Membership	Population 2023	2020 GDP (Billion $)	2021 GDP (Billion $)	2022 GDP (Billion $)	2023 GDP (Billion $)
Islamic Republic of Afghanistan	1969	42,239.854	20.136	14.288	14.467	veri yok
Albania	1992	2,832.439	15.192	17.984	19.083	22.743
Azerbaijan	1992	10,412.651	42.693	54.825	78.721	76.639
Kingdom of Bahrain	1972	1,485.509	34.622	39.289	44.383	44.674
People's Republic of Bangladesh	1974	172,954.319	373.902	416.265	460.201	446.349
Republic of Benin	1983	13,712.828	15.674	17.699	17.439	19.398
United Arab Emirates	1972	9,516.871	349.473	415.179	507.064	504.173
Brunei Darussalam	1984	452.524	12.006	14.006	16.682	15.128
Burkina Faso	1974	23,251.485	17.754	19.654	18.906	20.382
Algeria	1969	45,606.480	164.774	185.884	225.631	244.746
Djibouti	1978	1,136.455	3.185	3.386	3.726	4.023
Chad	1969	18,278.568	14.615	16.047	16.417	17.493
Indonesia	1969	277,534.122	1,059.055	1,186.510	1,319.076	1,371.171
Fas	1969	37,840.044	131.354	141.818	130.913	143.963
Ivory Coast (Côte d'Ivoire)	2001	28,873.034	63.119	72.833	72.046	79.978
Palestine	1969	5,371.230	15.532	18.109	19.166	18.602
Gabon	1974	2,436.566	15.337	20.229	21.076	20.524
Gambia	1974	2,773.168	1.809	2.045	2.161	2.362
Guinea	1969	14,190.612	14.089	16.320	19.589	23.005

Guinea-Bissau	1974	2,150.842	1.523	1.725	1.718	1.969
Cooperative Republic of Guyana	1998	813.834	5.471	7.662	14.529	17.050
Iraq	1975	45,504.560	181.402	206.372	261.369	254.416
Islamic Republic of Iran	1969	89,172.767	195.528	289.294	347.446	403.526
Cameroon	1974	28,647.293	40.863	45.391	44.508	48.958
Qatar	1972	2,716.391	144.411	179.732	236.258	234.218
Kazakhstan	1995	19,606.633	171.082	197.112	225.529	260.510
Kyrgyzstan	1992	6,735.347	8.283	9.256	11.672	12.775
Union of the Comoros	1976	852.075	1.218	1.273	1.225	1.340
Kuwait	1969	4,310.108	107.516	141.773	182.846	161.784
Libya	1969	6,888.388	46.921	35.224	43.289	45.011
Lebanon	1969	5,353.930	24.494	20.476	21.780	Veri yok
Maldives	1976	521.021	3.739	5.392	6.238	6.685
Malaysia	1969	34,308.525	337.456	373.832	407.027	415.569
Mali	1969	23,293.698	17.643	19.786	18.724	20.684
Egypt	1969	112,716.598	382.525	423.300	475.231	393.909
Islamic Republic of Mauritania	1969	4,862.989	8.464	9.126	9.799	10.543
Mozambique	1994	33,897.354	14.235	16.168	18.407	21.353
Niger	1969	27,202.843	13.764	14.923	15.448	16.528
Nigeria	1986	223,804.632	429.423	441.424	477.376	374.947
Republic of Uzbekistan	1996	35,163.944	60.225	69.934	81.167	90.882

(Continued)

Table 2.1. (*Continued*)

Countries	**Date of Membership**	**Population 2023**	**2020 GDP (Billion $)**	**2021 GDP (Billion $)**	**2022 GDP (Billion $)**	**2023 GDP (Billion $)**
Islamic Republic of Pakistan	1969	240,485.658	300.140	348.481	374.748	338.237
Senegal	1969	17,763.163	24.534	27.584	27.744	31.407
Sierra Leone	1972	8,791.092	4.059	4.148	4.095	3.906
Somalia	1969	18,143.378	9.204	9.839	10.420	11.680
Sudan	1969	48,109.006	34.470	34.800	33.762	25.716
Surinam	1996	623.236	2.912	3.084	3.631	3.751
Syria*	1972	23,227.014	Veri yok	Veri yok	Veri yok	Veri yok
Kingdom of Saudi Arabia	1969	36,947.025	734.271	874.156	1.108.572	1.067.583
Tajikistan	1992	10,143.543	8.134	8.934	10.493	11.855
Togo	1997	9,053.799	7.400	8.338	8.144	9.055
Tunisia	1969	12,458.223	42.540	46.688	46.265	51.283
Türkiye	1969	85,816.199	720.159	818.337	905.841	1.108.453
Turkmenistan	1992	6,516.100	52.385	60.934	77.963	77.106
Uganda	1974	48,582.334	37.901	42.747	47.567	51.819
Sultanate of Oman	1972	4,644.384	75.909	88.192	114.667	109.133
Hashemite Kingdom of Jordan	1969	11,337.052	43.762	46.362	48.722	50.989
Yemen	1969	34,449.825	20.220	19.394	23.534	18.824

Sources: *Date of Membership*; OIC (2024c); Worldometers (2024); IMF (2024).
*Membership was suspended at the 4th Extraordinary OIC Summit held on August 14–15, 2012.

Table 2.1 includes the dates of joining the OIC for member countries, their population figures for 2023, and their gross domestic product (GDP) for the pandemic period and beyond (2020–2023). When examining the population parameter for member countries in 2023, it is evident that the organization represents a total human resource of 2,027,459,763 people. Due to the geographical locations of OIC member countries, the population is mainly concentrated in the Middle East, Africa, and Central Asia. Considering the world's population is approximately 8,100,000,000, 25% of the global population are members of the OIC. Additionally, when reviewing the GDP levels of member countries, it is evident from the data that, except for a few countries (such as Afghanistan, Sierra Leone, and Yemen), GDP has continuously increased during the 2020–2023 period.

The total GDP of OIC member countries was \$6.678507 trillion in 2020, \$7.623563 trillion in 2021, \$8.754501 trillion in 2022, and \$8.838807 trillion in 2023. Considering that the total GDP of 196 countries in the world was \$101.334651 trillion in 2023, it can be understood from these figures that OIC member countries constitute approximately 8.72% of the world economy. Additionally, Indonesia, Saudi Arabia, and Turkey stand out in the table, with their GDPs exceeding the \$1 trillion level.

3. Decision-making Mechanism of the OIC

The OIC is considered the second-largest intergovernmental organization after the UN. As a large organization, the OIC has various bodies responsible for its operational principles and decision-making mechanisms. These bodies include the Islamic Summit, the CFM, the General Secretariat, and numerous subcommittees and units (Fig. 2.3).

The Islamic Summit, within the OIC's structure of working principles and decision-making mechanisms, is the highest decision-making body of the OIC. This Summit, attended by the heads of state or government of the member states, convenes every three years to consult on implementing the goals outlined in the OIC Charter and to make decisions regarding the policies to be followed. The Summit addresses essential political, economic, and social issues and determines the organization's general policies. It meets every three years in one of the member countries, but extraordinary meetings can also be held when necessary (Republic of Türkiye Ministry of Foreign Affairs, 2022).

The CFM, within the OIC's structure of working principles and decision-making mechanisms, is the second most crucial body responsible for implementing the decisions of the Islamic Summit and carrying out the OIC's objectives and policies. It also monitors the progress in implementing the decisions made at previous Summits and CFM Meetings and elects the Secretary-General. The Council meets regularly once a year and, like the Summit meetings, can hold extraordinary meetings when necessary. Its primary duties are policy formulation, budget approval, and oversight of the activities of the various organs within the OIC (Republic of Türkiye Ministry of Foreign Affairs, 2022).

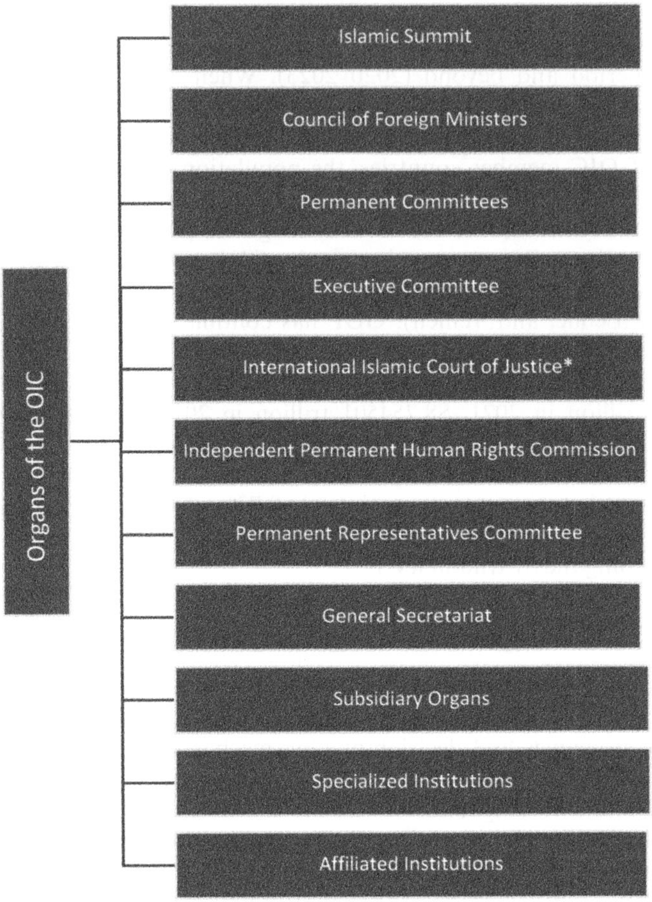

Fig. 2.3. Organs of the OIC. *Source*: Republic of Türkiye Ministry of Foreign Affairs (2022). *It is envisaged to become the principal judicial organ of the organization after its statute comes into force.

Within the OIC's structure of working principles and decision-making mechanisms, the General Secretariat serves as the administrative and executive body of the organization. It is led by the Secretary-General, elected from among citizens of member countries for five years, following fair geographical rotation and equal opportunity principles. The Secretary-General is recognized as the chief administrative authority of the organization, responsible for implementing OIC policies, organizing meetings, and ensuring coordination among member countries (Republic of Türkiye Ministry of Foreign Affairs, 2022).

Similarities and differences can be identified when comparing the operational structures of the OIC, UN, and European Union (EU). Both organizations work to promote international cooperation and maintain peace through diplomatic means. However, there are distinct differences as well. One notable difference is that the OIC represents countries with predominantly Muslim populations and focuses specifically on Islamic issues, operating solely within the scope of its member countries. In contrast, with its 193 member states, the UN has a broader global influence in terms of population and geographical coverage. The UN's inclusive structure allows it to approach global issues from various perspectives, not limited to religious considerations but also encompassing humanitarian aspects. This difference stems from the OIC's Islamic perspective and its 57 member countries, making it more regionally and religiously focused than the UN's global scope.

In terms of decision-making processes and organs, there are similarities between the two organizations. The OIC's decision-making process is generally consensus-based, emphasizing the importance of reaching agreement among member countries. In contrast, the UN often makes decisions based on majority voting, although the veto power of permanent members plays a critical role in the decision-making processes.

When evaluating the OIC and the EU, it is clear that these two organizations operate under different structures and pursue different objectives. The OIC aims to foster cooperation among member countries, address Islamic issues, and protect the interests of the Islamic world. In contrast, the EU is a regional organization of 27 member countries, with membership contingent upon meeting specific criteria for integration into the union. The EU primarily functions as an economic union to achieve economic and political integration among its member states, establish a common market, and ensure peace and prosperity in Europe.

Overall, the OIC's focus on Islamic issues and its membership of 57 predominantly Muslim countries distinguish it from the EU, which operates under a more integrated economic framework. The OIC's consensus-based decision-making process also contrasts with the EU's complex decision-making structure involving various organs and methods. For further clarity, Table 2.2 outlines the similarities and differences among the OIC, UN, and EU.

The OIC is a leading authority that provides guidance, mediation, and recommendations democratically and peacefully within the Muslim world. While the OIC cannot compel member states to act in a certain way, it endeavors to encourage such actions through dialogue and other peaceful means (Hashmat, 2011). Throughout its history, the OIC has played an active role as a mediator and has a solid track record of mediating international social disputes. The OIC maintains strong relationships with major world powers such as the UN, the EU, the United States, Russia, and the People's Republic of China. It collaborates extensively with the UN and other affiliated organizations worldwide. Despite its democratic structure, where all OIC members have equal status, this setup sometimes limits the OIC's ability to implement its agreements and decisions. Unlike the United Nations Security Council, where the five permanent members hold veto power, the OIC's decision-making process aims for consensus among member states, seeking to establish a unified position of the Islamic Ummah despite political differences (Akhmedova & Kornilov, 2019; Husain, 1997).

Table 2.2. Institutional Comparison.

	OIC	BM	AB
Number of member countries	57	193	27
Sphere of influence	Global (Religious)	Global	Regional
Goals	- Increasing cooperation among member countries.	- Promoting socio-economic development	- Promoting economic and political integration
	- Safeguarding the interests of the Islamic world	- Protecting human rights	- Creating a common market
	- Ensuring the proper representation of Islam	- Developing international law	- Ensuring peace and prosperity in Europe
Main organs	- Islamic Summit	- General Assembly	- Council of Europe
	- Council of Foreign Ministers	- Security Council	- European Parliament
	- Committee of Permanent Representatives	- Economic and Social Council	- European Commission
	- General Secretariat	- International Court of Justice	- Court of Justice of the EU
		- Secretariat	

Source: Compiled from sources utilized by the authors.

4. Conclusion

The OIC is the world's second-largest international organization, and every member of the OIC is also a member of the UN. Despite showing considerable capacity and potential, the organization faces criticism for its inability to fully mobilize its potential and respond effectively to global developments, which can be attributed to differences in levels of economic development, cultural and racial divides, regime incompatibilities, and sectarian differences.

Based on the data presented in Table 2.1, which includes membership dates, 2023 population figures, and GDPs during and after the pandemic period of OIC member countries, it is concluded that the total population of OIC member countries in 2023 was 2,027,459,763, with this population mainly concentrated in the Middle East, Africa, and Central Asia. Approximately 25% of the world's population are OIC members. It is also evident that the GDPs of OIC member countries generally increased during 2020–2023, with the total GDP in 2023 accounting for about 8.72% of the global economy. Furthermore, notable economies such as Indonesia, Saudi Arabia, and Türkiye have GDPs exceeding 1 trillion dollars.

The development levels of OIC member countries vary, presenting specific challenges in achieving collective action. Due to differences in governance, legal frameworks, and economic structures, the implementation processes of decisions made by the OIC can vary among member countries. Therefore, the OIC needs help in its decision-making process because decisions require unanimous consent. This situation often prolongs decision-making, making it advisable to consider adopting a majority voting system instead of consensus. The effectiveness of the OIC's decision-making mechanism is crucial for the organization's success and for strengthening cooperation among member countries. Implementing the above-mentioned recommendations would make the OIC a more robust and effective international actor.

Another noteworthy issue the study addresses is the importance of expediting the completion and activation of the "International Islamic Court of Justice." The functions performed by the UN's International Court of Justice and the EU's Court of Justice should also be carried out by the OIC's International Islamic Court of Justice. In other words, the International Islamic Court of Justice could serve as the ultimate authority on matters related to Islamic law among OIC member countries. This initiative would institutionalize the OIC further and provide it with a structure similar to that of the UN and the EU.

The differences in the working and decision-making mechanisms between the OIC and the UN are directly related to their purposes, membership structures, and roles in the international system. While the OIC focuses on issues specific to the Islamic world, the UN operates within a broader framework to ensure global peace and security. These differences shape each organization's contributions to international cooperation and peace.

Similarly, the differences in the working and decision-making mechanisms between the OIC and the EU stem from structural and functional disparities rooted in their distinct historical, cultural, and political contexts. While the OIC acts to protect the interests of the Islamic world and enhance cooperation among member states, the EU aims to ensure peace and prosperity in Europe through economic and political integration. These distinctions highlight how both organizations contribute uniquely to international cooperation and peace.

In conclusion, although the OIC is essential for fostering solidarity and cooperation among Muslim countries, it has not fully realized its potential. The organization needs reforms and enhanced cooperation among member countries to operate more effectively and efficiently. By restructuring to align with contemporary expectations, the OIC should play a more active role in protecting the rights and interests of Muslims, promoting economic development, and ensuring peace and security.

References

Akgül, M. S. (2013). Çekim Modeli Bulguları Işığında Türkiye'nin İslam İşbirliği Teşkilatı İle İlişkileri ve Ticari Potansiyeli. *Adam Akademi, 3*(2), 83–110.

Akhmedova, F. M., & Kornilov A. A. (2019). İslami İşbirliği Teşkilatı Ve Müslüman Ümmetinin Uluslararası Konumunun Geliştirilmesi. *Modern Dünyada İslam, 15*(1), 185–197 (Rusça.). https://doi.org/10.22311/2074-1529-2019-15-1-185-197

Arslan, K. (2014). İslam Ülkeleri Arasında İşbirliğine Giden Yolda Yeni Arayışlar. *Uluslararası Yönetim İktisat ve İşletme Dergisi, 10*(21), 179–198.

Ataman, M., & Gökşen, A. N. (2014). Analiz: Sembolizm ve Aktivizm Arasında İslam İşbirliği Teşkilatı, *SETA*, Ocak 2014, Sayı 76.

COMCEC. (2024, May 16). *History*. The Standing Committee for Economic and Commercial Cooperation of the Organization of the Islamic Cooperation. https://www.comcec.org/history/

Dağ, M. (2018). *İslam İşbirliği Teşkilatının Ekonomik ve Mali FaaliyetleriÜzerine Bir Değerlendirme*. Bitlis Uluslararası Sosyo-Ekonomik Araştırmaları ve Kalkınma Kongresi (USEAK).

Hashmat, S. A. (2011). The OIC's potential, capabilities and constraints for international conflict resolution. *Strategic Studies, 31*(1/2), 107–135.

Husain, S. S. (1997). The collaborative roles of the OIC and the UN in world affairs. *Pakistan Horizon, 50*(2), 21–27.

IMF. (2024, May 15). *World Economic Outlook database*. https://www.imf.org/en/Publications/WEO/weo-database/2024/April/select-country-group

Jeffery, M. (2018). *Issues and challenges of OIC in the 21st century*. https://doi.org/10.13140/RG.2.2.25284.12165; https://www.researchgate.net/publication/324056314_ISSUES_AND_CHALLENGES_OF_OIC_IN_THE_21_ST_CENTURY

Mustafa, G., & Bano, N. (2020, March). The Organization of Islamic Cooperation (OIC): Challenges for theIslamic World. *Journal of Development and Social Sciences, 1*(1), 1–11. http://doi.org/10.47205/jdss.2020(1-I)1.

OIC. (2024a, May 5). *History*. https://new.oic-oci.org/SitePages/CommonPage.aspx?Item=1

OIC. (2024b, May 12). *Subsidiary organs*. https://new.oic-oci.org/SitePages/OrganisationsEn.aspx?Item=9&

OIC. (2024c, May 15), *Member states*. https://new.oic-oci.org/SitePages/MemberStates.aspx.OrgType=Subsidiary%20Organs

OIC. (2024d, May 12). *Standing committees*. https://new.oic-oci.org/SitePages/CommonPage.aspx?Item=14

Öztürk, M. B. (2018). Türkiye ve Dünya Ticareti İçerisinde İslam İşbirliği. *Sakarya İktisat Dergisi*, *7*(3), 40–53.

Republic of Türkiye Ministry of Foreign Affairs. (2022, May 11). *Organisation of Islamic Cooperation (OIC)*. https://www.mfa.gov.tr/OIC.en.mfa

Uslu, N. (2018). *İslam İşbirliği Teşkilatı ve Çatışmaların Çözümü. IV. Uluslararası Orta Doğu Sempozyumu: Orta Doğu'da Barışı Tesis Etmek*. İstanbul Gelişim Üniversitesi.

Worldometers. (2024, May 15). *Countries in the world by population*. https://www.worldometers.info/world-population/population-by-country/

Chapter 3

Economic Integration and Cooperation from Systems Thinking Perspective: The European Union and the Organization of Islamic Cooperation

Mohammad Omar Farooq

United International University, Bangladesh

Introduction

In contemporary economic discourse, the concept of economic integration has garnered significant attention as a catalyst for fostering prosperity, stability, and cooperation among nations. Economic integration entails the gradual harmonization of economic policies, regulations, and institutions across borders, aimed at facilitating the seamless flow of goods and services as well as factors of production. This process, from the perspective of systems thinking, reflects the recognition that in an increasingly interconnected global economy, the pursuit of mutual interests through collaboration and cooperation can yield substantial benefits for participating countries. Moreover, economic integration has assumed heightened relevance amidst contemporary challenges such as technological advancements, environmental sustainability concerns, and geopolitical uncertainties, underscoring its role as a strategic imperative for promoting inclusive, ethical and sustainable development.

In the context of integration efforts during the twentieth century stand two prominent regional organizations: the European Union (EU) and the Organization of Islamic Cooperation (OIC). The EU, established in the aftermath of World War II, represents a paradigmatic example of successful economic integration, characterized by the stage-by-stage creation of a single market, a customs union, and a common currency among its member states. Through its ambitious integration agenda, the EU has fostered unprecedented levels of economic

The Economic Potential of Islamic Countries, Part A: Economics, Demographics and Financial Services, 39–51

Published under exclusive licence by Emerald Publishing Limited
doi:10.1108/978-1-83708-000-720251004

interdependence, institutional cooperation, and collective decision-making, contributing to decades of peace, prosperity, and stability in Europe.

In contrast, the OIC, founded in 1969, emerged from a shared sense of religious and cultural identity among its member states, encompassing predominantly Muslim-majority countries across the globe (Kamrava, 2018). While the OIC espouses principles of unity, cooperation, and solidarity among its members, its efforts toward economic integration have faced significant challenges and limitations. Despite a common religious and cultural heritage, the OIC member states have struggled to translate their shared aspirations into tangible economic integration outcomes, hindered by political divergences and tensions, socioeconomic disparities, and institutional weaknesses within the organization.

This chapter undertakes a comparative analysis of the EU and OIC's approaches to economic integration and collaboration, with a particular focus on elucidating the relatively poor success of the OIC in this regard. By examining the historical trajectories, institutional frameworks, and policy dynamics of both organizations, this comparative analysis seeks to unravel the underlying factors shaping their divergent experiences in collaboration. Through a nuanced exploration of successes, challenges, and lessons learned, this chapter aims to shed light on the intricate interplay between regional cooperation, institutional dynamics, and socioeconomic factors in shaping the envisioned outcomes. Ultimately, by drawing insights from the comparative analysis, this chapter endeavors to offer valuable perspectives for policymakers, scholars, and practitioners seeking to navigate the complexities of integration and collaboration in diverse regional contexts.

Historical Context and Foundations

The origins of economic integration in Europe can be traced back to the devastation wrought by World War I and World War II, which underscored the urgent need for mechanisms to foster peace, stability, and prosperity on the continent and beyond. In the aftermath of these conflicts, European leaders embarked on ambitious initiatives to promote economic cooperation and integration as a means to prevent future wars and promote collective prosperity. The Treaty of Paris in 1951, which established the European Coal and Steel Community (ECSC), marked the first step toward economic integration by pooling the coal and steel resources of six European countries – Belgium, France, Germany, Italy, Luxembourg, and the Netherlands. This initiative aimed to coordinate key industries essential for military production, thereby reducing the risk of future conflicts and fostering economic cooperation among former adversaries.

Subsequent milestones in European integration include the Treaty of Rome in 1957, which established the European Economic Community (EEC) and the European Atomic Energy Community (Euratom), laying the foundation for the creation of a common market and a customs union among member states. The Maastricht Treaty, signed in 1992, represented a significant milestone in the evolution of the EU, establishing the framework for economic and monetary union (EMU) and paving the way for the introduction of the euro as a single currency. The Lisbon Treaty, signed in 2007, further strengthened the institutional framework of the EU, enhancing its role in areas such as foreign policy, justice, and security cooperation.

In contrast to the EU, the OIC emerged from a different historical, especially post-colonial, context, with its foundational motives grounded in religious unity and solidarity among Muslim-majority countries. Established in 1969 following the arson attack on the Al-Aqsa Mosque in Jerusalem, the OIC aimed to promote cooperation and solidarity among member states, foster economic development, and safeguard as well as promote the interests of the Muslim world. While the OIC has held numerous summits and declarations addressing economic issues, such as the adoption of the Ten-Year Programme of Action to Strengthen Economic and Commercial Cooperation among Member States in 2005, its efforts toward economic integration have been constrained by political divisions, socioeconomic disparities, regional rivalries, and institutional weaknesses within the organization (Wilson, 2016).

The Theoretical Framework and EU as a Model of Economic Integration

The study of economic integration has been underpinned by a rich theoretical framework that elucidates the dynamics and implications of regional cooperation initiatives. Central to this discourse is the economics of integration theory, which provides analytical tools and frameworks for understanding the motivations, mechanisms, and outcomes of economic integration processes. Drawing on principles from international economics, game theory, political economy, and systems thinking, this theoretical perspective offers valuable insights into the determinants of regional integration, the distributional effects of integration policies, and the potential welfare gains for participating countries.

Key contributions to the economics of integration theory include important works such as "The Economics of European Integration" by Baldwin and Wyplosz (2019). This work provides an in-depth analysis of the economic principles underpinning European integration, encompassing topics such as trade liberalization, monetary integration, and regional policy coordination. Moreover, works such as "From Europeanisation to Diffusion" by Börzel and Risse (2018) offer insights into the processes of norm diffusion and institutional convergence within the EU, shedding light on the complex dynamics of integration across diverse policy and institutional domains.

Notably, the EU's evolution can be easily understood through the lens of the theory of economic integration, which delineates various stages of integration, each marked by increasing, cumulative levels of cooperation and integration among member states. The theory posits that economic integration progresses through several stages, starting from preferential trading arrangements and culminating in a full EMU. The EU's evolution can be mapped onto these stages, demonstrating the organization's trajectory toward deeper integration over time.

Preferential Trade Area (PTA): A PTA is a trading bloc in which member countries reduce or eliminate tariffs and other trade barriers on certain goods traded among themselves while maintaining their own individual tariff schedules for trade with non-member countries. PTAs aim to promote regional trade and economic cooperation among member states.

The EU went through the stage of a PTA in its journey toward economic integration with the establishment of the ECSC in 1951 and the subsequent formation of the EEC in 1957. These early initiatives aimed to create a common market for coal, steel, and other goods among member states, laying the foundation for a PTA characterized by the elimination of tariffs and quotas among member states. The Treaty of Rome, which established the EEC, committed member states to gradually eliminating trade barriers and promoting economic cooperation within the region.

As part of its PTA phase, the EU implemented various measures to foster trade liberalization and economic integration among member states. These measures included harmonization of trade policies, and the creation of institutions such as the European Commission and the Council of Ministers to oversee the integration process. Over time, the EU expanded its scope beyond the initial focus on coal and steel to encompass a wider range of goods and services, laying the groundwork for deeper economic integration in subsequent stages of its evolution (Baldwin & Wyplosz, 2019; Söderbaum, 2020).

Customs Union: The next stage in the EU's evolution involved the creation of a customs union. A customs union is a form of economic integration in which member countries eliminate tariffs and other trade barriers among themselves and adopt a common external tariff on imports from non-member countries. In addition to the elimination of internal trade barriers, customs unions also involve a common trade policy toward non-member countries.

The EU progressed through the stage of a customs union as part of its journey toward economic integration following the establishment of the EEC in 1957. The EEC aimed to create a common market for goods and services among member states, laying the foundation for deeper economic cooperation and integration within Europe.

Beyond what was achieved through the PTA stage, a key feature of the EU customs union included the establishment of a common external tariff. The Treaty of Rome, which established the EEC, committed member states to gradually eliminating trade barriers and promoting economic cooperation within the region.

As part of its customs union phase, the EU implemented various measures to facilitate trade liberalization and economic integration among member states. These measures included the creation of a common external tariff to regulate trade with non-member countries, the development of common trade regulations and standards, and the establishment of institutions at a broader level (Dinan, 2010).

Common Market: A common market is a form of economic integration where member countries not only eliminate tariffs and other trade barriers among themselves, as in a customs union, but also allow for the free movement of goods, services, capital, and labor within the market. In addition to the removal of internal trade barriers, a common market aims to create a level playing field for economic activity among member states by harmonizing regulations and standards.

The EU progressed through the stage of a common market as part of its journey toward economic integration following the establishment of the EEC in 1957. The EEC aimed to create a common market for goods and services among member states, laying the foundation for deeper economic cooperation and integration within Europe (Hix & Høyland, 2021).

EMU: The EMU is the highest form of economic integration, characterized by the adoption of a common currency, a coordinated monetary policy, and a high degree of economic convergence among member countries. In an EMU, member states relinquish control over their national currencies and entrust monetary policy decisions to a central authority, typically a central bank.

The EU progressed through the stage of an EMU as the culmination of its journey in economic integration. This phase was formalized with the signing of the Maastricht Treaty in 1992, which laid the groundwork for the establishment of the euro as the common currency of participating member states.

Key features of the EU's EMU included the adoption of the euro as the single currency, the establishment of the European Central Bank as the central monetary authority responsible for monetary policy, and the implementation of convergence criteria to ensure economic stability and convergence among member states (European Central Bank, 2020).

As part of its EMU phase, the EU underwent a rigorous process of economic convergence, with member states required to meet specific criteria related to inflation rates, government deficits and debt levels, exchange rate stability, and long-term interest rates before adopting the euro. The introduction of the euro in 1999 marked a significant milestone in the EU's economic integration journey, facilitating seamless trade and financial transactions among member states and enhancing economic stability and cooperation within the eurozone (Dyson & Featherstone, 1999).

Throughout its evolution, the EU has navigated challenges and opportunities associated with economic integration, adapting its institutional framework and policies to promote cohesion, stability, and prosperity among member states. The EU's trajectory from a PTA to a fully-fledged EMU reflects the organization's commitment to deepening integration and fostering cooperation among European nations. Of course, the establishment of the EU as a political entity went far beyond the scope of economic integration, which is beyond the scope of this chapter.

One of the EU's most significant successes is its role in promoting peace and stability in Europe. Founded in the aftermath of World War II, the EU was established with the aim of preventing future conflicts among European nations. Through economic integration and political cooperation, the EU has helped foster reconciliation and peaceful relations among its member states, contributing to the longest period of peace in European history. The EU's successes in promoting peace, prosperity, political cooperation, expansion, and global influence underscore its significance as a model of economic and political integration, offering valuable lessons and inspiration for other regions aspiring to achieve similar goals of cooperation and unity.

In parallel, the emergence of cooperation economics has offered a complementary perspective on economic integration, focusing on the role of collaboration and cooperative behavior in shaping economic outcomes. Cooperation economics encompasses interdisciplinary approaches and systems thinking that draw on insights from organizational theory, network analysis, and social psychology to understand the drivers and dynamics of collaboration within and across organizations (Axelrod, 2006). By emphasizing the importance of trust, reciprocity, and shared goals in fostering effective collaboration, this perspective offers valuable insights for analyzing the functioning and performance of regional organizations engaged in economic integration efforts.

In the context of assessing economic integration in regional organizations, various frameworks and methodologies have been developed to evaluate the extent and impact of integration initiatives. One such framework is the gravity model of trade, which has been widely used to analyze patterns of trade flows among countries and regions. Additionally, institutionalist approaches offer valuable insights into the role of institutions in shaping the incentives and constraints of economic integration processes (Botah, 2024). Moreover, frameworks such as the stages of regional integration model, developed by Ernst Haas (1961, 2004), provide a systematic framework for analyzing the evolution and dynamics of integration efforts over time.

Overall, the synthesis of the economics of integration theory, cooperation economics (Huxham & Vangen, 2005), and frameworks for assessing economic integration in regional organizations provides a robust analytical foundation for understanding the comparative dynamics of economic integration in the EU in achieving common goals and enhancing overall welfare. From economic integration to political cooperation, the EU's evolution reflects a commitment to deepening collaboration and solidarity among member states to promote peace, prosperity, and stability in Europe.

The OIC: A Journey in Economic Integration That Did Not Take Off

According to its official website, "The Organization is the collective voice of the Muslim world. It endeavors to safeguard and protect the interests of the Muslim world in the spirit of promoting international peace and harmony among various people of the world" (oic-oci.org). The establishment of OIC was not rooted in any proactive vision or agenda of systematic economic and political integration. Rather, it was more of a reaction to the historical humiliation the Muslim world in general and the Arab-Muslim world in particular suffered in the hands of Israel, when there was an arson incident targeting Al Aqsa mosque in Jerusalem.

Subsequently, it became a religious call to the members of OIC countries to unite and cooperate on issues of common interest. The Qur'an, as the sourcebook of guidance for Muslims, is quite explicit in its call toward unity, seeking common grounds and cooperating in good things.

> *And hold firmly together to the rope of Allahand do not be divided.* Remember Allah's favour upon you when you were enemies, then He united your hearts, so you – by His grace – became brothers. And you were at the brink of a fiery pit and He saved you from it. This is how Allah makes His revelations clear to you, so that you may be "rightly" guided. [3/Ale Imran/103]

> *Cooperate with one another in goodness and righteousness, and do not cooperate in sin and transgression.* And be mindful of Allah. [5/al-Maida/2]
>
> Say, O Prophet, "O People of the Book! *Let us come to common terms*: that we will worship none but Allah, associate none with Him, nor take one another as lords instead of Allah." But if they turn away, then say, "Bear witness that we have submitted 'to Allah alone'." [3/Ale Imran/64]

However, as the realities have unfolded, due to various reasons, both internal and external, religious imperatives do not seem to necessarily translate into meaningful action and substantive outcomes. Despite the very name containing "Cooperation", how OIC's legacy has evolved in terms of following a systematic approach toward genuine and practical cooperation is quite revealing.

The OIC's stated goals are to promote economic cooperation and integration among its member states, which comprise predominantly Muslim-majority countries spanning diverse regions across the globe. Within the framework of the OIC, various economic policies and initiatives have been pursued to foster collaboration and enhance economic development among member states. These initiatives include the negotiation of trade agreements, the convening of economic summits, and the promotion of joint investments aimed at facilitating economic integration and fostering shared prosperity among member states. However, all these initiatives were quite general and vague, not systematic as in accordance with the benchmarkable models of systematic economic integration. There was no free trade area, no customs union, no common market, and, of course, no economic union. In the realm of politics, the OIC has consistently struggled to take decisive and effective action on critical issues concerning the protection and promotion of the interests and integrity of the Muslim world.

One significant challenge stems from the political diversity and conflicts that characterize the organization's member states. Political tensions and conflicts within the Muslim world, fragmented into pieces as self-centered nation states since the post-colonial period, often impede the implementation of cohesive economic policies and hinder progress toward meaningful or deeper economic integration. Additionally, economic disparities among member states, stemming from differences in levels of development, resource endowments, and governance structures (mostly autocratic or pseudo-democracies), pose a significant obstacle to achieving meaningful economic cooperation and integration within the OIC (Kose & Yu, 2018).

Moreover, assessing the impact of whatever economic integration efforts within the OIC requires careful examination of trade volumes, economic cooperation initiatives, and development programs implemented by member states. While trade volumes among OIC member states have shown some growth in recent decades, they remain relatively modest compared to other regional groupings. Furthermore, economic cooperation initiatives, such as joint investment projects and infrastructure development programs, have been hampered by logistical challenges, financing constraints, and regulatory barriers, limiting their effectiveness in promoting structured and systematic economic integration and fostering sustainable development within the Muslim world.

Thus, while the OIC has some success on the economic front, in terms of meaningful economic cooperation and integration among its member states, significant challenges remain to be addressed. Overcoming political conflicts, reducing economic disparities, and enhancing the effectiveness of economic cooperation initiatives are essential steps toward realizing the full potential of economic integration within the OIC and fostering shared prosperity among its diverse member states.

Comparative Analysis

A comparative analysis of the EU and the OIC reveals stark differences in their structural and functional aspects, as well as their respective impacts on economic performance, member state benefits, and global influence. Structurally, the EU boasts a highly institutionalized framework characterized by supranational institutions, such as the European Commission and the European Parliament, which possess significant decision-making authority over member states. In contrast, the OIC operates on a more intergovernmental basis, with decision-making power residing primarily with sovereign member state governments, reflecting the diverse political, economic, and cultural landscape of its member states.

Functionally, the EU has achieved significant success in promoting economic integration among its member states through the establishment of a single market, a customs union, and a monetary union. These mechanisms have facilitated the free movement of goods, services, capital, and labor, leading to increased trade, investment flows, and economic growth within the union. Moreover, the EU's cohesion, systems-oriented policies have played a crucial role in reducing regional disparities and promoting economic convergence among member states, fostering social cohesion and solidarity across the union (El-Agraa, 2016).

In contrast, the OIC's economic integration efforts lacked a systematic, structured approach and have been hindered by political divisions, economic disparities, and institutional weaknesses among member states. As a result, the economic impact of the OIC on member states has been less pronounced compared to the EU, with trade volumes and investment flows remaining relatively modest and uneven across member states.

Furthermore, the role of cultural and religious factors in economic integration differs significantly between the EU and the OIC. While the EU's integration efforts are primarily driven by economic and political considerations, the OIC's foundation motives are rooted in religious unity and solidarity among Muslim-majority countries. While cultural and religious factors can serve as a potent source of cohesion and cooperation within the OIC, they can also pose challenges to economic integration by exacerbating political tensions and conflicts among member states. Indeed, despite the genuine messages of Islam regarding liberation, justice, unity, cooperation (*ta'awun*) and common welfare, the religious impetus has proven inadequate and hollow in achieving even the diluted stated goals.

One of the areas in which member countries of OIC have experienced substantive progress is Islamic banking and finance. However, even this success story is not desirably connected with the emphatic Qur'anic guidance about cooperation (*ta'awun*) (Farooq, 2019). Not seriously embracing the Islamic principle of cooperation in general, the journey of OIC toward an Islamic cooperation economy has been dismal.

While both the EU and the OIC aspire to promote economic integration and cooperation among their member states, their structural, functional, and cultural differences have resulted in divergent outcomes. Table 3.1 provides a concise overview of the key features of the EU and the OIC, highlighting their structural, economic, political, and cultural differences.

Table 3.1. Comparing and Contrasting the Key Features of the EU and the OIC.

Feature	**EU**	**OIC**
Structural aspect	Highly institutionalized framework with supranational institutions such as the European Commission and European Parliament	Inter-governmental organization where decision-making power rests primarily with member state governments
Economic integration	Single market, customs union, and monetary union promote free movement of goods, services, capital, and labor among member states	Trade agreements and economic cooperation initiatives aim to foster economic integration, but progress is limited
Cohesion policies	Comprehensive cohesion policies aim to reduce regional disparities and promote economic convergence among member states	Limited cohesion policies with focus on addressing socioeconomic disparities among member states
Political governance	Complex governance structure involving supranational institutions, national governments, and elected representatives	Decision-making power primarily rests with member state governments, reflecting diverse political landscape
Economic performance	Strong economic performance with high levels of intra-EU trade, investment flows, and economic growth	Varied economic performance across member states, with trade volumes and investment flows remaining relatively modest
Global influence	Significant global influence as a leading economic and political bloc, shaping international trade, investment, and governance	Limited global influence compared to the EU, with focus primarily on issues affecting Muslim-majority countries

(*Continued*)

Table 3.1. (*Continued*)

Feature	EU	OIC
Role of cultural/ religious factors	Cultural and religious factors play a minimal role in economic integration, with focus primarily on economic and political considerations	Religious unity and solidarity among member states serve as foundation motives, but can also pose challenges to economic integration
Systematic approach	EU has followed a systematic, structured, benchmarkable approach in transforming itself from disparate nation states into an economic and political union	OIC's goals and agenda are general, lacking a systematic, structured, benchmarkable approach, and the result is also much more limited

Comparative Analysis of Collaboration Performance: EU Versus OIC

Evaluating the relative performance and achievements of the EU and the OIC from a cooperation perspective involves considering various dimensions, including economic integration, political collaboration, institutional capacity, and socio-cultural factors (Table 3.2).

Lessons Learned and Policy Implications

The comparative analysis of the EU and the OIC offers valuable insights into the successes, challenges, and lessons learned from their respective experiences with economic integration. From the EU's trajectory, several key lessons emerge regarding the factors contributing to successful economic integration. Firstly, the EU's institutional framework, characterized by supranational institutions and binding legal frameworks, has played a crucial role in promoting cooperation, coordination, and enforcement among member states. Secondly, the EU's emphasis on solidarity and cohesion, as evidenced by its comprehensive cohesion policies, highlights the importance of addressing regional disparities and promoting inclusive growth within integrated regions. However, the EU has also faced significant challenges, including political tensions, institutional complexities, and socioeconomic disparities among member states, especially involving the western versus eastern Europe, underscoring the need for ongoing reforms and adaptive governance structures to address evolving challenges. Thirdly, EU's success can also be evaluated from systems thinking perspective, as the evolution of EU reflects the interplay of systems thinking frameworks, such as recognizing and comprehending interconnections and system structure, identifying and benefiting from feedback, identifying the leverage points to move the process in the desired direction, and effectively managing the dynamic behavior of the system components (Stave & Hopper, 2007).

Table 3.2. Comparative Analysis of Collaboration Performance.

Dimension	EU	OIC
Economic integration	Intra-EU trade accounts for approximately 67% of total EU trade (European Commission, 2022), indicative of a high level of economic integration	Intra-OIC trade remains relatively low, accounting for only around 16% of total OIC trade (Islamic Development Bank, 2021), indicating limited economic integration
Political cooperation	The EU operates with supranational institutions such as the European Commission and the European Parliament, facilitating policy coordination and decision-making among member states	Decision-making power within the OIC primarily resides with member state governments, leading to variations in political cooperation and collaboration (Heath-Brown, 2015)
Institutional Capacity	The EU boasts a robust institutional framework, including the European Commission, European Parliament, and European Central Bank, with comprehensive governance structures (Börzel & Risse, 2018)	The OIC's institutional capacity is relatively limited, with fewer supranational institutions and weaker governance structures compared to the EU (Kayaoglu, 2013)
Socio-cultural factors	The EU manages cultural and linguistic diversity through inclusive policies and social cohesion measures, fostering a sense of European identity and unity (Dinan, 2010)	Cultural and religious unity serve as foundation motives within the OIC, but differences in cultural and political contexts among member states can pose challenges to collaboration efforts (Milevski, 2018)

Conversely, the OIC's experiences offer important lessons for economic integration initiatives among diverse and heterogeneous member states, lacking the cohesion and efficacy derived from systems thinking. Despite facing numerous challenges, such as political divisions, economic disparities, and institutional weaknesses, the OIC has made some progress in fostering economic cooperation through trade agreements, joint investment projects, and development programs. One key lesson from the OIC's experiences is the importance of fostering political consensus, trust, and cooperation among member states to overcome political barriers and promote collective action toward economic integration. Additionally, the OIC's emphasis on cultural and religious unity as foundational motives underscores the significance of leveraging common identities and values to build solidarity and cooperation among member states, while exposing the weakness of religious imperatives when the underlying commitment is not authentic or compelling enough.

Conclusion

The comparative analysis of economic integration between the EU and the OIC offers valuable insights into the diverse approaches, challenges, and outcomes of regional cooperation initiatives. Through an examination of their structural, functional, and cultural aspects, as well as their impacts on economic performance, member state benefits, and global influence, several key conclusions can be drawn.

Firstly, the EU stands as a model of successful economic integration, characterized by a highly institutionalized framework, robust governance structures, and comprehensive cohesion policies. The EU's achievements in promoting economic convergence, fostering social cohesion, and enhancing global influence highlight the transformative potential of regional cooperation initiatives when accompanied by strong institutional frameworks and inclusive policies.

In contrast, the OIC's experiences underscore the complexities and challenges associated with economic integration efforts among diverse, often heterogeneous member states with petty rivalry. Despite its foundational motives based on religious unity and solidarity, the OIC has struggled to translate these aspirations into tangible beneficial outcomes, hindered by political divisions, economic disparities, and institutional weaknesses within the organization.

Moving forward, policymakers and stakeholders engaged in economic integration initiatives can draw upon the lessons learned from both the EU and the OIC to inform their strategies and policies. Emphasizing the importance of strong institutional frameworks, inclusive governance structures, and targeted policies to address regional disparities can help facilitate effective economic integration and promote sustainable development within diverse regional contexts. Moreover, fostering political dialogue, trust-building measures, and collaborative partnerships among member states are essential for overcoming political tensions and advancing shared objectives of economic cooperation and integration. By leveraging common identities and values tha Islam inculcates, policymakers can build solidarity and cooperation among member states, fostering an enabling environment for sustainable development, prosperity, and peace within integrated regions.

References

Axelrod, R. (2006). *The evolution of cooperation*. Basic Books.

Baldwin, R., & Wyplosz, C. (2019). *The economics of European integration*. McGraw-Hill Education.

Börzel, T. A., & Risse, T. (2018). *From Europeanisation to diffusion*. Westview Press.

Botah, K. (2024). Why institutions matter: Analysis of their significance in shaping economics, environmental, and policy transformation. *Journal of Social and Policy Issues*, *4*(2), 79–87.

Dinan, D. (2010). *Europe recast: A history of European Union*. Palgrave Macmillan.

Dyson, K., & Featherstone, K. (1999). *The road to Maastricht: Negotiating economic and monetary union*. Oxford University Press.

El-Agraa, A. M. (2016). *The European Union economics and policies*. Cambridge University Press.

European Central Bank. (2020). *Monetary policy*. https://www.ecb.europa.eu/mopo/strategy/pricestab/html/index.en.html

European Commission. (2022). *Intra-EU trade accounts for 67% of total EU trade*. https://ec.europa.eu/eurostat

Farooq, M. O. (2019). Banking structure and Riba-interest equation: The case for Ta'awuni (cooperation) finance. *Journal of Islamic Financial Studies*, *5*(2), 90–108.

Haas, E. B. (1961). International integration: The European and the universal process. *International Organization*, *15*(3), 366–392.

Haas, E. B. (2004). *The unity of Europe: political and economic integration reconsidered*. Stanford University Press.

Heath-Brown, N. (Ed.) (2015). Organization of the Islamic Conference (OIC). In *The statesman's yearbook 2016: The politics, cultures and economies of the world* (p. 57). Palgrave Macmillan UK.

Hix, S., & Høyland, B. (2021). *The political system of the European Union*. Palgrave Macmillan.

Huxham, C., & Vangen, S. (2005). *Managing to collaborate: The theory and practice of collaborative advantage*. Routledge.

Islamic Development Bank. (2021). *Intra-OIC trade remains at around 16% of total OIC trade*. https://www.isdb.org

Kamrava, M. (2018). *The political economy of the Persian Gulf*. Oxford University Press.

Kayaoglu, T. (2013). *The Organisation of Islamic Cooperation and human rights*. University of Pennsylvania Press.

Kose, M. A., & Yu, S. (2018). *The economic and social impact of the OIC: A regional integration perspective*. Springer.

Milevski, V. (2018). The 1969 Arson attack on the Al-Aqsa Mosque: An Islamic just war argument. *Journal of Religious Ethics*, *46*(1), 118–139.

Söderbaum, F. (2020). *Handbook of regional integration*. Routledge.

Stave, K., & Hopper, M. (2007, July 29–August 3). *What constitutes systems thinking? A proposed taxonomy* [Conference presentation]. Proceedings of the 25th international conference of the system dynamics society, Boston, MA. Retrieved May 2, 2024, fromhttp://www.systemdynamics.org/conferences/2007/proceed/index.htm

Wilson, R. (2016). *Economic development in the Middle East and North African countries: Contemporary issues*. Springer.

Section 2

Demography and Labor Market

Chapter 4

Future Demographic Dynamics: An Overview of the Islamic World's Projections*

Kais Hammami[a], *Ouiam Chafik*[a] *and Youssef Lazaare*[b]

[a]*ICESCO, Morocco*
[b]*Sidi Mohamed Ben Abdellah University, Morocco*

Introduction

In a world marked by increasing complexity and ambiguity, it is imperative to consider macro-forces and prevailing trends when analyzing the developmental possibilities of a state or region. Among these influential factors, demographics play a pivotal role. However, demographics are often misunderstood, being frequently reduced to mere population figures. While population is a fundamental aspect, it is merely one element among many that constitute the broader concept of demographics. To fully grasp the significance and impact of demographics, it is essential to consider various elements such as age distribution, gender, social classes, occupations and employment status, family structures, fertility, and mortality rates, among others.

Understanding the intricate dynamics of demographics provides valuable insights into the developmental trajectories of regions and nations. The interplay between these various elements shapes the social, economic, and political landscapes, influencing everything from policy decisions to resource allocation. For instance, the age structure of a population can determine the workforce availability, influence consumer behavior, and shape healthcare needs. Similarly, gender

*The findings presented in this chapter are primarily drawn from *Study of the Possible Futures of the Islamic World: The Demography of the Islamic World: Current Status and Future Prospects* by (Al-Masarweh et al., 2020) developed and revised under the supervision of the Center for Foresight and AI at ICESCO, and copyrighted by the ICESCO Center for Foresight and AI.

The Economic Potential of Islamic Countries, Part A:
Economics, Demographics and Financial Services, 55–100

doi:10.1108/978-1-83708-000-720251005

distribution affects labor market participation and educational attainment, while social classes can impact income distribution and access to opportunities.

As of November 15, 2022, the global population has surpassed 8 billion souls, with projections suggesting a figure of 9.8 billion by 2050, and 11.2 billion by 2100, placing the demographic dimension at the heart of the most pressing trends of our time (United Nations, 2020).

Amidst this demographic reality, a formidable youth population emerges, embodied by 1.8 billion individuals aged 15–24, constituting 16% of the global population. Significantly, 90% of this youth resides in developing countries (United Nations Educational, Scientific and Cultural Organization, 2022). Thus, the future of these young generations, tasked with shaping our collective future, becomes an imperative question to apprehend.

The Islamic World Educational Scientific and Cultural Organization (ICESCO) boasts a membership of 53 sovereign states, constituting a significant quarter (26%) of the world's nations. Presently, these member states collectively harbor a population of approximately 1.9 billion individuals, representing 24% of the global populace. It's noteworthy that this demographic estimate excludes an additional 300 million Muslim population lims residing in 25 countries, where Muslim population comprise at least one-tenth of their respective populations (Al-Masarweh et al., 2020).

The demographic distribution within the Islamic world reveals an intriguing pattern across its eight regions. Nearly half of the Islamic world's populace (49%), totaling roughly 1.87 billion individuals, is concentrated in 20 nations spanning South Asia (27%) and the West African and Sub-Saharan Africa region (22%). Moreover, 31% of the Islamic world's inhabitants reside in 17 countries situated within Southeast Asia (17%) and its Western counterpart (14%). The remaining segment, constituting 20% of the Islamic world's population, is dispersed across 15 nations, primarily encompassing North Africa, Central Asia, and East Africa. Additionally, a minute fraction, less than 1%, is found in two countries within South America (Pew Research Center, 2017).

The demographic profile of the Islamic World is characterized by significant diversity, reflecting varying stages of demographic transition. Some countries are experiencing rapid population growth due to high fertility rates, while others are witnessing aging populations and declining birth rates. These demographic shifts present both challenges and opportunities. High fertility rates can strain resources and infrastructure, necessitating investments in education, healthcare, and employment generation. Conversely, aging populations may require policy adjustments to address pension systems, healthcare services, and workforce management.

This distribution underscores the diverse demographic landscape and regional disparities within the Islamic world, reflecting varied historical, cultural, and geopolitical dynamics across its constituent regions.

Understanding demographic changes is crucial for comprehending the underlying structures of our world. For example, in the economic realm, demographics have profound and far-reaching effects. During the Cato Institute's 35th Annual Monetary Conference in 2018, Loretta J. Mester highlighted the intricate relationship between demographics and economic variables:

> demographic change can influence the underlying growth rate of the economy, structural productivity growth, living standards, savings rates, consumption, and investment; it can influence the long-run unemployment rate and equilibrium interest rate, housing market trends, and the demand for financial assets. (Mester, 2018)

The economy is just one facet of the broader societal structures influenced by demographic trends, underscoring the critical importance of demographic analysis.

Economic implications of demographic changes are vast and multifaceted. As populations age, the labor force shrinks, potentially slowing economic growth and increasing the dependency ratio. This shift necessitates policies to enhance productivity and adapt labor markets. Additionally, demographic trends influence housing markets, with younger populations driving demand for housing, while aging populations may lead to changes in housing preferences and needs. Savings rates and investment patterns are also affected, as different age cohorts exhibit varying financial behaviors.

By examining these various elements, we can better understand how demographics shape not only economic outcomes but also social and political dynamics, thus enabling more informed policy-making and strategic planning. Demographic analysis provides a foundation for anticipating future trends and addressing potential challenges, ensuring sustainable development and improved quality of life for populations across ICESCO member states. This comprehensive approach to understanding demographics highlights the interconnectedness of population dynamics with broader societal processes, emphasizing the need for holistic and forward-thinking strategies in addressing demographic shifts.

Among other shifts: Climate change and resource scarcity that has come at a time when most economies in the region are experiencing profound changes, rapid urbanization in addition to increasingly widespread adoption of technological advances such as Artificial Intelligence.

Indeed, the increasing scrutiny of global uncertainty has caught all our interest. It illustrates the extent of our collective naivety and forces us to focus our resources solely on responding to emergencies, to the detriment of the investments necessary for future development, which brings us to compel about the importance of strategic and strategic foresight studies.

Sources of Demographic Information in the Islamic World

Accurate demographic data is crucial for effective policy formulation and implementation. In Islamic World Countries, the primary sources of demographic information include national censuses, surveys, and international databases. National censuses are typically conducted every 10 years and provide comprehensive data on population size, distribution, and various demographic characteristics. Surveys, such as demographic and health surveys (DHS) and multiple indicator cluster surveys, offer more frequent updates and detailed information on specific aspects of the population, such as health, education, and living conditions (United Nations, Department of Economic and Social Affairs, Statistics Division, 2020).

International databases, like those maintained by the United Nations, World Bank, and other global organizations, compile and standardize data from national sources, making it accessible for comparative studies and international analysis.

According to the principles and recommendations of the Statistics Division of the United Nations Department of Economic and Social Affairs, countries should conduct a population and housing census every 10 years. The Division announces a 10-year round of censuses, the latest of which is the current round 2015–2024 (United Nations, Department of Economic and Social Affairs, Statistics Division, 2017), and monitors countries' compliance with their census dates and provides technical support for their implementation. It can be said that not all countries in the world, including a number of Islamic World Countries, have complied with international recommendations. Some developed countries conduct a census every five years, while others have no need to do so due to the quality of their civil registration data.

The reliability and accessibility of these data sources vary. National censuses are often considered highly reliable due to their comprehensive nature and official status. However, they can be expensive and logistically challenging to conduct, especially in countries with large or hard-to-reach populations. Surveys provide more targeted data but may face issues of sampling bias and limited coverage. International databases are useful for cross-country comparisons but rely on the quality and consistency of national data. Challenges associated with demographic data collection in Islamic World Countries.

Population Size – Trends and Growth Rates

Analyzing recent trends in population size and growth rates over the past decade (2010–2020) provides insights into current demographic conditions and helps forecast future developments. Over this period, the population of Islamic World Countries increased by about 330 million, reflecting an average annual growth rate of 1.9%. This growth is not uniform across all regions, as illustrated in Table 4.1, which presents population sizes in Islamic World Countries for 2010 and 2020.

We can categorize Islamic World Countries based on their adherence to conducting a population census every 10 years into the following groups:

- Countries that have adhered to the census schedule and conducted a census in both rounds: 12 countries: Azerbaijan, Bahrain, Oman, Palestine, Qatar (conducts a census every five years), Tajikistan, Indonesia, Iran (conducts a census every five years), Brunei, Malaysia, Egypt, and Burkina Faso.
- Countries that conducted a census in the first round but are not yet due for the second round: 12 countries expected to conduct a census between 2022 and 2024: Tunisia, Morocco, Mauritania, Benin, Togo, Senegal, Gabon, Gambia, Guinea, Uganda, Maldives, and Guyana.
- Countries that conducted a census in the first round and are overdue for the second round but have not conducted it yet are 13 countries: UAE (conducted two censuses in the first round), Turkiye, Saudi Arabia, Kazakhstan, Kyrgyzstan,

and Kuwait (conducted two censuses in the first round), Bangladesh, Algeria, Sudan, Libya, Chad, Guinea-Bissau, Cameroon, Ivory Coast, Mali, Niger, Nigeria, and Djibouti.

- Countries that did not conduct a census in the first round but have conducted or are expected to conduct a census in the second round: six countries: Jordan, Uzbekistan, Pakistan, Sierra Leone, Comoros, and Suriname.
- Countries that have not conducted a census in either round: six countries: Syria, Iraq, Lebanon, Yemen, Afghanistan, and Somalia.

From this classification, it is clear that various obstacles and challenges have prevented several Islamic World Countries from adhering to international recommendations to conduct a population census at least once every 10 years. Among these challenges are the scarcity of financial and human resources, as conducting a census is a significant statistical operation requiring extensive resources. In some countries, political challenges arise where governments hesitate to decide to conduct the census to avoid political repercussions, they consider undesirable or because the census is seen as a lower priority.

The data highlights significant regional variations in growth rates. East Africa experienced the highest growth rate at 38%, followed by West Africa and Sub-Saharan Africa at 32%. North Africa saw a growth rate of 22%, while West Asia grew by 21%. Central and South Asia had an 18% growth rate, and Southeast Asia and South America had the lowest growth rates at 13% and 7%, respectively. These variations reflect differing demographic trends and socio-economic conditions across regions.

Regional Distribution of the Islamic World by Population Size

The Islamic world's population, currently about 1.87 billion, is unevenly distributed across eight regions. Nearly half (49%) of this population resides in South Asia and West Africa/Sub-Saharan Africa, indicating these regions' significant demographic weight. Southeast Asia and West Asia also account for substantial proportions of the Islamic population. In contrast, North Africa, Central Asia, and East Africa have smaller shares of the population, with South America hosting the smallest Muslim population.

Table 4.2 ranks the regions by population size and highlights the top ten Islamic World Countries by population, which together represent 68% of the total Muslim population. The largest countries in terms of population are Indonesia, Pakistan, Nigeria, Bangladesh, and Egypt. This ranking underscores the demographic prominence of these nations within the Islamic world and their potential influence on regional and global demographic trends.

By examining these various sources and trends in demographic data, policymakers and researchers can better understand the population dynamics within Islamic World Countries. This understanding is essential for addressing the unique challenges and opportunities that arise from these demographic patterns, enabling more effective planning and resource allocation.

Table 4.1. Population Size in Millions at Mid-year and Percentage Change in Population Size and Annual Population Growth Rate for 2010–2020.

Region	Country	2010 Population	2020 Population	% Change 2010–2020	Annual Growth Rate (%)
North Africa	Tunisia	10.64	11.28	6.04	0.59
	Algeria	35.98	43.85	21.98	1.98
	Sudan	33.99	45.50	33.83	2.93
	Libya	6.35	7.40	16.51	1.54
	Mauritania	3.43	4.65	35.61	3.08
West Africa	Nigeria	158.50	206.14	30.08	2.66
	Ghana	24.66	31.07	25.97	2.33
	Senegal	12.46	16.74	34.29	3.02
	Guinea	10.45	13.56	29.77	2.64
	Sierra Leone	6.00	7.98	33.00	2.87
East Africa	Ethiopia	90.53	114.96	26.94	2.38
	Kenya	40.51	53.77	32.70	2.83
	Uganda	33.78	45.74	35.47	3.07
Southern Africa	South Africa	50.13	59.62	18.91	1.75
Middle East	Syria	21.02	17.50	–16.76	–1.83
	Iraq	31.33	40.22	28.39	2.52
	Yemen	24.05	30.20	25.54	2.29
	Jordan	6.11	10.20	67.09	5.23
	Lebanon	4.24	5.41	27.53	2.47
South Asia	India	1,210.19	1,366.42	12.90	1.22
	Pakistan	173.51	220.89	27.28	2.45
	Bangladesh	144.04	165.19	14.68	1.37
	Nepal	26.79	30.03	12.09	1.15
East Asia	China	1,341.00	1,402.00	4.55	0.45
	Japan	127.52	126.17	–1.06	–0.11
Southeast Asia	Indonesia	237.64	273.52	15.08	1.41
	Philippines	92.34	109.58	18.64	1.72
	Vietnam	87.84	97.34	10.80	1.03
Central Asia	Kazakhstan	16.30	18.40	12.88	1.21
	Uzbekistan	28.56	33.37	16.85	1.56
	Turkmenistan	5.10	6.03	18.24	1.69

Table 4.1. (*Continued*)

Region	Country	2010 Population	2020 Population	% Change 2010–2020	Annual Growth Rate (%)
South America	Brazil	195.71	212.56	8.60	0.83
North America	United States	309.33	331.00	6.98	0.68
Europe	Russia	142.86	144.10	0.87	0.09
	Germany	81.75	83.02	1.55	0.15
	France	65.03	67.39	3.62	0.36

Overall Totals:

- 2010 Population: 1,536.94 million
- 2020 Population: 1,867.32 million
- % Change 2010–2020: 21.52%
- Annual Growth Rate (%): 1.95

Source: United Nations, Department of Economic and Social Affairs, Statistics Division (2021).

Table 4.2. Top Ten Most Populous Islamic World Countries in Mid-2020.

Rank	Country	Population (millions)	Annual Population Growth Rate (%) 2010-2020	Number of Years for Population to Double
1	Indonesia	273.52	1.23	56
2	Pakistan	220.89	2.08	33
3	Nigeria	206.14	2.63	26
4	Bangladesh	164.69	1.10	63
5	Egypt	102.33	2.12	33
6	Turkiye	84.34	1.54	45
7	Iran	83.99	1.30	53
8	Uganda	45.74	3.44	20
9	Algeria	43.85	1.98	35
10	Sudan	43.85	2.39	29

Total Population of the Top 10 Countries: 1,269.34 million

Total Population of Islamic World Countries: 1,867.32 million

Percentage of Total Population: 68%

Source: United Nations, Department of Economic and Social Affairs, Population Division (2021).

Current Age Structure and Related Challenges

The demographic analysis of population characteristics encompasses not only the size and growth rates but also the age structure, which can be even more critical in understanding societal dynamics. The age structure is typically analyzed by dividing the population into broad age groups: children (usually those under 15) and the elderly (those 65 and older). This division helps in comprehensively understanding the demographic composition and its implications.

An inverse relationship exists between the proportions of children and the elderly in any given population. The proportion of children reflects recent demographic trends, particularly birth rates in the last 15 years. In contrast, the proportion of the elderly is connected to past demographic trends, specifically the birth rates from over 65 years ago and the subsequent survival rates of those cohorts. The recent level of births, as indicated by the birth rate, is the primary determinant of the age structure. It directly influences the number and proportion of children within a population. Consequently, the remaining proportions are allocated to the elderly and the working-age population. Life expectancy also plays a significant role, primarily affecting the proportion of the elderly. Additionally, international migration impacts the age structure by altering the composition of the working-age population (typically those aged 15–64 or 20–64).

The age structure significantly influences dependency ratios, which indicate the economic burden of supporting children and the elderly. Countries with high birth rates tend to have a high proportion of children and, consequently, a high child dependency ratio. Conversely, countries with low birth rates often have a higher proportion of elderly, leading to a higher elderly dependency ratio. This distribution impacts the nature of goods, services, and facilities required by the population, thus determining the resources and investments needed to meet these demands. For instance, a high proportion of children in the population affects labor force participation rates, often correlating with lower participation rates, particularly among women who might be engaged in child-rearing activities.

A detailed examination of the age composition of Islamic World Countries, as presented in Table 4.3, reveals the inverse relationship between the proportions of children and the elderly, with notable exceptions in Gulf Arab states due to their high proportions of young and adult foreign labor. Significant variations are evident, with the proportion of children ranging from less than a fifth in Gulf Arab states to 40% or more in West Africa and Sub-Saharan Africa.

Based on the data, Islamic World Countries can be classified into four groups according to their age structure. The first group consists of countries dominated by children (40% or more), including all West African and Sub-Saharan countries except Gabon, along with Sudan, Mauritania, Uganda, Somalia, Comoros, and Afghanistan. The second group comprises young societies (30–39% children) such as Jordan, Syria, Iraq, Palestine, Yemen, Tajikistan, Kyrgyzstan, Pakistan, Algeria, Libya, Egypt, and Gabon. The third group includes youthful societies (20–29% children) like Azerbaijan, Turkiye, Lebanon, Uzbekistan, Kazakhstan, Iran, Bangladesh, Maldives, Indonesia, Brunei, Malaysia, Tunisia, Morocco, Suriname, and Guyana. Notably, no Islamic World Countries fall into the category where children constitute less than 20% of the population, though some Gulf Arab states have low child proportions due to high rates of foreign labor.

Table 4.3. Percentage of Children and Elderly in Islamic World Countries for the Year 2020.

Region	Country	% Children	% Elderly
North Africa	Tunisia	22	7
	Algeria	34	4
	Sudan	41	3
	Libya	34	4
	Egypt	33	4
	Morocco	35	5
	Mauritania	44	3
West Africa and the Greater Sahara Desert	Burkina Faso	45	2
	Chad	46	2
	Nigeria	43	3
	Ghana	38	3
	Guinea	42	3
	Ivory Coast	39	3
	Senegal	41	3
	Togo	39	3
	Sierra Leone	39	3
	Gambia	44	3
	Guinea-Bissau	45	3
	Liberia	46	3
	Mali	44	4
	Niger	50	3
	Eritrea	44	3
East Africa	Uganda	47	2
	Somalia	47	2
	Djibouti	36	3
	Madagascar	47	2
	Comoros	45	3
	South America		
	Suriname	27	7
	Guyana	28	7
West Asia	Azerbaijan	22	8
	Saudi Arabia	30	4

(*Continued*)

Table 4.3. (*Continued*)

Region	Country	% Children	% Elderly
	United Arab Emirates	14	1
	Syria	33	4
	Iraq	40	3
	Palestine	39	3
	Jordan	34	3
	Kuwait	22	3
	Lebanon	25	7
	Yemen	39	3
Central Asia	Uzbekistan	30	4
	Kazakhstan	25	7
	Kyrgyzstan	34	4
	Tajikistan	35	3
	Turkmenistan	29	5
South Asia	Afghanistan	43	4
	Pakistan	35	3
	Bangladesh	28	5
	Maldives	31	5
Southeast Asia	Indonesia	27	6
	Malaysia	24	6
South America	Suriname	27	7
	Guyana	28	7

Source: Population Reference Bureau (2020).

Notes: Children are defined as those under the age of 15, while the elderly are those aged 65 and over. Total Percentage of Children in Islamic World Countries: 68% of the total population.

Three key concepts are associated with the implications of age structure: age dependency, potential for population growth, and the demographic dividend. Age dependency is particularly high in societies with a high proportion of children, as seen in the first two groups. The potential for population growth is evident in these groups as well, driven by large numbers of young people entering marriage and childbearing ages each year, ensuring sustained high birth rates even if the rates are declining. The demographic dividend, observed in Southeast Asian 'tiger' economies, arises from a demographic transition to low birth rates over several years. This transition reduces family size and child dependency, enabling families to save and invest more in education, health, and productivity, which in turn leads to economic growth and improved living standards.

By examining these various elements and trends in demographic data, policymakers and researchers can better understand the population dynamics within Islamic World Countries. This understanding is essential for addressing the unique challenges and opportunities that arise from these demographic patterns, enabling more effective planning and resource allocation.

Elements of Demographic Change

Fertility and Its Regulation

Fertility, one of the three critical elements determining the trajectory of population growth and age composition in any society, alongside mortality and external migration, plays a particularly significant role in shaping the demographic landscape of most Islamic World Countries. The exception lies with countries that receive substantial numbers of foreign labor, such as the Gulf Arab states. Fertility levels in any society are typically measured by two key indicators: the crude birth rate and the total fertility rate (TFR). The crude birth rate refers to the number of live births per 1,000 people in a given year, while the TFR represents the average number of children a woman is expected to have over her reproductive lifetime, assuming she experiences the current age-specific fertility rates.

Vital statistics, population censuses, and household surveys in Islamic World Countries provide data on fertility levels, which are published periodically, sometimes annually. International and regional organizations collect, evaluate, and disseminate these data through their databases. To obtain the most recent data on fertility levels in Islamic World Countries for the base year of 2020, we relied on international sources. Table 4.4 presents the crude birth rate and the TFR for Islamic World Countries in 2020, revealing significant variations in fertility levels among these countries. This disparity indicates that the future demographic trajectories of these nations will be diverse, unless those with high fertility rates implement effective programs to assist families in regulating fertility.

Based on the statistics in Table 4.4, Islamic World Countries can be classified according to their current fertility levels into several groups:

- Countries with Very Low Fertility (Near or Below Replacement Level, TFR 1.8–2.2): Azerbaijan, Lebanon, Iran, Maldives, Brunei, Malaysia, Tunisia, and Morocco.
- Gulf Arab States with Very Low Fertility (Due to High Male Labor Migration, TFR 1.8–2.2): United Arab Emirates, Bahrain, Saudi Arabia, Qatar, and Kuwait.
- Countries with Low Fertility (TFR 2.3–2.9): Jordan, Turkiye, Oman, Uzbekistan, Kazakhstan, Bangladesh, Indonesia, Djibouti, Suriname, and Guyana.
- Countries with Moderate Fertility (TFR 3.0–3.5): Syria, Palestine, Tajikistan, Kyrgyzstan, Algeria, Libya, Egypt, and Gabon.
- Countries with High Fertility (TFR 3.6–4.0): Iraq, Yemen, and Pakistan.
- Countries with Very High Fertility (TFR 4.1–4.9): Afghanistan, Sudan, Mauritania, Togo, Sierra Leone, Senegal, Gambia, Guinea, Guinea-Bissau, Cameroon, Côte d'Ivoire, and Comoros.
- Countries with Extremely High Fertility (TFR 5.0 or more): Benin, Burkina Faso, Chad, Mali, Niger, Nigeria, Uganda, and Somalia.

Table 4.4. Crude Birth Rate and Total Fertility Rate in Islamic World Countries for the Year 2020.

Region	**Country**	**Crude Birth Rate**	**Total Fertility Rate**
North Africa	Tunisia	17	2.1
	Algeria	24	3.0
	Sudan	31	4.4
	Libya	18	2.3
	Egypt	25	3.3
	Morocco	19	2.4
	Mauritania	35	4.5
West Africa and the Greater Sahara Desert	Burkina Faso	42	5.7
	Chad	45	6.2
	Nigeria	38	5.2
	Ghana	28	3.7
	Guinea	37	4.8
	Ivory Coast	36	4.6
	Senegal	36	4.7
	Togo	33	4.3
	Sierra Leone	34	4.2
	Gambia	39	5.0
	Guinea-Bissau	35	4.9
	Liberia	37	4.8
	Mali	44	6.3
	Niger	50	7.1
	Eritrea	33	4.6
East Africa	Uganda	42	5.5
	Somalia	41	6.0
	Djibouti	23	3.2
	Madagascar	35	4.4
	Comoros	29	3.7
South America	Suriname	17	2.4
	Guyana	20	2.5
West Asia	Azerbaijan	14	1.8
	Saudi Arabia	18	2.3

Table 4.4. (*Continued*)

Region	Country	Crude Birth Rate	Total Fertility Rate
	United Arab Emirates	10	1.4
	Syria	23	3.2
	Iraq	30	4.2
	Palestine	31	3.8
	Jordan	24	3.0
	Kuwait	14	2.1
	Lebanon	16	1.8
	Yemen	31	4.1
Central Asia	Uzbekistan	21	2.5
	Kazakhstan	22	2.7
	Kyrgyzstan	25	3.3
	Tajikistan	27	3.6
	Turkmenistan	21	2.9
South Asia	Afghanistan	34	4.3
	Pakistan	28	3.6
	Bangladesh	18	2.1
	Maldives	20	2.5
Southeast Asia	Indonesia	17	2.4
	Malaysia	16	2.0
South America	Suriname	17	2.4
	Guyana	20	2.5

Source: Population Reference Bureau (2020).

The Islamic World Countries in West Africa and Sub-Saharan Africa exhibit the highest fertility levels, indicating a potential for significant population growth, particularly among children, in the coming years.

Family Planning and Reproductive Rights

Discussing the demographics of the Islamic world necessitates addressing family planning, as fertility is a major determinant of population growth and age structure. Family planning practices significantly influence fertility levels. In many Islamic societies, couples voluntarily use various methods to regulate their fertility, a practice commonly known as family planning. These methods are employed for three primary reasons: delaying the first childbirth, spacing between births, and stopping childbirth after achieving the desired number of children.

Family planning methods are broadly categorized into modern and traditional methods. Information on the use of these methods is available from administrative records of family planning services provided by governmental and non-governmental organizations and from periodic household surveys, especially DHS conducted in several Islamic World Countries. These surveys, part of a global initiative started in the 1980s, have been conducted in over 90 countries, including 33 Islamic World Countries at least once (Ahbab & Kabir, 2014).

For the latest data on family planning practices in Islamic societies, we referred to international databases. Additionally, data on the use of family planning methods in countries participating in the global DHS program can be accessed online, though some data may be outdated. Table 4.5 presents the usage rates of family planning methods in Islamic World Countries, showing the prevalence of both modern and traditional methods. The usage rates reflect the percentage of couples currently using any method to regulate their fertility.

The availability and use of family planning methods vary significantly among Islamic World Countries, explaining the disparities in fertility levels. There is a strong inverse relationship between fertility rates and the usage of family planning methods, as evidenced by numerous studies. The usage rate of modern methods ranges from 5% to about 62%, while traditional methods vary from less than 0.5% to about 37%. Traditional methods, despite not requiring a service provider, have higher failure rates, adding another layer of explanation for the variation in fertility rates.

Unmet need for family planning is another critical aspect. This term refers to the proportion of couples who do not wish to have more children or who want to delay their next child but are not using any method to achieve their reproductive goals. The existence of unmet need contributes to unintended pregnancies, high population growth rates, and increased numbers of children. Table 4.5 indicates that unmet need for family planning varies among Islamic World Countries, ranging from about 6% to 34%. The countries with high fertility rates, particularly in West Africa and Sub-Saharan Africa, also have high levels of unmet need for family planning.

In summary, addressing the unmet need for family planning falls under reproductive rights, which international conventions recognize. These rights ensure that couples can decide freely and responsibly the number and spacing of their children, guaranteeing adequate care and health for both mothers and children.

Mortality Rates

The latter half of the 20th century witnessed a rapid decline in mortality rates across Islamic World Countries, driven largely by the widespread immunization of children against epidemics and the introduction of advanced medications and medical technologies from developed nations. This decline led to a population explosion in several countries, particularly those where birth rates remained high, as discussed

Table 4.5. Rate of Use of Modern and Traditional Contraceptive Methods (%) and Unmet Need for These Methods in Islamic World Countries for the Year 2019.

Region	Country	Unmet Need	Traditional Methods	Modern Methods
North Africa	Tunisia	15.4	36.8	14.3
	Algeria	14.2	7.6	49.5
	Sudan	N/A	1.6	11.5
	Egypt	N/A	4.0	58.0
	Morocco	15.6	8.8	58.6
	Mauritania	16.4	2.3	18.4
West Africa and Sub-Saharan Africa	Benin	17.8	10.9	10.1
	Burkina Faso	22.1	12.4	31.4
	Chad	N/A	1.5	7.8
	Togo	25.6	8.2	18.1
	Sierra Leone	N/A	3.4	24.2
	Niger	28.7	4.3	14.8
	Ghana	N/A	3.8	21.7
	Gambia	7.8	3.0	12.8
	Guinea-Bissau	N/A	5.2	11.1
	Côte d'Ivoire	19.8	3.1	21.1
	Mali	24.5	2.7	15.7
	Nigeria	N/A	3.3	19.0
	Uganda	28.6	7.8	36.3
East Africa	Somalia	N/A	N/A	N/A
	Comoros	14.5	2.2	58.7
	Djibouti	2.7	7.9	14.2
	Sudan	N/A	N/A	N/A
South Asia	Afghanistan	N/A	0.4	23.4
	Pakistan	17.3	9.3	20.2
	Bangladesh	N/A	7.8	54.1
	Maldives	5.7	5.1	33.2
	Indonesia	11.6	2.2	57.0
	Brunei	N/A	2.2	58.7
	Malaysia	N/A	7.9	23.4

(*Continued*)

Table 4.5. (*Continued*)

Region	**Country**	**Unmet Need**	**Traditional Methods**	**Modern Methods**
Central Asia	Turkiye	7.8	30.1	61.9
	Kazakhstan	12.7	21.6	27.7
	Uzbekistan	7.8	2.1	40.0
Middle East	Jordan	14.3	14.3	39.3
	Saudi Arabia	N/A	12.4	34.4
	UAE	N/A	N/A	N/A
	Qatar	N/A	N/A	N/A
	Lebanon	N/A	7.6	28.4
	Yemen	23.0	10.3	21.5
South Asia	Maldives	5.1	7.8	33.2
	Indonesia	11.6	2.2	57.0
	Malaysia	N/A	7.9	23.4
East Africa	Sudan	N/A	N/A	N/A

Source: Population Reference Bureau, Family Planning Data Sheet 2019.

Notes: "N/A" indicates data not available.

in the fertility section. Consequently, these countries, especially those with limited resources, faced significant challenges in adapting to the rapid population growth and the high proportions of children and adolescents within their societies.

Unlike fertility and international migration, mortality is unique in that it primarily acts to reduce population growth through the annual loss of life. Furthermore, due to ethical and humanitarian considerations, mortality can only be addressed through policies aimed at enhancing and protecting the health of citizens and extending their life spans. Therefore, mortality does not serve as a tool for countries aiming to slow population growth, necessitating a focus on fertility and migration policies instead.

Mortality levels in any society are commonly measured using several indicators: the crude death rate, infant mortality rate, and life expectancy at birth. The crude death rate indicates the number of deaths per 1,000 individuals in a given year. The infant mortality rate refers to the number of infants who die before reaching their first birthday per 1,000 live births. Life expectancy at birth summarizes age-specific mortality rates and represents the average number of years a newborn is expected to live if current age-specific mortality rates remain constant throughout their lifetime. There is an inverse relationship between the infant mortality rate and life expectancy at birth; improvements in infant survival rates often lead to higher life expectancy.

Life expectancy is calculated using life tables, a demographic tool that synthesizes age-specific mortality rates into a single measure (Kintner, 1976). This metric also reflects the health dimension of the Human Development Index (HDI) and is considered an indicator of national progress. Typically, life expectancy is higher among females than males due to biological and social factors. In Islamic World Countries, the gap between male and female life expectancy ranges from one to nine years, favoring females. This disparity is attributed to women's biological advantages, improved maternal care, reduced childbearing, and the predominance of men in hazardous occupations.

Table 4.6 provides estimates for the three key mortality indicators across Islamic World Countries. The crude death rate varies widely, ranging from 1 to 11 deaths per 1,000 people, reflecting differences in living conditions and healthcare system efficiency, as well as population age structures. For instance, the crude death rate is particularly low in Gulf Arab states due to their youthful populations, who are less susceptible to death.

However, the crude death rate alone is insufficient for comparative analysis between Islamic World Countries and with developed nations, as it is influenced by the age composition of the population. Developed countries often have higher crude death rates due to larger elderly populations, who are more prone to death, despite overall better living conditions and healthcare systems.

To facilitate a more accurate comparison of mortality levels, the infant mortality rate is a more appropriate measure. Table 4.6 shows significant variations in infant mortality rates among Islamic World Countries, ranging from 5 to 75 deaths per 1,000 live births. These disparities highlight differences in household conditions, healthcare service efficiency, especially maternal and child care, fertility levels, and birth spacing.

For a broader perspective on infant mortality levels, Islamic World Countries can be grouped into five categories based on their infant mortality rates:

- Very Low Infant Mortality (<10 deaths per 1,000 live births): Includes UAE, Bahrain, Turkiye, Oman, Qatar, Kuwait, Lebanon, Kazakhstan, Iran, Maldives, Brunei, and Malaysia.
- Low Infant Mortality (10–19 deaths per 1,000 live births): Includes Azerbaijan, Jordan, Saudi Arabia, Syria, Palestine, Uzbekistan, Kyrgyzstan, Tunisia, Libya, Egypt, Morocco, and Suriname.
- Moderate Infant Mortality (20–34 deaths per 1,000 live births): Includes Iraq, Tajikistan, Bangladesh, Indonesia, Algeria, Gabon, Djibouti, and Guyana.
- High Infant Mortality (35–49 deaths per 1,000 live births): Includes Yemen, Sudan, Togo, Senegal, Gambia, Cameroon, and Uganda.
- Very High Infant Mortality (50–75 deaths per 1,000 live births): Includes Afghanistan, Pakistan, Mauritania, Benin, Burkina Faso, Chad, Sierra Leone, Guinea, Guinea-Bissau, Côte d'Ivoire, Mali, Niger, Nigeria, Somalia, and Comoros.

Table 4.6. Crude Death Rate, Infant Mortality Rate, and Life Expectancy at Birth in 17 Islamic World Countries for the Year 2020.

Region	**Country**	**Life Expectancy at Birth**	**Infant Mortality Rate**	**Crude Death Rate**
North Africa	Tunisia	76	14	6
	Algeria	76	17	6
	Sudan	65	42	7
	Egypt	72	17	6
	Libya	73	10	5
	Morocco	76	18	5
	Mauritania	65	52	9
West Africa and Sub-Saharan Africa	Benin	61	52	9
	Burkina Faso	61	52	8
	Chad	58	72	11
	Togo	60	62	8
	Sierra Leone	61	82	11
	Senegal	68	39	7
	Côte d'Ivoire	59	66	10
	Ghana	64	44	7
	Mali	65	50	10
	Niger	59	62	11
	Nigeria	54	66	12
East Africa	Uganda	63	45	6
	Ethiopia	67	32	7
	Somalia	57	80	13
	Comoros	64	52	7
South America	Suriname	72	17	6
	Guyana	70	26	8
Middle East	Jordan	74	13	5
	Saudi Arabia	75	12	4
	Iraq	70	25	4
	Lebanon	78	7	4
	Palestine	74	17	3
	Qatar	80	6	1
	Kuwait	78	7	2
	Yemen	66	43	6

Table 4.6. (*Continued*)

Region	Country	Life Expectancy at Birth	Infant Mortality Rate	Crude Death Rate
Central Asia	Uzbekistan	75	11	4
	Tajikistan	71	26	5
	Kazakhstan	73	12	8
	Kyrgyzstan	72	15	5
South Asia	Afghanistan	65	60	6
	Iran	76	12	5
	Pakistan	67	60	7
	Bangladesh	73	24	5
	Maldives	78	7	4
South East Asia	Indonesia	71	25	6
	Brunei	78	6	4
	Malaysia	75	7	4

Source: Population Reference Bureau (2020).

Notes: Crude Death Rate: Number of deaths per 1,000 population. Infant Mortality Rate: Number of infant deaths (under 1 year) per 1,000 live births.

Life Expectancy in Islamic World Countries

Life expectancy at birth varies significantly among Islamic World Countries, as detailed in Table 4.6. These variations can be categorized into the following groups:

- Low Life Expectancy (<60 years): Includes five countries in West Africa and Sub-Saharan Africa, and one in East Africa.
- Moderate Life Expectancy (60–64 years): Includes 10 countries in West and East Africa.
- Above Average Life Expectancy (65–69 years): Includes eight countries.
- High Life Expectancy (70–74 years): Includes 11 countries.
- Very High Life Expectancy (≥75 years, up to 82 years): Includes 19 countries.

These classifications highlight the diverse health outcomes and longevity across the Islamic world, influenced by various factors such as healthcare quality, socio-economic conditions, and public health policies.

The study of mortality in Islamic World Countries reveals significant progress in reducing death rates over the past few decades, largely due to advancements in medical technology and healthcare services. However, substantial disparities remain, particularly in infant mortality rates and life expectancy, underscoring the need for continued efforts to improve healthcare access and quality. Understanding these mortality trends is crucial for policymakers to develop targeted strategies that address health inequalities and promote sustainable population growth and development.

International Migration

In addition to the vital demographic processes of fertility and mortality, spatial movement, specifically international migration, plays a significant role in shaping the demographic landscape of Islamic World Countries. International migration involves the movement of individuals between Islamic World Countries and between Islamic World Countries and the rest of the world. This type of migration not only changes the size of the population but also alters its composition by sex, age, and ethnicity. These changes depend on the demographic characteristics of the incoming and outgoing migrants, as evidenced by the age and ethnic composition of countries like the Gulf Arab states. These countries host large numbers of migrants, primarily young and adult males from South Asian countries such as Bangladesh, Pakistan, and India, who are both Muslim and non-Muslim population.

The impact of international migration on the size, distribution, and composition of populations in both sending and receiving Islamic World Countries does not become apparent over a short period. Instead, its effects accumulate over a long period. Large numbers of migrants have moved in and out of countries over several decades, making it challenging to capture the full scope of this historical process with current data. However, it is possible to provide estimates of current annual net migration in Islamic World Countries. Net migration refers to the difference between the number of people entering a country to reside for a significant period and those leaving the country for an extended period.

Not all Islamic World Countries are net receivers of migrants; some are net senders. To provide an overview of international migration in the Islamic world, net migration is used, which is the difference between the number of incoming and outgoing migrants. Based on this concept and available data, Islamic World Countries can be categorized into three groups according to their current net migration trends.

- Countries with Negative Net Migration: This group includes 36 countries that send more migrants abroad than they receive. These countries are Afghanistan, Algeria, Bangladesh, Benin, Burkina Faso, Cameroon, Comoros, Egypt, Gambia, Guinea, Guinea-Bissau, Guyana, Indonesia, Iran, Jordan, Kyrgyzstan, Lebanon, Libya, Maldives, Mali, Morocco, Nigeria, Pakistan, Senegal, Sierra Leone, Somalia, Palestine, Sudan, Suriname, Tajikistan, Togo, Tunisia, Turkiye, Uganda, Uzbekistan, and Yemen.
- Countries with Zero Net Migration: This group includes five countries with balanced migration flows, meaning the number of migrants entering and leaving is roughly equal. These countries are Azerbaijan, Chad, Côte d'Ivoire, Kazakhstan, and Brunei.
- Countries with Positive Net Migration: This group includes 13 countries that receive more migrants than they send abroad. These countries are Bahrain, Djibouti, Gabon, Iraq, Malaysia, Mauritania, Niger, Oman, Qatar, Saudi Arabia, Syria, the United Arab Emirates, and Kuwait.

- The effects of international migration on the demographic composition of these countries are substantial. In the Gulf Arab states, the influx of young, male migrant workers has significantly altered the demographic profile, creating an age and gender imbalance that affects various socio-economic dynamics. These migrants contribute to the labor force and the economy but also present challenges related to social integration and resource allocation.

Migration Trends and Implications

Countries with positive net migration, particularly those in the Gulf region, face unique demographic challenges. The high influx of migrants can strain infrastructure, public services, and housing. Additionally, these countries must address issues related to the social and cultural integration of diverse migrant populations. The reliance on migrant labor also raises questions about long-term sustainability and the need for policies that balance economic growth with social cohesion.

Countries with zero net migration present a balanced scenario, where migration does not significantly alter the population size but still impacts demographic composition. These countries might experience both the benefits and challenges of migration, such as cultural exchange and the need for effective integration policies.

Understanding the patterns and effects of international migration is crucial for policymakers in Islamic World Countries. Effective management of migration flows can enhance economic development, social stability, and overall demographic balance. By fostering cooperation and dialogue among Islamic World Countries, there can be a more coordinated approach to managing migration and its impacts, ensuring that migration serves as a catalyst for growth and development across the Islamic world.

Demographic Conditions and Socio-economic Development in the Islamic World

In understanding the pathways to achieving socio-economic development in the Islamic World, it is essential to explore the intricate correlations between demographics and development. Analyzing the demographics of the member states of the Islamic World presents significant challenges, as demographic trends are influenced by numerous factors, both internal and global. Disruptions such as wars, pandemics, and other unforeseen events can profoundly impact state demographics, and consequently, the demographic landscape of the Islamic World as a whole. Despite these complexities, a thorough understanding of the role of demographics in achieving development necessitates examining key elements such as population growth and age structure, gender disparities, fertility and mortality rates, education and employment, and GDP per capita.

Many states within the Islamic World experience rapidly growing populations with a substantial proportion of young people. Typically, such demographic conditions suggest a dynamic workforce and increased productivity, which could lead to significant socio-economic development. However, this potential advantage comes with substantial challenges. The critical question is whether these states can provide adequate education and employment opportunities for their burgeoning youth population. Without sufficient investment in these areas, the potential benefits of a young population may not be realized, and rapid population growth could strain resources and infrastructure, exacerbating socio-economic challenges.

Delving deeper into population growth necessitates an examination of fertility and mortality rates. Numerous studies indicate that Muslim countries tend to have higher fertility rates, contributing to the overall population growth. However, it is crucial to note that fertility rates across many states in the Islamic World are gradually declining. This trend represents a significant demographic shift that requires careful study. While some countries continue to maintain relatively high fertility rates, the overall decline in fertility rates could have profound implications for future demographic and socio-economic landscapes. On the other hand, mortality rates in many Islamic World Countries are low, contributing to population growth. Nonetheless, there are notable disparities in healthcare quality and access between different countries, which impact mortality rates and overall demographic trends.

Education and employment opportunities are vital for achieving socio-economic development, and this issue must be approached with caution due to the significant variability in education quality and employment opportunities across Islamic World Countries. Higher levels of education are associated with increased innovation, entrepreneurship, and economic growth, which are essential for socio-economic development. However, disparities in education levels among Islamic World Countries, and within countries, particularly in terms of gender, pose significant challenges. Girls and women often have fewer opportunities for education and employment, limiting the development prospects of entire communities and nations.

Focusing on the economic dimension, GDP per capita is a critical indicator of the correlation between demographics and socio-economic development. GDP per capita reflects the average income and standard of living within a country, highlighting disparities in economic development and prosperity among the Organization of Islamic Cooperation (OIC) member states. Various factors, including natural resource wealth, investment in infrastructure, quality of governance, and economic diversification, influence GDP per capita levels. Enhancing GDP per capita requires sustained efforts to promote economic growth, create jobs, reduce poverty, and improve social welfare.

Addressing these multifaceted challenges and opportunities necessitates comprehensive strategies that integrate demographic analysis into development planning. Policymakers must prioritize investments in education, healthcare, and employment creation while also addressing gender disparities and ensuring equitable access to resources and opportunities. By doing so, the Islamic World can harness its demographic potential to achieve sustainable socio-economic development, fostering a more prosperous and equitable future for its populations.

In conclusion, understanding and leveraging the demographic dynamics within the Islamic World is critical for driving socio-economic development. The interplay between population growth, age structure, gender disparities, fertility and mortality rates, education and employment, and economic indicators like GDP per capita shapes the development trajectories of these countries. Addressing these elements with targeted policies and investments will enable the Islamic World to overcome challenges and unlock its full potential for growth and development.

Differences Between Countries of the Islamic World

Analyzing the demographics of the Islamic World necessitates acknowledging the significant variations among its countries across multiple dimensions (Table 4.7). While these nations share common religious ties, they exhibit inherent differences in demographic characteristics, economic development, governance structures, and social dynamics. As highlighted in the study *The Demography of the Islamic World – Current Status and Future Prospects* (Al-Masarweh et al., 2020), these disparities are evident when comparing countries such as Saudi Arabia, Afghanistan, Morocco, and Niger. Despite being part of the Islamic World, these nations differ substantially in their demographic profiles and socio-economic contexts, with religion often being the primary commonality among them. The following analyses are derived from the same study and aim to further illustrate these differences, offering a data-driven foundation for understanding the diverse trajectories of demographic development within the Islamic World:

- Population Size and Growth: Countries of the Islamic World vary widely in terms of population size and growth rates. Countries like Indonesia, Pakistan, and Bangladesh have large populations with high growth rates, while smaller states like Brunei and Maldives have relatively smaller populations. These differences influence resource allocation, infrastructure planning, and socio-economic development strategies.
- Economic Diversity and GDP per Capita: The economic diversity among countries of the Islamic World is significant. Some countries, like Saudi Arabia, Qatar, and the United Arab Emirates, have high GDP per capita levels due to abundant natural resources such as oil and gas. Others, like Afghanistan, Yemen, and Niger, have lower GDP per capita levels and rely on agriculture or remittances. Economic disparities impact standards of living, access to services, and opportunities for development.
- Urbanization and Rural–Urban Divide: Urbanization rates vary across countries of the Islamic World, with some countries experiencing rapid urban growth while others remain predominantly rural. For example, Saudi Arabia and Qatar have highly urbanized populations, whereas countries like Afghanistan and Sudan have significant rural populations. Urbanization affects infrastructure needs, employment patterns, and social dynamics.
- Education and Literacy Rates: Educational attainment levels differ among countries of the Islamic World, reflecting variations in access to schooling, quality of education, and cultural attitudes toward learning. Countries like

Table 4.7. Demographic and Socio-economic Indicators of Islamic Countries.

Country	Population (2024)	Population Growth Rate (%)	Male Population (%)	Female Population (%)	Fertility Rate (Children per Woman)	Literacy Rate (%)	Employment Rate (%)
Afghanistan	43,372,950	2.68	51.7	48.3	3.741	38.39	35.9
Albania	2,826,020	−0.23	50.1	49.9	1.534	97.61	51.6
Algeria	46,278,751	1.47	50.5	49.5	2.749	80.17	35.1
Azerbaijan	**10,462,904**	0.48	49.5	50.5	1.978	99.81	59.6
Bahrain	1,498,712	0.89	62.6	37.4	1.873	95.65	69
Bangladesh	174,701,211	1.01	50.6	49.4	1.908	61.38	54
Benin	14,080,072	2.68	49.3	50.7	4.486	38.44	69.8
Brunei	455,858	0.74	50.5	49.5	1.744	96.38	–
Burkina Faso	23,840,247	2.53	49.7	50.3	4.763	36.09	61.8
Cameroon	**29,394,433**	2.61	49.9	50.1	4.241	75.02	72.5
Chad	18,847,148	3.11	49.7	50.3	5.231	39.52	57.2
Comoros	867,605	1.82	50.4	49.6	3.872	77.7	39.3
Djibouti	**1,152,329**	1.4	50	50	2.486	–	–
Egypt	114,484,252	1.57	50.2	49.8	3.097	75.34	60.7
Gambia	2,841,803	2.47	49.4	50.6	4.831	55.61	51
Guinea	14,528,770	2.38	50.5	49.5	4.313	30.37	58.2
Guinea-Bissau	**687,000**	3.46	49.6	50.4	4.104	59.54	66
Indonesia	**279,798,049**	0.82	49.9	50.1	2.204	–	64.7

Iran	89,809,781	0.71	50.7	49.3	2.081	86.9	–
Iraq	46,523,657	2.24	50.2	49.8	3.406	79.75	–
Jordan	11,384,922	0.42	51.4	48.6	2.541	96.66	30.8
Kazakhstan	19,828,165	1.13	48	52	2.598	99.79	65.7
Kuwait	4,349,380	0.91	59.6	40.4	2.022	96.13	67.9
Kyrgyzstan	6,946,242	–	49.3	50.7	–	99.52	51.4
Lebanon	5,219,044	–2.52	48.8	51.2	2.005	93.84	36.3
Libya	6,964,197	1.10	50.4	49.6	2.094	91.29	38.3
Malaysia	34,671,895	1.06	50.7	49.3	1.910	94.71	61.7
Maldives	517,887	–0.60	50.4	49.6	1.759	99.4	–
Mali	24,015,789	3.1	50	50	5.372	38.48	63.3
Mauritania	4,993,922	2.69	50.3	49.7	4.274	51.41	39.6
Morocco	38,211,459	0.98	49	51	2.276	72.33	38.6
Mozambique	34,858,402	2.84	48.7	51.3	4.475	58.55	75.1
Niger	28,238,972	3.81	50.3	49.7	6.414	19.1	72.4
Nigeria	229,152,217	2.39	50.6	49.4	5.009	59.6	48.5
Oman	4,713,553	1.49	59	41	2.548	93.89	66.1
Pakistan	245,209,815	1.96	50.8	49.2	3.189	58.75	47.9
Palestine	5,494,963	2.30	50.8	49.2	3.307	96.66	–
Qatar	2,737,061	0.76	75.9	24.1	1.760	97.7	87.1
Saudi Arabia	37,473,929	1.43	55.2	44.8	2.148	94.41	56.1

(*Continued*)

Table 4.7. (*Continued*)

Country	Population (2024)	Population Growth Rate (%)	Male Population (%)	Female Population (%)	Fertility Rate (Children per Woman)	Literacy Rate (%)	Employment Rate (%)
Senegal	18,221,567	2.58	49.6	50.4	4.288	55.41	42.9
Sierra Leone	8,977,972	2.13	48.9	51.1	3.778	47.41	53
Somalia	18,706,922	3.11	49.6	50.4	5.576	–	38.5
Sudan	49,358,228	2.60	50.4	49.6	4.104	75.86	–
Suriname	628,785	0.89	50.1	49.9	2.296	95.57	48.7
Syria	24,348,053	4.83	50.6	49.4	2.610	86.41	–
Tajikistan	10,331,513	1.85	49.2	50.8	3.367	99.77	37.2
Togo	9,260,864	2.29	49.5	50.5	4.010	66.63	55.1
Tunisia	12,564,689	0.85	50	50	2.080	81.83	38.2
Turkiye	90,121,841	–	49.9	50.1	–	95.12	43.5
Turkmenistan	6,598,071	1.26	49.2	50.8	2.598	99.7	43.5
Uganda	49,924,252	2.76	50	50	4.334	73.87	65.5
United Arab Emirates	11,027,129	0.79	69.5	30.5	1.346	93.83	73.9
Uzbekistan	35,673,804	1.45	49.7	50.3	2.289	99.59	53.6
Yemen	35,219,853	2.24	50.3	49.7	3.360	70.27	31.8

Source: This table is based on data from multiple sources including World Bank et al. (n.d.).

Turkiye, Iran, and Malaysia have relatively high literacy rates and well-developed education systems, whereas others face challenges in providing universal education, particularly for girls and women.

- Healthcare Infrastructure and Access: The availability and quality of healthcare services vary among countries of the Islamic World, impacting population health outcomes and life expectancy. Countries like Saudi Arabia, Qatar, and the United Arab Emirates have advanced healthcare systems with modern facilities, while others struggle with limited healthcare infrastructure and inadequate access to medical services.
- Gender Equality and Women's Empowerment: Gender disparities persist in many countries across the Islamic World, although the degree varies. Some countries, such as Bangladesh and Indonesia, have made significant strides in promoting gender equality and women's empowerment through legislative reforms and social programs. Others, like Afghanistan and Yemen, continue to face challenges related to women's rights, education, and participation in the workforce.
- Political Stability and Governance: Political stability and governance structures differ across countries of the Islamic World, ranging from democratic systems to authoritarian regimes and fragile states. Countries like Turkiye, Malaysia, and Indonesia have relatively stable political environments and democratic institutions.

Muslim Population Outside the Member States of the Islamic World Educational, Scientific and Cultural Organization

As previously mentioned, not all countries classified as Islamic are members of the Islamic World Educational, Scientific and Cultural Organization (ICESCO), and not all countries with a high percentage of Muslim population are considered Islamic states. Some of these countries are secular, with constitutions that do not reference an official religion, and they are not members of the OIC. Nevertheless, this section is dedicated to those countries where Muslim population form a significant portion of the population but are not officially recognized as Islamic states.

Table 4.8 reveals that there are 25 countries where Muslim population make up more than 10% of the population. Notably, in nine of these countries, Muslim populations constitute over a third of the population. The total number of Muslim populations in these 25 countries amounts to approximately 311 million, with India alone accounting for 63% of this figure. India hosts the largest Muslim population outside the Islamic world, highlighting its significant Muslim demographic.

Given the special interest in the Russian Federation as an observer state in ICESCO, it is pertinent to discuss Russia as a country with a considerable Muslim population. The history of Islam and its civilization in the countries that were part of the Soviet Union is noteworthy. Following the dissolution of the Soviet Union, six republics gained independence: one in the Caucasus (Azerbaijan) and five in Central Asia (Uzbekistan, Kazakhstan, Turkmenistan, Kyrgyzstan, and Tajikistan). All these republics, except Turkmenistan, are members of ICESCO.

Table 4.8. Countries Outside the Islamic World Organization for Education, Science, and Culture with a Muslim Population Percentage Exceeding 10% in 2021.

Country	Number of Muslim Population (Million)	% of Muslim Population	Country	Number of Muslim Population (Million)	% of Muslim Population
Côte d'Ivoire	0.1	19.1	Mayotte	0.3	97.0
Ghana	5.1	18.0	Kosovo	1.7	95.6
Mozambique	3.8	17.9	Azerbaijan	8.5	93.4
Cyprus	0.2	17.3	Northern Cyprus	0.3	99.1
Central African Republic	0.9	15.0	Tanzania	2.6	35.2
Singapore	0.8	14.7	India	195.0	14.2
India	195.0	14.2	Russia	19.7	13.5
Russia	19.7	13.5	Bulgaria	0.9	13.4
Bulgaria	0.9	13.4	Kenya	5.5	11.2
Kenya	5.5	11.2	Georgia	0.4	10.7
Georgia	0.4	10.7			
Total	310.8				

Source: World Population Review, https://worldpopulationreview.com/country-rankings/muslim-population-by-country.

During the Soviet era, various levels of local governance included autonomous republics, many of which are now part of the Russian Federation. Most of these are Islamic republics, differing little from the six main ones except in size and their proximity to central Russia. Prominent autonomous Islamic republics within Russia include Chechnya, Ingushetia, and Dagestan in the Russian Caucasus. Other significant republics with high Muslim populations include Kabardino-Balkaria and Karachay-Cherkessia in the North Caucasus, as well as Tatarstan and Bashkortostan in the Ural region.

Overall, approximately 20 million Muslim population reside in the Russian Federation, which has a total population of about 146 million. Russia, the largest country in the world by area, shares land and sea borders with 20 countries, including Islamic World Countries such as Turkiye, Azerbaijan, and Kazakhstan. Islam is the second-largest religion in Russia, with Muslim population currently constituting about 14% of the population. This percentage is expected to increase due to generally higher birth rates among Muslim population compared to other groups. Islam is legally recognized and acknowledged by Russian political leadership as part of the country's historical heritage alongside Orthodox Christianity.

The presence of significant Muslim populations in countries outside the traditional Islamic world, such as India and Russia, underscores the global diversity of Islam and its adherents. These populations contribute to the cultural and religious mosaic of their respective countries while also facing unique challenges and opportunities. In India, for instance, Muslim population play a vital role in the country's social, economic, and political spheres, despite often facing socio-economic disparities and political marginalization. In Russia, the historical legacy of Islam and its integration into the broader fabric of Russian society highlight the complexities of religious coexistence and the importance of recognizing and addressing the needs of minority populations.

Moreover, the increasing Muslim populations in these countries necessitate comprehensive policies that promote social inclusion, religious tolerance, and economic opportunities. This involves not only recognizing the contributions of Muslim communities but also addressing issues such as discrimination, inequality, and access to education and employment. By fostering an inclusive environment, these countries can harness the potential of their diverse populations, leading to more cohesive and prosperous societies.

In conclusion, the demographic presence of Muslim population outside the member states of ICESCO, particularly in secular and non-OIC countries, reflects the widespread and diverse nature of the Muslim population globally. Understanding and addressing the unique circumstances of these communities is crucial for promoting inclusive development and social harmony. This approach aligns with the broader goals of ICESCO and similar organizations in fostering mutual understanding, cooperation, and respect among different cultural and religious groups worldwide.

The Islamic World Scenarios of Unity or Divide?

Shedding the light on the differences among countries of the Islamic World leads to a question that is extremely important and relevant to the matter of development: Do these differences mean that each country is supposed to seek its own growth and development regardless of what the situation is like in other countries, or should collective efforts be made in order for the Islamic World to rise as a whole? This question provides the perfect opportunity to look into some possible scenarios for the evolution of the dynamics between countries of the Islamic World in the future (Fig. 4.1).

Scenario 1: Unity Through Economic Integration

- Description: In this scenario, countries of the Islamic World prioritize economic cooperation and integration as a means to foster unity and solidarity. They establish regional trade agreements, investment partnerships, and infrastructure projects to promote economic growth and development. Shared economic interests incentivize collaboration and build trust among member states, leading to greater unity and cohesion within the Islamic World.

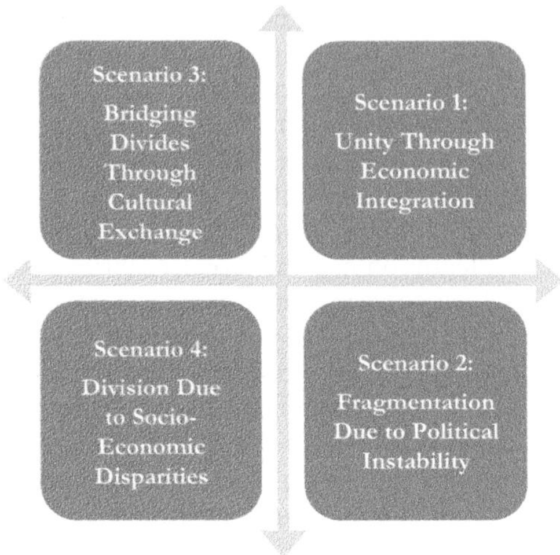

Fig. 4.1. Future Scenarios for Cooperation and Socio-economic Dynamics in the Islamic World.

- Implications: Economic integration strengthens intra-regional trade, stimulates investment flows, and creates opportunities for joint ventures and technology transfer. Enhanced economic ties pave the way for closer diplomatic relations and cultural exchanges, fostering a sense of common identity and purpose among countries of the Islamic World.

Scenario 2: Fragmentation Due to Political Instability

- Description: This scenario is leading to fragmentation and discord within the Islamic World. External interventions and geopolitical rivalries further exacerbate tensions, leading to the emergence of regional blocs and alliances based on competing interests.
- Implications: Political fragmentation hampers efforts to address shared challenges such as poverty, terrorism, and climate change. Divisions along sectarian, ethnic, or ideological lines deepen, fueling sectarianism and extremism. Lack of trust and cooperation among member states impede progress toward common goals, resulting in missed opportunities for collective action and mutual benefit.

Scenario 3: Bridging Divides Through Cultural Exchange

- Description: In this scenario, countries of the Islamic World prioritize cultural exchange, dialogue, and mutual understanding as a means to bridge divides and promote unity. They invest in educational and cultural initiatives that highlight shared heritage, values, and traditions, fostering a sense of belonging and solidarity among diverse populations. People-to-people exchanges, interfaith dialogues, and cross-cultural partnerships build trust and empathy, transcending political and ideological differences.

- Implications: Cultural exchange initiatives promote tolerance, diversity, and social cohesion within the Islamic World. They challenge stereotypes, misconceptions, and prejudices, fostering empathy and understanding across borders. Shared cultural experiences strengthen social bonds and create opportunities for collaboration in areas such as education, tourism, and the arts, contributing to a more cohesive and resilient Islamic World.

Scenario 4: Division Due to Socio-economic Disparities

- Description: This scenario depicts widening socio-economic disparities among countries of the Islamic World, leading to divisions and tensions within the Islamic World. Countries with higher levels of economic development and prosperity become increasingly isolated from those facing poverty, inequality, and underdevelopment.
- Implications: Socio-economic disparities undermine efforts toward unity and cooperation within the Islamic World. Divisions along economic lines deepen, leading to distrust and suspicion among member states. Inequality fuels social discontent and extremism, posing challenges to regional stability and security. Addressing socio-economic disparities becomes imperative to prevent further fragmentation and promote inclusive development.

These scenarios illustrate potential pathways for the unity or divide of the Islamic World based on key drivers and uncertainties related to economic, political, cultural, and socio-economic factors. By considering these scenarios, policymakers, analysts, and stakeholders can anticipate future challenges and opportunities and develop strategies to promote unity, resilience, and prosperity within the Islamic World.

Correlation Between the Demographics of the Member States of the Islamic World

- Population Growth and Urbanization: Demographic trends such as population growth and urbanization can influence the dynamics of economic integration, political stability, and cultural exchange within the Islamic World. Rapid population growth and urbanization may strain resources, exacerbate socio-economic disparities, and contribute to political instability, potentially leading to scenarios of fragmentation or division. Conversely, effective management of urbanization and population growth through sustainable development strategies can promote unity and cooperation among countries of the Islamic World.
- Education and Human Capital Development: Educational attainment levels and human capital development are essential factors in fostering unity

or divide within the Islamic World. Countries with higher levels of education and investment in human capital are more likely to promote cultural exchange, dialogue, and mutual understanding, as depicted in the scenario of bridging divides through cultural exchange. Conversely, disparities in education and human capital development may exacerbate socio-economic inequalities, leading to scenarios of division due to socio-economic disparities.

- Healthcare Infrastructure and Access: Disparities in healthcare infrastructure and access can impact socio-economic development, political stability, and social cohesion within the Islamic World. Countries with advanced healthcare systems and universal access to healthcare services are better positioned to address public health challenges and promote unity through collective action against shared threats such as pandemics or disease outbreaks. In contrast, countries with inadequate healthcare infrastructure and limited access to medical services may face greater challenges in addressing health-related crises, potentially leading to scenarios of fragmentation due to political instability or socio-economic disparities.
- Economic Development and GDP per Capita: Economic development levels and GDP per capita also play a significant role in shaping scenarios for the unity or divide of the Islamic World. Countries with higher levels of economic development and prosperity are more likely to promote economic integration, cooperation, and mutual benefit among countries of the Islamic World. In contrast, disparities in economic development and GDP per capita may lead to scenarios of division due to socio-economic disparities, where wealthier countries become increasingly isolated from those facing poverty and underdevelopment.

By examining how demographic factors intersect with scenarios for the unity or divide of the Islamic World, policymakers and stakeholders can better understand the underlying drivers and dynamics shaping future outcomes and develop strategies to promote unity, resilience, and prosperity within the Islamic World.

Education, Employment, and Investment Opportunities as Crucial Elements for Development in the Islamic World

It has previously been established that education and employment opportunities hold significant importance to the matter of socio-economic development of the Islamic World. Though it may seem that these topics steer away from the realm of demographics, they are actually very closely related to it. In this sense, we must once again look into possible scenarios while accounting for the ways in which the key involved factors may evolve (Fig. 4.2).

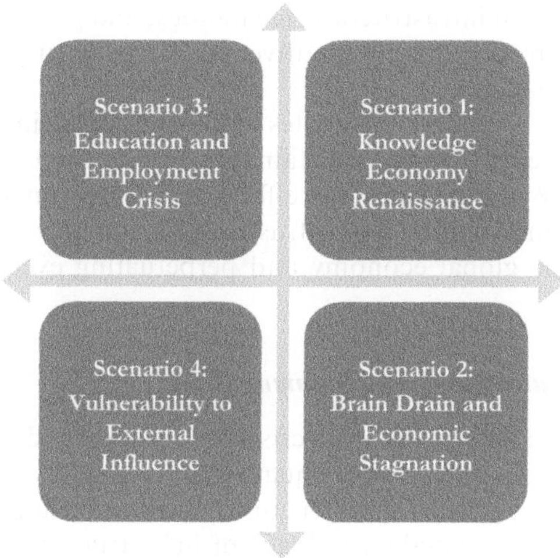

Fig. 4.2. Future Scenarios for Education, Employment, and Socio-Economic Development.

Scenario 1 – Knowledge Economy Renaissance

- Description: This scenario envisions countries of the Islamic World prioritizing investment in education, research, and innovation, leading to the emergence of a vibrant knowledge economy. High levels of education and employment opportunities fuel creativity, entrepreneurship, and technological advancement, attracting domestic and foreign investment. This scenario fosters sustainable development, economic diversification, and human capital accumulation, positioning the Islamic World as a global leader in innovation and prosperity.
- Implications: Investments in education and innovation capitalize on the demographic dividend, fostering social mobility, economic empowerment, and social cohesion within countries of the Islamic World. Enhanced research and development drive technological innovation and industrial competitiveness, attracting investment and creating high-value jobs. Collaboration among governments, academia, and the private sector fosters knowledge exchange and accelerates progress toward shared development goals, ensuring inclusive growth and resilience.

Scenario 2 – Brain Drain and Economic Stagnation

- Description: In this scenario, brain drain and economic stagnation characterize the Islamic World, marked by inadequate investment in education, employment, and development. Limited opportunities for higher education and skilled employment drive talented individuals to seek opportunities abroad, resulting in a loss of human capital and innovation potential. The

lack of investment in infrastructure, technology, and productive sectors hampers economic growth and competitiveness, perpetuating cycles of poverty and underdevelopment.
- Implications: Brain drain exacerbates skills shortages, impedes innovation, and undermines efforts toward sustainable development in countries of the Islamic World. Without concerted efforts to address underlying challenges and invest in human capital and infrastructure, the Islamic World risks falling behind in the global economy and perpetuating cycles of poverty and inequality.

Scenario 3 – Education and Employment Crisis

- Description: This scenario depicts a crisis in education and employment within the Islamic World, marked by inadequate access to quality education, training, and employment opportunities. Structural barriers, including gender disparities, socio-economic inequality, and lack of infrastructure, hinder educational attainment and skills development.
- Implications: The education and employment crisis undermine human capital development, social cohesion, and economic progress in countries of the Islamic World. Inadequate investment in education and workforce development perpetuates cycles of poverty, exclusion, and vulnerability. Addressing the education and employment crisis requires holistic approaches that prioritize inclusive education, vocational training, and job creation initiatives, empowering individuals and communities to participate in and benefit from economic development.

Scenario 4 – Vulnerability to External Influence

- Description: This scenario highlights the vulnerability of the Islamic World to external influence and exploitation due to inadequate investment in education, employment, and development. Limited opportunities for education and employment drive marginalized populations toward extremism, radicalization, and violence, creating fertile ground for external actors to exploit divisions and pursue geopolitical agendas. Weak governance structures, corruption, and lack of social cohesion further exacerbate vulnerabilities, undermining sovereignty and stability.
- Implications: Vulnerability to external influence poses significant risks to the sovereignty, security, and development of countries of the Islamic World. Strengthening resilience and self-reliance through investment in education, employment, and development is essential to safeguarding the Islamic World against external threats and fostering sustainable peace and prosperity.

Future Prospects of the Islamic World's Population Until the Mid-century – The Medium/Likely Scenario

Government agencies in many Islamic countries periodically conduct projections or future population estimates for their nations. In addition, international organizations such as the United Nations Population Division and the U.S. Census Bureau regularly prepare population forecasts for the world, regions, and countries. In developing these projections, demographers make assumptions about future trends in fertility, mortality, and migration. These assumptions, while based on data, research, and expert opinions, are not certainties.

Population projections represent the future size and distribution of populations by age and gender if the underlying assumptions hold true. Therefore, it is essential for users of these projections to have a fundamental understanding of these assumptions and their plausibility before utilizing them. Uncertainty in projections can arise from a variety of sources, and generally, uncertainty in results increases with time. Long-term projections are less certain than short-term forecasts due to the compounded effects of the accuracy of assumptions over time (Kaneda & Bremner, 2014).

The population of a country or region changes through the interaction of three demographic factors: birth rates, death rates, and migration, in addition to another underlying factor, which is the aging of the population year by year. To predict the future population, demographers make assumptions about how current rates of births, deaths, and migration will change in the future. Based on these assumptions, the population is calculated by age and sex, increasing or decreasing over the years and periods following the base year.

Population projections are important because they help policymakers in government and business leaders in the private sector make decisions and prepare for the future in all aspects of human society. The size and composition of a population are primary inputs in estimating the basic needs of humans and the resources required to meet them, such as the demand for food, water, energy, health services, education, infrastructure, and other facilities.

Each set of projections produced by government and international organizations is based on its own set of assumptions about birth rates, death rates, and migration, and they are likely to differ from one another. Some organizations, most notably the United Nations Population Division, address the uncertainty in projections by presenting several estimates of the likelihood that the future population size will fall within a certain range, reflecting potential scenarios for the future paths of birth, death, and migration rates.

Expert demographers at the United Nations Population Division typically propose at least four scenarios or alternatives for the future population of every country in the world: the high scenario, the medium scenario, the low scenario, and the constant scenario. Each scenario has its own assumptions about the future paths of birth rates, death rates, and international migration. However, past experiences have shown that the medium scenario is the one that most often materializes and is the most widely used by policymakers and decision-makers. Therefore, we will use the population projections for Islamic countries according to this most likely scenario.

In the past, conducting population projections using standard computational tools was a laborious process. However, with technological advancements, it became possible to convert demographic mathematical equations into computerized software, which is currently used to execute population projections by age and gender for several years into the future (see the footnote for information on these demographic software programs and the organizations that utilize them).[1]

The statistics presented in Table 4.9 regarding the population size for the years 2020, 2035, and 2050 are based on the results of the latest national census, national official data, analyses by national statistical offices, or estimates by regional and international organizations working in this field, such as the Population Reference Bureau and the United Nations Population Division. These estimates, to the greatest extent possible, account for the impacts of refugee movements, large numbers of foreign workers, and current population fluctuations due to ongoing political and security events. The future population projections provided here are based on reasonable assumptions about the expected future trajectory of demographic variables that directly influence the population size and age structure, namely fertility, mortality, and net international migration.

Table 4.9 illustrates the future population size of the countries in the Islamic world and its eight regions, using data from two sources, over the next thirty years and until the mid-century, divided into two periods: the first ending in 2035 and the second ending in 2050. All countries and regions in the Islamic world will experience an increase in their population sizes, albeit to varying degrees. Generally, according to the medium scenario of the United Nations Population Division, the population of the Islamic world will increase by 498 million people by 2035 and by approximately another 482 million by 2050. In other words, the population of the Islamic world will grow by about one billion people (980 million) over the next three decades. Consequently, the proportion of the population of Islamic countries relative to the global population will rise from 24% to 27% by 2035 and to 29% by 2050.

Discussing the future prospects of the demographic situation in Islamic countries leads us to the implications and goals of population policies implemented by these nations. Such policies will determine the future demographic state of the population. Therefore, the subject of population policies warrants dedicated research. Before we conclude this section, it is important to note that projecting the future demographic situation of the population in Islamic countries depends on the scope and objectives of the population policies adopted by these nations, based on their priorities. These policies aim to influence the future trends of direct and indirect factors affecting demographic variables.

Experts recommend that countries, when formulating their population policies, should consider the current state of these variables and determine their stance toward them, i.e., what policy they will adopt regarding each variable.

To understand the variables of population policy as seen by experts from the United Nations Population Division, we must consider factors such as: age of marriage for both genders, marriage and divorce rates and their legislation, celibacy; population growth rate; age structure of the population and concerns about

[1]MortPak Software is used by the United Nations Population Division; Demographic Analysis & Population Projection System (DAPPS) Software is used by U.S. Bureau of Census; SPECTRUM/DemProj Software is used by Avenir Health.

Table 4.9. Population Size (millions) in Islamic Countries in Mid-Years 2020, 2035, and 2050.

Region/Country	**According to Population Reference Bureau A**			**According to United Nations Population Division B**		
	2020	**2035**	**2050**	**2020**	**2035**	**2050**
West Asia	**263.7**	**324.1**	**367.2**	**262.7**	**319.3**	**361.9**
Republic of Azerbaijan	10.1	10.9	11.0	10.1	10.9	11.1
Hashemite Kingdom of Jordan	10.7	12.9	13.9	10.2	11.2	12.9
United Arab Emirates	9.8	10.6	10.3	9.9	10.7	10.4
Kingdom of Bahrain	1.5	1.8	2.0	1.7	2.1	2.3
Republic of Turkiye	83.7	97.2	105.0	84.3	91.9	97.1
Kingdom of Saudi Arabia	35.0	43.1	48.1	34.8	41.1	44.6
Syrian Arab Republic	19.4	28.1	33.2	17.5	28.6	33.1
Republic of Iraq	39.7	52.4	64.3	40.2	55.3	70.9
Sultanate of Oman	4.7	5.7	6.4	5.1	6.2	6.9
State of Palestine	5.0	6.8	8.7	5.1	7.0	8.8
State of Qatar	2.8	3.4	3.8	2.9	3.5	3.8
State of Kuwait	4.7	5.4	5.9	4.3	5.0	5.4
Lebanese Republic	6.8	6.2	6.5	6.8	6.2	6.5
Republic of Yemen	29.8	39.6	48.1	29.8	39.6	48.1
Central Asia	**68.9**	**81.9**	**93.0**	**68.3**	**81.1**	**92.2**

(*Continued*)

Table 4.9. *(Continued)*

Region/Country	**According to Population Reference Bureau A**			**According to United Nations Population Division B**		
	2020	**2035**	**2050**	**2020**	**2035**	**2050**
Republic of Uzbekistan	34.2	39.9	43.8	33.5	39.1	42.9
Republic of Tajikistan	9.4	12.5	16.0	9.5	12.6	16.2
Republic of Kazakhstan	18.7	21.5	24.0	18.8	21.5	24.0
Kyrgyz Republic	6.6	8.0	9.2	6.5	7.9	9.1
South Asia	**514.3**	**631.8**	**729.1**	**509.0**	**616.2**	**699.0**
Islamic Republic of Afghanistan	38.9	54.7	70.7	38.9	52.6	64.7
Islamic Republic of Iran	84.2	92.5	94.6	84.0	95.8	103.1
Islamic Republic of Pakistan	220.9	287.2	347.8	220.9	282.9	338.0
People's Republic of Bangladesh	169.8	196.9	215.5	164.7	184.4	192.6
Republic of Maldives	0.5	0.5	0.5	0.540	0.538	0.586
Southeast Asia	**305.0**	**346.2**	**370.3**	**306.3**	**347.9**	**372.0**
Republic of Indonesia	271.7	307.7	328.7	273.5	309.8	330.9
Brunei Darussalam	0.5	0.5	0.5	0.437	0.482	0.492
Malaysia	32.8	38.0	41.1	32.4	37.6	40.6
South America	**1.4**	**1.5**	**1.6**	**1.3**	**1.5**	**1.5**
Republic of Suriname	0.6	0.7	0.8	0.587	0.650	0.680

Cooperative Republic of Guyana	0.8	0.8	0.8	0.747	0.832	0.825
North Africa	**249.0**	**312.5**	**376.3**	**250.1**	**315.0**	**379.6**
Republic of Tunisia	11.9	12.5	12.7	11.8	13.1	13.8
People's Democratic Republic of Algeria	44.4	53.4	61.4	43.8	53.0	60.9
Republic of the Sudan	43.8	61.5	81.2	43.8	61.5	81.2
State of Libya	6.9	8.3	9.6	6.9	7.9	8.5
Arab Republic of Egypt	100.8	128.6	157.8	102.3	130.3	160.0
Kingdom of Morocco	36.6	41.5	44.6	36.9	42.5	46.2
Islamic Republic of Mauritania	4.6	6.7	9.0	4.6	6.7	9.0
West Africa and Sub-Saharan Africa	**405.5**	**598.7**	**839.2**	**405.5**	**590.8**	**813.9**
Republic of Benin	12.2	19.8	30.6	12.1	17.7	24.3
Burkina Faso	20.9	31.1	43.4	20.9	31.1	43.4
Republic of Chad	16.9	26.2	37.5	16.4	24.6	34.0
Togolese Republic	8.3	12.0	16.8	8.3	11.6	15.4
Republic of Sierra Leone	8.0	10.9	14.2	8.0	10.5	12.9
Republic of Senegal	16.7	25.1	35.9	16.7	24.2	33.2
Republic of Gabon	2.2	3.1	4.1	2.2	3.0	3.8
Republic of The Gambia	2.4	3.5	4.5	2.4	3.6	4.9

(*Continued*)

Table 4.9. (*Continued*)

Region/Country	**According to Population Reference Bureau A**			**According to United Nations Population Division B**		
	2020	**2035**	**2050**	**2020**	**2035**	**2050**
Republic of Guinea	12.6	18.9	27.6	13.1	19.1	26.0
Republic of Guinea-Bissau	1.9	2.8	4.0	2.0	2.7	3.6
Republic of Cameroon	26.6	39.4	55.0	26.5	37.7	50.6
Republic of Côte d'Ivoire	26.2	37.5	50.9	26.4	37.8	51.3
Republic of Mali	20.3	31.9	47.1	20.2	30.8	43.6
Republic of Niger	24.2	41.5	66.3	24.2	41.4	65.6
Federal Republic of Nigeria	206.1	295.0	401.3	206.1	295.0	401.3
East Africa	**63.5**	**96.2**	**135.4**	**63.458**	**93.6**	**127.1**
Republic of Uganda	45.7	69.5	97.7	45.7	66.9	89.4
Republic of Djibouti	1.0	1.2	1.3	0.988	1.2	1.3
Federal Republic of Somalia	15.9	24.3	34.9	15.9	24.3	34.9
Union of the Comoros	0.9	1.2	1.5	0.870	1.2	1.5
General total	**1871.3**	**2392.9**	**2912.1**	**1867.32**	**2365.40**	**2847.20**

Sources: Population Reference Bureau (2020); United Nations, Department of Economic and Social Affairs, Population Division (2021).

the proportion of children and their dependency, the size of the working-age population, and measures to address aging; stance on fertility levels and related policies; comprehensive birth registration measures; balancing family and work concerning maternity leave, breastfeeding, and institutional childcare; concerns about teenage pregnancies and policies to limit them; government support for family planning and policies to facilitate access to reproductive services; reproductive and sexual health measures for adolescents, including educational curriculum content; legislative regulations permitting abortion; concerns about unsafe abortions and rape; reproductive infertility rates; family size, child allowances, taxes, and government support; concerns about violence against women and policies to eliminate domestic violence and women's inheritance rights; life expectancy at birth; under-five mortality rates; child malnutrition concerns; maternal mortality and measures to address neonatal and maternal deaths; concerns about traffic accidents and their victims; concerns about overweight and obesity among the population; concerns about non-communicable diseases, tuberculosis, malaria, sexually transmitted infections, especially HIV/AIDS, and measures to address them; stance on the spatial and geographical distribution of the population and policies to manage it; internal migration trends; international migration trends both outbound and inbound; non-national labor force, their nationalities, and rights; unemployment levels, particularly among youth; retirement age and social security; disabilities, ways to reduce them, and the rights of disabled individuals; and finally, measures related to the COVID-19 pandemic, which are general across all countries and not exclusive to Islamic nations.

Conclusion: Summary of Findings and Approaches to Addressing the Demographic Challenge and Overcoming the Current Situation

Currently, the population of the Islamic world constitutes 24% of the global population, unevenly distributed across its eight regions. Half of this population, approximately 1.87 billion people, reside in 20 countries in South Asia, West Africa, and Sub-Saharan Africa. Thirty percent are found in 17 countries in Southeast Asia and Western Asia. The remaining fifth (20%) are primarily located in 15 countries in North Africa, Central Asia, and East Africa, with less than 1% in two countries in South America.

Over 500 million people from the Islamic world live in four major Islamic countries in South Asia alone (excluding approximately 200 million Muslim population in India, a non-Islamic state in the same region). West Africa and Sub-Saharan Africa follow, with a population exceeding 400 million. Southeast Asia ranks third, with over 300 million people, followed by Western Asia with over 262 million. North Africa has a population of 250 million, while 130 million people reside in Central Asia, East Africa, and South America.

Regarding fertility, the most crucial variable determining natural population growth and the age structure, the TFR per woman remains above replacement level in 40 Islamic countries. In half of these countries, the rate exceeds four births per woman, predominantly in African countries, especially in West Africa and Sub-Saharan Africa. Consequently, these societies have youthful populations with high child dependency ratios, preventing them from entering the demographic dividend phase experienced by some Southeast Asian tiger economies. The challenges associated with high birth rates in many Islamic countries necessitate systematic efforts by responsible institutions to assist couples in achieving their reproductive desires and rights. This can be done by providing accessible services that meet their unmet needs for modern family planning methods.

Mortality rates vary among Islamic countries, particularly infant mortality rates, which range from 5 to 75 deaths per thousand live births. This disparity reflects differences in living conditions, the efficiency of health services, particularly maternal and child care, fertility levels, and birth spacing. There is also a wide variation in life expectancy at birth among Islamic countries, ranging from less than 60 years to over 75 years.

The impact of international migration on the current demographic state of Islamic countries has been cumulative over several years, not just the result of recent trends. Generally, except for the Gulf states, all Islamic countries are primarily migrant-sending countries, particularly those with large populations. Therefore, emigration does not significantly affect their age structure. Net international migration is negative or zero in almost all Islamic countries except for the Gulf states, where it is positive, with the number of immigrants exceeding the number of citizens, and immigrants forming the majority of the workforce.

Data indicates significant differences in the age structure among Islamic countries. The proportion of children varies from less than one-fifth of the population in the Gulf states to 40% or more in West Africa and Sub-Saharan Africa. This youthful age structure presents three challenges: a high child dependency burden, a driving force for population growth, and the inability of countries to benefit from the demographic dividend.

All Islamic countries and regions are expected to experience population growth, albeit at varying degrees. Overall, the population of the Islamic world will increase by 498 million by 2035 and by about 482 million more by 2050. In other words, the population will grow by approximately one billion (980 million) over the next three decades, raising the proportion of the Islamic world's population from 24% to 27% by 2035 and to 29% by 2050.

A significant portion of the global population increase over the next 30 years will come from the Islamic world (46% and 57% for the two periods, respectively). The largest growth within the Islamic world itself will be in West Africa and Sub-Saharan Africa, followed by South Asia, with lesser contributions from the other six regions.

By mid-century, West Africa and Sub-Saharan Africa will surpass South Asia to become the most populous region, North Africa will rise from fifth to third place, Southeast Asia will fall from third to fourth, and West Asia from fourth to fifth. East Africa, Central Asia, and South America will occupy the sixth, seventh, and eighth places, respectively, in terms of population size.

Due to varying population growth rates among Islamic countries, the ranking of the ten most populous countries will change by mid-century. Nigeria will

Table 4.10. Comparison of Population Size and Growth in Islamic Countries, Developed, and Developing Nations (2020–2035).

Region	Population Size (Million) 2020	%	Population Size (Million) 2035	%	Average Annual Increase (Million) 2020–2035
Developed Countries	1,272	16.4	1,311	14.7	3
Developing Countries	6,501	83.6	7,626	85.3	75
World	7,773	100.0	8,937	100.0	78
Islamic World Countries	1,871	24.1	2,393	26.8	35

Source: Population Reference Bureau (2020).

become the most populous, followed by Pakistan, while Indonesia will drop to third place. Bangladesh and Egypt will maintain their fourth and fifth positions, respectively. Iran, Turkiye, Uganda, Sudan, and Algeria will rank sixth to tenth. The populations of these ten countries will constitute about two-thirds of the total population of the member states of the ICESCO by mid-century. In general, the population of these ten countries will increase by 585 million by mid-century, accounting for approximately 60% of the total population growth of the member states over the next 30 years.

The demographic information presented in this chapter highlights the significant policy and governance challenges Islamic countries must address to manage current and future demographic changes and their political, economic, and social implications. In terms of demographic data challenges, Islamic countries need to establish policies and strategies based on reliable and up-to-date data, primarily obtained from regular national censuses and surveys. The United Nations Population Division recommends that countries conduct population and housing censuses at least every 10 years. However, many Islamic countries have not adhered to this decennial schedule and require technical, logistical, and financial support to meet this requirement. Additionally, Islamic countries need to conduct more household surveys to regularly collect data on reproductive behavior and the use of family planning methods.

Addressing the challenges of rapid current and anticipated population growth, and the accompanying youthful age structure, is crucial. Over the past decade alone, the population of member states increased by 330 million (22%), with an annual growth rate of 1.95%, which is high by global standards. East Africa recorded the highest population growth rate at 38%, followed by West Africa and Sub-Saharan Africa at 32%, North Africa at 22%, West Asia at 21%, and Central and South Asia at 18%. Southeast Asia and South America experienced the lowest growth rates, at 13% and 7%, respectively.

Thirty-four Islamic countries experienced rapid annual population growth of at least 2%, including fifteen in West Africa and Sub-Saharan Africa, ten in West Asia (where migration, not natural increase, contributed to rapid growth in Gulf countries), three each in South Asia and North Africa, two in East Africa, and one in Central Asia. Eighteen countries experienced moderate annual growth, none of which were in West Africa and Sub-Saharan Africa, while only two countries had low or negative annual growth.

Our world today is divided not only politically, economically, and socially but also demographically. To understand this demographic divide and the current and anticipated challenges faced by Islamic countries related to population size and growth, one can refer to the comparative data summarized in Table 4.10. At least four out of five people globally live-in developing countries, and 96% of the expected global population increase in the next fifteen years will occur in developing countries, with 45% of that increase in Islamic countries, whose populations will grow by over 500 million by 2035, averaging an annual increase of 35 million.

Oil-rich Islamic countries in the Arabian Gulf face challenges related to the high proportion of expatriates from South Asia, including maintaining national cultural identity, protecting expatriates' rights, managing substantial remittance outflows, and addressing the administrative burden of expatriate affairs. In contrast, most other Islamic countries face resource shortages needed to meet the demands of growing populations and achieve economic and social development, while also contending with political instability and public debt burdens.

Thus, the solution for Gulf countries is to encourage population growth among their citizens, evaluate marriage fund outcomes, and diversify expatriate labor by increasing the proportion of Arab workers. For other Islamic countries, mitigating the consequences of rapid population growth requires prudent population policies and programs to meet families' needs for information and services related to family planning. This approach aims to slow the pace of population growth, transitioning to smaller families and younger communities to capitalize on the "demographic dividend" previously discussed in this chapter.

Finally, the demographic trends observed in Islamic countries over the past decade and the future outlook for the next three decades present significant internal challenges requiring substantial resources and good governance to meet the needs of increasing young populations. It may be beneficial for these countries to adopt strong programs to moderate population growth rates and achieve demographic transitions toward lower fertility rates and smaller families, following the successful examples of some Islamic countries like Malaysia, which have achieved remarkable social and economic development.

Demographic challenges will not only affect Islamic countries but also neighboring countries with aging populations, characterized by high proportions of the elderly and low proportions of children. These neighboring countries will also face the impacts of rapid population growth and economic and political development issues in Islamic countries. Illegal migration from African countries to aging

European countries is a clear indication of the challenges this continent will face due to the demographic explosion in West Africa and Sub-Saharan Africa.

In conclusion, the demographic trends observed in the Islamic world over the past decade, along with the projected future outlook for the next three decades, present significant internal challenges for many of these nations. Addressing and overcoming these challenges will necessitate substantial resources and effective governance to meet the needs of the burgeoning young population. It may prove advantageous for these countries to incorporate robust programs within their policies aimed at moderating the pace of population growth and achieving a demographic transition toward lower fertility rates and smaller family sizes. This approach has been successfully implemented by some Islamic World Countries, such as Malaysia, which have achieved remarkable social and economic development milestones.

Furthermore, the demographic challenges will not be confined solely to the Islamic World Countries. The repercussions will extend to neighboring nations characterized by an aging population structure, with a high proportion of elderly individuals and a low proportion of children. These countries will not be immune to the effects of rapid population growth and stalled economic and political development in the Islamic world. The phenomenon of illegal migration from African countries to the aging European continent underscores the potential impact of demographic trends in adjacent regions, particularly the population explosion in West Africa and the Sahel.

Ultimately, the future demographics of the Islamic world will be shaped by complex interactions between fertility, mortality, migration, and aging trends. These factors will collectively influence population size, structure, and distribution. Policymakers must utilize population projections to make informed decisions and develop strategic responses to the challenges and opportunities posed by these demographic changes. By doing so, they can pave the way for a prosperous and sustainable future for the Islamic world.

References

Al-Masarweh, I.S.I. et al. (2020). *Study of the possible futures of the Islamic world: The demography of the Islamic world: Current status and future prospects*. Foresight and AI Center, ICESCO.

Kaneda, T., & Bremner, J. (2014). *Understanding population projections: Assumptions behind the numbers* [Policy Brief]. Population Reference Bureau. https://www.worldometers.info/world-population/population-by-country/

Mester, L. J. (2018). *Cato Institute's 35th annual monetary conference*. Cato Institute. https://www.cato.org/events/35th-annual-monetary-conference

Pew Research Center. (2017). *The future of world religions: Population growth projections, 2010–2050*. https://www.pewresearch.org/

Population Reference Bureau. (2020). *World population data sheet 2020*. https://www.prb.org/wp-content/uploads/2020/07/letter-booklet-2020-world-population.pdf

United Nations. (2020). *La population mondiale atteindra 8 milliards d'habitants en novembre (ONU)*. Nations Unies. https://www.un.org/fr/desa-fr/la-population-mondiale-atteindra-8-milliards-dhabitants-en-novembre-onu

United Nations, Department of Economic and Social Affairs, Population Division. (2021). *World population prospects (WPP) 2021 upgrade – Towards a more open and reproducible WPP (medium variant)*. https://population.un.org/wpp/Download/Standard/CSV/

United Nations, Department of Economic and Social Affairs, Statistics Division. (2017). *Principles and recommendations for population and housing censuses* (Rev. 3). United Nations.

United Nations, Department of Economic and Social Affairs, Statistics Division. (2021, October 1). *The 2020 world population and housing census programme: Census dates for all countries*. https://unstats.un.org/unsd/demographic-social/census/censusdates/

United Nations, Department of Economic and Social Affairs, Statistics Division. (2020). *2020 demographic yearbook* (71st Issue). United Nations.

United Nations Educational, Scientific and Cultural Organization. (2022). *Youth*. https://www.unesco.org/fr/youth

Section 3

Fiscal Policy and Public Debt Management

Chapter 5

Enhancing Economic Stability: Fiscal Choices and Their Implications on External Balance in OIC and OPEC Nations

Tsegaye Assayew

Consultant, Economic Policy Department, World Bank, USA

1. Introduction

Fueled by health crises like the COVID-19 pandemic, conflict, and climate-related disasters, among others, the global debt stock has been surging over the past few decades and has reached a record high of USD315 trillion in Q1 2024 (IIF, 2024). This is equivalent to 333% of the global gross domestic product (GDP).[1] Public debt accounts for more than 39% of the global overall debt – at least as of 2022, as per the IMF data – causing a severe fiscal constraint to many governments. Governments employ their fiscal firepower to address the acute social and economic risks from the different cocktails of shocks in addition to addressing chronic development challenges, which severely constrain their fiscal space. A sustained shock to the fiscal balance (FB) adversely impacts the country's external position in the long term, also commonly known as a twin-deficits phenomenon in the literature.

Grounding on Mundell–Fleming's (Fleming, 1962; Mundell, 1963) theoretical foundation, the twin-deficits literature argues that an increase in budget deficit will cause an upward shift in the interest rate and exchange rate, in effect, encouraging foreign investment that leads to an increase in the domestic demand and hence

[1]IIF, 2024. Global Debt Monitor. The Institute of International Finance, Inc. All rights reserved.iif.com©Copyright2024. https://www.iif.com/portals/0/Files/content/Global%20Debt%20Monitor_May2024_vf.pdf

The Economic Potential of Islamic Countries, Part A:
Economics, Demographics and Financial Services, 103–146

doi:10.1108/978-1-83708-000-720251006

appreciation of the currency, which in turn creates a negative trade imbalance. The increase in imports will eventually lead to a current account deficit (Leachman & Francis, 2002; Salvatore, 2006). Opponents of the twin-deficits hypothesis (TDH), on the other hand, reject this claim and argue that, in an open economy setting, there is no correlation between the budget and current account deficits, and hence, the former would not cause the latter (Barro, 1989; Neaime, 2008).

Given these competing two schools of thoughts, the twin-deficits empirical literature is not still conclusive, with mixed findings depending on the choice of model assumptions and sample compositions, among others. The literature is also heavy on advanced economies (AEs) with high access to market-based financing, flexible exchange rate regimes, and dynamic private sector.

There are limited, if non-existent, studies of twin deficits in certain economic groups, like the Organization of the Islamic Cooperation (OIC), which have unique macroeconomic conditions. The OIC group includes the majority – 9 out of the current 12 – Organization of the Petroleum Exporting Countries (OPEC). The OIC and OPEC member states are uniquely situated to test the universality of the TDH as the Islam-dominated cultural and historical context extensively shapes their financial, fiscal and external sectors and their overall economic trajectories uniquely. The OPEC countries, in particular, render a peculiar country group as they play a crucial role in setting the global energy market – the international oil price – and hence their balance of payment position.

This study makes a significant contribution to the twin-deficits literature by filling a crucial evidence gap. It does so by examining the state of twin deficits across a unique group of OIC member states. Additionally, it provides a defining benchmark by separating the OPEC countries from the rest of the OIC members and comparing the results between the two groups, thereby offering a fresh perspective on the TDH.

In this study, we employ the latest panel data analysis techniques, which account for slope heterogeneity and cross-sectional dependence between panel members. While our data range from 2000 through 2022, we also consider the effects of the business cycle and trade openness. We also analyze the effects of different forex exchange regimes, which serve as a primary transmission mechanism of the effect of fiscal policy on the external sector, thereby ensuring the robustness of our research approach. To provide a more nuanced understanding, we conduct three case studies focusing on Azerbaijan and Türkiye, which have geographic proximity and economic similarities, and Saudi Arabia, which is an OPEC member.

We find strong evidence of twin deficits across both the OIC and OPEC member countries, which are also OIC members (OIC–OPEC group). While a 1% increase in overall fiscal balance (OFB) causes close to a triple (a 2.8%) lasting effect in the current account balance (CAB) in the full sample of OIC group, it causes a 2.4% increase for the OIC–OPEC group. This is a relatively large impact compared to the literature confirming that the OIC member countries are indeed unique in their macroeconomic context. We also observe a strong presence of twin deficits in managed Fx regimes, such as the OIC–OPEC countries, than flexible Fx regimes consistent with the literature. The complementary case study from the three countries, nevertheless provides conflicting evidence against the results obtained from the panel data analysis, highlighting country heterogeneity notwithstanding the broader similarities as a group.

The chapter is organized as follows. Section 2 discusses the literature. Sections 3 and 4 provide the empirical framework and the data description, respectively. Section 5 presents the results, followed by a conclusion in Section 6.

2. Literature Review

Since the seminal Corsetti and Müller's (2006) paper, the twin-deficits empirical literature is growing faster primarily focusing on AEs because of availability of a relatively adequate historical data. Nevertheless, the literature is not yet conclusive and at times conflicting. Corsetti and Müller's (2006) paper, for instance, find that a twin deficits is more likely if the economy is more open and if the spending shock is more persistent. That is, in an open economy, a fiscal policy shock will increase output and consumption thereby hurting net exports via higher imports (and lower exports) that leads to a rise in current account deficit. In a closed economy, on the other hand, the domestic agents will have a harder time increasing their purchases of foreign goods, and the response of the current account will be lower. Builds on the identification approach of Sims (1980) and Blanchard and Perotti (2002), Corsetti and Müller (2006) employed a structural VAR estimation method using government spending that does not respond to other variables contemporaneously to determine the size of the impact. They find that the response of the current account has the expected sign, and the magnitude is statistically different than zero.

Using a recursive identification scheme as in Sims (1980), Kim and Roubini (2008), on the other hand, find a contrasting result that an increase in the government spending improves the current account and depreciates the exchange rate, which is contradicting to the simple intuition of a small open economy perspective. The mechanism comes from an increase in private savings and a decrease in the private investment. The contrasting findings between the two studies primarily originate from different sample they considered. While Corsetti and Müller (2006) focus Australia, Canada, UK, and the USA, Kim and Roubini (2008) focus on the USA, all AEs. Falling in between these two contradicting findings, Monacelli and Perotti (2010) also find that a rise in government spending induces a depreciation of the real exchange rate and a trade balance deficit. Monacelli and Perotti (2010) employ a recursive identification method following Blanchard and Perotti (2002).

Focusing on the European Union (EU), Beetsma et al. (2008) investigate the consequences of an increase in public expenditure for trade balances and budget deficits using a panel vector auto-regression approach based on annual. The main identification assumption is that public spending within the year does not react to unexpected output shocks, also building on Blanchard and Perotti (2002).[2]

---

[2]It is harder to argue that the fiscal policy does not respond to shocks to the current account within a one-year period. For example, because of a negative demand shock on exports, the government might adjust fiscal policy as a precaution.

They find that a 1% increase in public spending causes an on-impact fall in trade balance by 0.5% of GDP that peaks at 0.8%, primarily driven by rising imports and falling exports.

Ramey (2011) highlights one of the critical problems in the approach to identification based on timing assumptions as economic agents might anticipate fiscal policy, and is labeled as *anticipation effects*.[3] Thus, part of what studies based on timing assumption identify as a shock is expected by the agents, who modify their behaviors in advance. This will bias the results toward obtaining smaller multipliers. Consequently, several twin-deficit studies in the literature tried to address the timing restrictions and anticipation effects problems. Corsetti et al. (2006), for instance, address the anticipation effects and construct an instrument for fiscal policy by identifying fiscal shocks as residuals from an estimated spending rule. The authors find an output increases by 0.7 percentage points with a one percentage point impulse and that next exports deteriorate in the case of OECD countries. In line with the hypothesis of state dependence, they find that the conditional responses differ systematically across exchange rate regimes, finding that real appreciations and external deficits mainly occur under currency pegs.

Taking a quite different route, Romer and Romer (2010) use a narrative approach to construct an instrument and address the problem of anticipation effects. Similarly, Bluedorn and Leigh (2011) investigate the effect of fiscal consolidations on the current account by examining policy documents (Budget Speeches, Budgets, and IMF and OECD reports) and identify changes in fiscal policy motivated primarily by the desire to reduce the budget deficit and not as a response to current macroeconomic conditions to construct exogenous innovations to fiscal policy. They find that a 1% of GDP fiscal consolidation is associated with a 0.6 percentage points raise in the CAB-to-GDP ratio, supporting the TDH. They find that the effect is substantially larger than that obtained using standard measures of the fiscal policy stance, such as the change in the cyclically adjusted primary balance.

Combine different identification schemes, Ali Abbas et al. (2011) study the relationship between fiscal policy and the current account, focusing on a large group of countries (advanced, emerging, and low-income economies). They use three alternative methods (panel regressions, an analysis of large fiscal policy and current account changes, and panel vector auto-regressions). Using panel regressions, they find that one percentage point of GDP fiscal consolidation is associated with a reduction of the current account deficit of around 0.3 percentage points of GDP. Using a quarterly structural VAR, as in Blanchard and Perotti (2002), they find a multiplier in the 0.3–0.5 range. They also find that the multiplier is larger in emerging markets and low-income countries, countries that are more open to trade, and when the economy is operating over capacity. One of the key findings is that the multiplier is lower during large fiscal policy and current account changes, which suggests that fiscal policy might have a smaller role in correcting large and persistent imbalances.

[3]See also Forni and Gambetti (2010) and Leeper et al. (2013).

Diverting from AEs, where most of the twin-deficits literature focuses on, Furceri and Zdzienicka (2018) investigate the situation in low-income countries context. Following Auerbach and Gorodnichenko (2013a & 2013b), the authors identify shocks to the budget balance using the forecast errors in the WEO projections. They employ the local projection method (Jordà, 2005), and find that the multiplier from government budget balance into the current account is 0.8 and that the effect is larger during recessions, in countries that are more open to trade, that have less flexible exchange rate regimes, and with lower initial public debt-to-GDP ratios.

More interestingly, Nickel and Tudyka (2014) find a non-linear relationship between fiscal policy and the external balance highlighting the state dependence of the relationship. Using panel VAR with time varying parameters that depend on the amount of debt, they find a non-linear effect of a spending shock on trade balance where the effect is negative at first but switches sign at higher levels of debt.

This study adds several values to the literature. First, it focuses on a unique group of OIC member states whose overall financial and economic trajectories are highly shaped by Islam-dominated cultural and historical backgrounds – providing a cultural perspective into the economy. Most of the OPEC countries are also members of the OIC and deserves a separate investigation as they have a pivotal role in influencing the global energy market, thereby impacting their external sector position. Their fiscal decisions are also heavily dependent on their external position, making them highly relevant group to study the twin-deficits argument. Moreover, this study employs the latest panel data analysis techniques, which account for slope heterogeneity and cross-sectional dependence between panel members that the literature omits often. The study also analyzes the effects of different forex exchange regimes, which serve as a primary transmission mechanism of the effect of fiscal policy on the external sector, thereby ensuring the robustness of our research approach. Finally, the study analyzes two case countries to provide a nuanced understanding of the twin deficits such complex country groups.

3. Methodological Framework

3.1. A Stylized Theoretical Model

In an open economy, the nexus between FB and current account originates from the national account identity:

$$Y = C + I + G + \text{TB} + \text{NFI} + \text{NCT}, \tag{1}$$

where Y is the gross national disposable income (GNDI), C is private consumption, I is total investment, G is government consumption, TB is trade balance or net exports of goods and services, NFI is the net factor income from abroad, and NCT is net current transfers. The difference between income (Y) and total consumption ($C+G$) represents national saving (S), whereas the sum of TB, NFI, and NCT is the CAB. Hence, the identity in Eq. 1 can be rewritten as:

$$\text{CAB} = S - I. \tag{2}$$

By further disaggregating the national saving (S) into government (S^g) and private (S^p) savings and I *in* private investment I^p and government investment I^g, Eq. 2 can be reformulated as:

$$\text{CAB} = (S^g + S^p) - (I^g + I^p), \tag{3}$$

where $S^g - I^g = T - G - I^g$ is the government FB), with T taxes collected by the government. Subsequently, we can rewrite Eq. 3 as:

$$\text{CAB} = \text{FB} + S^p - I^p, \tag{4}$$

where $S^p - I^p$ is the private balance (*PB*).

Eq. 4 shows that, under a balanced *PB*, a fiscal deficit (− FB) must equate to the current account deficit (− CAB), and both move together in the same direction – also known as the TDH. In contrast, if changes in private balance fully offset changes in the fiscal deficit, then the Ricardian equivalence hypothesis (REH) holds – the absence of a nexus between fiscal and current account movements.

The theoretical foundation of the TDH originates from the Mundell–Fleming's model (Fleming, 1962; Mundell, 1963), which argues that an increase in budget deficit will cause an upward shift in interest rate and exchange rate. The increase in interest rates encourages foreign investment that leads to increase in the domestic demand and hence appreciation of the currency, which in turn creates a negative trade imbalance. The increase in imports will eventually lead to a current account deficit (Leachman & Francis, 2002; Salvatore, 2006).

The REH, on the other hand, argues that in an open economy setting, there is no correlation between the budget and current account deficits and hence the former would not cause the latter. That is, a change in governmental tax structure will not have any impact on real interest rate, investments or consumption (Barro, 1989; Neaime, 2008). As per the life cycle model of Modigliani and Ando in 1957, current consumption depends on the expected lifetime income rather than on the current income as proposed by the Keynesian model. Moreover, lending from the permanent income hypothesis developed by Milton Friedman in 1957, the REH support their claim of no linkage between current account and primary deficit by arguing that private consumption will increase only with a permanent increase in income. A temporary rise in income fueled by tax cuts or deficit-financed public spending will increase private savings rather than spending (Barro, 1989, p. 39; Hashemzadeh & Wilson, 2006). This, in turn, discourages foreign capital inflow, and strengthens the CAB (Khalid & Guan, 1999, p. 390).

3.2. Empirical Strategy for Estimating the Long-run Effects

Most macroeconomic variables with large time observations are known to be non-stationary processes with heterogeneous parameters across groups, deviating from the standard distribution assumptions of the traditional homogeneous panel VAR model estimation. In this case, Pesaran and Smith (1995), Pesaran (1997), Pesaran and Shin (1999), and Pesaran et al. (2001) demonstrated that the traditional panel autoregressive distributed lag (ARDL) estimation approach could be used to test the existence of a level relationship between a dependent variable and a set of regressors using a bounds test approach when it is not known with certainty whether regressors are trend- or first-difference stationary, but with the dependent variable being an $I(1)$ process. The ARDL approach is also robust to omitted variables bias and bi-directional feedback effects between dependent and independent variables.

Assume an (ARDL) ($p, \lambda_1, \ldots, \lambda_k$) dynamic panel specification of the form:

$$y_{it} = \sum_{j=1}^{p} \lambda_{ij} y_{i,t-j} + \sum_{j=0}^{q} \delta' X_{i,t-j} + \mu_i + \varepsilon_{it}, \tag{5}$$

where the number of groups $i = 1, 2, \ldots, N$; the number of periods $t = 1, 2, \ldots, T$; y_{it} is a dependent variable for country i, period t; $X_{i,t}$ is a $(k \times 1)$ vector of explanatory variables; δ_{it} are the $(k \times 1)$ coefficient vectors; λ_{ij} are scalars; and μ_i is the group-specific effect. T must be large enough such that the model can be fitted for each group separately. Time trends and other fixed regressors may be included.

If the variables in Eq. 5 are of the form $I(1)$ and cointegrated, for instance, then the error term is an $I(0)$ process for all i, with error correction equation representation of the form:

$$\Delta y_{it} = \phi_i \left(y_{i,t-1} - \theta_i' X_{it} \right) + \sum_{j=1}^{p-1} \lambda_{ij}^{*} \Delta y_{i,t-1} + \sum_{j=0}^{q-1} \delta_{ij}^{\prime *} \Delta X_{i,t-j} + \mu_i + \varepsilon_{it}, \tag{6}$$

where $\phi_i = -\left(1 - \sum_{j=1}^{p} \lambda_{ij}\right), \theta_i = \sum_{j=0}^{q} \delta_{ij} \Big/ \left(1 - \sum_{k} \lambda_{ik}\right), \lambda_{ij}^{*} = -\sum_{m=j-1}^{p} \lambda_{im}, j = 1, 2, \ldots, p-1,$

and $\delta_{ij}^{*} = -\sum_{m=j+1}^{q} \delta_{im}, j = 1, 2, \ldots, q-1$.

In our bivariate case, Eq. 6 can be rewritten as:

$$\begin{aligned} \Delta \mathrm{CAB}_{it} &= \phi_i \left(\mathrm{CAB}_{i,t-1} - \theta_i' \mathrm{OFB}_{it} \right) + \sum_{j=1}^{p-1} \lambda_{ij}^{*} \Delta \mathrm{CAB}_{i,t-1} \\ &+ \sum_{j=0}^{q-1} \delta_{ij}^{\prime *} \Delta \mathrm{OFB}_{i,t-j} + \mu_i + \varepsilon_{it}. \end{aligned} \tag{7}$$

The parameter ϕ_i is the error-correcting speed of adjustment term, with $\phi_i = 0$ implying no evidence for a long-run relationship. This parameter is expected to be significantly negative under the priori assumption that the variables show a return to a long-run equilibrium. The vector θ_i' contains the long-run relationships between the variables.

The dynamic heterogeneous panel in Eq. 6 or 7 can be estimated in at least three ways: (i) using the fixed-effects (FE), in which the time series data for each group are pooled and only the intercepts are allowed to differ across groups, (ii) using mean group (MG) estimator, in which the model is fitted separately for each group, and a simple arithmetic average of the coefficients could be calculated as proposed by Pesaran and Smith (1995), and iii) using the pooled mean group (PMG) estimator that combines both pooling and averaging as indicated by Pesaran et al. (1997, 1999). The PMG estimator allows the intercept, short-run coefficients, and error variances to differ across the groups (as would the MG estimator) but constrains the long-run coefficients to be equal across groups (as would the FE estimator).

3.2.1. Dynamic Common Correlated Effects (CCE) Estimator

The (Pesaran et al., 1999, 2001) PMG or MG ARDL model estimation fails to account for possible cross-sectional dependence that could, for instance, originate from exogenous shocks and other economic spillovers between units in the panel. Failing to account for this dependence could lead to biased and inconsistent estimation results. In response, we employed the dynamic CCE estimator, which uses cross-sectional averages of the independent and dependent variables to control for cross-sectional dependency as proposed by Chudik and Pesaran (2015) and Karabiyik et al. (2017).

For simplicity, consider an ARDL(1,1) representation of Eq. 5 (with minor notation change here):

$$y_{i,t} = \mu_i + \lambda_i y_{i,t-1} + \beta_{0,i} x_{i,t} + \beta_{1,i} x_{i,t-1} + u_{i,t}, \tag{8}$$

$$u_{i,t} = \sum_{l=t}^{m} \varrho_{y_{i,l}} f_{t,l} + e_{i,t}, \tag{9}$$

where $y_{i,t}$ is the dependent variable, $x_{i,t}$ is an observed independent variable, $f_{t,l}$ are m unobserved common factors, $\varrho_{y_{i,l}}$ are factor loadings with $i = 1, \ldots, N$ and $t = 1, \ldots, T$. $e_{i,t}$ is a cross-section unit-specific *IID* error term.

To allow for correlation between the m unobserved factors, $f_{t,l}$, and the k observed regressors, $x_{i,t}$, we assume that the latter is generated according to the following factor model:

$$x_{i,t} = \sum_{l=1}^{m} \varrho_{x_{i,l}} f_{t,l} + \xi_{i,t} \tag{10}$$

with $i = 1,\ldots, N$ and $t = 1,\ldots, T$, where $\xi_{i,t}$ are the idiosyncratic components of $x_{i,t}$ which are assumed to be distributed independently of the idiosyncratic errors, $u_{i,t}$. The factor loadings $\varrho_{y_{i,l}}$ and $\varrho_{x_{i,l}}$ are heterogeneous across units and μ_i is a unit-specific fixed effect (FE). The heterogeneous coefficients are randomly distributed around a common mean, such that $\beta_i = \beta + v_i$, and $\lambda_i = \lambda + a_i$, where v_i and a_i are random deviations with mean zero, independent of the error term and the common factors. λ_i lies strictly inside the unit circle to ensure a non-explosive series.

Pesaran (2006) and Chudik and Pesaran (2015) demonstrate that Eq. 8 could be estimated consistently by approximating the common factors with the floor of $p_T = \sqrt[3]{T}$ lags of the cross-sectional averages of the (dependent and explanatory) variables. The estimated equation becomes:

$$y_{i,t} = \mu_i + \lambda_i y_{i,t-1} + \beta_0 x_{i,t} + \beta_1 x_{i,t-1} + \sum_{l=0}^{p_T} \gamma'_{i,l} \bar{z}_{t-l} + \varepsilon_{i,t}, \tag{11}$$

where $\bar{z}_t = (\bar{y}_t, \bar{x}_t)' = \left(\frac{1}{N}\sum_{i=1}^{N} y_{i,t}, \frac{1}{N}\sum_{i=1}^{N} x_{i,t} \right)'$ are the cross-sectional averages of the dependent and explanatory variables and $\gamma_{i,l} = (\gamma_{y,i,l}, \gamma_{x,i,l})'$ are the estimated coefficients of the cross-sectional averages and generally treated as nuisance parameters.

Eq. 7 can be estimated by either an MG estimator (Chudik & Pesaran, 2015; Pesaran, 2006; Pesaran & Smith, 1995) or by a pooled estimator (Karabiyik et al., 2020; Pesaran, 2006), also known as the common correlated effects mean group estimator (CCE-MG) or common correlated effects pooled estimator (CCE-PM), respectively.

Recall that our main objective is estimating the long-run relationship between overall fiscal and CABs for the OIC and OIC–OPEC member states with heterogenous country context. With the steady state assumption of Eq. 8 where $y_t^* = y_{t-1}^* = y^*$ and $x_t^* = x_{t-1}^* = x^*$, the long-run effect of variable x is defined as:

$$\theta_i = \frac{\beta_{0,i} + \beta_{1,i}}{1 - \lambda_i}. \tag{12}$$

The long-run effect in Eq. 12 can be estimated in three ways (by augmenting cross-sectional averages of the dependent and explanatory variables to approximate cross-sectional dependence): (i) cross-sectional ARDL (CS-ARDL), distributed lag (CS-DL), and Error Correction Model (CS-ECM) approach. However, in this study we focus on the first two estimation methods since the CS-ARDL model can be rewritten as an ECM and therefore the long-run estimates from both CS-ECM and CS-ARDL approaches are numerically equivalent.

3.2.2. The CS-ARDL Estimator

A more generalized representation of Eq. 11 with the cross-sectional averages to accommodate cross-sectional dependence leads to:

$$y_{i,t} = \mu_i + \sum_{l=1}^{p} \lambda_{l,i} y_{i,t-l} + \sum_{l=0}^{q} \beta_{l,i} x_{i,t-l} + \sum_{l=0}^{p_T} \gamma'_{i,l} \bar{z}_{t-l} + e_{i,t}, \tag{13}$$

where p, q, and p_T are $\sqrt[3]{T}$ lags of the dependent variable, the explanatory variables, and the cross-sectional averages of the dependent and explanatory variables ($\bar{z}$), respectively.

The CS-ARDL regression representation of Eq. 13 follows the form of:

$$\Delta y_{it} = \mu_i + \sum_{l=1}^{p} \lambda_{li} \Delta y_{i,t-l} + \sum_{l=0}^{q} \beta'_{il} x_{i,t-l} + \sum_{l=0}^{p_T} \gamma' \bar{z}_{t-l} + e_{i,t}. \tag{14}$$

The individual long-run coefficients are calculated as:

$$\hat{\theta}_i = \frac{\sum_{l=0}^{q} \hat{\beta}_{l,i}}{1 - \sum_{l=1}^{p} \hat{\lambda}_{l,i}}. \tag{15}$$

As indicated above, the coefficients can be estimated by the MG or PMG estimator.

3.2.3. The CS-DL Estimator

The general representation of an ARDL(p, q) model can be written in the following distributed lag form under the assumption that λ_i lies in the unit circle:

$$y_{i,t} = \mu_i + \theta_{1,i} x_{i,t} + \delta_i(L) \Delta x_{i,t} + \tilde{u}_{i,t}, \tag{16}$$

where $\delta_i(L) = -\sum_{l=0}^{\infty} \left[\lambda_i^{l+1} (1-\lambda_i)^{-1} \beta_{1,i} \right] L^l$, $\theta_{0,i} = (1-\lambda_i L)^{-1}$, and L is the lag operator.

Following Chudik et al. (2016), Eq. 16 can be directly estimated by the CCE estimator, also known as the CS-DL approach by augmenting the regression with the differences of the explanatory variables (x), their lags and the cross-sectional averages. The estimation is consistent even if the errors are serially correlated (Pesaran, 2006).

The CS-DL estimator for a general representation of the ARDL(p, q), with added cross-sectional averages to take out strong cross-sectional dependence, follows the below equation:

$$y_{i,t} = \mu_i + \theta_{1,i} x_{i,t} + \sum_{l=0}^{p-1} \delta_{i,l} \Delta x_{i,t-l} + \sum_{l=0}^{\bar{q}} \gamma_{y,i,l} \bar{y}_{t-1} + \sum_{l=0}^{\bar{p}} \gamma_{x,i,l} \bar{x}_{t-1} + e_{i,t}, \tag{17}$$

where $\bar{y}_{t-1}$ and $\bar{x}_{t-1}$ are the cross-sectional averages and $\bar{p} = T^{1/3}$ and $\bar{q} = 0$.

In this study, however, we prefer to primarily employ the first method (CS-ARDL) as it has several advantages over the rest two. Compared to the CS-DL estimator, the panel CS-ARDL estimator is robust to endogeneity problems (or simultaneity bias) and has superior small-sample performance when the time dimension is sufficiently large and the underlying ARDL model is correctly specified (Chudik et al., 2013, 2016). Most importantly, unlike the CS-DL estimator, the CS-ARDL allows feedback effects from (lagged) dependent variable onto the regressors (reverse causality), which is relevant to our variables of concern (current and FBs) and provides a complete set of estimates for the long and short-run coefficients. The CS-DL estimator provides only the estimate of the long-run coefficients. The long-run estimates of the CS-ARDL estimator are also consistent irrespective of whether the underlying variables are $I(0)$ or $I(1)$.[4]

3.3. Case Study

To contextualize the evidence from the panel study at country levels, we analyzed three country cases: Azerbaijan and Türkiye, which share similar economic background and geographic proximities, and Saudi Arabia, which is an OPEC member states with large influence in setting the global oil price. To ensure methodological continuity, we continue to employ the time series ARDL model with bound tests at country-level by limiting the dimension (number of groups) in Eq. 9 to one. That is, $i = 1$. (See Kripfganz & Schneider, 2022, for better understanding of the time series model implementation.) In such country-level studies, cross-sectional dependence and slope heterogeneity become no longer concerns unlike with panel data. However, the bounds test for cointegration become problematic if there is a structural break in the series.

Structural breaks are very common in most macroeconomic series. Shocks like the Global Financial Crisis cause structural breaks, which affected our case countries alike the rest of the world. Data visualizations of the CAB and OFB of the three countries also reveal potential structural break in the mid-2000s. To this end, we employ time-dummy variables to capture the impact of the possible structural breaks in our ARDL model estimations. (We discuss the time-dummy generation in the *ARDL estimations* section, under Section 6, Results.) Finally, we employ the ARDL error correction models to estimate the short- and long-run coefficients and the speed of adjustments after accounting for exogenous shocks (captured through World real GDP growth) and structural breaks as appropriate (Kripfganz & Schneider, 2022; Pesaran et al., 2001).

---

[4]For the panel data analyses, we employed the Stata xtdcce2 command generously prepared by Ditzen (2018). For the country case studies, we used the Stata ardl commond kindly prepared by Sebastian Kripfganz, University of Exeter Business School, S.Kripfganz@exeter.ac.uk; and Daniel C. Schneider, Max Planck Institute for Demographic Research, schneider@demogr.mpg.de.

4. Data and Sample Context

We analyzed 53 OIC members using unbalanced panel data for the period ranging from 1980 through 2022.[5] The data for the main variables (CAB, OFB, and real GDP growth) were obtained from the October 2023 IMF's World Economic Outlook (WEO) database. While the trade openness data was obtained from the WDI,[6] the Fx regime data was obtained from Ilzetzki et al. (2021).[7] The data are all in nominal terms (as a share of GDP) unless stated otherwise and no (seasonal) adjustments or transformations of the data have been performed.

The OIC members are heterogeneous covering five continents, all income groups, fragile states, small states, energy exporters, commodity exporters, and some with history of HIPC and sovereign debt restructurings. Over the past two decades, the median CAB and OFB for the member countries stood at –3.1% and –2.5% of GDP, respectively, despite volatilities. (See Table AI and Fig. 5.1.) While countries like Kuwait experienced more than 30% of GDP overall fiscal surplus (during 2001–2014), Djibouti enjoyed close to 50% of GDP current account surplus in the early 2000s. On the other hand, the median public debt ended its declining trajectory during the great financial recession and started its upward trend to reach 50% of GDP by 2022. Following a similar pattern, the median debt service on external debt more than doubled since 2012 (0.8% of GDP) and reached 1.8% of GDP in 2022. The increasing openness to the international market witnessed in the 2000s by the OIC member states, however, deteriorated after the great financial crisis. (See Fig. 5.1.)

---

[5]At the time of conducting the data only 53 out of the 56 member countries have enough data to analyze. Most of the econometric analyses also use data from 2000 to 2022 as many countries miss relevant data before 2000.

[6]The Trade data (the share of both import and export to GDP) in the WDI database has large missing values for many countries over the years. However, the Merchandise trade (% of GDP) [TG.VAL.TOTL.GD.ZS] and the Trade in services (% of GDP) [BG.GSR.NFSV.GD.ZS] data for many countries and years fairly exist. Hence, we revised the Trade (openness) indicator as the sum of the two sub-indicators. In the event where there is a Trade data from the WDI database but different from the revised computed data, we use the original Trade data from the WDI database.

[7]The Fx regimes are obtained from the coarse classification of Ilzetzki et al. (2021), where we classify country-period into fixed and flexible Fx regimes. While the fixed exchange rate regimes constitutes the score of 1 (No separate legal tender, Pre announced peg or currency board arrangement, Pre announced horizontal band that is narrower than or equal to ±2%, and De facto peg) and score 2 (Pre announced crawling peg, Pre announced crawling band that is narrower than or equal to ±2%, De factor crawling peg, and De facto crawling band that is narrower than or equal to ±2%), whereas the flexible regime are those score 3 (Pre announced crawling band that is wider than or equal to ±2%, De facto crawling band that is narrower than or equal to ±5%, Moving band that is narrower than or equal to ±2%, and Managed floating), score 4 (Freely floating) and score 5 (Freely falling).

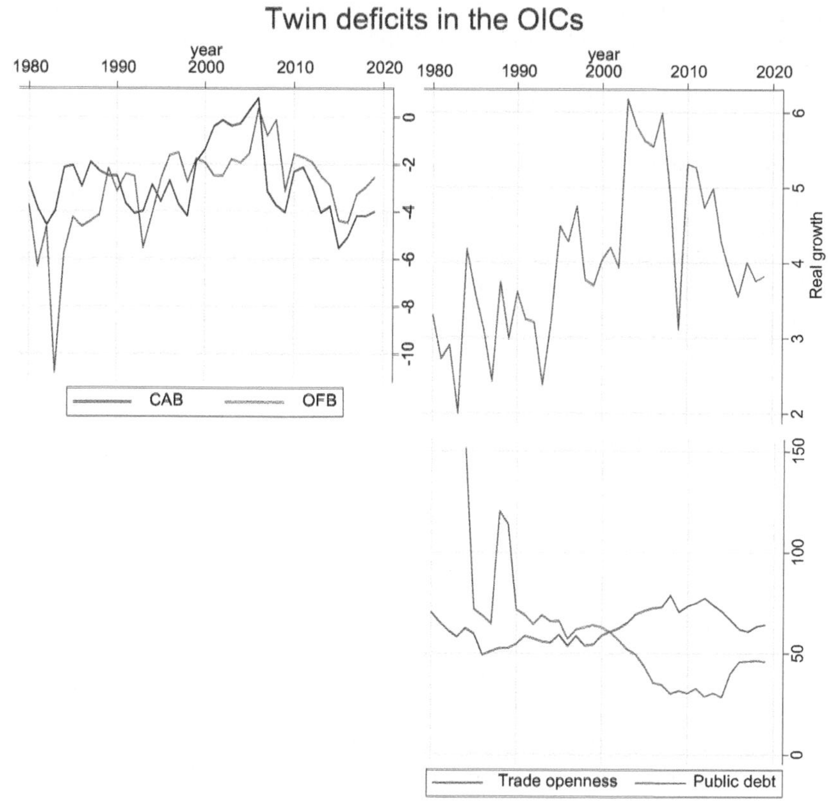

Fig. 5.1. Twin Deficits Across OIC Members.
Source: OCT 2023 WEO, IMF. All, except Real growth, are as a % share of GDP and are median values for the OIC members.

5. Results

5.1. Unit Root, Cross-sectional Dependence (CSD), Structural Break

Following the standard practice, we first tested for the presence of unit root in our series (CAB, OFB, real Growth, and Openness). First, we employed the Im et al. (2003) first-generation unit root test, after including 1 lag of the series in the ADF regressions. The results reveal that all the four series (CAB, OFB, real Growth, and Openness) are stationary in levels across some countries in the panel, that is, the null of *all panels contain unit roots* is rejected. (Table AII, in the Appendix, presents the Unit Root test results.) Nevertheless, rejecting the null hypothesis in these tests does not guarantee that there are no countries in our panel with a non-stationary process. The test only confirms that there are countries with stationary (CAB, OFB, real Growth, and Openness) processes. A validation test using the Hadri (2000) maximum likelihood (ML) test rejects the null of *all the panels are stationary at levels* but fails to do so at difference for all the four variables implying that all series are $I(1)$ processes. (See Table AIII, Annex.)

Since the Hardi ML panel unit root test requires strongly balanced panel, we limited the tests for the period between 2000-2022/3 for all series except OFB, which was limited between 2004 and 2022/2023.

Next, we conducted the Pesaran and Xie (2021) weak cross-sectional dependence test between units in our sample for each series, CAB, OFB, Growth and Openness, separately. This test is superior to the Pesaran (2015) test as it is a bias-corrected CD test for error cross-sectional dependence in panel data models with latent factors. We applied the test on the full sample as the test is valid only with the cross-sectional data (N) larger than the time period (T), where N is 55 and T is as long as 23 years in this study. The test rejects the null of weak cross-sectional dependency for all series implying possible violation of the basic ordinary least-squares assumption of an independent and identically distributed error term. (See the results on Table AIV, Annex.)

Given the strong evidence of the presence of cross-sectional dependence in our panel, we employ the Pesaran (2007) panel unit root tests – a second-generation panel unit root tests – that assumes/allows for heterogeneity in the autoregressive coefficient of the Dickey–Fuller regression and allows for the presence of a single unobserved common factor with heterogeneous factor loadings in the data. Table AV, Annex, presents the results from the Pesaran (2007) panel unit root tests and shows that CAB and real Growth are stationary in levels and first difference with and without a trend term, at either lag 0 or 1. However, the OFB is found to be an $I(1)$ process when a trend term and one lag included. On the other hand, Openness is found to be an $I(1)$ process in levels and first difference with and without a trend term, at either lag 0 or 1.

To address the possible structural breaks in the series, which cover up to 23 years of observations for many countries in the study, we employ the Karavias and Tzavalis (2014) panel unit root test that takes structural breaks into account. Table AVI, Annex, presents the result. It shows that while CAB and real Growth are unit root processes, OFB and Openness are found to be stationary processes with breaks in the early 1980s.

Overall, from the first-generation (Hardi) and the second-generation unit root tests accounting for structural breaks, there is strong evidence that the CAB and real Growth series in our panel are unit root, $I(1)$, processes. The OFB and Openness series, on the other hand, are found to be stationary process with structural breaks in the early 1980s.

5.2. Slope Homogeneity

Next, we test for slop homogeneity to address any biased estimation originating from parameter heterogeneity (Pesaran & Smith, 1995). We employ the Pesaran and Yamagata (2008) test for slope heterogeneity after accounting for autocorrelation in the residual using the heteroskedasticity- and autocorrelation-consistent (HAC) robust standard errors following Blomquist and Westerlund (2013). We also employed prewhitening to reduce small-sample bias in HAC estimation following (Andrews & Monahan, 1992). As shown in Table AVII, Annex (first two columns) the tests reject the null of slope homogeneity for CAB and Openness, while it fails to reject for OFB and Growth as dependent variables. However, when we account for cross-sectional dependence, which is prevalent in our panel, the test rejects the null for all series confirming that not all slope coefficients are identical across our cross-sectional units and calls for a careful estimation of parameters for our sample.

5.3. Cointegration

Given the mixed unit root test results and growing body of literature that most macroeconomic time series are non-stationary, we proceed with testing for cointegration between our series. We employ two tests: the first-generation Pedroni (1999, 2004) panel cointegration tests as well as the second-generation Westerlund (2007) error-correction-based panel cointegration test, which accounts for cross-sectional dependency in our sample.

All the seven Pedroni (1999, 2004) test statistics reject the null of no cointegration in our panel at 5% or lower level of significance except the panel-v and group rho statistics when a trend term is included. (See Table AVIII, Annex.) We apply the Akaike information criterion (AIC) lag selection (2 lags) and demeaned the dependent variables, that is, included time dummies to remove the effect of the cross-section dependence of error terms. Either of the AIC or Bayesian information criterion (BIC) lag-length selection methods provide similar results except with the only minor difference in the ADF-statistic, which still rejects the null either way.

The Westerlund (2007) error-correction-based cointegration panel and group mean statistics, on the other hand, reject the null of no error correction or no cointegration at a 1% level of significance when the standard *p*-values are used – in both cases when the CAB and OFB are regressed one over the other. However, in the presence of strong evidence of cross-sectional dependence that was detected in our sample, we preferred to use the bootstrapped *p*-values, which are more robust to cross-sectional dependence. Subsequently, all the test statistics fail to reject the null of no cointegration using the robust bootstrap *p*-values. (See Table AIX, Annex.) The mixed evidence from the first- and second-generation cointegration tests call for a careful estimation of our panel data.

5.4. Panel Model Estimation Results: CS-ARDL Results

5.4.1. OIC Member Countries

We start our analysis by estimating the CS-ARDL model for the bivariate specification of CAB and OFB using the full sample, 53 OIC countries with adequate size of data. As indicated in the methodology section, the CS-ARDL estimator has relevant advantages, including superior small-sample performance, robust to endogeneity problems (or simultaneity bias) and, most importantly, it allows feedback effects from (lagged) dependent variable onto the regressors (reverse causality), which is relevant to our variables of concern (current and FBs). However, one of the known limitations of the CS-ARDL model is identifying the right lag orders for the variables in the model (p for CAB – the dependent variable – and q for the regressors) need to be known. Since we do not have a credible theoretical or empirical foundation to determine the values of p and q for now, we run 18 ARDL(p, q) model specifications with $p \in [1, 2]$ and $q \in [0, 2]$ and selected the results with better model qualities. We also loop the model estimations by adding 0 (contemporaneous), 1 and 2 lags of the cross-sectional means of the dependent and all independent variables.

Out of the 18 model estimations we conducted, we selected the ARDL (2, 0) which meets critical model quality criteria, including week cross-sectional dependence of the error terms and acceptable error-correction speed of adjustment parameter. Table 5.1, column 1, presents the results from the CS-ARDL(2,0) estimation. The result shows strong evidence supporting to the TDH. A 1% increase in OFB is associated with a 0.2% (and 0.3%) increase in the CAB in the long (and short) run across the OIC member countries. The partial adjustment to the long-run equilibrium appears to be very quick, with 100% of the gap closing in less than one year.

Next, we estimate more than 162 models of the form ARDL (p, q, r, s) accounting for the business cycle (real growth, r lags) and openness (s lags), where $p \in [1, 2]$ and $q, r, s \in [0, 2]$. Like the bivariate model above, we also loop the model estimations over 0 (contemporaneous), 1 and 2 lags of the cross-sectional means of the dependent and all independent variables. Consequently, we selected the ARDL(2,2,1,0) estimator with contemporaneous lags of cross-sectional means as it meets all model qualities, also discussed in the bivariate estimation above. The results show strong evidence of long-run causal relationship running from OFB to CAB across OIC member countries. See Table 5.1, column 2. We find that a 1% increase in OFB causes close to a triple effect (a 2.8%) increase in the CAB in the long run. The effect appears rather smaller (0.3% increase) in the short run. The partial adjustment to the long-run equilibrium is very quick, with 100% of the gap closing in a year. This is relatively strong evidence of large impact of fiscal decisions on external balance compared to the literature confirming that OIC member countries indeed have unique macroeconomic context.

5.4.2. Fx Regimes

As indicated in the literature review section, the Fx exchange regime is the primary transmission channels for the impact of fiscal policy to current account. To this end, we investigate the case of twin deficits by dividing the OIC member countries into two groups of managed/fixed versus flexible/floating Fx regimes based on data obtained from the Ilzetzki et al. (2021). We followed the same procedure above and loop the ARDL (p, q, r, s) model estimations over a range of [1, 2] lags for the dependent variable and [0, 2] lags of the regressors over a range of [0, 2] lags of the means of cross-sectional averages to account for cross-sectional dependence for the managed/fixed Fx regimes group. Consequently, we selected the results from the ARDL(2,2,1,0) estimator because of the desired model qualities. As shown in Table 5.1, column 3, the result reveals some evidence of twin deficits despite a relatively lower coverage of OIC countries. This is consistent with the literature. In the 15 countries analyzed where there was enough Fx regime data, a 1% OFB shock is associated with a similar 1% increase in CAB in the long

Table 5.1. Cross-section Augmented ARDL (CS-ARDL).

Variables (Dependent: Δ CAB)	(1) Bivariate ARDL(2,0), Full Sample	(2) Controlling Key Variables ARDL(2,2,1,0), Full Sample	(3) Managed Fx Regime ARDL(2,2,1,0)	(4) Flexible Fx Regime ARDL(1,1,0,2)	(5) OPEC ARDL(1,1)	(6) OPEC ARDL(1,1,0,1)
Short-Run Estimates						
L Δ CAB	–0.096**	0.0604	0.118	0.169	–0.206	–0.222
	(0.037)	(0.388)	(0.304)	(0.369)	(0.187)	(0.413)
L2 Δ CAB	–0.142***	–0.117**	–0.153		–0.292*	
	(0.000)	(0.027)	(0.226)		(0.092)	
Δ OFB	0.294***	0.275***	–0.148	–0.836***	0.643***	1.060***
	(0.000)	(0.008)	(0.617)	(0.000)	(0.009)	(0.002)
L Δ OFB		0.0397	0.230	–1.372	0.130	0.205
		(0.687)	(0.234)	(0.320)	(0.501)	(0.195)
L2 Δ OFB		0.066	0.225			
		(0.605)	(0.215)			
Δ Growth		0.147	0.121	–0.519		0.248
		(0.309)	(0.593)	(0.104)		(0.169)
LΔ Growth		0.0512	–0.550			
		(0.660)	(0.395)			

(*Continued*)

Table 5.1. (*Continued*)

Variables (Dependent: Δ CAB)	**(1) Bivariate ARDL(2,0), Full Sample**	**(2) Controlling Key Variables ARDL(2,2,1,0), Full Sample**	**(3) Managed Fx Regime ARDL(2,2,1,0)**	**(4) Flexible Fx Regime ARDL(1,1,0,2)**	**(5) OPEC ARDL(1,1)**	**(6) OPEC ARDL(1,1,0,1)**
L2 Δ Growth						
Δ Openness		–0.044	–0.208*	–0.130		0.003
		(0.422)	(0.067)	(0.120)		(0.989)
L Δ Openness				0.238***		0.203**
				(0.009)		(0.020)
L2 Δ Openness				0.113		
				(0.324)		
Long-run estimates						
ECT (adjust. Term)	*–1.237****	–1.056***	–1.034***	–0.831***	–1.206***	–1.222***
	(0.000)	(0.000)	(0.000)	(0.005)	(0.000)	(0.000)
OFB	0.224***	2.766**	0.972*	–2.436*	0.736***	2.201**
	(0.003)	(0.030)	(0.061)	(0.072)	(0.005)	(0.046)

Growth		1.203	0.284	–0.584**		0.736
		(0.426)	(0.743)	(0.030)		(0.162)
Openness		–0.0172	–0.238	0.283**		0.413
		(0.932)	(0.160)	(0.022)		(0.252)
Observations	952	946	510	29	144	152
Number of countries	53	53	34	2	9	9
R-squared	0.651	0.290	0.236	0.404	0.454	0.162
CD	–1.317	0.487	–1.319	–1.353	–1.342	–0.00492
p-Value (CD)	0.188	0.627	0.187	0.176	0.180	0.996
Period (years of observations)	18	18	15	15	16	17

Notes: We applied recursive small-sample time series bias correction as appropriate. All models meet (semi-)weak cross-sectional dependency of residuals test. Standard errors in parentheses. *** $p<0.01$, ** $p<0.05$, * $p<0.10$.

run. The long-run relationship also retains its equilibrium in about one year after a shock to the equilibrium.

In the case of flexible/floating group, where we have enough data only for three countries (Malaysia, Türkiye, and Uganda), the result shows a long run but reverse feedback mechanism between the two balances. (See Table 5.1, column 4.) That is, a 1% increase in overall FB causes a 2.4% decrease in CAB in the long run and a 0.8% decrease in the short run. The partial adjustment to the long-run equilibrium also indicates that 83% of the disequilibrium adjusts every period for this flexible/floating Fx regime group.

5.4.3. OPEC Members of OIC Countries

As 9 out of the 12 OPEC member states also constitute the critical elements of the OIC group, we separately study this unique group – nine OPEC member countries which are also members of the OIC. Interestingly, the results for these OPEC and OIC members show impeccable evidence of twin deficits irrespective of the choice of lags, ARDL(p, q, r, s) for $p \in [1, 2]$ and $q, r, s \in [0, 2]$. The bivariate CS-ARDL(1, 1) model estimation, Table 5.1, column 5, shows that a 1% increase in OFB is strongly associated with a 0.7% increase in CAB in the long term and a 0.6% increase in the short term. The steady state long-run relationship also quickly retains its long-term equilibrium in less than a year after a shock to the equilibrium. The twin-deficits evidence becomes even stronger when we control the business cycle and trade openness in this OPEC-OIC group. As shown in column 6 of Table 5.1, a 1% increase in OFB causes a double (2%) lasting impact in CAB after controlling for the business cycle and trade openness. The partial adjustment to the long-run equilibrium is very quick, with 100% of the gap closing in 10 months, witnessing a strong and large impact of fiscal decisions on external balance across OPEC-OIC member countries.

The nine OPEC and OIC member countries are predominantly managed Fx regimes. Since 2000, these countries run a managed (peg or crawling peg) Fx regime for 83% of the time. If we included the periods when they run a managed floating arrangement, the duration of the time they would be considered as managed Fx regime jumps to 89%. That is, between 2000 and 2019 – the last year we have data on Fx regime – these nine countries had a managed/fixed Fx regime for 89% of the time. This is equivalent to 18 years out of the 20 years between 2000 and 2019. The literature shows that twin deficits are more prevalent in fixed/managed Fx regime situations (Furceri & Zdzienicka, 2018). Our evidence from these nine OPEC-OIC member states with predominantly managed Fx regimes also strongly supports the claim.

5.5. Panel Model Estimation Results: CS-DL Results

Notwithstanding its extensive merits, including simultaneous estimations of both the short- and long-term effects, and accounting reverse feedback, among others, the CS-ARDL estimator has some limitations, such as determining the lags selection. (See the discussion in the methodology section.) To verify the findings from the CS-ARDL estimations, we also employ a CS-DL estimator for the model specification accounting for the business cycle and openness for our full sample of OIC member countries and the OPEC group separately. One of the major advantages of CS-DL is that the estimation is consistent even if the errors are serially correlated. The CS-DL(2, 2,1,0) estimation for the full sample, using similar model specification in the CS-ARDL estimation above, confirms the presence of twin deficits across the OIC. (See Table 5.2, column 1.) We find that a 1% increase in OFB pushes the CAB up by 0.6% in the long term. For the OPEC-OIC group, in particular, the long-term impact of fiscal decision on external balance is even higher with a 1% increase in OFB causing 1 1.3% positive impact on CAB (see Table 5.2, column 2).

Table 5.2. Cross-Section Augmented Distributed Lag (CS-ARDL) Estimator.

Variables	**(1)**	**(2)**
	Full Sample CS-DL, ARDL(2, 2,1,0),	**OPEC CS-DL, ARDL(1,2,0,0),**
	Δ.CAB	**Δ.CAB**
Δ2.CAB	0.817***	
	(0.000)	
LΔ2.CAB	0.513***	
	(0.000)	
L2Δ2.CAB	0.267***	
	(0.000)	
Δ.OFB	0.546**	1.285**
	(0.013)	(0.024)
Δ2.OFB	–0.558***	–0.925
	(0.000)	(0.104)
LΔ2.OFB	–0.322***	–0.360
	(0.003)	(0.353)
L2Δ2.OFB	–0.144**	–0.089
	(0.022)	(0.540)
Δ. Growth	–0.247*	0.150
	(0.099)	(0.441)
Δ2.Growth	–0.110	–0.039
	(0.537)	(0.820)
LΔ2.Growth	–0.203	
	(0.374)	

(*Continued*)

Table 5.2. (*Continued*)

Variables	**(1)**	**(2)**
	Full Sample CS-DL, ARDL(2, 2,1,0),	**OPEC CS-DL, ARDL(1,2,0,0),**
	Δ.CAB	**Δ.CAB**
Δ. Openness	–0.0482	–0.124
	(0.335)	(0.532)
Δ2.Openess	0.0426	–0.217
	(0.260)	(0.125)
Observations	899	128
Number of countries	50	8
R-squared	0.015	0.148
Period (years)	18	16
CD	1.295	–1.554
p-Value (CD)	0.195	0.120

Notes: *p*-Value in parentheses; *** $p<0.01$, ** $p<0.05$, * $p<0.10$. While the number of lags of cross-section averages for CAB, OFB, Growth, and Openness is (2,2,1,0) for result (1), it is (2,1,2,0) for result (2), respectively.

Overall, the panel data analyses using both CS-ARDL and CS-DL estimation methods are conclusive that there is strong evidence of twin deficits in the OIC member countries, across the OPEC group, in particular. Compared to countries with flexible Fx regime, there is more evidence of presence of twin deficits in managed/fixed Fx regime member countries, such as OPEC, consistent with the literature. The evidence indicates that a flexible Fx regime helps to absorb fiscal shocks from transmitting to the external sector with full impact. Similarly, for those countries setting the international oil price, the impact of their fiscal decision transmits quickly and strongly to their external position exacerbated by their managed/fixed Fx regime.

5.6. Case Study

To contextualize the evidence from the panel study at country levels, we analyzed three country cases: Azerbaijan, Türkiye, and Saudi Arabia. While Azerbaijan and Saudi Arabia are predominantly managed Fx regimes, Türkiye is considered as a flexible Fx regime. Azerbaijan and Türkiye have geographic proximities and are relatively in a similar level of economic status – with both countries being upper middle income as of 2024. On the other hand, Saudi Arabia is a high-income country and a member of OPEC group with high influence of setting the international oil price. In this section, we investigate further the relationship between fiscal and CABs by zooming in to these three countries, Azerbaijan, Saudi Arabia, and Türkiye.

5.6.1. County Context: Azerbaijan

Azerbaijan enjoyed a sound economic growth at an average of 4.8% real GDP growth over the past three decades. The country graduated to lower middle-income country in 2005 and to upper middle-income in 2009 based on World Bank income group classification. However, since the financial crisis, real growth has been declining from a peak of 35% in 2006 to an average of 1.7% in the past decade, 2013–2022. The FB, on the other hand, experienced some turbulence over the past three decades despite remaining in a surplus at an average of 3.7% of GDP 1994–2022. Since the financial crisis, the fiscal account has been deteriorating accompanied by an increasing public borrowing. The overall public debt has been declining from a peak of 25.4% of GDP in 1999 to a low of 3.2% in 2008. However, the debt trajectory reversed in 2009 and reached a high of 26.4% in 2021 surpassing historical highs. The year 2005 seems a defining year for Azerbaijan's external sector with the historically large current account deficit – at an average of 16.5% of GDP between 1992 and 2004 – dramatically shifting to a large surplus resulting in an average of 15.3% since then, between 2005 and 2022. Most interestingly, the divergence between the CAB and OFB seems to shift in the mid-2000s and started co-movement. (See Fig. 5.2.) The country's trade openness, on the other hand, remains high with trade (import plus export) to GDP ratio averaging at 88% between 1990 and 2022.

5.6.2. County Context: Saudi Arabia

Saudi Arabia (henceforth, Saudi, for simplicity) has been a high-income country since 2004 with an average real growth rate of 3.7% of GDP. The FB, on the other hand, experienced continuous decline since the financial crisis, from a peak of 30% of GDP in 2008 to as low as 16% deficit in 2015. Since 2016, the balance improved to reach 2.5% in 2022.

The overall public debt has been declining steadily since the end of the last century – from a peak of more than 100% of the GDP in the late 1990s until it reached a trough of 1.5% in 2014. However, the debt started its upward trajectory in 2015 and reached 23.8% in 2022.

Since 2000, Saudi enjoyed a current account surplus at an average rate of 11.4% of GDP except a couple of deficits it experienced in 2015 (year of commodity shock) and 2020 (the COVID-19 pandemic).

The divergence between the fiscal and current account came to an end in 2006 and the two balances comoved since then with a pairwise correlation of 0.9. (See Fig. 5.3.) Saudi's trade openness, on the other hand, remains high with trade (import plus export) to GDP ratio averaging at 73% between 2000 and 2022.

5.6.3. Country Context: Türkiye

Türkiye benefited from a strong economic performance over the past four decades – with an average real growth of 4.7%. As per the World Bank income group classification, Türkiye transitioned from a lower middle-income country to an upper middle-income country in fiscal year 1999 although it relapsed back to a

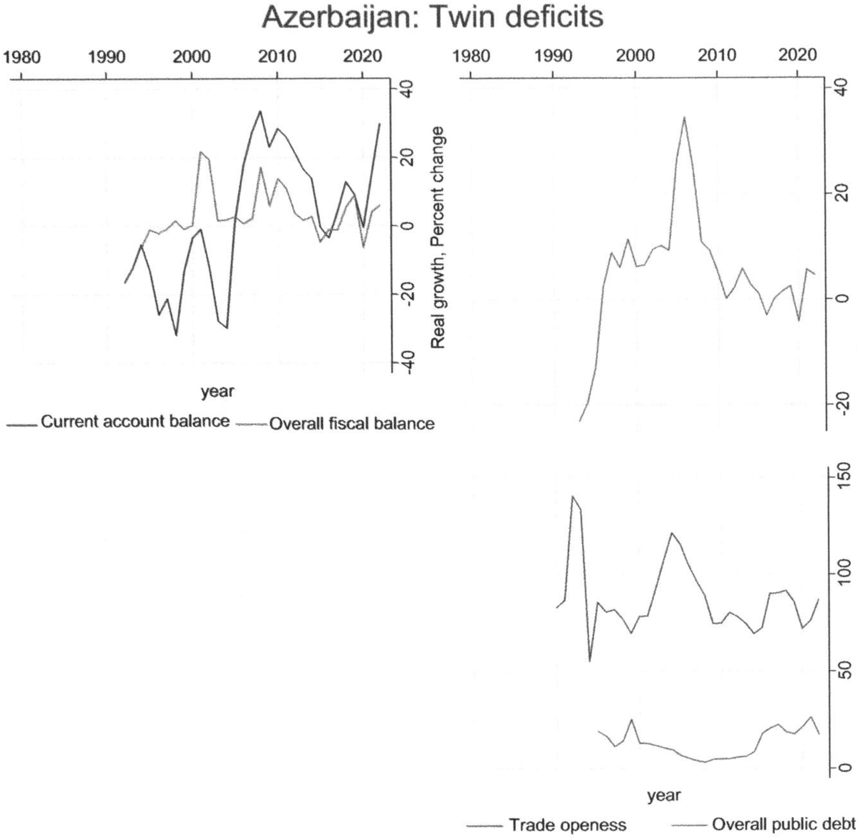

Fig. 5.2. Real Growth, Fiscal and External Balances in Azerbaijan.
Source: OCT 2023 WEO, IMF. All, except Real growth, are as a % share of GDP.

lower middle income in fiscal year 2001. The country rejoined the upper middle-income group in fiscal year 2006 once again and maintained it to date. Nevertheless, the country sustained a fiscal deficit of 3.9 between 2000 and 2022 despite some improvement over the past one decade – excluding the pandemic years (2019 and 2020). (See Fig. 5.4.) Türkiye's external sector also experienced high volatility over the past four decades. Since the start of the century, in particular, the current account deficits remain high and stood at 3.6% of GDP (between 2000 and 2022) compared to the 0.8% in the last two decades of the last century. There is strong co-movement between the current account and FB as shown in Fig. 5.4. Türkiye's openness to the external market witnessed a monotonous growth over the past four decades and reached at 81% of external trade as a share of GDP in 2022.

5.6.4. Unit Root Tests

Ahead of the country-level ARDL estimation, in this section, we investigate the presence of unit roots across the four series we already discussed in the panel

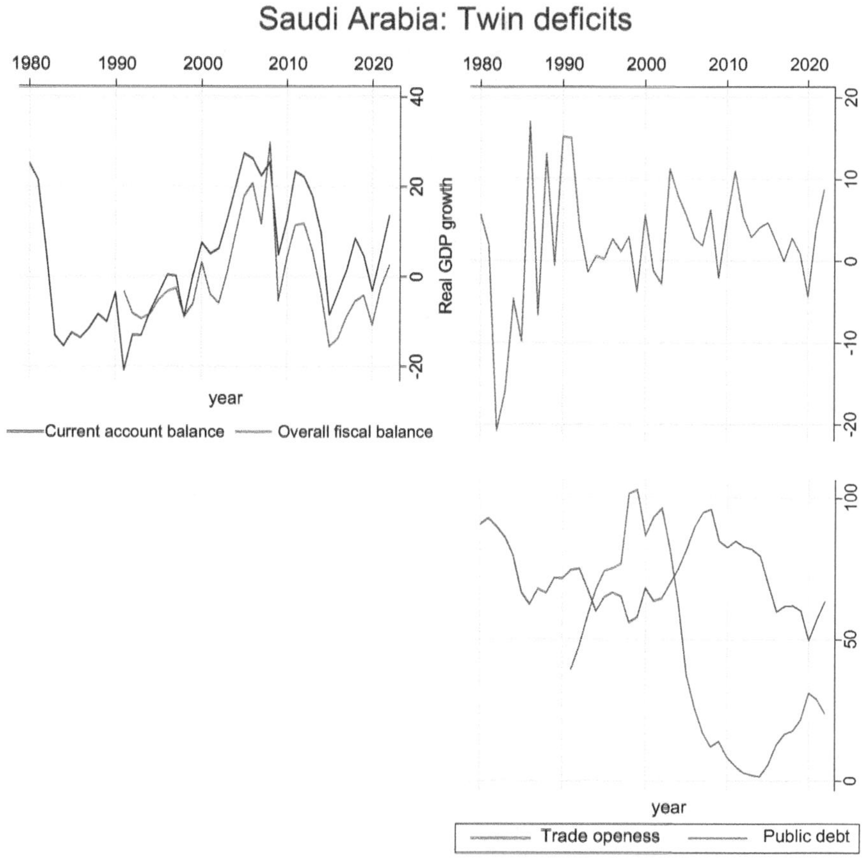

Fig. 5.3. Real Growth, Fiscal and External Balances, Saudi Arabia.
Source: OCT 2023 WEO, IMF. All, except Real growth, are as a % share of GDP.

analyses, for the three case countries: Azerbaijan, Saudi Arabia, and Türkiye. To this end, we employ the most common modified Dickey-Fuller *t*-test (GF-GLS). Table 5.3 presents the results.

As shown in Table 5.3, the CAB is found to be an $I(1)$ process across the three case countries, whereas the OFB and Openness are found to be an $I(1)$ process only in the case of Saudi Arabia. While Openness is a stationary, $I(0)$, processes in Azerbaijan, it is an $I(2)$ process in the case of Türkiye. On the other hand, Growth is found to be an $I(2)$ process across all three countries.

5.6.5. ARDL Estimations

The unit root test results justify the appropriateness of using ARDL models as it allows mixed $I(0)$ and $I(1)$ regressors as long as the dependent variable, in our case, the CAB, is an $I(1)$ process. In this section, we estimate the short- and/or long-run impact of OFB on the CAB for our three case countries, also controlling for the business cycle and trade Openness, using the ARDL models.

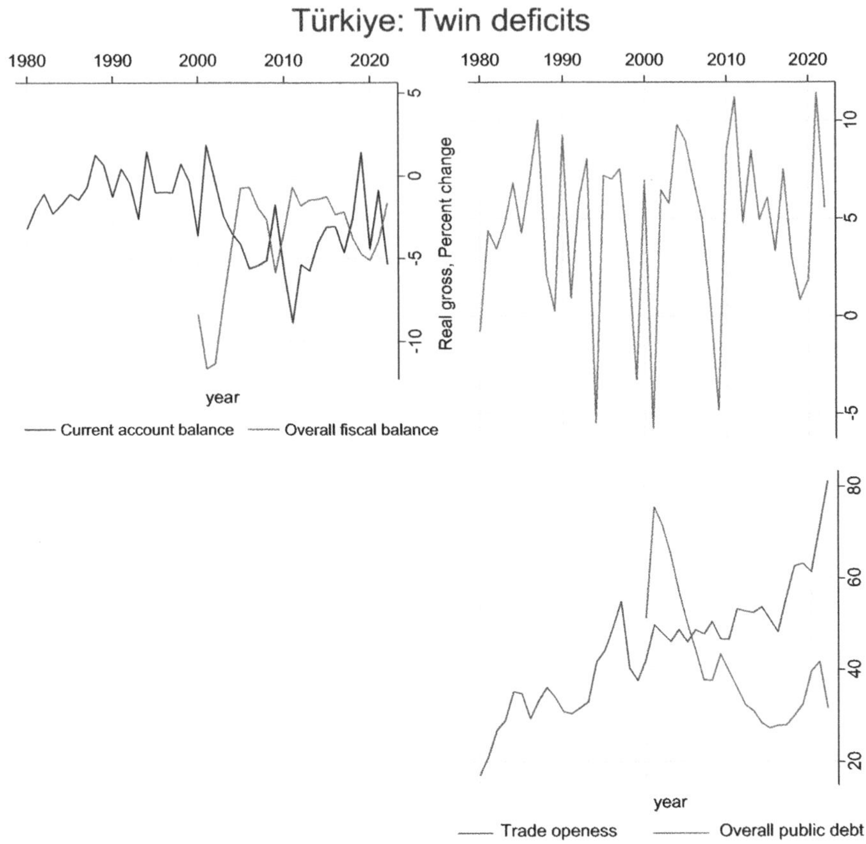

Fig. 5.4. Real Growth, Fiscal and External Balances in Türkiye.
Source: OCT 2023 WEO, IMF. All, except Real growth, are as a % share of GDP.

ARDL models are known to be inconsistent in the presence of breaks in the series under estimation. To overcome this challenge, we will introduce a year-dummy variable in the model to capture the period before and after the break. This dummy variable is included in the model as exogenous variable since such structural breaks are more often driven by exogenous shocks, such as regime changes. We also capture yearly exogeneous shocks using world's real GDP growth. The year-dummy is defined as:

$$\text{dummy} = \begin{cases} 0 \text{ if year} < \textit{breakyear} \\ 1 \text{ if year} \geq \textit{breakyear} \end{cases}.$$

It should be also noted that the reported t-statistic for the speed-of-adjustment coefficient in the ARDL model estimates does not have a standard distribution under the null hypothesis that it equals zero. Instead, we obtain the appropriate critical values (or t-statistic) and the p-values (under a one-sided alternative hypothesis) based on the Kripfganz and Schneider (2022) approximations. These

Table 5.3. GL-ADF Unit root Test (Optimal Lag Based on SIC).

Country/ Variable	**Levels**		**First difference**	
	DF-GLS tau	***p*-Value (5%)**	**DF-GLS tau**	***p*-Value (5%)**
Azerbaijan				
CAB	–2.722	–3.428	–3.567**	–3.443
OFB	–3.806***	–3.457		
Growth	–1.579***	–3.443		
Openness	–2.162[a]	–2.513	–2.561	–3.443
Saudi Arabia				
CAB	–2.095	–3.293	–4.281***	–3.303
OFB	–1.687	–3.428	–3.881***	–3.428
Growth	–3.767***	–2.364		
Openness	–1.835	–3.293	–4.247***	–3.303
Türkiye				
CAB	–2.722	–3.428	–3.567**	–3.443
OFB	–3.806***	–3.457		
Growth	–1.579***	–3.443		
Openness	–2.162[a]	–2.513	–2.561	–3.443

[a]Azerbaijan's Openness is an $I(2)$ process.

*** $p<0.01$, ** $p<0.05$, * $p<0.10$.

appropriate values can be obtained after running the bound test estimations based on the Stata *ARDL* command. We inserted these approximated values ex post in the following regression output tables.

5.6.6. Azerbaijan

A close observation of the data visualization indicates that the Azerbaijan's current account and FBs persistently co-move around constant means with a possible structural break in 2005. (see Fig. 5.2.) To this end, we first fit a bivariate ARDL(p, q) model of OFB on CAB with no deterministic model components. Optimal lags are selected based on the AIC, which tends to select less parsimonious models and has certain superiority over the BIC especially when serial correlation is a concern. Subsequently, we estimate more model specifications accounting for key macrovariables (real Growth and Openness) and time dummies to capture possible structural breaks in the economy.

As presented in Table 5.4, there is no evidence of a twin deficits in the case of Azerbaijan. Table 5.4, column (1), for instance, presents the results from an ARDL(1,4) estimation of the bivariate CAB-OFB model, with the optimal lags

Table 5.4. Azerbaijan: ARDL Estimations.

Dependent Variable: Δ CAB	**(1)** *ARDL(1,4) f(OFB)*	**(2)** *ARDL(2,1) f(OFB, time-dummy)*	**(3)** *ARDL (3,3,3,1) f(OFB, Growth, Openness)*	**(4)** *ARDL (3,3,3,1) f(OFB, Growth, Openness, time-dummy)*
Long-run coefficient				
L. OFB	–0.669	–1.771	–1.808	0.644
	(0.864)	(0.475)	(0.403)	(0.392)
L. Growth			0.608	0.301
			(0.662)	(0.482)
L. Openness			–0.137	–0.251***
			(0.396)	(0.00289)
Short-run coefficient				
ECT	–0.144	–0.241	–0.357*	–1.031*
	(0.210)	(0.241)	(0.0880)	(0.0558)
Bound test's *t*-stat and *p*-values[a]	–1.148	–1.212	..	..
	0.593	0.190	..	..
L ΔCAB		0.293	0.165	0.437
		(0.117)	(0.604)	(0.230)
L2 ΔCAB			0.463	0.506
			(0.176)	(0.126)
ΔOFB	0.309	0.229	–0.181	0.167
	(0.339)	(0.494)	(0.622)	(0.691)
L ΔOFB	–0.209		–0.0401	–0.539
	(0.634)		(0.929)	(0.332)
L2 ΔOFB	–0.585*		–0.683	–0.921**
	(0.0933)		(0.103)	(0.0417)
L3 ΔOFB	–0.516			
	(0.108)			
ΔReal Growth			0.0614	–0.0944
			(0.908)	(0.854)

Table 5.4. (*Continued*)

Dependent Variable: Δ CAB	**(1)** *ARDL(1,4) f(OFB)*	**(2)** *ARDL(2,1) f(OFB, time-dummy)*	**(3)** *ARDL (3,3,3,1) f(OFB, Growth, Openness)*	**(4)** *ARDL (3,3,3,1) f(OFB, Growth, Openness, time-dummy)*
L ΔReal Growth			–0.186	–0.404
			(0.622)	(0.307)
L2 ΔReal Growth			–1.086**	–1.017**
			(0.0194)	(0.0225)
Δ Openness			–0.478	–0.534
			(0.160)	(0.107)
Real world GDP growth	1.207 (0.161)	0.846 (0.484)	3.025* (0.0938)	2.670 (0.121)
Time dummy (structural break in 2004)		3.653 (0.529)		21.84 (0.158)
Observations	25	25	25	25
R-squared	0.563	0.495	0.810	0.846
Adj. *R*-squared	0.393	0.335	0.569	0.615

[a]Kripfganz and Schneider (2022) approximations critical values (*t*-statistic) and the *p*-values (under a one-sided alternative hypothesis).

.. Empty cell refers to no results because of low degree of freedom to estimate the parameters.

p-Values in parentheses. *** $p<0.01$, ** $p<0.05$, * $p<0.10$.

selected based on AIC criteria. The bound test for the presence of a long-run relationship between OFB and CAB reveals no such long-run level relationship in the case of Azerbaijan. The negative sign of the coefficient – although not statistically significant – also indicates possible reverse impact of OFB on CAB in Azerbaijan case. Even after controlling for the possible structural break in the two series in 2005, the result remains the same – no long-run relationship between OFB and CAB. (See Table 5.4, column 2.) This is true even after controlling for the business cycle (real Growth) and Openness (see Table 5.4, column 3) or the structural break in 2004 (see Table 5.4, column 4).

Azerbaijan is a predominantly managed/fixed Fx regime country. As per the data from Ilzetzki et al. (2021), between 2000 and 2019, where we have data for our twin deficits study in the country, the currency (manat) has been mostly (for 15 years) pegged to the US dollar. The currency also run a dual market for four years and it was freely falling in 2016. Despite the literature that the fiscal shocks strongly transmit to external balance in less flexible Fx regimes, the evidence from Azerbaijan does not corroborate it.

5.6.7. Saudi Arabia

Alike the case of Azerbaijan above, the data visualization for Saudi Arabia also indicates that the current account and FBs persistently co-move around constant means with a possible structural break during the global financial crisis. (See Fig. 5.3.) Consequently, we first fit a bivariate ARDL(p, q) model of OFB on CAB with no deterministic model components, that is, unrestricted constant, but no trend, using AIC optimal lags selection. We estimate more model specifications accounting for key macrovariables (real Growth and Openness) and time dummies to capture possible structural breaks in the economy.

Table 5.5, column (1) presents the results from an ARDL(1,2) estimation of the bivariate CAB-OFB model. Despite the strong statistically significant long-run and error-term adjustment coefficients, the Bound's test statistics reject a long-run relationship between the fiscal and external balances in the case of Saudi Arabia (see the Kripfganz and Schneider (2022) approximations critical values (t-statistic) and the p-values). Nevertheless, when we account for the possible structural break in 2009, we find a strong long-run relationship between the two balances (see Table 5.5, Column 2). The evidence reveals that a 1% increase in the overall FB is associated with a similar magnitude, 1% increase, in the external balance with the long-run equilibrium adjusting by 79% every year after the shock. The evidence also suggests a 0.8% increase in the short run.

Table 5.5, column 3, presents the result after accounting for the key macrovariables, real growth and trade openness. Alike the first specification, the result shows statistically significant long-run relationship between OFB and CAB. Nevertheless, the Bound's test reject the claim based on the Kripfganz and Schneider (2022) approximations. However, when we account for the structural break in the 2009, the result reveals a strong relationship between overall FB and CAB in the case of Saudi Arabia. A 1% increase in OFB is found to cause a 0.85% and a 0.61% improvement in the external balance in the long and short run, respectively. (See Table 5.5, column 4.) The long-run equilibrium also adjusting by 72% every year after the shock.

In general, our empirical evidence highlights strong presence of twin deficits in the case of Saudi Arabia. As discussed in the previous sections, alike Azerbaijan, Saudi Arabia is a solely managed Fx regime. A shock to the FB, hence, has paramount impact on the external balance aligning with the empirical evidence.

Table 5.5. Saudi Arabia: ARDL Estimations.

Dependent Variable: Δ CAB	**(1)** *ARDL(1,2) f(OFB)*	**(2)** *ARDL(1,0) f(OFB, time-dummy)*	**(3)** *ARDL(1,1,1,1) f(OFB, Growth, Openness)*	**(4)** *ARDL(1,1,1,1) f(OFB, Growth, Openness, time-dummy)*
Long-run coefficient				
L. OFB	0.780***	1.014***	0.275	0.853***
	(0.002)	(1.35e–10)	(0.486)	(0.001)
L. Growth			0.897*	0.192
			(0.010)	(0.530)
L. Openness			0.257	0.009
			(0.329)	(0.957)
ECT	–0.422**	–0.790***	–0.539***	–0.716***
	(0.029)	(0.000)	(0.003)	(0.000)
Bound test's *t*-stat and *p*-values[a]	–2.339 (0.152)	–7.841*** (0.000)	–3.357 (0.114)	–6.138*** (0.001)
ΔOFB	0.713***	0.801***	0.462***	0.611***
	(0.000)	(0.000)	(0.003)	(0.000)
L ΔOFB	0.110			
	(0.210)			
ΔReal Growth			0.137	0.137
			(0.551)	(0.524)
Δ Openness			0.655**	0.472*
			(0.025)	(0.068)
Real-world GDP growth	0.542 (0.295)	0.696 (0.160)	–0.563 (0.366)	–0.128 (0.826)
Time dummy (structural break in 2004)		3.355** (0.044)		3.530** (0.029)
Constant	2.106	2.726	–4.635	3.776
	(0.354)	(0.206)	(0.617)	(0.627)

(*Continued*)

Table 5.5. (*Continued*)

Dependent Variable: Δ CAB	**(1)** *ARDL(1,2) f(OFB)*	**(2)** *ARDL(1,0) f(OFB, time-dummy)*	**(3)** *ARDL(1,1,1,1) f(OFB, Growth, Openness)*	**(4)** *ARDL(1,1,1,1) f(OFB, Growth, Openness, time-dummy)*
Observations	28	28	29	29
R-squared	0.822	0.820	0.868	0.868
Adj. *R*-squared	0.782	0.789	0.815	0.824

[a]Kripfganz and Schneider (2022) approximations critical values (*t*-statistic) and the *p*-values (under a one-sided alternative hypothesis).

.. Refers to no results because of low degree of freedom to estimate the parameters.

p-Values in parentheses. *** $p<0.01$, ** $p<0.05$, * $p<0.10$.

5.6.8. Türkiye

In this section, we present the results for the case of Türkiye. We followed similar approach as in the case of Azerbaijan above and estimated four types of model specifications of the form ARDL(*p*,*q*,*r*,*s*) with no deterministic model components – informed by the strong co-movement between CAB and OFB around constant means – for Türkiye. Optimal lags are again selected based on the AIC method.

Table 5.6, column (1), shows the results from an ARDL(2,1) estimation of the bivariate CAB-OFB model for the full sample. The bound test for the presence of a long-run relationship between the two series reveals no such long-run level relationship in the case of Türkiye. However, the result indicates a significant contemporaneous (short run) effect if the system was still in equilibrium. That is, a 1% increase in OFB is associated with a similar but reverse impact on the external balance (CAB) in the short run. In this estimation, the appropriate *t*-statistic and the *p*-values for the negative speed-of-adjustment coefficient (or ECT) are found to be 0.208 and 0.686, respectively, suggesting that the speed-of-adjustment coefficient is statistically weakly significant, hence, less informative[8] (see the grey highlighted rows in Table 5.6). The results remain the same even after accounting for possible structural break in the OFB-CAB series. (See Table 5.6, column 2.)

[8]Recall that the reported t-statistic for the speed-of-adjustment coefficient in the ARDL model estimates does not have a standard distribution under the null hypothesis that it equals zero. Instead, we use the appropriate critical values (or *t*-statistic) and the *p*-values (under a one-sided alternative hypothesis) from the bound test estimations, and they are inserted ex post in the regression output table.

Table 5.6. Türkiye: ARDL Estimations.

Dependent Variable: Δ CAB	**(1)** *ARDL(2,1)*	**(2)** *ARDL(1,4)*	**(3)** *ARDL(1,0,0,0)*	**(4)** *ARDL(2,1,1,0)*
Long-run coefficient				
L. OFB	–0.803	–0.257	–0.334	0.662
	(0.896)	(0.554)	(0.169)	(0.153)
L. Growth			–0.755*	–1.133**
			(0.0829)	(0.0286)
L. Openness			–0.0776**	0.177*
			(0.0194)	(0.0856)
Short-run coefficient				
ECT	0.0473	–0.559**	–0.588***	–0.641**
	(0.838)	(0.0298)	(0.00612)	(0.0236)
Bound test's t-stat and p-values[a]	0.208 (0.686)	–2.495** (0.022)	–3.129* (0.084)	–2.592* (0.018)
L ΔCAB	–0.483**			–0.279
	(0.0235)			(0.110)
ΔOFB	–1.015**	–1.566***	–0.196	–0.449
	(0.0224)	(0.00175)	(0.224)	(0.304)
L ΔOFB		–0.222		
		(0.410)		
L2 ΔOFB		–0.184		
		(0.468)		
L3 ΔOFB		–0.299		
		(0.203)		
ΔReal Growth			–0.444***	–0.397*
			(0.00626)	(0.0500)
Δ Openness			–0.0456*	0.114*
			(0.0644)	(0.0615)
Real world GDP growth	0.228 (0.468)	0.658** (0.0280)	0.677** (0.0413)	0.564* (0.0612)

(*Continued*)

Table 5.6. (*Continued*)

Dependent Variable: Δ CAB	**(1)** *ARDL(2,1)*	**(2)** *ARDL(1,4)*	**(3)** *ARDL(1,0,0,0)*	**(4)** *ARDL(2,1,1,0)*
Time dummy (structural break in 2004)		–4.482*** (0.00263)		–5.751** (0.0158)
Observations	20	19	22	21
R-squared	0.580	0.819	0.693	0.828
Adj. R-squared	0.441	0.688	0.603	0.699

[a]Kripfganz and Schneider (2022) approximations critical values (t-statistic) and the p-values (under a one-sided alternative hypothesis).

.. Refers to no results because of low degree of freedom to estimate the parameters.

p-Values in parentheses. *** $p<0.01$, ** $p<0.05$, * $p<0.10$.

When we account for the real growth and trade openness in the model specifications, the bound test for the ARDL(1,0,0,0)[9] specification reveals once again no evidence of twin deficits in Türkiye (see Table 5.6, column 3).[10] Yet, the evidence shows that shocks on the real growth and trade openness cause external sector imbalance in the long-term for the case of Türkiye (see Table 5.6, column 3). The impact of openness, however, becomes positive when we control the possible structural breaks in the mid-2000s (see Table 5.6, column 4).

Unlike Azerbaijan, Türkiye has been predominantly a flexible/floating Fx regime between 2000 and 2019, the period of analysis in this study. As per the data from Ilzetzki et al. (2021), during this period, the country runs a managed floating policy for 11 years and a freely floating policy for six years. The country also had a freely falling policy for three years, in early 2000s (2001 and 2002) and in 2019. Türkiye's flexible Fx regime might have contributed to the absence of statistically significant long-run relationship between OFB and CAB in the country as fiscal shocks are automatically stabilized by the foreign exchange rate resulting in minimal impact on the external balance.

---

[9]Optimal lags are based on AIC selection.

[10]All post-estimation diagnosis tests meet the criteria to conduct a bound test post model estimation. That is, the Breusch–Godfrey LM and the Durbin's alternative test for autocorrelation both show no serial correlation of the error terms. The White's test and the Cameron and Trivedi's (1990) decomposition of information matrix (IM)-test also confirm no issues of heteroskedasticity with the model specification. Moreover, the recursive cumulative sum test for parameter stability shows that the model is stable.

6. Conclusion

This study provides crucial empirical evidence on the TDH, particularly in the context of OIC and OPEC member states. The OIC and OPEC constitute intriguing country groups with their unique Islam-dominated cultural and historical backgrounds playing a significant role in shaping their financial, fiscal and external balances, thereby influencing the overall economic trajectory. The OPEC countries, in particular, are a must-study group as they have a pivotal role in influencing the global energy market, thereby impacting their external sector position. Their fiscal decisions are also highly dependent on their external positions, making them a relevant group to study the twin-deficits argument.

We have employed a robust cross-sectionally augmented panel data analysis, following the approach proposed by Chudik et al. (2016), using panel data ranging from 2000 through 2022. This method is particularly effective in handling slope heterogeneity and cross-sectional dependence, which are prevalent in our panel. To further strengthen our analysis, we have included three case studies using data from Azerbaijan, Saudi Arabia, and Türkiye. Azerbaijan and Türkiye share extensive economic similarities and geographic proximity, making the comparison of the results fair and reliable, whereas Sausi Arabia provides a high-income-country perspective.

The pre-panel data analyses of the causal relationship between OFB and CAB reveal that the CAB and real Growth series in our panel are unit root, $I(1)$, processes. In contrast, the OFB and Openness series are stationary processes, $I(0)$. This invites employing the ARDL model estimation methods, which allow mixed stationary and non-stationary series given that the dependent variable is an $I(1)$ process, which is the case in our panel. Further investigations also reveal strong evidence of cross-sectional dependence between units in our sample, implying a possible violation of the basic ordinary least-squares assumption of an independent and identically distributed error term in the classical panel data analysis methods. We also find strong evidence of slope heterogeneity in our series after accounting for autocorrelation in the residuals using the HAC robust standard errors and small-sample bias implying that the standard panel data regression models, such as FEs and random effects, will lead to biased results. However, the first- and second-generation cointegration tests between CAB and OFB render mixed evidence, requiring careful estimation of our panel data.

The panel data analyses using both CS-ARDL and CS-DL estimation methods, as proposed by Chudik et al. (2016), reveal strong evidence of twin deficits across both the OIC and OIC–OPEC member countries. We find that a 1% increase in OFB causes close to a triple effect (a 2.8% increase) in the CAB in the long run after accounting for the business cycle and trade openness in the full OIC sample. The partial adjustment to the long-run equilibrium is very quick, with 100% of the gap closing in a year. For the OIC–OPEC group, a 1% increase in OFB is associated with a lasting 2.4% increase in CAB. This is a relatively stronger impact than the evidence provided in the literature confirming that the OIC member countries have unique macroeconomic contexts.

Compared to OIC members with flexible Fx regimes, there is more evidence of the presence of twin deficits in managed/fixed Fx regime countries, such as OPEC member states, consistent with the literature. The evidence shows that a 1% increase in OFB is associated with an equivalent (1%) increase in the CAB in the long term for the managed/fixed Fx regimes as opposed to a reverse (negative) impact in the flexible/floating regimes. However, the evidence is not statistically significant for the latter group.

The complementary case studies from the three countries, Azerbaijan, Saudi Arabia, and Türkiye, provide mixed results highlighting country heterogeneity even within OIC member states despite the broader similarity they share as a group. We find strong evidence of twin deficits in Saudi Arabia after controlling for the structural break during the global financial crisis, while there is no such strong evidence of causality running from OFB to CAB in the case of Azerbaijan and Türkiye. The results remain the same even after controlling for the business cycles, trade openness, and possible structural breaks in the latter two country cases. It worth recalling that both Saudi Arabi and Azerbaijan are predominantly managed/fixed Fx regimes, while Türkiye is a flexible/floating Fx regime.

Türkiye's relatively strong private sector, as evidenced by more than double (58%) the size of private credit to the GDP ratio of a representative country in the OIC (29% of GDP) and OPEC (23% of GDP), might be filling the public deficit gap and rebalance the current account, reinforcing the REH. However, the Azerbaijan case may not be as trivial as stated in the twin-deficits literature. Even after controlling the real interest rate, we find no statistically significant long-term impact of OFB on CAB for the case of Azerbaijan, although the sign of the coefficient is positive, aligning with the literature that shows a stronger twin-deficits phenomenon in less flexible Fx regimes.[11]

References

Ali Abbas, S. M., Bouhga-Hagbe, J., Fatás, A., Mauro, P., & Velloso, R. C. (2011). Fiscal policy and the current account. *IMF Economic Review*, *59*(4), 603–629.

Andrews, D. W. K., & Monahan, J. C. (1992). An improved heteroskedasticity and autocorrelation consistent covariance matrix estimator. *Econometrica*, *60*, 953–966.

Auerbach, A. J., & Gorodnichenko, Y. (2013a). Output spillovers from fiscal policy. *American Economic Review*, *103*(3), 141–146.

Auerbach, A. J., & Gorodnichenko, Y. (2013b). Fiscal multipliers in recession and expansion. In A. Alesina & F. Giavazzi (Eds.), *Fiscal policy after the financial crisis* (National Bureau of Economic Research Conference Report, pp. 63–98). University of Chicago Press.

Barro, R. J. (1989). The Ricardian approach to budget deficits. *Journal of Economic Perspectives*, *3*(2), 37–54.

[11]The results of the estimation accounting for real interest rate for the case of Azerbaijan is not presented in this study as there is no enough data on real interest rate for the majority of the countries in our sample.

Beetsma, R., Giuliodori, M., & Klaassen, F. (2008). The effects of public spending shocks on trade balances and budget deficits in the European Union. *Journal of the European Economic Association, 6*(2–3), 414–423.

Blanchard, O., & Perotti, R. (2002). An empirical characterization of the dynamic effects of changes in government spending and taxes on output. *The Quarterly Journal of Economics, 117*(4), 1329–1368.

Bluedorn, J., & Leigh, D. (2011). Revisiting the twin deficits hypothesis: The effect of fiscal consolidation on the current account. *IMF Economic Review, 59*(4), 582–602.

Blomquist, J., & Westerlund, J. (2013). Testing slope homogeneity in large panels with serial correlation. *Economics Letters, 121*(3), 374–378.

Cameron, A. C., & Trivedi, P. K. (1990). Regression-based tests for overdispersion in the poisson model. *Journal of Econometrics, 46*(3), 347–364.

Chudik, A., Mohaddes, K., Pesaran, M. H., & Raissi, M. (Eds.). (2016). Long-run effects in large heterogeneous panel data models with cross-sectionally correlated errors. In *Essays in honor of Aman Ullah*. Emerald Group Publishing Limited.

Chudik, A., Mohaddes, K., Pesaran, M. H., Raissi, M. (2013). *Debt, inflation and growth: Robust estimation of long-run effects in dynamic panel data models*. Tech. Rep., Faculty of Economics, University of Cambridge.

Chudik, A., & Pesaran, M. H. (2015). Common correlated effects estimation of heterogeneous dynamic panel data models with weakly exogenous regressors, *Journal of Econometrics, 188*, 393–420.

Corsetti, G., & Müller, G. J. (2006). Twin deficits: Squaring theory, evidence and common sense. *Economic Policy, 21*(48), 598–638.

Ditzen, J. (2018). Estimating dynamic common-correlated effects in Stata. *The Stata Journal, 18*(3), 585–617.

Fleming, J. M. (1962). Domestic financial policies under fixed and under floating exchange rates. *International Monetary Fund, 9*, 369–379. https://doi.org/10.2307/3866091.

Forni, M., & Gambetti, L. (2010). *Fiscal foresight and the effects of government spending*. CEPR Discussion Paper No. 7840. CEPR Press.

Furceri, D., & Zdzienicka, A. (2018). *Twin deficits in developing economies*. IMF Working Papers 2018, 170. https://doi.org/10.5089/9781484364000.001.

Hadri, K. (2000). Testing for stationarity in heterogeneous panel data. *The Econometrics Journal, 3*(2), 148–161.

Hashemzadeh, N., & Wilson, L. (2006). The dynamics of current account and budget deficits in selected countries in the Middle East and North Africa. *International Research Journal of Finance and Economics, 15*, 111–129.

Ilzetzki, E., Reinhart, C. M., & Rogoff, K. (2021). *Rethinking exchange rate regimes*. NBER Working Papers 29347, National Bureau of Economic Research, Inc.

Im, K. S., Pesaran, M. H., & Shin, Y. (2003). Testing for unit roots in heterogeneous panels. *Journal of Econometrics, 115*, 53–74. https://doi.org/10.1016/S0304-4076(03)00092-7

Jordà, Ò. (2005). Estimation and inference of impulse responses by local projections. *American Economic Review, 95*(1), 161–182.

Karabiyik, C., Lee, M. J., & Rubinsztein, D. C. (2017). Autophagy impairment in Parkinson's disease. *Essays in Biochemistry, 61*(6), 711–720.

Karabiyik, H., Westerlund, J., & Juodis, A. (2020). On the robustness of the pooled CCE estimator. *Journal of Econometrics, 220*(2), 325–348.

Karavias, Y., & Tzavalis, E. (2014). Testing for unit roots in short panels allowing for a structural break. *Computational Statistics & Data Analysis, 76*(C), 391–407.

Khalid, A. M., & Guan, T. W. (1999). Causality tests of budget and current account deficits: Cross-country comparisons. *Empirical Economics, 24*(3), 389–402. https://doi.org/10.1007/s001810050062

Kim, S., & Roubini, N. (2008). Twin deficit or twin divergence? Fiscal policy, current account, and real exchange rate in the US. *Journal of International ECONOMICS*, 74(2), 362–383.

Kripfganz, S., & Schneider, D. (2022). *ardl: Estimating autoregressive distributed lag and equilibrium correction models* [Tohoku University Research Center for Policy Design Discussion Paper]. https://www2.econ.tohoku.ac.jp/~PDesign/dp.html

Leachman, L. L., & Francis, B. (2002). Twin deficits: Apparition or reality? *Applied Economics*, *34*, 1121–1132. https://doi.org/10.1080/00036840110069976

Leeper, E. M., Walker, T. B., & Yang. S-C. S. (2013). Fiscal foresight and information flows. *Econometrica*, *81*(3), 1115–1145.

Monacelli, T., & Perotti, R. (2010). Fiscal policy, the real exchange rate and traded goods. *The Economic Journal*, *120*(544), 437–461.

Mundell, R. (1963). Capital mobility and stabilization policy under fixed and fixed and flexible exchange rates. *Canadian Journal of Economics and Political Science*, *29*, 475–485. https://doi.org/10.2307/139336

Neaime, S. (2008). *Monetary policy transmission and targeting mechanisms in the MENA region*. Working Papers 395, Economic Research Forum.

Nickel, C., & Tudyka, A. (2014). Fiscal stimulus in times of high debt: Reconsidering multipliers and twin deficits. *Journal of Money, Credit and Banking*, *46*(7), 1313–1344.

Pedroni, P. (1999). Critical values for cointegration tests in heterogeneous panels with multiple regressors. *Oxford Bulletin of Economics and Statistics*, *61*, 653–670. https://doi.org/10.1111/1468-0084.61.s1.14

Pedroni, P. (2004). Panel cointegration: Asymptotic and finite sample properties of pooled time series tests with an application to the Ppp hypothesis. *Econometric Theory*, *20*, 597–625. https://doi.org/10.1017/S0266466604203073

Persyn, D., & Westerlund, J. (2008). Error correction based cointegration tests for panel data. *Stata Journal*, *8*, 232–241. https://doi.org/10.1177/1536867X0800800205

Pesaran, M. H. (1997). The role of economic theory in modelling the long run. *The Economic Journal*, *107*, 178–191. https://doi.org/10.1111/1468-0297.00151

Pesaran, M. H. (2006). Estimation and inference in large heterogeneous panels with a multifactor error structure. *Econometrica*, *74*(4), 967–1012.

Pesaran, M. H. (2007). A simple panel unit root test in the presence of cross section dependence. *Journal of Applied Econometrics*, *22*, 265–312. https://doi.org/10.1002/jae.951

Pesaran, M. H. (2015). *Time series and panel data econometrics*. Oxford University Press. https://doi.org/10.1093/acprof:oso/9780198736912.001.0001

Pesaran, M. H., & Shin, Y. (1999). Chapter 11: An autoregressive distributed lag modelling approach to cointegration analysis. In: S. Strom (Ed.), *Econometrics and Economic Theory in the 20th Century the Ragnar Frisch Centennial Symposium* (pp. 371–413). Cambridge University Press.

Pesaran, M. H., Shin, Y., & Smith, R. P. (1997). *Pooled estimation of long-run relationships in dynamic heterogeneous panels*. University of Cambridge, Department of Applied Economics, Cambridge.

Pesaran, M. H., Shin, Y., & Smith, R. P. (1999). Pooled mean group estimation of dynamic heterogeneous panels. *Journal of the American Statistical Association*, *94*(446), 621–634.

Pesaran, M. H., Shin, Y., & Smith, R. P. (2001, May–June). Bounds testing approaches to the analysis of level relationships. *Journal of Applied Econometrics*, *16*(3), 289–326. https://www.jstor.org/stable/2678547

Pesaran, M. H., & Smith, R. (1995). Estimating long-run relationships from dynamic heterogeneous panels. *Journal of Econometrics*, *68*(1), 79–113.

Pesaran, M. H., & Xie, Y. (2021). *A bias-corrected CD test for error cross-sectional dependence in panel data models with latent factors* [Cambridge Working Papers in Economics 2158].

Pesaran, M. H., & Yamagata, T. (2008). Testing slope homogeneity in large panels. *Journal of Econometrics*, *142*(1), 50–93.

Ramey, V. A. (2011). Identifying government spending shocks: It's all in the timing. *The Quarterly Journal of Economics*, *126* (1), 1–50.
Ravn, M. O, Schmitt-Grohé, S., & Uribe, M. (2012). Consumption, government spending, and the real exchange rate. *Journal of Monetary Economics*, *59*(3), 215–234.
Romer, C. D., & Romer, D.H. (2010). The macroeconomic effects of tax changes: Estimates based on a new measure of fiscal shocks. *American Economic Review*, *100*(3), 763–801.
Salvatore, D. (2006). Twin deficits in the G-7 countries and global structural imbalances. *Journal of Policy Modeling*, *28*(6), 701–712. https://doi.org/10.1016/j.jpolmod.2006.06.003
Sims, C. A. (1980). Macroeconomics and reality. *Econometrica: Journal of the Econometric Society*, *48*, 1–48.
Smith, L. T. (1999). *Decolonizing methodologies: Research and indigenous peoples*. Zed Books.
Westerlund, J. (2007). Testing for error correction in panel data. *Oxford Bulletin of Economics and Statistics*, *69*, 709–748. https://doi.org/10.1111/j.1468-0084.2007.00477

Annex: Background Data

Table AI. OIC members: Summary Statistics of the Sample (2000–2022).

Indicator	Average	Median	p5	p95	SD	Min	Max	Obs.
Current account bal.	(1.04)	(3.05)	(18.89)	24.74	13.35	(84.11)	63.39	1,247
Overall fiscal bal.	(1.46)	(2.51)	(10.07)	11.47	7.38	(35.40)	43.17	1,239
Real growth	4.42	4.36	(2.77)	10.87	6.83	(50.34)	86.83	1,248
Trade openness	76.53	68.70	31.58	148.32	40.43	2.70	348.00	1,250
Public debt	49.63	42.45	5.67	121.72	40.47	–	349.88	1,189

Source: October 2023 WEO and author's computation.

Table AII. IPS Unit Root Test Results.

	IPS (W-t-bar statistic)	
	Level	
	Constant, lag (1)	Constant, Trend, lag (1)
CAB	–4.787***	–2.808***
OFB	–5.799***	–4.182***
Growth	–10.310***	–10.581***
Openness	–1.922**	–1.906**

Notes: *H0*: All panels contain unit roots.
*** $p<0.01$, ** $p<0.05$, * $p<0.10$.

Table AIII. Hadri (2000) Maximum Likelihood (ML) Unit Root Test.

	Hadri ML (Z_T statistic)							
	Level				first-difference			
	No trend	***p*-value**	**Trend**	***p*-value**	**No trend**	***p*-value**	**Trend**	***p*-value**
CAB	15.379***	0.0000	13.927***	0.0000	–3.8412	0.9999	0.2726	0.3926
OFB	21.1098***	0.0000	11.6076***	0.0000	–3.9437	1.0000	–0.2848	0.6121
Growth	9.9587***	0.0001	–0.4697	0.6807	–5.7497	1.0000	–5.1745	1.0000
Openness	40.3841***	0.0000	21.9088***	0.0000	–2.4538	0.9929	0.9083	0.1819

Notes: *H0*: All panels are stationary. Two countries (Afghanistan and Somalia) with small time series observations were excluded as the Hardi test requires strongly balanced panel.
*** $p<0.01$, ** $p<0.05$, * $p<0.10$.

Table AIV. Pesaran and Xie (2021) CD*, a Bias-corrected CD Test for Error Cross-sectional Dependence in Panel Data Models with Latent Factors.

	Statistics	***p*-Value**
CAB	2.39**	0.017
OFB	15.79***	0.000
Growth	14.29***	0.000
Openness	2.05**	0.041

Notes: *H0*: weak cross-section dependence.
*** $p<0.01$, ** $p<0.05$, * $p<0.10$.

Table AV. Pesaran (2007) Second-generation Unit Root Test (CIPS).

		IPS (W-t-bar statistic)	
		Level	
	Lags	Without Trend	With Trend
CAB	0	–3.894***	–2.522***
CAB	1	–4.847***	–2.532***
OFB	0	–9.329***	–7.012***
OFB	1	–4.507***	–1.098
Growth	0	–12.974***	–10.104***
Growth	1	–6.953***	–2.978***
Openness	0	1.563	0.206
Openness	1	2.168	1.399

Notes: *H0*: series is *I*(1).
*** $p<0.01$, ** $p<0.05$, * $p<0.10$.

Table AVI. Karavias and Tzavalis (2014) Panel Unit Root Test with (Possible) Structural Breaks.

	Level Without Trend		Level with Trend	
	min *Z*-statistic	Structural break	min *Z*-statistic	Structural break
CAB	–18.8443	–	–8.2808	–
OFB	–21.2017***	1981	–11.8937***	1995
Growth	–39.6280***	1981	–25.2695***	–
Openness	–10.6309	–	–7.4906	–

Notes: *H0*: All panel time series are unit root processes.
*** $p<0.01$, ** $p<0.05$, * $p<0.10$.

Table AVII. Blomquist and Westerlund (2013) Test for Slope Heterogeneity.

Dependent variable		**IPS (W-t-bar Statistic)** **Without Accounting for Cross-Sectional Dependence**			**IPS (W-t-bar Statistic)** **Accounting for Cross-Sectional Dependence**	
		Delta	***p*-Value**		**Delta**	***p*-Value**
CAB		8.171***	0.000		10.675***	0.000
CAB	adj.	9.594***	0.000	adj.	14.622***	0.000
OFB		1.145	0.252		15.204***	0.000
OFB	adj.	1.346	0.178	adj.	20.976***	0.000
Growth		–0.784	0.433		16.656***	0.000
Growth	adj.	–0.784	0.357	adj.	22.814***	0.000
Openness		6.341***	0.000		12.032***	0.000
Openness	adj.	7.445***	0.000	adj.	16.480***	0.000

Notes: *H0*: Slope coefficients are homogenous.
The *p*-values for the non-adjusted and adjusted delta test imply that the null of slope homogeneity can be rejected. *** $p<0.01$, ** $p<0.05$, * $p<0.10$.

Table AVIII. Pedroni (1999, 2004) Residual-Based Cointegration Test.

Test Stats.	**Panel (Within Dimension)**	***p*-Value**	**Group (Between Dimension)**	***p*-Value**
Case 1: Constant				
v	3.539***	0.0000	.	
rho	–6.313***	0.0000	–3.163***	0.0000
t	–7.436***	0.0000	–6.511***	0.0000
adf	–5.585***	0.0000	–3.884***	0.000
Case 2: Constant and Trend Terms Included				
v	–1.293	0.902	.	
rho	–3.237***	0.0000	0.1377	0.555
t	–7.176***	0.0000	–5.29***	0.0000
adf	–1.771**	0.038	–0.3369***	0.368

Notes: We employed the Stata xtpedroni command. Panel statistic: *H0*: No Cointegration in all panels; *Ha*: Cointegration in all panels. Group mean statistic: *H0*: No Cointegration in all panels; *Ha*: Cointegration in some panels. The test statistics follow a normal distribution of $N(0,1)$. The large negative (for ρ, t, and ADF) and positive value (only for panel v) of test statistic will lead to the rejection of null hypothesis (see Pedroni, 1999). The AIC lag selection criteria were used to select the lags for each individual panel.

Table AIX. Westerlund (2007) ECM-based Cointegration Test.

Dependent Variable: CAB; Constant with Trend				
Statistic	**Value**	***Z*-Value**	***p*-Value**	**Robust *p*-Value**
gt	–2.798	–4.007	0.000	0.970
ga	–13.470	–1.721	0.043	1.000
pt	–27.426	–14.028	0.000	0.710
pa	–19.389	–12.719	0.000	0.620
Dependent Variable: OFB; Constant with Trend				
gt	–3.414	–9.586	0.000	0.530
ga	–19.376	–8.185	0.000	0.830
pt	–21.871	–7.558	0.000	0.630
pa	–17.907	–10.912	0.000	0.600

Notes: The Stata command xtwest developed by Persyn and Westerlund (2008) was used to apply the above test. (The ga and gt test statistics test *H0*: $a\_i = 0$ for all *i* vs *H1*: $a\_i < 0$ for at least one *i*. The pa and pt test statistics pool information over all the cross-sectional units to test *H0*: $a\_i = 0$ for all *i* vs *H1*: $a\_i < 0$ for all *i*.) Bootstrap *p*-values were obtained with 100 bootstrap replications. AIC is used to determine the optimal lag-length between 1 or 2 lags and the optimal lead value between 0 and 1, respectively.

Chapter 6

Fiscal Policies in Islamic Countries: An Evaluation with a Focus on the Pandemic Era

Mehmet Yüce[a], *Mehmet Fatih Aslantaş*[b] *and Hüseyin Akkaya*[c]

[a]*Faculty of Economics and Administrative Sciences, Department of Finance, Bursa Uludağ University, UNEC-TUDIFAK, Azerbaijan*
[b]*Susuz Vocational School, Kafkas University, Turkey*
[c]*Artova Vocational School, Department of Finance, Banking, and Insurance, Tokat Gaziosmanpaşa University, Turkey*

1. Introduction

Despite pursuing different economic policies, it is observed that the state's role in the economy is generally significant across Islamic countries. This naturally implies that the state directs the economy. The state's intervention in the economy is possible through economic policy and fiscal policy. Since Islamic countries exhibit a heterogeneous structure, state intervention in the economy varies depending on the country's economic system, cultural structure, and religious rules. In countries that prefer a liberal economic system, state intervention in the economy occurs within the framework of market economy regulations. In countries where economic systems are primarily tied to Islamic rules, the state intervenes in the economy based on principles such as zakat (almsgiving), sadaqah (charitable giving), halal–haram (permissible and forbidden), and the prohibition of interest.

In some Islamic countries, the state also uses its authority to plan and regulate the economy. For example, the state controls the oil industry and its revenues in oil-rich countries like Saudi Arabia. In some Islamic countries, the state makes direct investments in strategic sectors and thus holds significant ownership. For instance, in countries like the United Arab Emirates (UAE), the state plays an active role in major infrastructure projects and tourism investments. In some Islamic countries, the state emphasizes various policies to provide social welfare

The Economic Potential of Islamic Countries, Part A:
Economics, Demographics and Financial Services, 147–174

doi:10.1108/978-1-83708-000-720251007

to its citizens, such as healthcare services, education, and housing. Conversely, the state primarily determines foreign trade policies in other Islamic countries, regulating import and export activities. Therefore, speaking of a single fiscal policy in Islamic countries is impossible.

In this study, the subject of fiscal policy in Islamic countries will be examined in general terms, and then the fiscal policy followed during the pandemic period in selected Islamic countries will be analyzed. In this context, public expenditures in these countries will be examined, focusing on the trend of healthcare expenditures.

2. Fiscal Policy in General in Islamic Countries

The term "fiscal policy" was conceptually used for the first time by Edwin R. A. Seligman in the early 19th century to critique Adolph Wagner's view that governments should regulate income distribution through budgets (Şen & Kaya, 2015). *Fiscal policy* can be defined as the adjustments needed in the size and composition of public expenditures and revenues to achieve the fundamental macroeconomic goals of an economy. It refers to the policies implemented by the state to achieve full employment, economic stability, and equitable wealth and income distribution using fiscal policy tools (public expenditures, taxes, debts, and budgets).

Islamic countries do not have a homogeneous structure. They vary based on their administrative structures, economic systems, Islamic principles, and historical, cultural, geographical, and political factors. It is possible to classify Islamic countries based on their economic structures, sources of income, economic policies, and the degree to which they apply Islamic principles. While some of these countries have shaped their socio-economic structures entirely according to secular principles, others are entirely governed by Sharia law, with some following a mixed structure. Countries with a mixed structure shape their socio-economic systems based on modern economic and governance principles while considering Islamic law and values. From this perspective, Islamic countries can be divided into three groups: countries with a liberal system, countries with an Islamic economic system, and countries with a mixed economic system (Islamic + market economy). Each Islamic country uses fiscal policy tools based on its economic system.

Traditional fiscal policies are used alongside Islamic economic tools in countries where the Islamic economy prevails. For instance, zakat is used as a fiscal policy tool in these countries. Zakat is considered a compulsory type of tax in these countries and plays a vital role in correcting income distribution and ensuring social justice. Charitable giving, social assistance, and services balance income distribution, reduce poverty, and ensure social justice.

In addition to traditional fiscal policy, the waqf (endowment) system is also a unique fiscal policy tool in Islamic countries. The waqf institution, whose practice dates back to the early periods of Islam, provides socially oriented public services. Waqfs emerged as philanthropists who supported these services voluntarily in areas where the state needed to provide public services or provide them more adequately. Thus, waqfs fill the gap in areas where the state is insufficient and provide the beneficiaries with economic contributions and social assistance. With this structure, the waqf institution functions as a fiscal policy tool to ensure social justice.

Another criterion for classifying Islamic countries is based on their economic resources and natural assets. According to this criterion, the economic structures of Islamic countries such as Saudi Arabia, Kuwait, and Qatar largely depend on oil and natural gas exports. Therefore, in these countries, the state assumes the functions of planning and regulation. The state generally controls the energy sector and uses revenues for economic development and welfare. Consequently, these countries are not expected to implement Keynesian fiscal policy tools.

Although the market economy generally prevails in countries like Türkiye, Egypt, Indonesia, and Pakistan, private and public economies operate simultaneously. In some of these countries, the private economy is more dominant, while in others, state intervention plays a significant role in economic activities. The industrial, agricultural, and service sectors have developed balanced in these countries. Among these countries, Türkiye stands out as an industrialized country with a significant share of the economy in the industrial and manufacturing sectors, emphasizing technological developments. The most crucial feature of industrialized countries is that they adopt growth strategies based on industry and exports. Therefore, contemporary fiscal policy practices are observed to be effective in these countries.

Countries like Iran, Iraq, and Libya are undergoing significant changes and reforms in their economic structures and policies, transitioning to a free market economy. Given that the state is prominent in the economy, shaped by oil and natural gas, and political stability has not been fully achieved in these countries, it is challenging to speak of an effective fiscal policy.

The economies of countries like Sudan and Niger are primarily based on agriculture and other natural resources. The agricultural sector is a significant source of employment and income. These countries, which exhibit the characteristics of a traditional agrarian society, face challenges such as high inflation, debt, political instability, severe difficulties like poverty, infrastructure deficiencies, and climate change. Therefore, these countries' fiscal policy priorities and features differ significantly from those of developed Islamic countries.

Spread across a vast geography encompassing the Middle East, North Africa, South Asia, and Southeast Asia, Islamic countries vary significantly regarding development levels and economic systems. They encompass diverse nations and cultures and are governed under different forms such as monarchies (e.g., Saudi Arabia, UAE, Qatar, Jordan), Republics (e.g., Türkiye, Azerbaijan, Kazakhstan, Kyrgyzstan, Uzbekistan, Iran, Indonesia, Egypt), and federations (e.g., Pakistan and the UAE).

As a result of this diversity, Islamic countries do not have a homogeneous structure, and it is impossible to assert that they follow a standard or similar fiscal policy. Therefore, discussing a general fiscal policy application for these countries is not feasible. However, insights into their fiscal policies can be derived from their budgets, revenues, and expenditures. Based on this understanding, we will attempt to provide a general overview of the fiscal policies of some sampled Islamic countries by analyzing their income and expenditure patterns.

3. View on Fiscal Policies in OIC Countries During the Pandemic Period

Fiscal policy aims to achieve economic policy objectives such as economic growth, development, stability, and fair income distribution by regulating the quantity and composition of public sector financial variables like public expenditures and revenues (Kısa, 2021, p. 104). In this context, many countries have implemented expansionary fiscal measures to revive and support the economy in response to the COVID-19 pandemic. These measures include tax cuts, increased transfer payments, wage subsidies, financing support, employment subsidies, and tax deferrals, which directly increase budgetary burdens (Çelik, 2022, p. 8).

The economic downturn caused by the COVID-19 crisis has underscored the importance of fiscal policy. The significant impact of the crisis on households and businesses necessitated extensive fiscal policy responses. The prominence of fiscal policy during this crisis has pushed monetary policies into the background. Given the uncertainty surrounding the duration of the crisis, its total economic impact remains unclear, potentially prolonging its effects on households and businesses. This situation enhances the importance of fiscal policies (Fırat, 2020, p. 210).

The COVID-19 pandemic emerged against pre-existing sluggish global growth, historically low nominal interest rates, and a low inflation environment. The pandemic has escalated the need for fiscal policy action to unprecedented levels. However, high debt levels and tightening financing conditions have constrained policy responses in some countries. Unlike previous economic downturns, where the primary goal of fiscal policy was to stimulate demand, this crisis is unique. Initially, the priority objectives were to increase resources for healthcare services, provide emergency living spaces for individuals and firms, protect the worst affected from income losses, unemployment, and bankruptcies, and reduce the likelihood of the pandemic leading to a deep and prolonged collapse. Therefore, the role of fiscal policy in saving lives and safeguarding against a potential deep and long-lasting economic collapse has become crucial. Policy measures under fiscal policy encompass increasing transfer expenditures, wage subsidies, tax reductions, and various guarantees and measures to prevent corporate insolvencies and provide liquidity support to companies (International Monetary Fund, 2020, p. 9).

Many countries have implemented expansive fiscal policies in response to the economic crisis caused by COVID-19. According to the IMF report released in October 2020, the amount of fiscal support had reached 12% of global GDP by September, highlighting that nearly all of the public spending aimed at mitigating the economic effects of the pandemic was undertaken by advanced economies and large emerging market economies. This was primarily due to the initial spread of the pandemic in these countries, its transition to a health crisis, the credibility of central banks in these countries ensuring that their monetary expansion would not create inflation, and their ability to finance large deficits at low interest rates (Öz, 2020, p. 1).

In discussing fiscal policies implemented in Organization of Islamic Cooperation (OIC) countries during the pandemic, it is essential to note that the OIC is a political organization in terms of its founding philosophy. However, this organization has incorporated social, fiscal, and economic objectives into its structure over time. The OIC's objectives include social and fiscal policy goals such as "combating hunger, eliminating poverty, and ensuring access to basic nutrition for every country" (Sey, 2020, p. 61).

The Coordination Office of the Islamic Development Bank Group (CCO) initiated the IDB COVID-19 Response Program (CCR) in 2020 to mitigate the current and potential adverse effects of the COVID-19 pandemic on member country public institutions. The CCR was primarily designed to alleviate the negative impact of the pandemic on member country economies in sectors such as agriculture, finance, poverty reduction, trade, transportation, and tourism. Under the program, CCO financed specific project types focusing on needs assessment, expertise sharing, and direct grants to ultimate beneficiaries. In 2020 and 2021, CCO launched project proposal calls under the CCR, and public institutions registered with IDB Working Groups submitted project proposals within this framework. In this context, eight projects were implemented under the 1st Call in 2021, and six projects were implemented under the 2nd Call in 2022 to reduce the adverse effects of the COVID-19 global pandemic on OIC Member Country economies. During the program implementation period, CCR focused on six sectors: Agriculture, Finance, Poverty Reduction, Tourism, Trade, and Transportation and Telecommunications. As of early 2023, the CCR Program has been completed (IDB, 2024).

From OIC member countries, Indonesia announced a stimulus package of $725 million in February 2020, allocating $324 million to low-income households to support the tourism, aviation, and real estate sectors. Following this initial package, the Indonesian government announced a second emergency stimulus package worth $8 billion on March 3, 2020. The package includes special incentives for small and medium-sized enterprises (SMEs) alongside a range of financial and non-financial incentives, primarily targeting the manufacturing sector and including corporate and personal income tax reductions (Medina, 2020).

In Türkiye, numerous measures were implemented in response to the COVID-19 pandemic, and several decisions were made within this context. A comprehensive package totaling 100 billion Turkish liras under the "Economic Stability Shield" was announced, encompassing various measures and precautions. The following are some of the critical decisions highlighted within the scope of public finance (Sakarya Ekonomik ve Sosyal Araştırmalar Merkezi, 2024):

- Continuing the minimum wage support.
- Activating the short-time work allowance.
- Increasing the minimum pension to 1,500 TL.
- Paying retirees' holiday bonuses at the beginning of April.
- Cash support of 1,000 TL will be announced to approximately 2 million families.

In Türkiye, measures taken due to the COVID-19 pandemic were not limited to the "Economic Stability Shield" financial support package; various institutions also announced support and aid packages. In this context, tax expenditure measures announced by the Ministry of Treasury and Finance can be listed as follows:

- The income tax declaration and payment deadline for 2019 has been postponed by one month.
- Value Added Tax declaration and payment deadlines have been postponed.
- The declaration of force majeure has been facilitated for taxpayers.
- Tax obligations of segments of society subject to curfew due to personal circumstances have been postponed.
- The deadlines for submission of Ba and Bs forms related to purchases and sales of goods and services by taxpayers to the Ministry of Treasury and Finance units have been extended.

Saudi Arabia has announced a fiscal stimulus package amounting to US$31.9 billion to mitigate the economic impacts of the COVID-19 pandemic. This package includes US$18.6 billion to support the private sector and US$13.3 billion to bolster the banking sector through the Central Bank. The Saudi Social Development Bank has also unveiled a separate stimulus package worth US$3.2 billion to support low-income families and owners of small and developing businesses in priority sectors (BSA Ahmad Bin Hazeem & Associates LLP, 2020).

The Government of Pakistan declared an economic relief package of 1.2 trillion PKR in response to the COVID-19 pandemic to assist businesses. Of this amount, 150 billion PKR is allocated primarily to low-income groups, including workers, and 280 billion PKR (approximately US$1.76 billion) is earmarked for wheat procurement. Credit interest payments for exporters have been temporarily deferred, and a package totaling 100 billion PKR (US$63 million) has been implemented to support small industries and the agricultural sector. Significant reductions in oil prices have occurred, and installment payments for public electricity and natural gas bills below a certain amount have been facilitated (Board of Investment, 2024).

Azerbaijan has established an inter-agency COVID-19 Task Force under the Prime Minister, along with working groups attached to key ministries, to alleviate the socio-economic impacts of the COVID-19 pandemic. The government allocated 3.5 billion AZN (US$2.06 billion or 4.8% of GDP) to implement a pandemic intervention package focusing on health-related, social protection, and macroeconomic stability measures. Responding to a recent surge in new COVID-19 cases in 2021, the government approved an additional budget of US$1.77 billion (3.6% of GDP) to expand the implementation of the pandemic response program initiated in 2020 (Asian Infrastructure Investment Bank (AIIB), 2021).

The UAE announced a fiscal stimulus package of 33 billion Dirhams (approximately US$9 billion or 2.5% of GDP) to combat COVID-19. The federal government has implemented measures to reduce certain state revenues. Approximately 16 billion AED worth of projects supporting infrastructure investments and boosting the private sector have been approved. Dubai's administration launched a package worth 1.5 billion AED, reducing taxes and increasing water and electricity services subsidies. Abu Dhabi's government announced a 9 billion AED initiative under the Ghadan-21 economic stimulus program, providing credit and liquidity support to new ventures and SMEs. The package includes obligations such as deferring tenant collections and delaying payments to credit cards for three months. Additionally, Abu Dhabi's government has implemented reductions or deferrals in various government fees. The Dubai government announced a package of 1.5 billion AED, including canceling penalties imposed by the government and customs departments, tax refunds for hotels and restaurants, and various banking facilities. Furthermore, in late October 2020, the Dubai government announced an additional 500 million Dirhams to support the local economy and a further 315 million Dirhams from January to June (International Monetary Fund (IMF), 2021).

In 2020, through the Ministry of Finance, additional packages were announced for the real estate sector, which experienced a decline in 2020. Moreover, incentives were implemented for the insurance sector to ensure the continuation of infrastructure services. Various measures were also accepted to operate e-commerce and digital banking effectively during the pandemic (Saputri & Hamzah, 2021, pp. 514–515).

Bangladesh, like many other countries, has faced significant public health and livelihood challenges during the COVID-19 pandemic, substantially damaging both global and local economies. The Bangladeshi economy, heavily reliant on the ready-made garment sector, suffered due to measures such as travel bans and quarantines (Alam et al., 2020, p. 10). To facilitate economic recovery, the government swiftly implemented fiscal and monetary stimuli, including an economic stimulus package totaling 23 billion Bangladeshi Taka (Alam & Mohammad, 2021, p. 23). Additionally, the Ministry of Health allocated an additional 2.5 billion Tk for the COVID-19 Preparedness and Response Plan. Furthermore, the Ministry of Finance announced a stimulus package of approximately US$588 million on March 31, 2020, to address issues faced by export sectors during the pandemic. The government also initiated a package of US$250.9 million for housing allocation to the homeless and US$176.7 million for poor families experiencing job losses (IMF, 2021).

The primary impact of the pandemic on Egypt's economy included slowdowns in all domestic activities, significant declines in tourism, remittances, and revenue from the Suez Canal, severely undermining household incomes and pushing millions below the poverty line (Elkhasen et al., 2021, p. 83). The Egyptian government responded to these challenges with expansive fiscal policies, allocating a budget increase of 100 billion Egyptian pounds under comprehensive fiscal policies. Moreover, various tax reductions were implemented (Alatrash & Nurmukhametov, 2021, p. 2), Corresponding to 1.8% of GDP. The coverage of social programs like Takaful and Karama was extended, and a cash aid plan for pandemic-affected sector workers for three months was established. Approximately 5 billion pounds were earmarked for purchasing new medical supplies and providing bonuses to healthcare workers. Furthermore, subsidy payments to exporters were increased, and energy costs were reduced (IMF, 2021).

Like other countries, Iran suffered negative economic and social impacts from the pandemic. To mitigate these impacts, the Iranian government implemented expansive fiscal policies. Significant support measures were included in the 2020 relief packages to ensure various sectors could navigate the pandemic successfully. The health sector received a share equivalent to 2% of GDP in the package. Additional funds were allocated to the unemployment insurance fund to support citizens who lost their jobs. Additional payments were made to manage the process through the National Development Fund. The package also provided proportional loans to businesses and households affected by the pandemic, amounting to 4.7% of GDP (IMF, 2021).

Senegal's government took several measures to control the increasing number of COVID-19-positive cases (Diallo et al., 2022, p. 110). Measures included nationwide curfews, closure of schools for 14 weeks, and travel restrictions. To mitigate the pandemic's impact, the government implemented a package totaling US$801 million, including cash and food assistance. The government's response package focused on four main areas:

- Improving the healthcare system.
- Strengthening social protection.
- Stabilizing the economy by supporting the private sector.
- Ensuring the supply and distribution of products like medicine, energy, food, and hygiene items.

Measures such as deferrals in some public debts for citizens and funds allocated for healthcare treatments and testing were part of the implemented measures (IMF, 2021).

Albania experienced production declines during the pandemic due to curfews and quarantine measures. These production declines led to income reductions for individuals, decreasing demand. Additionally, disruptions in the supply chain negatively impacted the economy (Leka, 2020, p. 5). The tourism sector in Albania was another severely affected sector during the pandemic, experiencing a 60% decrease compared to the previous year. The transportation and service sectors were also affected (Leka, 2020, p. 11). The Albanian government responded to the adverse developments in the economy by revising institutional budgets and increasing expenditures (Shahini & Grabova, 2023, p. 10). In 2020, the Albanian government approved two packages equivalent to 2.8% of GDP for individuals and businesses affected by the pandemic. An additional 2.5 billion Lek was allocated for the health sector. The second package included a payment plan of 7 billion Lek for employees in sectors affected by the pandemic that were not included in the first package (IMF, 2021).

The Algerian government responded swiftly to mitigate the pandemic's effects, focusing on preventing the virus's spread and ensuring stability through the financial law enacted on June 4, 2020 (Shu & Hussain, 2020, p. 383). The financial package cost the government 70 billion dinars, covering unemployment benefits and protection for vulnerable individuals. In 2021, due to the support provided for daily life return, the Algerian government budget faced a deficit of US$22 billion. Alongside a decrease in global demand and the oil, banking, and tourism crisis, the damage caused by isolation in 2020 was expected to be US$8.4 billion (Chibi et al., 2022, p. 11).

The Board of Governors of the Islamic Development Bank (IsDB) approved a $2.3 billion aid package for the IsDB Group Strategic Preparedness and Response Program for the global COVID-19 pandemic in March 2020. The program received contributions from various IsDB entities, including US$1.52 billion from IsDB itself, US$50 million from the Islamic Solidarity Fund for Development, US$300 million from the International Islamic Trade Finance Corporation, US$250 million from the Islamic Corporation for the Development of the Private Sector (ICD), US$8.5 million from the King Abdullah bin Abdulaziz Fund (KAAP), US$1 million from the Science, Technology, and Innovation Transformation Fund, and an additional US$150 million from the Islamic Corporation for the Insurance of Investment and Export Credit (ICIEC) (ISDB, 2020).

4. Evaluation of Expenditure Sizes of Selected OIC Countries

Fiscal policy involves the state's public revenue and expenditure to achieve economic objectives such as ensuring economic stability, regulating income distribution, and promoting economic growth. One of the critical fiscal policy tools is public expenditure, where expenditures on essential sectors like education and health, termed "investment expenditures," play a crucial role. The level of these expenditures relative to total public spending provides significant insights into the fiscal policies pursued by respective countries.

Health expenditures hold critical importance within fiscal policy. These expenditures serve several pivotal goals, such as enhancing societal well-being, increasing labor productivity, promoting economic growth, regulating income distribution, and ensuring social stability. Therefore, effective and efficient planning and management of health expenditures are vital for the success of fiscal policies.

As investment expenditures, health expenditures contribute to enhancing societal well-being. They serve to improve the overall health levels of individuals and society. A healthier population translates into a higher quality of life and longer life expectancy, thereby increasing societal welfare and supporting economic development. Furthermore, one of the direct benefits of health expenditures is their positive impact on labor productivity. A healthy workforce is inherently more productive and efficient. Reducing diseases and health issues minimizes labor losses and enhances labor productivity, positively contributing to overall economic performance. Considering these impacts of health expenditures, it can be concluded that such expenditures enhance social and economic stability. A healthy population reduces societal unrest and economic uncertainties. Additionally, ensuring adequate resources for managing pandemic diseases and health crises helps maintain social and economic order.

This study primarily emphasizes the importance of public expenditure policies in national economies. The impact of the unprecedented COVID-19 pandemic, which occurred globally and had rare effects on this vast geography, on expenditure policies in OIC countries has been evaluated in the previous section, focusing on expenditure policies. One of the common grounds where Islamic countries with different geographical locations, different administrative models, and cultural and social infrastructures converge is the expansive fiscal policies they applied to mitigate the social and economic aspects caused by the pandemic. The pandemic not only adversely affected public health but also disrupted the fundamental elements of the economic system. This situation led countries to adopt aggressive programs that increased interventions over time. This study section will analyze the increase in public expenditures resulting from the expansive fiscal policy pursued in selected countries.

Based on the data in Table 6.1, considering the widespread onset of the pandemic in 2020 and its peak in 2021, there was an increase in total government expenditures as a percentage of GDP among OIC member countries. In 2020, the average ratio of total government expenditures to GDP for member countries was 27.95%, which increased to 30.98% in 2021. By 2022, as the normalization process began, there was a general decrease in government expenditures across these countries. The average ratio of total government expenditures to GDP for member countries was 25.07% in 2022, slightly increasing to 25.97% in 2023.

During the pandemic, governments worldwide responded with unprecedented fiscal policies to strengthen healthcare systems and provide emergency support to households and businesses. This approach helped mitigate economic contraction. Many countries continued to provide fiscal support to mitigate the impact of the COVID-19 pandemic and support their recovery, although the size and composition of support varied from country to country. According to the IMF, as of September 27, 2021, global fiscal measures related to the pandemic amounted to $16.9 trillion, comprising $10.8 trillion in additional spending and $6.1 trillion in liquidity support provided through equity injections, loans, and guarantees. Both forms of fiscal support were approximately four times larger in advanced economies compared to developing countries as a percentage of GDP.

OIC countries, on average, provided relatively limited support compared to advanced and developing countries. In advanced economies, support in the form of additional spending and forgone revenues amounted to 17.8% of GDP, while in developing countries, it was 4.7%. In OIC countries, these supports amounted to an average of 4.0% of GDP. Similarly, OIC countries' support provided through equity, credit, and guarantee mechanisms amounted to 2.0% of GDP, compared to 11.3% in advanced economies and 2.5% in developing countries. The COVID-19 pandemic led to extraordinary fiscal needs for government spending while reducing tax revenues through economic downturns, resulting in historically high fiscal deficits globally. The general government fiscal deficit as a percentage of GDP increased from 3.0% in 2019 to 10.8% in 2020 in advanced economies and from 4.6% to 9.3% in developing countries (SESRIC, 2022, p. 22).

When examining the trend of current healthcare expenditures as a percentage of GDP across OIC countries from 2013 to 2020, it is observed that there were fluctuating changes in different countries across various regions from 2013 to 2019 (Table 6.2). However, in 2020, marked by the pandemic's impact on national budgets, there

Table 6.1. Ratio of Total Public Expenditure to GDP (%) in Member Countries of the OIC.

Countries	**Total Public Expenditure/GDP 2020**	**Total Public Expenditure/GDP 2021**	**Total Public Expenditure/GDP 2022**	**Total Public Expenditure/GDP 2023**
Islamic Republic of Afghanistan	27.937	17.934	16.116	N/A
Republic of Albania	32.552	32.124	30.445	29.059
Republic of Azerbaijan	40.157	32.540	32.030	34.054
Kingdom of Bahrain	35.803	31.8038	28.817	29.155
People's Republic of Bangladesh	13.308	12.967	13.011	12.934
Republic of Benin	19.071	19.855	19.864	19.327
UAE	31.131	26.390	22.936	25.946
Brunei Darussalam	33.235	39.284	26.376	28.840
Burkina-Faso	25.542	27.886	32.435	29.043
Algeria	37.506	32.540	32.030	34.054
Djibouti	25.463	23.172	20.046	20.154
Chad	14.346	13.810	13.873	20.359
Indonesia	18.427	18.124	17.361	16.636
Morocco	34.145	31.279	34.074	32.969
Ivory Coast (Côte d'Ivoire)	20.370	20.454	21.556	21.192

(Continued)

Table 6.1. (*Continued*)

Countries	Total Public Expenditure/GDP 2020	Total Public Expenditure/GDP 2021	Total Public Expenditure/GDP 2022	Total Public Expenditure/GDP 2023
State of Palestine	33.054	30.830	29.055	28.187
Gabon	19.811	16.594	19.101	21.684
Gambia	25.348	21.496	22.318	24.601
Guinea	17.131	15.168	14.535	15.472
Gine Bissau	25.034	24.957	21.306	21.518
Cooperative Republic of Guyana	30.544	26.009	20.549	23.481
Iraq	42.176	37.098	37.403	43.853
Islamic Republic of Iran	13.008	14.186	13.817	13.543
Cameroon	16.580	19.940	17.056	16.628
Qatar	34.699	29.368	24.273	24.431
Kazakhstan	24.546	22.070	21.718	23.340
Kyrgyzstan	64.557	50.335	39.614	50.795
Union of the Comoros	18.767	19.952	18.278	21.821
Kuwait	64.557	50.335	39.614	50.795
Libya	57.342	64.706	62.189	63.351
Lebanon	19.552	9.133	12.673	Veri yok
Maldives	49.899	39.479	41.510	45.723

Malaysia	25.040	24.448	24.682	23.250
Mali	25.889	26.272	25.154	26.327
Arab Republic of Egypt	25.695	25.543	24.701	22.737
Islamic Republic of Mauritania	18.532	20.780	28.013	24.840
Mozambique	32.222	30.765	33.634	30.645
Niger	22.366	24.260	21.588	15.977
Nigeria	12.095	12.559	14.378	13.842
Uzbekistan	28.714	30.485	34.811	33.755
Islamic Republic of Pakistan	20.296	18.458	19.959	19.195
Senegal	26.564	25.796	26.573	26.148
Sierra Leone	25.726	28.254	29.072	24.384
Somalia	5.130	4.677	6.906	6.297
Sudan	10.728	9.742	17.696	8.604
Suriname	30.204	32.051	29.537	26.417
Syria*	–	–	–	–
Kingdom of Saudi Arabia	39.068	31.693	28.250	32.282
Tajikistan	29.164	27.642	27.954	28.754
Togo	34.031	30.504	28.203	27.740

(Continued)

Table 6.1. (*Continued*)

Countries	**Total Public Expenditure/GDP 2020**	**Total Public Expenditure/GDP 2021**	**Total Public Expenditure/GDP 2022**	**Total Public Expenditure/GDP 2023**
Tunisa	34.495	33.293	35.175	34.113
Turkiye	34.112	30.822	27.700	33.852
Turkmenistan	11.754	10.681	9.442	10.459
Republic of Uganda	21.438	21.512	20.128	19.121
Sultanate of Oman	44.538	36.134	29.618	26.220
Hashemite Kingdom of Jordan	31.243	32.285	32.633	33.374
Yemen	10.646	8.221	12.172	11.439

Source: IMF, World Economic Outlook Database, 2024, https://www.imf.org/en/Publications/WEO/weo-database/2024/April/select-country-group (May 21, 2024).

Table 6.2. Current Health Expenditure in Selected OIC Countries (% of GDP).

Country	2013	2014	2015	2016	2017	2018	2019	2020	Mean
Afghanistan	8.81	9.53	10.11	11.82	12.62	14.21	14.83	15.53	12.18
Albania	6.27	6.44	6.48	6.67	6.55	6.66	..	..	6.51
Algeria	6.04	6.55	6.98	6.61	6.28	6.16	6.25	6.32	6.40
Bahrain	4.31	4.41	4.98	4.86	4.51	4.13	3.96	4.72	4.49
Bangladesh	2.75	2.73	2.72	2.86	2.78	2.72	2.62	2.63	2.73
Benin	2.86	2.67	2.68	2.47	2.60	2.48	2.32	2.59	2.58
Brunei Darussalam	1.90	1.91	2.39	2.55	2.27	2.41	2.19	2.39	2.25
Burkina Faso	5.56	5.00	5.13	5.95	6.06	4.95	5.38	6.72	5.59
Chad	4.07	4.27	4.52	5.05	4.56	4.57	4.48	5.41	4.62
Cameroon	3.63	3.79	3.60	3.59	3.40	3.62	3.65	3.77	3.63
Cote d'Ivoire	3.72	3.73	3.22	3.35	3.31	3.12	3.29	3.72	3.43
Djibouti	2.92	2.97	3.08	2.73	2.46	2.26	2.02	2.01	2.56
Gabon	2.84	2.53	2.66	3.11	2.78	2.75	2.77	3.43	2.86
Gambia	3.91	3.05	3.18	3.20	3.35	3.34	3.16	2.61	3.23
Guinea	3.46	4.79	5.81	5.40	3.92	3.74	4.07	4.04	4.40
Guinea-Bissau	7.04	9.97	8.13	8.33	7.00	7.62	8.35	8.41	8.11
Guyana	3.80	3.95	4.02	4.02	4.32	4.90	4.93	5.51	4.43
Indonesia	2.87	2.96	2.92	3.02	2.90	2.87	2.90	3.41	2.98

(*Continued*)

Table 6.2. *(Continued)*

Country	2013	2014	2015	2016	2017	2018	2019	2020	Mean
Iran. Islamic Rep.	5.55	6.35	7.25	7.82	7.75	7.53	5.95	5.34	6.69
Iraq	2.82	2.80	3.14	3.28	4.19	4.06	4.26	5.08	3.70
Jordan	7.17	7.21	7.46	7.16	7.98	7.85	7.57	7.47	7.48
Kazakhstan	2.66	2.97	3.04	3.42	3.05	2.82	2.79	3.79	3.07
Comoros	5.10	5.24	4.60	4.65	5.27	4.90	5.18	5.35	5.04
Kuwait	2.49	2.92	4.21	4.73	4.65	5.19	5.36	6.31	4.48
Lebanon	7.06	7.52	7.40	7.89	7.76	8.02	7.90	7.95	7.69
Maldives	8.16	7.91	8.73	10.31	9.27	7.44	7.66	11.35	8.85
Malaysia	3.51	3.71	3.82	3.70	3.71	3.76	3.84	4.12	3.77
Mali	3.96	4.48	4.11	3.77	3.67	3.73	3.88	4.31	3.99
Egypt. Arab Rep.	4.92	5.03	5.34	5.36	5.63	4.99	4.84	4.36	5.06
Mauritania	2.87	3.47	3.67	3.10	3.32	3.44	3.35	3.36	3.32
Mozambique	6.13	6.33	6.72	7.28	7.84	8.09	7.95	7.62	7.24
Niger	4.47	4.45	5.35	4.53	5.57	5.29	5.67	6.20	5.19
Nigeria	3.42	3.35	3.58	3.65	3.75	3.09	2.99	3.38	3.40
Oman	2.86	3.59	4.66	4.79	4.53	3.69	4.39	5.33	4.23
Pakistan	2.40	2.46	2.46	2.57	2.79	2.83	2.85	2.95	2.66
Saudi Arabia	4.47	5.23	6.00	6.43	6.26	5.54	..	..	5.65
Senegal	4.39	4.39	4.38	4.26	4.16	4.43	4.50	5.15	4.46

Sierra Leone	11.57	19.73	20.41	16.53	9.40	8.29	8.85	8.76	12.94
Sudan	6.96	5.68	7.27	5.48	5.92	4.46	4.63	3.02	5.43
Suriname	4.49	4.52	5.81	5.99	5.32	6.69	8.43	6.77	6.00
Tajikistan	6.53	6.67	6.91	6.96	6.85	7.01	6.95	8.18	7.01
Togo	4.94	5.08	4.96	6.60	6.41	6.00	5.64	5.96	5.70
Turkiye	4.37	4.33	4.12	4.28	4.18	4.12	4.36	4.62	4.30
Turkmenistan	3.94	4.31	5.12	5.74	5.94	5.69	5.68	5.68	5.26
Tunisia	6.51	6.45	6.24	6.26	6.19	5.94	5.47	6.34	6.18
Uganda	5.78	5.34	5.08	4.96	4.00	4.02	3.80	3.96	4.62
Uzbekistan	5.72	4.43	4.74	4.72	4.84	5.08	5.43	6.75	5.21
Yemen. Rep.	4.96	4.84	4.25	..	..	..	..	..	4.69
UAE	3.59	3.63	3.58	3.47	4.06	4.15	4.30	5.67	4.06
Kyrgyz Republic	8.19	7.36	7.15	6.41	6.19	5.01	4.49	5.26	6.26
Morocco	5.69	5.86	5.57	5.50	5.39	5.33	5.37	5.99	5.59
Azerbaijan	3.04	3.38	4.11	4.04	3.74	3.56	4.07	4.61	3.82
Qatar	2.08	2.42	3.69	3.68	3.44	3.25	3.51	4.18	3.28

Source: Made by us using data from www.worldbank.org (May 12, 2024).

was a general increase in current healthcare expenditures as a percentage of GDP among the countries examined, as seen in the above table. The Maldives notably showed the most dramatic increase. This increase indicates that expansive spending policies were implemented during the pandemic period to ensure overall welfare. Despite being managed under different governance styles and having variations in the needs of their citizens, OIC countries tended to adopt effective expenditure policies to manage their processes during the global pandemic.

The general government's current consumption expenditures are a crucial tool of fiscal policy. These expenditures play a critical role in various areas, such as economic stability, provision of public services, income distribution, demand management, and support for the labor market. Effectively managing current expenditures is essential for governments to achieve their economic and social objectives.

Among current consumption tools, general government expenditures are vital for the state's effective, efficient, and transparent functioning. These expenditures fulfill significant functions in areas such as the rule of law, public safety, economic stability, improvement of the investment climate, and social justice. Therefore, efficient planning and management of the general government's current consumption expenditures are vital for fiscal policy success and for achieving societal goals.

Looking at the ratio of current consumption expenditures of the general government to GDP, one of the findings from the created table is that 36 countries with available data showed an increase in this ratio in 2020 compared to the previous year. Governments increased their consumption expenditures in 2020 compared to the previous year. The highest increase in expenditure from the previous year in 2020 was observed in Libya. In Libya, the ratio of general government current consumption expenditures to GDP was 39.83% in 2019, which increased to 61.17% in 2020. This suggests that the government prioritized expenditure policies during the COVID-19 period. These comments can be made from Table 6.3.

An essential indicator of expenditure trends for OIC countries is the share of domestic health expenditures within total expenditures. This dataset is crucial for understanding changes in health expenditures and overall expenditures within each country. Upon examining the general situation of the 52 countries in the dataset, it is observed that in 2020, compared to the previous year, 29 countries experienced an increase in the share of domestic health expenditures within total expenditures. Conversely, seven countries saw a decrease in this share compared to the previous year. Additionally, no change was observed in this ratio compared to the previous year in 14 of the examined OIC countries. These comments can be made from Table 6.4.

During the pandemic, governments faced significant challenges in ensuring social welfare, preventing the spread of the virus, and providing necessary treatments. Public expenditures played a crucial role in these efforts. From the perspective of general fiscal theory, financing public expenditures relies heavily on government revenues, with taxes being the primary source. Due to factors like quarantine measures, lockdowns, and disruptions in supply chains, global trade weakened, leading to economic challenges in various countries. Consequently, tax revenues saw substantial declines during this period. Table 6.5 provides the tax

Table 6.3. General Government Final Consumption Expenditure in Selected OIC Countries (% of GDP).

Country	2013	2014	2015	2016	2017	2018	2019	2020	2021	2022	Mean
Albania	11.03	11.45	11.11	11.27	11.50	11.29	11.35	11.85	11.91	10.18	11.29
Algeria	19.14	19.53	21.56	20.89	18.95	17.26	18.34	18.79	17.42	15.48	18.74
Bahrain	15.55	16.13	17.69	17.11	16.63	16.29	15.69	17.14	15.81	..	16.45
Bangladesh	5.12	5.34	5.40	5.87	6.02	5.96	6.24	5.97	5.88	5.70	5.75
Benin	11.04	10.18	11.41	10.28	10.48	10.41	10.34	11.40	10.08	10.06	10.57
Brunei Darussalam	20.16	21.42	25.06	26.22	26.48	24.14	25.04	25.43	22.47	20.12	23.65
Burkina Faso	14.66	15.47	15.94	16.51	17.74	18.42	20.50	19.78	20.29	19.87	17.92
Chad	7.92	6.23	5.15	4.21	4.33	3.60	3.59	4.74	4.68	3.95	4.84
Cameroon	12.26	12.06	12.25	12.12	11.68	11.92	12.10	12.28	12.05	10.96	11.97
Cote d’Ivoire	..	..	8.74	9.23	9.60	9.40	10.26	10.43	..	..	9.61
Djibouti	19.67	19.09	19.91	22.23	21.77	21.35	19.81	19.59	18.18	..	20.18
Gabon	14.46	14.85	14.82	14.64	13.23	10.57	10.99	13.17	11.37	10.48	12.86
Gambia	9.27	8.84	8.33	8.45	7.87	6.82	8.24	8.99	9.81	9.41	8.60
Guinea	18.87	17.79	19.50	16.88	15.28	15.48	15.40	17.30	16.34	16.59	16.94
Guinea-Bissau	7.12	13.83	11.33	9.82	9.30	12.62	14.78	16.51	..	..	11.91
Indonesia	9.52	9.43	9.75	9.53	9.12	9.02	8.81	9.66	9.25	7.66	9.17
Iran. Islamic Rep.	12.97	12.82	15.57	15.78	16.06	15.75	15.30	14.43	14.23	12.73	14.57
Iraq	17.46	18.00	18.67	18.39	16.31	15.88	19.32	22.51	17.89	..	18.27

(Continued)

Table 6.3. *(Continued)*

Country	**2013**	**2014**	**2015**	**2016**	**2017**	**2018**	**2019**	**2020**	**2021**	**2022**	**Mean**
Jordan	18.26	18.22	17.82	17.25	16.95	16.74	16.37	..	..	..	17.37
Kazakhstan	10.17	10.69	11.63	11.63	10.54	8.32	9.13	12.74	11.27	11.26	10.74
Comoros	9.33	10.28	10.59	10.61	10.82	10.23	10.09	10.56	10.15	9.61	10.23
Kuwait	16.39	17.76	24.19	25.71	24.42	23.05	25.22	..	..	..	22.39
Lebanon	12.93	12.75	12.53	12.98	13.21	15.34	15.63	9.14	2.36	..	11.87
Malaysia	13.72	13.33	13.09	12.56	12.19	11.97	11.65	12.96	12.71	11.66	12.58
Mali	16.88	16.26	16.37	16.24	16.18	15.88	15.74	15.81	16.25	16.71	16.23
Egypt. Arab Rep.	11.35	11.85	11.76	11.43	9.58	7.94	7.29	7.54	7.56	7.27	9.36
Mauritania	11.69	13.63	14.62	13.44	13.38	12.98	13.30	12.30	14.97	17.89	13.82
Niger	15.30	17.94	16.50	15.27	15.46	15.17	15.66	15.76	17.34	15.75	16.01
Oman	18.90	21.62	24.64	26.12	24.53	21.56	23.11	26.07	22.14	..	23.19
Pakistan	10.26	10.03	9.79	10.61	10.75	10.99	10.75	11.79	10.93	10.50	10.64
Saudi Arabia	22.23	25.71	29.32	25.01	23.53	23.60	23.40	27.96	23.80	20.83	24.54
Senegal	14.60	14.73	14.30	14.03	13.63	13.78	14.01	14.28	15.05	16.30	14.47
Sierra Leone	8.71	7.15	10.17	11.83	10.47	9.24	8.57	8.09	7.32	11.68	9.32
Somalia	4.65	4.88	4.69	5.29	5.89	5.98	5.61	6.46	6.88	7.28	5.76
Sudan	6.40	6.08	6.17	5.59	6.43	6.71	6.17	14.45	10.96	17.85	8.68
Tajikistan	13.30	14.04	11.56	11.76	11.39	11.22	11.15	11.57	10.88	..	11.87
Togo	12.41	12.08	13.03	15.48	13.98	13.20	13.25	13.63	13.14	13.37	13.36

Turkiye	14.02	14.02	13.81	14.73	14.38	14.51	15.27	14.99	12.95	11.65	14.03
Turkmenistan	6.06	6.58	8.46	8.60	9.37	10.02	9.70	10.02	10.17	9.81	8.88
Tunisia	17.30	17.33	17.91	18.72	19.12	18.39	18.82	21.61	20.98	20.34	19.05
Uganda	7.10	7.43	8.95	7.35	8.01	8.64	8.77	9.51	9.93	9.79	8.55
Uzbekistan	13.32	13.25	13.62	14.14	12.60	13.43	16.15	16.15	16.59	16.82	14.61
Yemen. Rep.	13.09	12.19	10.80	8.80	6.11	9.14	..	..	..	..	10.02
UAE	10.71	10.64	12.02	12.11	13.05	11.69	12.26	14.45	..	..	12.11
Libya	31.66	42.65	50.84	48.42	40.27	35.34	39.83	61.17	24.50	..	41.63
Kyrgyz Republic	18.45	17.47	17.76	17.43	17.13	17.17	..	..	..	..	17.57
Morocco	18.33	19.11	18.16	18.36	17.98	18.00	18.18	19.40	19.00	19.22	18.57
Azerbaijan	10.28	10.89	12.41	12.83	11.34	10.47	11.12	16.22	13.87	10.93	12.04
Qatar	14.56	15.47	20.23	19.54	17.61	16.28	18.46	21.96	16.65	12.85	17.36

Source: Created using data from www.worldbank.org (May 12, 2024).

Table 6.4. Domestic General Government Health Expenditure in Selected OIC Countries (% of General Government Expenditure).

Country	2013	2014	2015	2016	2017	2018	2019	2020	Mean
Afghanistan	1.78	1.86	2.01	2.14	2.32	1.91	1.78	4.25	2.26
Albania	8.83	8.17	8.88	9.62	9.11	9.80	9.84	9.00	9.16
Algeria	11.85	11.61	10.73	10.73	10.73	10.73	10.73	10.73	10.98
Bahrain	8.46	10.09	8.87	8.53	7.98	7.23	7.06	8.29	8.31
Bangladesh	3.62	3.59	3.38	4.10	4.11	3.75	3.30	3.08	3.61
Benin	5.13	4.04	3.23	3.73	4.58	2.96	3.71	4.55	3.99
Brunei Darussalam	5.12	5.20	5.86	6.15	5.87	7.14	6.39	6.78	6.06
Burkina Faso	6.38	7.77	7.15	11.03	9.99	8.78	9.58	11.46	9.02
Chad	5.04	5.55	5.25	5.73	4.68	4.87	4.87	4.87	5.11
Cameroon	2.50	2.94	1.81	1.81	0.73	1.96	2.18	3.70	2.20
Cote d'Ivoire	4.59	5.11	4.87	4.85	5.15	5.12	5.73	6.66	5.26
Djibouti	6.74	6.07	4.07	4.07	4.07	4.31	4.28	4.28	4.74
Gabon	5.26	6.38	7.03	9.20	9.72	9.42	9.59	9.59	8.27
Gambia. The	6.31	5.75	5.10	6.66	4.49	5.14	5.48	5.48	5.55
Guinea	2.62	3.03	1.98	4.11	3.46	3.85	6.15	6.15	3.92
Guinea-Bissau	4.44	2.60	2.50	2.36	2.75	2.75	2.75	2.75	2.86
Guyana	8.75	9.35	10.77	10.00	10.55	10.61	10.33	13.09	10.43

Indonesia	4.28	5.34	6.63	8.18	8.15	8.39	8.68	10.10	7.47
Iran, Islamic Rep.	16.05	22.60	22.60	21.08	21.07	22.54	21.40	22.07	21.18
Iraq	2.38	2.37	1.68	1.68	5.00	6.19	5.99	6.32	3.95
Jordan	13.13	13.06	12.22	12.22	12.40	12.63	12.76	11.88	12.54
Kazakhstan	9.32	10.03	8.39	9.48	7.86	9.10	8.25	10.21	9.08
Comoros	4.45	3.82	2.45	3.04	3.59	3.99	4.12	4.12	3.70
Kuwait	5.48	5.57	6.57	7.51	7.76	8.98	9.06	8.65	7.45
Lebanon	10.79	12.39	12.46	12.98	11.86	11.55	11.44	13.43	12.11
Maldives	15.93	16.86	18.45	19.75	21.47	17.68	17.85	18.17	18.27
Malaysia	6.82	7.82	8.23	8.26	8.72	8.45	8.52	8.61	8.18
Mali	4.13	4.45	4.39	5.43	5.14	5.67	5.67	5.67	5.07
Egypt. Arab Rep.	4.16	4.16	5.06	5.06	5.42	4.72	4.82	5.16	4.82
Mauritania	5.39	5.24	5.53	5.76	6.07	6.98	6.98	6.98	6.11
Mozambique	4.73	4.32	5.55	6.00	6.00	5.76	6.17	7.29	5.73
Niger	6.56	5.40	4.59	5.69	9.66	8.35	9.38	10.23	7.48
Nigeria	3.46	3.34	5.33	4.87	4.44	3.88	3.75	4.22	4.16
Oman	5.58	6.81	8.26	8.41	8.95	7.25	8.59	10.24	8.01
Pakistan	3.25	3.34	3.85	3.96	4.77	4.90	4.95	5.12	4.27
Saudi Arabia	8.75	9.28	10.06	12.61	13.51	11.05	..	..	10.88
Senegal	5.30	4.68	4.70	4.46	4.50	4.96	4.37	6.48	4.93

(Continued)

Table 6.4. (*Continued*)

Country	2013	2014	2015	2016	2017	2018	2019	2020	Mean
Sierra Leone	5.15	7.58	7.91	7.91	3.63	3.60	5.82	5.29	5.86
Sudan	7.52	10.62	18.29	12.94	8.05	6.17	5.37	9.59	9.82
Suriname	7.03	6.90	10.86	13.71	11.39	17.45	14.51	13.76	11.95
Tajikistan	6.83	7.54	6.41	5.14	5.88	6.14	6.58	7.38	6.49
Togo	4.69	4.59	4.22	4.26	6.45	5.49	5.38	5.38	5.06
Turkiye	10.09	10.15	9.69	9.65	9.74	9.23	9.50	10.72	9.85
Turkmenistan	8.71	8.71	8.71	8.71	8.71	8.71	8.71	8.71	8.71
Tunisia	12.50	13.54	12.29	12.63	11.66	10.88	9.52	10.78	11.72
Uganda	7.32	7.01	5.08	5.18	3.92	4.17	3.14	3.14	4.87
Uzbekistan	9.52	9.30	9.60	8.82	8.98	7.77	8.28	10.79	9.13
UAE	8.53	7.78	7.89	7.89	7.36	7.40	7.40	10.45	8.09
Kyrgyz Republic	10.35	7.14	7.12	6.42	6.34	7.33	7.09	6.92	7.34
Morocco	7.65	6.84	6.98	7.02	7.12	7.18	7.39	7.22	7.18
Azerbaijan	2.81	3.10	3.37	3.29	2.82	2.81	3.95	3.95	3.26
Qatar	6.18	6.50	8.29	7.59	7.83	8.68	8.39	9.54	7.87

Source: Created using data from www.worldbank.org (May 12, 2024).

Table 6.5. Tax revenue in Selected OIC Countries (% of GDP).

Country	2013	2014	2015	2016	2017	2018	2019	2020	2021
Albania	16.50	18.30	18.52	17.59	18.89	18.55	18.14	16.98	18.20
Bangladesh	8.96	8.64	8.50	7.32	7.00	7.73	7.64	7.00	7.64
Burkina Faso	14.95	13.66	13.28	14.14	15.26	15.29	15.64	13.43	15.98
Cameroon	11.52	12.29	12.11	11.65	11.88	12.35	12.03	10.87	11.35
Cote d'Ivoire	10.64	10.12	11.18	11.46	11.76	11.67	11.76	11.80	12.56
Indonesia	11.29	10.84	10.75	10.34	9.88	10.23	9.75	8.31	9.09
Kazakhstan	16.03	14.19	9.84	9.92	10.30	11.72	11.79	8.32	9.45
Lebanon	14.07	14.11	13.47	13.53	15.36	15.33	15.41	8.90	5.68
Malaysia	15.31	14.84	14.06	13.55	12.95	12.02	11.94	10.88	11.21
Mali	13.03	12.65	14.10	15.40	15.88	11.67	14.50	14.16	..
Mozambique	21.54	23.97	20.01	20.08	22.11	21.19	26.68	21.53	22.75
Saudi Arabia	2.71	2.73	3.26	3.28	3.26	8.29	7.00	8.24	..
Senegal	..	..	15.77	16.37	15.91	16.38	18.42	17.45	17.52
Turkiye	18.36	17.95	18.18	18.27	17.72	17.27	16.52	17.66	17.86
Uganda	..	..	10.80	11.12	11.60	11.68	12.24	11.39	12.46
Uzbekistan	13.80	13.47	13.56	13.43	11.64	14.09	12.62	14.79	..
UAE	0.36	0.35	0.06	0.04	0.07	0.06	0.97	0.68	0.54
Kyrgyz Republic	..	17.55	16.80	16.95	17.05	18.00	15.96	14.04	16.49
Morocco	20.63	20.35	19.44	19.87	20.13	20.29	19.91	20.02	19.69
Azerbaijan	13.39	14.21	15.60	14.56	13.16	12.97	14.22	15.19	13.42

Source: Created using data from www.worldbank.org (May 12, 2024).

revenue as a percentage of GDP for certain OIC countries. Overall, the dataset indicates that in 2020, many countries experienced a decrease in tax revenue as a percentage of GDP compared to the previous year.

Considering all these findings, while it is acknowledged that the economic structures of Islamic countries are not homogeneous, it is evident that these countries implemented expansionary fiscal policies in line with the global economic context. These expansionary fiscal policies led to increased public expenditures and decreased government revenues. Consequently, this naturally resulted in more significant budget deficits.

5. Conclusion and Evaluation

As is well known, governments employ two critical tools, namely monetary and fiscal policies, when undertaking economic regulation. Fiscal policies have gained increased significance with the onset of economic downturns. In response to the economic crisis triggered by the emergence of economic disruptions, fiscal policy measures have been presented as a remedy. One of the significant tools of fiscal policies is public expenditure policies. Public expenditures profoundly impact the social and economic structures of countries. During the pandemic, public expenditure policies have come to the forefront in OIC countries. The expenditure policies implemented during this period have mitigated the adverse effects of the pandemic while positively impacting societal welfare. Despite having different administrative structures and demographic profiles, OIC countries have actively utilized fiscal policy tools, particularly expenditure policies, during the pandemic. Consequently, OIC countries have alleviated negative impacts on critical areas such as health and the economy through their expenditure policies.

With their diverse governance models and societal needs, OIC countries generally adopt unique expenditure policies. Therefore, it is deemed necessary to establish an index that distinguishes OIC countries economically, administratively, or socially. Expenditures, as a process, emphasize the establishment of societal welfare and the effective utilization of national resources. The effective utilization of resources by an organization as extensive as the OIC, with its broad geography and production factors, will strengthen its global position in the future. The authors propose the creation of an index to determine the welfare levels of countries and guide expenditure policies accordingly. While indices such as the Human Development Index are utilized, we believe that the OIC should create a new index utilizing parameters from an Islamic perspective to reflect its dynamics better.

References

Alam, M. F., & Mohammad, N. (2021). Fiscal measures for tackling the economic fallout in Bangladesh: An assessment of stimulus measures during the COVID-19 pandemic era. *AIUB Journal of Business and Economics*, *18*(1), 15–35.

Alam, S. A., Bhuiyan, J., & Solaiman, M. (2020). The impact of Covid-19 pandemic on the economic growth in Bangladesh: A conceptual review. *American Economic & Social Review*, *6*(2), 1–12.

Alatrash, Y., & Nurmukhametov, G. (2021, December). *Fiscal policy effectiveness under different debt regimes: The case of Egypt* [ERF Working Paper No. 1527, pp. 1–14]. Retrieved from https://erf.org.eg/publication/fiscal-policy-effectiveness-under-different-debt-regimes-the-case-of-egypt/

Asian Infrastructure Investment Bank (AIIB). (2021). COVID-19 Active Response and Expenditure Support (CARES) Program: Azerbaijan Republic. Retrieved May 23, 2024, from https://www.aiib.org/en/projects/details/2021/approved/Azerbaijan-Republic-of-Azerbaijan-COVID-19-Active-Response-and-Expenditure-Support-CARES-Program.html

BSA Ahmad Bin Hazeem & Associates LLP. (2020). Saudi Arabia announces USD 31.9 billion stimulus package to mitigate the economic crisis caused by the COVID-19 outbreak. Retrieved May 23, 2024, from https://bsabh.com/saudi-arabia-announces-usd-31-9-billion-stimulus-package-to-mitigate-the-economic-crisis-caused-by-the-covid-19 outbreak/#:~:text=The%20Saudi%20Arabian%20government%20has, 19%20outbreak%20in%20the%20Kingdom

Çelik, Ş. Ç. (2022). Covid-19 Pandemisi Sonrasında Maliye Politikaları Uygulamaları: Türkiye Özelinde Bir Değerlendirme. *İslâm İktisadı Araştırmaları Dergisi*, *2*(1), 4–27.

Fırat, M. (2020). Covid-19 Krizi ve IMF Destekli Maliye Politikalarının Gerekliliği. *Ekonomi İşletme Ve Maliye Araştırmaları Dergisi*, *2*(3), 209–222. https://doi.org/10.38009/ekimad.776850

International Monetary Fund. (2020). *Fiscal monitor: Policies to support people during the COVID-19 pandemic*. IMF.

International Monetary Fund. (IMF). (2021). *Bangladesh: Policy response to the COVID-19 pandemic and economic recovery.* IMF

Islamic Development Bank (ISDB). (2020). İslam Kalkınma Bankası Grubu'nun COVID-19 Stratejik Hazırlık və Müdahale Programı Kapsamında Üye Ülkelere 2,3 Milyar USD Tahsis Ediliyor [In Turkish]. Retrieved May 24, 2024, from https://www.isdb.org/tr/node/44551

Islamic Development Bank. (2024). The Coordination Office of the Islamic Development Bank Group (CCO) and the IDB COVID-19 Response Program (CCR). Islamic Development Bank.

Kısa, Ö. (2021). Salgın Döneminde Maliye Politikası. *Vergi Raporu*, *267*, 93–110.

Leka, B. (2020). An overview of the pandemic impact in the economy of Albania. *Romanian Economic Journal*, *23*(78), 2–12.

Medina, A. F. (2020). *Indonesia issues second stimulus package to dampen COVID-19 impact* [ASEAN Briefing]. Retrieved May 22, 2024, from https://www.aseanbriefing.com/news/indonesia-issues-second-stimulus-package-dampen-covid-19-impact/

OECD. (2020). *Coronavirus (COVID-19) living with uncertainty*. Economic Outlook Interim Report: 107, Eylül 2020.

Öz, S. (2020). *COVID-19 Salgını ve Maliye Politikası*. Retrieved May 19, 2024, from https://eaf.ku.edu.tr/wp-content/uploads/2020/12/eaf_an20-05.pdf

Sakarya Ekonomik ve Sosyal Araştırmalar Merkezi (SESAM). (2024, May 23). Türkiye'de COVID-19'la Mücadelede Alınan Kamu Maliyesi Tedbirlerinin Değerlendirilmesi. Retrieved from https://sesam.sakarya.edu.tr/tr/duyuru/goster/91540/turkiye-de-covid-19-la-mucadelede-alinan-kamu-maliyesi-tedbirlerinin-degerlendirilmesi

Saputri, O. B., & Hamzah, M. Z. (2021, November 22–23). United Arab Emirates fiscal policy facing global economic crisis during the Covid-19 pandemic. In W. Saputri & M. Z. Hamzah (Eds.), *Proceedings of the 5th International Conference of Zakat (ICONZ)* (pp. 507–522). BAZNAS Indonesia.

Şen, H., & Kaya, A. (2015). Ekonomik Krizlerin Değişmeyen İmdatçısı: Maliye Politikası. *Sosyoekonomi*, *23*(23), 55–86.
Sey, N. (2020). İslam İşbirliği Teşkilatı Üzerine Bir Değerlendirme: Ekonomik Sorunlar Ve Fırsatlar. *İslam Ekonomisi ve Finansı Dergisi*, *6*(1), 55–74.
Shahini, L., & Grabova, P. (2023). Economic role of government budget revision in the presence of COVID-19. *Economies*, *11*(4), 118.
Shu, M., & Hussain, A. (2020). Political turbulence converged with Covid-19 – Algeria's structural development dilemma. *Asian Journal of Middle Eastern and Islamic Studies*, *14*(3), 383–395.
Statistical, Economic, and Social Research and Training Centre for Islamic Countries. (SESRIC). (2022). Title of the report. SESRIC. https://www.sesric.org/

Section 4

State of Global Islamic Financial Services Industry

Chapter 7

Central Bank Digital Currencies and Their Prospects for the OIC Countries

Ahmet Faruk Aysan and Muhammad Fazlurrahman Syarif

Hamad Bin Khalifa University, Qatar

1. Introduction

Central Bank Digital Currencies (CBDCs) are digital currencies issued by central banks (Jung & Jeong, 2021). They represent a digital form of central bank money and differ from traditional reserves and settlement account balances (Bakar et al. 2022). CBDCs are essentially a digital version of domestic currency, with a unit of account equivalent to the respective domestic currency (Sethaput & Innet, 2023). The concept of CBDCs has gained significant global attention with discussions revolving around their drivers, approaches, and technologies (Auer et al., 2020).

The evolution of digital currencies has paved the way for the development of CBDCs. The rise of cryptocurrencies, such as Bitcoin, has demonstrated the potential of digital currencies (Härdle et al., 2020). Blockchain technology is instrumental in enabling the creation and functioning of CBDCs (Arthur et al., 2018). Blockchain technology offers new opportunities for CBDC development by providing secure and transparent transaction mechanisms (Ko et al., 2018). Global trends in CBDC development indicate a growing interest among central banks in exploring the implementation of CBDCs (Koshelev, 2022). Research shows that a significant percentage of central banks are actively researching the potential of CBDCs (Doğan & Övenç, 2021). The implementation of CBDCs is seen as a way to modernize payment systems and enhance financial inclusion (Semeko, 2022). Furthermore, the issuance of CBDCs is motivated by various factors, including the need for efficient cross-border payments and improved monetary policy transmission (Garg & Kumar, 2023).

The Organization of Islamic Cooperation (OIC) comprises 57 member countries that share a common bond of Islamic faith and work toward mutual cooperation in various fields. When examining the financial landscape of OIC countries in terms of CBDC, it is essential to consider the current financial systems in these

The Economic Potential of Islamic Countries, Part A:
Economics, Demographics and Financial Services, 177–190

doi:10.1108/978-1-83708-000-720251008

nations. OIC countries often face challenges in terms of financial inclusion, with many individuals lacking access to basic financial services. However, there is a growing interest in digital financial inclusion within the OIC region, with the potential for CBDCs to play a significant role in enhancing financial access for underserved populations (Kim et al., 2018; Sarma & Pais, 2010).

The introduction of CBDCs in OIC countries presents both challenges and opportunities for the financial sector. While some nations have faced difficulties in implementing CBDC programs, countries such as China, the European Union, Japan, and Russia are actively exploring the development of their own digital currency payment networks (Wu et al., 2022). CBDCs have the potential to increase financial inclusion by providing secure and efficient means of conducting transactions, especially in regions where traditional banking services are limited (Ozili, 2021). However, there are concerns about the impact of CBDCs on existing financial systems and the need for robust regulatory frameworks to support their implementation (Ozili, 2021).

CBDC initiatives are gaining traction globally, with central banks around the world considering the issuance of digital currencies. The emergence of CBDCs presents an opportunity for central banks to enhance financial inclusion, improve payment systems, and contribute to the transition toward a more digital economy (Ozili, 2022). As countries such as Nigeria explore the opportunities and risks associated with CBDCs, it is crucial to address challenges related to regulation, security, and interoperability to ensure the successful adoption of digital currencies (Ozili, 2021).

In this comprehensive study, we explore the evolving landscape of CBDCs, focusing on their relevance and implications within the OIC countries. The document begins with an introduction to CBDCs, setting the stage for a deeper examination through various global case studies that highlight pioneering CBDC initiatives. It then transitions into an analysis of the unique opportunities that CBDCs present to OIC member states, addressing their potential to enhance financial inclusion and streamline economic transactions. Following this, this study examines the challenges and risks associated with the adoption of CBDCs, such as concerns related to privacy, cybersecurity, and financial stability. Building on this analysis, the next section proposes targeted policy recommendations and strategic approaches to effectively navigate the complexities of CBDC implementation. The discussion culminates in a forward-looking perspective on the future of CBDCs in the OIC region before concluding with a summary that encapsulates the key findings and underlines the transformative potential of digital currencies in these economies.

2. Case Studies of CBDC Initiatives in OIC Countries

CBDC initiatives have garnered significant global attention, with various countries exploring their implementation. Within the OIC countries, there have been notable case studies and initiatives regarding CBDCs. For example, Uruguay conducted tests on the potential implementation of a CBDC known as the "e-Peso," while the Bahamas initiated "Project Sand Dollar" to explore the effects of a CBDC (Alonso et al., 2020). These initiatives highlight the increasing interest in and experimentation with CBDCs in OIC countries. Moreover, research shows that the implementation of CBDCs can impact the payment industry's open innovation. Malaysia and South Africa have been identified as optimal areas for CBDC implementation in Asia and Africa, respectively (Alonso et al., 2021). This highlights the strategic considerations and potential benefits that OIC countries are assessing regarding CBDC adoption.

Additionally, studies have stressed the importance of understanding the economic dynamics and growth factors within OIC countries regarding initiatives such as CBDCs. Research has investigated the impact of economic globalization on economic growth in OIC countries (Samimi & Jenatabadi, 2014), as well as the determinants of economic growth within the OIC context, considering factors such as inflation, population, and exchange rates (Nugroho & Herianingrum, 2022). These insights offer a comprehensive view of the economic landscape within OIC countries and how CBDC initiatives align with broader economic development strategies.

Below are the case studies and research within OIC countries concerning CBDC initiatives that reflect a growing trend toward exploring digital currency solutions in the region. These initiatives aim not only to enhance financial inclusion and innovation but also to address specific economic growth challenges unique to OIC countries. As more countries within the OIC explore and implement CBDCs, it will be crucial to continue studying and analyzing the impacts and implications of these initiatives on their economies and financial systems.

The exploration of CBDCs by countries of the OIC signifies a considerable step toward financial innovation and economic reform in the Muslim world (see Table 7.1). The document outlines various statuses, ranging from research and development to pilot projects within these nations. This progression reflects an academic understanding of the role that CBDCs could potentially play in enhancing economic strategies within OIC member states.

Case studies within OIC countries demonstrate a keen interest in harnessing the potential of CBDCs to address specific financial system challenges, from enhancing retail and wholesale payment efficiencies to contributing to financial inclusion. Nations such as the UAE, Indonesia, and Saudi Arabia have initiated pilots and developmental projects, showcasing a forward-leaning posture toward CBDCs. The inclusion of technological partnerships and cross-border projects such as mBridge and Project Aber indicates a strategic approach toward interoperability and innovation. However, the document also highlights that many OIC countries remain in the research phase, with decisions on use-case architecture and technology infrastructure still undecided. This indicates a cautious approach, weighing the challenges and risks such as cybersecurity, impact on existing financial institutions, and regulatory complexities against potential opportunities.

The emergence of digital currencies presents a unique set of policy implications for OIC countries. This necessitates the development of new frameworks that can support digital innovations while maintaining financial stability and security. Policymakers are advised to craft strategies that promote collaboration both within and beyond OIC borders, ensuring that the evolution of CBDCs is harmonized with global financial systems and standards. Hence, the academic assessment of CBDC initiatives across OIC member states suggests a expanding

Table 7.1. CBDCs Initiative in OIC Countries.

Country	Membership	CBDC Status	Announcement	Use Case	Architecture	Cross-Border Project	Infrastructure	Technology	Technology Partnerships
Republic of Azerbaijan	Member since 1992	Research	June 2022		Undecided		Undecided		Visa
Hashemite Kingdom of Jordan	Member since 1969	Research	January 2022		Undecided		Undecided		
Islamic Republic of Afghanistan	Member since 1969								
Republic of Albania	Member since 1992								
State of The United Arab Emirates	Member since 1972	Pilot	2019	Retail, Whole-sale	Undecided	mBridge	DLT	Fabric	
Republic of Indonesia	Member since 1969	Development-Project Name: Digital Rupiah	May 2021	Retail, Whole-sale	Undecided		Undecided		
Republic of Uzbekistan	Member since 1996	Research	2023	Un-decided	Undecided		Undecided		
Republic of Uganda	Member since 1974	Research	February 2022		Undecided		Undecided		Temtum Group
Islamic Republic of Iran	Member since 1969								
Islamic Republic of Pakistan	Member since 1969	Research	April 2019	Retail	Undecided		Undecided		

Kingdom of Bahrain	Member since 1972	Development	Early 2020	Wholesale	Intermediated	Both	JP Morgan Onyx
Brunei-Darussalam	Member since 1984						
People's Republic of Bangladesh	Member since 1974	Research	July 2022	Undecided	Undecided	Undecided	
Republic of Benin	Member since 1983	Inactive	2016	Undecided	Undecided	Undecided	
Burkina-Faso (then Upper Volta)	Member since 1974						
Republic of Tajikistan	Member since 1992						
Republic of Türkiye	Member since 1969	Pilot	December 2022	Retail	Undecided	Both	Aselsan, Havelsan, Tubitak Bilgem
Turkmenistan	Member since 1992						
Republic of Chad	Member since 1969	Research		Undecided	Undecided	Undecided	
Republic of Togo	Member since 1997						
Republic of Tunisia	Member since 1969	Pilot	July 2021	Wholesale	Undecided	Undecided	ProsperUs

(*Continued*)

Table 7.1. (*Continued*)

Country	Membership	CBDC Status	Announcement	Use Case	Architecture	Cross-Border Project	Infrastructure	Technology	Technology Partnerships
People's Democratic Republic of Algeria	Member since 1969	Research-Project Name: Digital Dinar	December 2022	Undecided	Undecided		Undecided		
Republic of Djibouti	Member since 1978								
Kingdom of Saudi Arabia	Member since 1969	Pilot-Project Name: Project Aber	2019	Wholesale	Undecided	Project Aber	DLT	Fabric	
Republic of Senegal	Member since 1969	Cancelled	2016	Retail	Direct			Undecided	eCurrency Mint
Republic of The Sudan	Member since 1969								
Syrian Arab Republic	Member since 1972								
Republic of Suriname	Member since 1996								
Republic of Sierra Leone	Member since 1972								
Republic of Somalia	Member since 1969								
Republic of Iraq	Member since 1975								

Sultanate of Oman	Member since 1972	Research	May 2022	Retail, Wholesale	Undecided		Undecided	
Republic of Gabon	Member since 1974	Research		Undecided	Undecided		Undecided	
Republic of The Gambia	Member since 1974							
Republic of Guyana	Member since 1998							
Republic of Guinea	Member since 1969							
Republic of Guinea-Bissau	Member since 1974							
Union of The Comoros	Member since 1976							
State of Palestine	Member since 1969	Inactive	2022	Retail	Undecided		Undecided	
Kyrgyz Republic	Member since 1992							
State of Qatar	Member since 1972	Research	November 2023	Wholesale, Retail	Undecided		Undecided	
Republic of Kazakhstan	Member since 1995	Pilot-Project Name:Digital tenge	2021	Retail	Intermediated	R3 Corda	Both	Binance
Republic of Cameroon	Member since 1974	Research			Undecided		Undecided	

(Continued)

Table 7.1. (*Continued*)

Country	Membership	CBDC Status	Announcement	Use Case	Architecture	Cross-Border Project	Infrastructure	Technology	Technology Partnerships
Republic of Cote D'ivoire	Member since 2001								
State of Kuwait	Member since 1969	Inactive	December 2022	Retail	Undecided		Undecided		
Republic of Lebanon	Member since 1969	Inactive	November 2020	Retail	Undecided		Undecided		
Libya	Member since 1969								
Republic of Maldives	Member since 1976								
Republic of Mali	Member since 1969								
Malaysia	Member since 1969	Pilot	June 2021	Wholesale	Undecided	Project Dunbar	Undecided		
Arab Republic of Egypt	Member since 1969	Research, Project Name:E-pound	December 2018	Undecided			Undecided		
Kingdom of Morocco	Member since 1969								
Islamic Republic of Mauritania	Member since 1969	Research, Project Name: Digital Ouguiya	March 2023	Undecided	Undecided				

Republic of Mozambique	Member since 1994				
Republic of Niger	Member since 1969				
Federal Republic of Nigeria	Member since 1986	Research	August 2022	Undecided	Undecided
Republic of Yemen	Member since 1969				

Source: Authors data analysis. Adapted from https://www.atlanticcouncil.org/cbdctracker/.

interest, coupled with careful consideration of the potential transformative impact on their economies. The future of CBDCs in these countries rests on the balance between embracing technological advancement and addressing inherent challenges through comprehensive, strategic policy planning.

3. Opportunities for CBDCs

CBDCs offer significant opportunities for OIC countries across various dimensions. First, CBDCs can play a crucial role in enhancing financial inclusion by providing improved monetary policy transmission, efficient payments, and increased access to financial services (Ozili, 2021). The adoption of CBDCs in emerging countries is often driven by the goal of promoting financial inclusion, which is essential for economic development (Ozili, 2022). Efforts to increase financial inclusion in OIC countries can not only lead to providing financial access to the community, but also create opportunities for benefits such as tax revenues (Nur et al., 2022).

Furthermore, CBDCs can strengthen cross-border payments and remittances, which are vital in many OIC countries. By enabling safe, efficient, and inexpensive cross-border transactions, CBDCs can facilitate international remittances and improve fund flows (Themistocleous et al., 2023). This is particularly important for OIC countries, where a significant portion of remittances occurs through informal channels (Sarma & Pais, 2010). Moreover, the adoption of CBDCs can enhance the economic growth and stability of OIC countries. CBDCs can contribute to economic development and stability by promoting financial inclusion and by providing a more efficient payment system (Kim et al., 2018). Additionally, CBDCs can help reduce the size of the informal economy, which is crucial for improving economic governance and stability (Oh & Zhang, 2022). Furthermore, CBDCs support digital transformation in the financial sector by digitizing value chains, improving access to digital financial services, enlarging the digital economy, enhancing the efficiency of digital payments, and offering low transaction costs (Ozili, 2022). Digital transformation can lead to more transparent and cost-efficient financial transactions, thus benefiting both individuals and businesses in OIC countries.

Interestingly, the compatibility of CBDCs with Islamic financial principles lies in their potential to enhance financial inclusion, efficiency, and transparency. CBDCs can align with Islamic finance by promoting financial stability, reducing costs, and enhancing access to financial services, which is in line with the principles of fairness and social welfare in Islamic finance (Andolfatto, 2020). The potential impact of CBDCs on Islamic banking and finance is significant. CBDCs may streamline payment systems, reduce transaction costs, and enhance financial inclusion, thus benefiting Islamic banks and their customers. However, challenges such as cybersecurity risks, regulatory frameworks, and the impact on monetary policy need to be addressed to ensure the smooth integration of CBDCs in Islamic banking systems (Mnohoghitnei et al., 2021). Islamic finance principles emphasize ethical and moral values, prohibiting interest (riba), uncertainty (gharar), and gambling (maysir). Islamic banking operates on profit-sharing principles, focusing on asset-backed transactions to ensure fairness and risk-sharing (Kabir et al., 2015). In OIC countries, the adoption of CBDCs in

Islamic banking could revolutionize the financial landscape by providing a digital alternative to cash, promoting financial inclusion, and enhancing transaction efficiency. However, careful consideration must be given to ensuring that CBDCs comply with Islamic finance principles, such as avoiding interest-based transactions and upholding ethical standards (Mnohoghitnei et al., 2021).

4. Challenges and Risks

CBDCs pose various challenges and risks to countries within the OIC. One significant challenge is regulatory compliance (Mahardika et al., 2023). Implementing CBDCs requires adherence to strict regulations to ensure financial stability and prevent illicit activities. Moreover, technological challenges and cybersecurity concerns are paramount (Mahardika et al., 2023). The digital nature of CBDCs exposes them to cyber threats, including cyber-attacks and IT failures, necessitating robust cybersecurity measures to safeguard financial systems.

Economic and monetary policy implications are also critical considerations for OIC countries exploring CBDCs. The introduction of CBDCs can affect monetary policies, exchange rates, and financial stability (Mahardika et al., 2023). Therefore, careful evaluation and planning are essential to mitigate any adverse effects on the economy. Cultural and societal considerations also play a vital role in the successful implementation of CBDCs. Cultural values and practices influence managerial decisions and societal acceptance of new financial technologies, highlighting the importance of aligning CBDC initiatives with local cultural norms (Minelgaite et al., 2017).

5. Policy Recommendations and Strategies

To develop and implement CBDCs in OIC countries, a framework is essential. This framework should adhere to internationally acceptable standards to guide policy development and implementation and ensure consistency across diverse local contexts (Alonso et al., 2021). Collaboration and cooperation among OIC member states are crucial for the successful establishment of CBDCs, as they can facilitate knowledge sharing, resource pooling, and collective decision-making processes (Lee et al., 2021; Wang & Gao, 2023). Moreover, balancing innovation with regulation is a key consideration. While innovation drives progress, effective regulation is necessary to ensure stability, security, and compliance within the financial system (Ozili, 2022; Philippon, 2019).

Strategies for public engagement and education play vital roles in the adoption of CBDCs. Public awareness campaigns, educational programs, and transparent communication can help build trust, address concerns, and promote an understanding of the benefits of CBDCs among the general population (Alonso et al., 2020; Ozili, 2022). Additionally, involving stakeholders in the design and implementation process can enhance acceptance and a sense of ownership among the public (Ozili, 2022).

In the context of CBDCs, it is crucial to consider their implications for financial inclusion, monetary policy, and the international financial system. CBDC adoption can have significant effects on financial stability, payment industry innovation, and power dynamics within the global financial landscape (Themistocleous et al., 2023).

Therefore, continuous evaluation, adaptation, and collaboration with international bodies such as the Bank for International Settlements and the International Monetary Fund are essential to successfully navigate the evolving CBDC ecosystem.

6. The Future of CBDCs

CBDCs are gaining significant attention globally, including in OIC countries. The future adoption of CBDCs in the OIC region is likely to be influenced by various factors. Research by Bordo and Levin (2017) discusses how CBDCs can impact monetary policy, indicating a shift toward digital currencies. Auer et al. (2020) highlight the drivers and technologies behind the rise of CBDCs, emphasizing their potential to reshape the financial landscape.

In OIC countries, the adoption of CBDCs can have a substantial impact on the global financial system. Mohieldin et al. (2011) emphasize the role of Islamic finance in enhancing financial inclusion in OIC countries, suggesting that CBDCs could further this goal. Agur et al. (2022) discuss the design aspects of CBDCs, pointing toward their potential to enhance financial intermediation and inclusivity. The role of CBDCs in shaping the future of digital finance in OIC countries is crucial. Ozili (2022) highlights the importance of financial inclusion in the adoption of CBDCs, especially in emerging economies. Furthermore, Maryaningsih et al. (2022) underline the significance of cross-border transactions in influencing wholesale CBDC adoption, which could have implications for OIC countries.

7. Conclusion

In conclusion, the exploration of CBDCs within the OIC countries has illuminated a path toward significant financial advancement and reform. Diverse case studies from OIC nations have demonstrated varying degrees of readiness and implementation strategies, revealing the nuances and complexities of adopting digital currencies in different socio-economic contexts. Opportunities presented by CBDCs, such as enhanced financial inclusion, streamlined transactions, and improved monetary policy mechanisms, offer compelling incentives for OIC countries to pursue digital currency initiatives. However, the challenges and risks associated with CBDCs – chief among them cybersecurity, potential destabilization of conventional banking, and intricacies of monetary policy adjustments – cannot be overlooked.

This analysis culminates in strategic policy recommendations tailored for OIC member states. It advocates robust digital infrastructure, a collaborative regulatory approach that accommodates international standards, and initiatives aimed at enhancing public trust and the understanding of digital currencies. The trajectory of the CBDCs within the OIC region was poised at a critical juncture. While the digitalization of currency presents a horizon brimming with promise, it necessitates careful navigation, judicious policymaking, and international cooperation. If these elements are successfully integrated, the future of CBDCs in the OIC region could signal a new era of economic innovation, offering a blueprint for financial prosperity in the digital age.

References

Alonso, S., Jorge-Vázquez, J., & Forradellas, R. (2020). Detection of financial inclusion vulnerable rural areas through an access to cash index: Solutions based on the pharmacy network and a CBDC. *Evidence Based on Ávila (Spain). Sustainability, 12*(18), 7480. https://doi.org/10.3390/su12187480

Alonso, S., Jorge-Vázquez, J., & Forradellas, R. (2021). Central banks digital currency: detection of optimal countries for the implementation of a CBDC and the implication for payment industry open innovation. *Journal of Open Innovation Technology Market and Complexity*, *7*(1), 72. https://doi.org/10.3390/joitmc7010072

Agur, I., Ratnovski, L., & Dell'Ariccia, G. (2022). Designing central bank digital currencies. *Journal of Monetary Economics*, *125*, 62–79. https://doi.org/10.1016/j.jmoneco.2021.05.002

Andolfatto, D. (2020). Assessing the impact of central bank digital currency on private banks. *The Economic Journal*, *131*(634), 525–540. https://doi.org/10.1093/ej/ueaa073

Arthur, M., Treccani, A., & Moyano, J. (2018). A 9-dimension grid for the evaluation of central bank digital currencies. *SSRN Electronic Journal.* https://ssrn.com/abstract=3248909 or http://dx.doi.org/10.2139/ssrn.3248909

Auer, R., Cornelli, G., & Frost, J. (2020). Rise of the central bank digital currencies: Drivers, approaches and technologies. *SSRN Electronic Journal.* https://doi.org/10.2139/ssrn.3724070

Bakar, N., Yahya, N., Khairuddin, I., Abidin, A., Zain, J., Idris, N., & Ali, E. (2022). The Central Bank Digital Currency in Malaysia: A Literature Review. In: B. Alareeni & Hamdan, A. (Eds.), *Innovation of businesses, and digitalization during covid-19 Pandemic. ICBT 2021*. Springer. https://doi.org/10.1007/978-3-031-08090-6_18

Bordo, M., & Levin, A. (2017). *Central bank digital currency and the future of monetary policy*. NBER Working Paper Series. National Bureau of Economic Research. https://doi.org/10.3386/w23711

Doğan, E., & Övenç, E. (2021). Central bank digital currencies under Blockchain technology: Discussion of digital bank runs and design principles. *European Journal of Science and Technology*, (27), 699–709. https://doi.org/10.31590/ejosat.916233.

Garg, S., & Kumar, R. (2023).To get insight into issuance motivations behind introducing CBDC in India. *Sachetas*, *2*(2), 73–77. https://doi.org/10.55955/220008.

Härdle, W., Harvey, C., & Reule, R. (2020). Understanding cryptocurrencies. *Journal of Financial Econometrics*, *18*(2), 181–208. https://doi.org/10.1093/jjfinec/nbz033

Jung, H., & Jeong, D. (2021). Blockchain implementation method for interoperability between cbdcs. *Future Internet*, *13*(5), 133. https://doi.org/10.3390/fi13050133

Kabir, M., Worthington, A., & Gupta, R. (2015). Comparative credit risk in Islamic and conventional bank. *Pacific-Basin Finance Journal*, *34*, 327–353. https://doi.org/10.1016/j.pacfin.2015.06.001

Kim, D., Yu, J., & Hassan, M. (2018). Financial inclusion and economic growth in OIC countries. *Research in International Business and Finance*, *43*, 1–14. https://doi.org/10.1016/j.ribaf.2017.07.178

Ko, T., Lee, J., & Ryu, D. (2018). Blockchain technology and manufacturing industry: Real-time transparency and cost savings. *Sustainability*, *10*(11), 4274. https://doi.org/10.3390/su10114274

Koshelev, S. (2022). Trends in the evolution of the digital financial assets market in the context of the digital transformation of the global economy. *Finance Theory and Practice*, *26*(4), 80–94. https://doi.org/10.26794/2587-5671-2022-26-4-80-94.

Lee, D., Li, Y., & Wang, Y. (2021). A global perspective on central bank digital currency. *China Economic Journal*, *14*(1), 52–66. https://doi.org/10.1080/17538963.2020.1870279

Mahardika, Z., Permana, R., & Maulisa, N. (2023). Going digital rupiah: Some considerations from sovereignty and cybersecurity perspectives. *Journal of Central Banking Law and Institutions*, *2*(1), 25–54. https://doi.org/10.21098/jcli.v2i1.42

Maryaningsih, N., Nazara, S., Kacaribu, F., & Juhro, S. (2022). Central bank digital currency: What factors determine its adoption? *Buletin Ekonomi Moneter Dan Perbankan*, *25*(1), 1–24. https://doi.org/10.21098/bemp.v25i1.1979

Minelgaite, I., Edvardsson, I., & Littrell, R. (2017). Societal culture in Iceland and Lithuania: Managerial implications. *Sage Open*, *7*(2), 215824401770402. https://doi.org/10.1177/2158244017704023

Mnohoghitnei, I., Neguț, C., & Horobet, A. (2021). The future is near: On the prospects of central bank digital currency adoption in central and eastern European countries. *KNE Social Sciences*, *2021*, 1–15. https://doi.org/10.18502/kss.v5i9.9882

Mohieldin, M., Iqbal, Z., Rostom, A., & Fu, X. (2011). *The role of islamic finance in enhancing financial inclusion in organization of Islamic cooperation (OIC) countries*. https://doi.org/10.1596/1813-9450-5920

Nugroho, A., & Herianingrum, S. (2022). Determinant of economic growth in organization of Islamic cooperation (OIC) countries. *Karachi Islamicus*, *2*(1), 28–42. https://doi.org/10.58575/ki.v2i1.19

Nur, M., Febriyanti, A., Rusgianto, S., & Herianingrum, S. (2022). Islamic banking financial inclusion and tax revenue in OIC countries: To what extent do they correlate? *Shirkah Journal of Economics and Business*, *7*(3), 302–317.

Oh, E., & Zhang, S. (2022). Informal economy and central bank digital currency. *Economic Inquiry*, *60*(4), 1520–1539. https://doi.org/10.1111/ecin.13105

Ozili, P. (2021). Can central bank digital currency increase financial inclusion? Arguments for and against. *SSRN Electronic Journal*. https://doi.org/10.2139/ssrn.3963041.

Ozili, P. (2022). CBDC, Fintech and cryptocurrency for financial inclusion and financial stability. *Digital Policy Regulation and Governance*, *25*(1), 40–57. https://doi.org/10.1108/dprg-04-2022-0033.

Philippon, T. (2019). The FinTech opportunity. In J. Agnew, & O. S. Mitchell (Eds.), *The Disruptive Impact of FinTech on Retirement Systems* (pp. 190–218). Oxford Academic. https://doi.org/10.1093/oso/9780198845553.003.0011

Samimi, P., & Jenatabadi, H. (2014). Globalization and economic growth: Empirical evidence on the role of complementarities. *PLoS One*, *9*(4), e87824. https://doi.org/10.1371/journal.pone.0087824

Sarma, M., & Pais, J. (2010). Financial inclusion and development. *Journal of International Development*, *23*(5), 613–628. https://doi.org/10.1002/jid.1698.

Semeko, A. (2022). Central bank digital currency: New opportunities for cross-border payments. *Financial Journal*, *14*(4), 108–121. https://doi.org/10.31107/2075-1990-2022-4-108-121.

Sethaput, S., & Innet, A. (2023). Blockchain application for central bank digital currencies (CBDC). *Cluster Computing*, *26*(4), 2183–2197. https://doi.org/10.1007/s10586-022-03962-z.

Themistocleous, M., Cunha, P., Tabakis, E., & Papadaki, M. (2023). Towards cross-border CBDC interoperability: Insights from a multivocal literature review. *Journal of Enterprise Information Management*, *36*(5), 1296–1318. https://doi.org/10.1108/jeim-11-2022-0411

Wu, B., An, X., & Shin, H. (2022). Extending UTAUT with national identity and fairness to understand user adoption of DCEP in china. *Scientific Reports*, *12*(1), 6856. https://doi.org/10.1038/s41598-022-10927-0

Wang, H., & Gao, S. (2023). The future of the international financial system: The emerging CBDC network and its impact on regulation. *Regulation & Governance*, *18*(1), 288–306. https://doi.org/10.1111/rego.12520

Chapter 8

Enhancing Financial Inclusion Through Fintech in OIC Member Economies

Shabeer Khan

Al Yamamah University, Saudi Arabia

Introduction

A highly observed but less understood phenomenon, the informal economy, is on a roll in many countries, most dominantly in the OIC member states. This is an industry that contribution toward economic activity in a momentous way. According to Capasso and Ohnsorge (2022) and Schneider et al. (2010), this industry forms the crux of jobs and means of subsistence for a considerable percentage of the population. However, the lack of official documents and developed credit histories leads the informal economy to often operate outside the formal financial system (Aterido & Osmani, 2018; Demir & Karamanos, 2016). The exclusion by this phenomenon limits the access to important financial services and hamper the capacity of the informal sector to contribute significantly toward the growth of the national economy.

Financial technology, or FinTech, has recently made great strides and offers one possible remedy. The term fintech describes a vast host of the most advanced technologies that are changing the face of the financial services industry. These technologies can lead to bridging the gap separating the formal and informal sectors by providing inclusive and, of course, readily available financial instruments that are explicitly tailored to meet the needs of informal enterprises. Only by considering the behavioral interactions between financial development, FinTech adoption, and an informal economy in OIC countries can such policy decisions include financial inclusion, which would spur economic growth.

The Economic Potential of Islamic Countries, Part A:
Economics, Demographics and Financial Services, 191–201

doi:10.1108/978-1-83708-000-720251010

The Informal Economy: A Complex and Dynamic Landscape

The informal economy[1] is a significant category that includes unregistered enterprises of independent contractors. Street vendors, home-based enterprises, micro-enterprises, and seasonal agricultural workers are just a few examples among the many players in this industry (Schneider, 2011). Although the informal-sector-led economy varies in size and composition across countries, it tends to be a weighty proportion when the total economic activity is considered, especially in developing countries where most people lack access to banking (Schneider et al., 2010).

The informal economy provides a place to work and earn a living for those who would otherwise not be able to make it through the formal labor market due to a lack of education, stringent restrictions, or limited skill sets. It also lessens poverty through income-generating opportunities for the backward classes. The unorganized sector also often begets entrepreneurship and innovation by introducing new goods and services into the market at cheap rates.

However, the unofficial sector is also facing many difficulties. One of the most significant barriers is the inaccessibility of official financial services. Credit rarely becomes available to the informal firm; no formal loans or credit records exist, and they often exercise difficulties conducting secure transactions, managing their money, as well as getting access to this money. Their capacity to grow, which involves making investments, expanding on its operations, and being formalized, is heavily constrained by this financial exclusion.

Besides this, a large part of the informal sector is unorganized, which again results in it being not circulated under statutory cover, creating problems like tax evasion or unfair competition for the registered businesses. Above all, all the related social securities and safeguards available to workers in the formal sector may go astray from employees working in the informal sector.

Financial Development and the Informal Economy

Financial development, therefore, plays a key supporting role in economic development and growth, explained mainly in the literature by the robust banking system, the properly functioning financial system with easy access to credit, and wide-ranging classes of financial instruments and products (Beck et al., 2009; Demirguc-Kunt & Levine, 2009). A well-developed financial system makes resources available to the unorganized sector in a variety of ways:

- *Access to credit*: Financial institutions can provide loans to the informal sector, whereby they can use the money to invest in their inventory, equipment, and expansion. As Beck et al. (2009) argue, this eventually leads to higher productivity and the creation of jobs.

---

[1]According to WIEGO (https://www.wiego.org/informal-economy), "The informal economy is the diversified set of economic activities, enterprises, jobs, and workers that are not regulated or protected by the state."

- *Financial exclusion*: With more bank accounts and active usage of mobile money platforms and other financial service methods, even more informal enterprises are effectively managing their finances conducting safe transactions, and begin establishing credit records. This, according to Demirguc-Kunt and Klapper (2012), might motivate people to legalize their enterprises and interact more actively within the official economy.
- *Risk management tools*: Various risk management tools, such as insurance policies, can be extended by these financial institutions to protect unofficial enterprises from things like fires, theft, and natural calamities. This would lead to empowerment in the field of entrepreneurship when it comes to the unorganized sector and also make them feel more financially secure. But a lot of moving parts are involved here, and the nature of financial development theory in explaining the informal sector is anything but clear. Others have also claimed that a well-developed financial system may raise pretty much the regulatory requirements and sediments of the cost of the same, which can equally inhibit the development of unofficial enterprises (De Soto, 2000).

Furthermore, since most unofficial enterprises do not have official records and a proven credit history, most formal financial institutions view this as a risky involvement. They hence will not easily extend credit lines to them. This chapter thus attempts to fill this particular knowledge gap by interrogating the intricate linkage between financial growth, FinTec adoption, and the informal sector in OIC nations. It will look into the ways against which the size and productivity of the informal sector depend on variables like bank penetration, availability of loans, and the overall financial infrastructure. It is also our intent to explore further how some FinTech solutions could encourage and so empower these informal companies within the OIC economies and promote financial inclusion. An example of these solutions is perhaps a digital payment platform, over and above that of mobile money, and an alternative credit scoring system. We attempt to understand the way in which a propitious financial environment and innovation within the domain of FinTech can help formalize and grow the unorganized sector so that it translates into higher economic activity and prosperity, by looking at the relationship between financial development and FinTech adoption.

This research would have a good deal of potential to contribute to the comprehensive understanding of the subject of informal economy and financial inclusion in the member states of the Organization of Islamic Cooperation (OIC). This research, in that case, therefore, will help provide empirical information while giving light on the effects brought about by the adoption of Fintech and financial growth as a way of bringing to a better clarification the characteristics and workings of the informal sector. This knowledge is, hence, invaluable to policymakers and scholars who are trying to understand this critical component of the economy and therefore work toward its integration. The results from this study will help formulate effective plans and policies to promote financial inclusion and help the unorganized sector grow.

The effective utilization of such a vibrant and innovative FinTech ecosystem will enable this research to contribute toward the overall economic development of OIC countries by closing the gap between informal and formal sectors. This will raise the level of employment, reduce poverty, and improve the livelihoods of a large number of the population. In addition to enhancing our understanding of the mechanisms at play, we hope that our research will bring on board some enlightening information that may, in all effect, make the knowledge gap between the formal and informal sectors thinner as a course that could lead to ways in which the eventual evolution of more prosperous and inclusive economies might arise in the Organization of the Orient.

Literature Review

The informal economy is a resilient, enigmatic force operating just beneath the surface to official markets worldwide. It encompasses everyone from street vendors who peddle their wares amid howling city streets to subsistence farmers who till the land, covering all types of unregistered enterprises and independent workers along the way. Especially among its OIC members, this dynamic sector is a powerful yet often-overlooked development dynamo in many developing countries. Surveys conducted by Schneider et al. (2010) and Capasso and Ohnsorge (2022) suggest "that the informal economy is a large share of these countries' total economic activity, often exceeding an astonishing 30% of GDP." This hidden engine hence provides employment and livelihood for an extensive section of the population. It serves as a vital safety net, which provides opportunities to people who may have difficulty gaining entry into the official labor market either because they lack education, lack skills, or perhaps due to laws that are too strict and cannot allow them to exceed them.

The informal economy also operates on the fringes of the official financial system and is invariably excluded from finance. This marginalization is mainly caused by the fundamental traits of the unorganized sector itself. Informal firms frequently lack the official documentation – like company licenses and tax registrations – that is required to build credit histories with financial institutions to enable them to avail themselves of institutional credit in times of need. Demir and Karamanos (2016) argue that banks do not advance their loans or even provide other financial services as they consider them risk-prone borrowers due to the lack of documentation. Besides that, formal financial institutions, who are used to more extensive and more stable income flows, find the informal enterprises – which, as noted, are characterized by small and erratic cash flow – not particularly attractive as customers.

This financial exclusion has some significant implications. Thus, firms lack access to critical financial services that could expand and develop informal firms. For example, without access to finance, firms will be unable to invest in inventory, marketing efforts, or equipment, which are essential for business growth and attracting new customers (Beck et al., 2009). Demirguc-Kunt and Levine (2009) add that the deepening of the informal sector has limited contribution to the growth of the national economy since it has minimal avenues of employment creation and productivity enhancement. Also, they are least capable of controlling their income and expenditure as a result of improper use of digital payment methods or bank accounts, which places them at increased risk of financial mismanagement and reduced profitability as a result (Aterido & Osmani, 2018).

Delving Deeper: Drivers and Dynamics of the Informal Economy

An in-depth analysis of the various factors that explain the prevalence and characteristics of the informal economy is thus necessary for understanding it. Researchers have identified multiple factors that nudge firms toward informality. For example, based on the analysis undertaken by De Soto (2000), one of the critical barriers to formalization is the excessive bureaucratic hurdles and regulations. Firms will be induced to operate informally to avoid the costly, time-consuming, and non-transparent process of obtaining permits and licenses and complying with complicated rules. On the other hand, researchers emphasizing the role of lax property rights and enforcement procedures include Maloney (2004). Firms might be unwilling to register in an economy with weak property rights and no legal penalty for breach of contract because companies will then face the risk of expropriation or unfair treatment. Moreover, Schneider's work also suggests that corrupt economies with weak institutional structures may cause a higher informality rate. Of course, in countries where corruption and rent-seeking activities are most prevalent, there is less incentive for firms to formalize their production since they could always bribe their way out, thus urging them to shift their productive capacity into the underground economy to dodge these extra costs. Beyond these over-arching causes, there is also a great deal of regional and national variation in the informal sector.

Researchers such as Schneider (2007) group the informal economy into three sectors: own-account workers, home enterprises, and unincorporated companies. In some contexts, the household enterprise refers to small-scale family below-registered firms producing goods or services for self-consumption or minor trade. Own-account workers are self-employed who sell their services directly to consumers. Now, unincorporated enterprises are small and informal outfits and may also have some employees. The specific economic environment of a country may affect the relative prevalence of different types of informal enterprises. For instance, in economies where the rural sector is significant, a higher proportion of home-based enterprises engage in agriculture. The proportion of own-account workers in urban economies in repair work or transportation is probably higher. More than that, gender and the degree of talent involved, apart from access to technology, explain the dynamics of this informal sector.

As per Chen (2004), some studies show the critical role women play in the unorganized sector, especially in developing nations. Certain cultural practices promote male employment, and a lack of source of proper education that may cause-specific challenges that inhibit women from taking place in the formal employment system. Therefore, this factor makes many people engage in unofficial ways of earning their livelihood, either by street vending, home production, or domestic work, to put food on the family table.

In effect, this phenomenon shows that, besides serving just as a source of economic activity, the informal sector is also significant for purposes of poverty reduction and women empowerment. Add to that, the kinds of activities people engage in and their chances of progressing up the ladder are tied, therefore, to their skill level in the informal sector. As the low-skilled labor will find minimal opportunities in the formal employment sector, they will join the informal sector where often, skills need to be learned informally on the job or through informal apprenticeships-something already witnessed in the construction industries where "the high proportion of labor working informally, in any case, means that neither formal certification criteria nor training provisions apply" (ILO, 2013). Technology affects the Informal economy in two ways. Development of digital technology and mobile links allows access to markets, information, and financial services that led to the rise in Unofficial enterprises, Awais and Hassan (2023), for instance, in most the developing countries, mobile money networks have drastically refuted the manner in which payments are found to be carried. As such, informal business people can accept digital payments and more securely manage their cash flow, as capitalized, (Christiaensen et al, 2013). On the contrary, due to affordability, lower levels of infrastructure, or poor literacy in terms of digital consideration, substantial numbers of informal or unemployed labors are still excluded from the use of digital technology (World Bank, 2016).

The Role of Policy and Regulation

Widely diverging policy responses toward the informal sector can be traced back to institutional capability, economic conditions, and national goals. As Portes et al. (1989) state, countries can opt to utilize tactics ranging from repression and punitive measures up to accommodation and formalization incentives. Repressive policies generally include strict law enforcement and crackdowns on unofficial activity to fines for noncompliance. These policies attempt to promote formalization and impede informality. Still, in their implementation, they often have many problems with enforcement and other unintended outcomes, such as more corruption or social unrest.

On the other hand, accommodation and formalization methods adapt to envelop these informal companies into the formal economy, providing necessary measures that recognize their resilience and advantages in terms of economic contributions. Simplified registration procedures, tax incentives for formalization, and targeted support for access to finance and skill development are some indicative examples of this. These approaches acknowledge that formalization is a complex process, influenced by much more than simply the regulations, that affects many informal workers and businesses in ways other. Those factors involve social norms, institutional trust, and economic viability, among others, according to Chen and Carré (2001).

Any governmental measures will only be effective if it is understood just what kind of incentives and constraints these unofficial enterprises confront. According to Tokman (2017), there is an extreme case to be made about following context-specific approaches fine-tuned to the unique characteristics of different informant sectors and the various local dynamics. For example, urban formalization projects can develop a focus on increased accessibility to services and infrastructure, and the rural areas may very well benefit from market links and farm extension services.

In addition, development agencies and international organizations play an essential role in determining the policy objectives and then providing the technical support to the countries suffering from the informal economy problems. For instance, the ILO has been advocating for inclusive growth plans that offer social protection and suitable employment to informal workers as the first priority. This, in turn, is ensured by the World Bank and regional development banks through efforts to increase financial inclusion, fortify legal frameworks, and create inclusive growth across all walks of society, including such segments that participate via the informal economy.

Case Studies and Regional Perspectives

Analyzing regional differences in the informal sector offers important insights into the many ways it manifests itself and the variables affecting its dynamics. For example, informal work is widespread in Latin America due to variables including economic instability, labor market fragmentation, and urbanization (Maloney, 2004). Social protection programs and microenterprise assistance initiatives have been put in place in countries like Brazil and Mexico with the goal of enhancing the lives of informal workers and promoting their transition to formal employment (ECLAC, 2018).

The informal economy accounts for a sizeable portion of economic activity in sub-Saharan Africa, especially in industries like services, retail commerce, and agriculture (McKay, 2010). Urban planning, service delivery, and social cohesion are facing problems as a result of the expansion of informal urban settlements and informal employment, which has been exacerbated by population trends and rapid urbanization (UN-Habitat, 2016). The region's policy solutions frequently center on developing infrastructure, expanding access to education and skill-building opportunities, and encouraging inclusive economic growth that integrates unorganized laborers into value chains in the formal sector (African Development Bank, 2019).

From high-tech hubs to rural agricultural economies, the characteristics of the informal sector are diverse across Asia (ADB, 2017). Along with using digital payment efforts and microfinance programs, countries such as Bangladesh and India are working to expand financial inclusion and help unregistered business owners (ADB, 2020). Yet, challenges such as unplanned city urbanization and mass-production still present formidable development problems that can be addressed by innovative policy reform (UNESCAP, 2018).

Despite the vast size and economic significance of the informal sector in the member countries of the OIC, little has been done to address the drivers that shape its behavior. The impact of financial development on informal economy activities is one of the areas that experience a large literature gap. Previous studies have focused on the role of financial institutions in the expansion of the formal sector (Beck et al., 2009; Demirguc-Kunt & Levine, 2009) but have not been able to translate how improvements in financial infrastructure and access to credit would affect informal enterprises. To fill this gap, we empirically investigate in this chapter how enhanced financial development in a sample of OIC contexts might spur formalization efforts, improve productivity, and mitigate informal economic activity risks.

Yet the role of financial technology (FinTech) in the informal economies of OIC countries remains understudied. While FinTech innovations are reshaping access to financial services globally (Awais & Hassan, 2023), their implications for informal sectors—especially in OIC member states—are rarely addressed not much is known about the impact of these innovations on the informal sector in OIC countries. We examine how FinTech-based innovations (e.g., digital payment systems, mobile banking) can promote financial inclusion and greater formalization within the informal economy, thus narrowing the gap. Through this examination of these technological developments, we hope and have to find out how FinTech has the potential to enable unregistered business owners to get better access to financial services or even can make it easier for them to become part of the formal economy.

Moreover, through the use of a panel data set that covers the OIC member countries, we are able to conduct a more investigation than mere informal glance of the economy. This enables us to identify country-specific causes, trends, and variations of informal economic activity. We deploy advanced panel econometrics for exploring the subtle relationships that exist between FinTech adoption, financial development, and informal economy dynamics. Through statistical methods which are systematic in nature, our works provide fine nuances for better understanding of policy prescriptions that enhance inclusive economic growth and resilience within the OIC area with no compromise on methodological rigor of studies in the informal sector.

Summing up, our research is based on a review of literature, presenting new perspective together with empirical evidence and filling the gap prevailing as to how workings, causes, and impacts of informality should be understood at OIC member countries level. In particular, we aim at providing decision-makers and those concerned with practical strategies promoting formalization, better economic opportunities, and improvement of life conditions for workers/entrepreneurs involved in informal economy across various socioeconomic settings. This will be undertaken through integrating findings of empirical analysis and literature review system.

Conclusion

The informal economy is a significant but often-overlooked segment of economic activity, particularly in the member states of the OIC. Despite its substantial contribution to employment and sustenance for a large portion of the population, the informal economy faces numerous challenges that limit its growth and integration into the formal financial system. The absence of official documentation and established credit histories often leads to financial exclusion, preventing informal enterprises from accessing critical financial services necessary for their expansion and formalization. Recent advancements in financial technology (FinTech) present an opportunity to address these challenges. FinTech innovations, including digital payment systems and alternative credit scoring mechanisms, have the potential to bridge the gap between the formal and informal sectors. By providing inclusive, accessible, and tailored financial instruments, FinTech can empower informal enterprises, enabling them to manage their finances more effectively, conduct secure transactions, and establish credit histories.

Financial development plays a pivotal role in economic growth by offering a robust banking system, accessible credit, and diverse financial instruments. However, the relationship between financial development and the informal sector is complex. While a well-developed financial system can provide resources and support to informal enterprises, it can also impose regulatory burdens that may inhibit their growth. This research aims to explore the intricate dynamics between financial development, FinTech adoption, and the informal economy in OIC countries. Through empirical analysis and literature review, this study highlights several key insights:

Role of FinTech in financial inclusion: FinTech can significantly enhance financial inclusion for informal enterprises. Digital payment platforms and mobile banking services provide informal businesses with tools to manage their finances, conduct transactions, and build credit histories. This can encourage formalization and integration into the formal economy.

Access to credit and risk management: Financial institutions, leveraging FinTech innovations, can extend credit and risk management tools to informal enterprises. This access to financial resources can enable informal businesses to invest in inventory, equipment, and expansion, leading to higher productivity and job creation.

Challenges of financial exclusion: The lack of access to official financial services remains a significant barrier for the informal sector. Without formal loans or credit records, informal enterprises struggle to secure the necessary funding for growth. FinTech solutions can mitigate this challenge by providing alternative credit assessments and digital financial services.

Policy implications: Policymakers need to adopt context-specific approaches that recognize the unique characteristics of the informal sector. Simplified registration procedures, tax incentives for formalization, and targeted support for access to finance and skill development can encourage the transition of informal enterprises into the formal economy.

Regional perspectives and case studies: The informal economy varies significantly across regions, influenced by factors such as economic instability, labor market fragmentation, and urbanization. Case studies from Latin America, sub-Saharan Africa, and Asia highlight the diverse manifestations of the informal sector and the different policy responses required to address its challenges.

Empirical evidence and future research: This study provides empirical evidence on the relationship between financial development, FinTech adoption, and the informal economy in OIC countries. It underscores the need for further research to explore how specific FinTech solutions can support the growth and formalization of informal enterprises, thereby contributing to overall economic development.

In summary, the informal economy represents a vital component of many developing countries' economic landscapes, particularly within OIC member states. While it provides essential employment and entrepreneurial opportunities, its exclusion from formal financial systems limits its potential contribution to national economic growth. FinTech offers a promising avenue to bridge this gap, providing tailored financial services that can facilitate the formalization and expansion of informal enterprises. By fostering financial inclusion through FinTech innovations, policymakers can enhance the productivity and growth of the informal sector, contributing to overall economic development and poverty reduction in OIC countries. This research highlights the importance of integrating financial development and technological advancements to create more inclusive and resilient economies.

References

ADB. (2017). Asian Development Outlook 2017: Meeting Asia's Infrastructure Needs. Asian Development Bank.

ADB. (2020). Financial Inclusion in the Digital Economy. Asian Development Bank. Retrieved from https://www.adb.org/publications/financial-inclusion-digital-economy

African Development Bank. (2019). Creating Decent Jobs: Strategies, Policies, and Instruments. Retrieved from https://www.afdb.org/en/documents/creating-decent-jobs-strategies-policies-and-instruments

Aterido, R., & Osmani, A. R. (2018). Informal economy and financial inclusion: Evidence from OIC countries. *Islamic Economic Studies*, *26*(1), 45–67.

Awais, M., & Hassan, S. (2023). Role of FinTech in bridging the financial inclusion gap: Evidence from OIC countries. *Journal of Islamic Business and Management*, *3*(1), 45–62.

Beck, T., Demirguc-Kunt, A., & Levine, R. (2009). *Financial institutions and markets across countries and over time: Data and analysis* [Policy Research Working Paper No. 4943]. World Bank.

Capasso, S., Ohnsorge, F., & Yu, S. (2022). Informality and financial development: A literature review. *Manchester School, 90*(5), 587–608.

Christiaensen, L., & Raza, W. (2013). Pathways out of informality: The role of FinTech in the financial inclusion of informal sector workers in OIC countries. *Journal of Development Economics*, *103*, 62–78.

Demir, F., & Karamanos, I. (2016). Financial inclusion and the informal economy: Evidence from OIC countries. *Journal of Economic Development*, *41*(2), 123–145.

Demirguc-Kunt, A., & Klapper, L. (2012). Measuring financial inclusion: Explaining variation in use of financial services across and within countries. *Brookings Papers on Economic Activity*, *2012*(1), 279–321.

Demirguc-Kunt, A., & Levine, R. (2009). *Finance and inequality: Theory and evidence* [NBER Working Paper No. 15275]. National Bureau of Economic Research.

De Soto, H. (2000). *The mystery of capital: Why capitalism triumphs in the West and fails everywhere else*. Basic Books.

Economic Commission for Latin America and the Caribbean. (ECLAC). (2018). Social Panorama of Latin America, 2018 (LC/PUB.2019/3-P). Santiago. Retrieved from https://www.cepal.org/en/publications/43928-social-panorama-latin-america-2018

International Labour Organization (ILO). (2013). Transitioning from the informal to the formal economy (Report V(1), International Labour Conference, 102nd Session, Geneva). Retrieved from https://www.ilo.org/wcmsp5/groups/public/---ed_emp/documents/meetingdocument/wcms_456553.pdf

Maloney, W. F. (2004). Informality revisited. *World Development*, *32*(7), 1159–1178.

McKay, A. (2010). The rise of the urban informal sector in Africa: Macro-dynamics and micro outcomes. *Urban Forum*, *21*(3), 297–315.

Portes, A., Castells, M., & Benton, L. A. (1989). *The informal economy: Studies in advanced and less developed countries*. Johns Hopkins University Press.

Schneider, F. (2007). Shadow economies of 145 countries all over the world: What do we really know? *International Journal of Public Policy*, *3*(1/2), 1–17.

Schneider, F. (2011). *Size and development of the shadow economy of 31 European and 5 other OECD countries from 2003 to 2011: A further decline* [Discussion Paper No. 5355]. IZA Institute of Labor Economics.

Schneider, F., Buehn, A., & Montenegro, C. E. (2010). *Shadow economies all over the world: New estimates for 162 countries from 1999 to 2007* [IZA Discussion Paper No. 5230]. IZA Institute of Labor Economics.

Tokman, V. E. (2017). The role of the informal sector in national development strategies: Lessons from Latin America. *World Development*, *95*, 246–257.

UNESCAP. (2018). *Economic and social survey of Asia and the Pacific 2018: Ambitions beyond growth*. United Nations Economic and Social Commission for Asia and the Pacific.

UN-Habitat. (2016). *The new urban agenda*. United Nations Human Settlements Programme.

World Bank. (2016). *World development report 2016: Digital dividends*. World Bank.

Section 5

Energy Transition and Cooperation

Chapter 9

Challenges and Opportunities Associated with Energy Transition in Islamic Countries

Benuka Ferdousi

Bangladesh Institute of International and Strategic Studies, Bangladesh

1. Introduction

A great energy transition is in the horizon. The triumphant advance in renewable technology, amidst the background of increasingly threatening evidences of climate change worldwide, have created an irreversible momentum for a global energy transformation (IRENA et al., 2018). To keep the global temperature in the track of Paris Agreement, the share of renewables needs to be raised to 65% of the world's primary energy supply by 2050 up from 15% today (IEA & IRENA, 2017). Such targets are no more deemed to be impossible, at least technologically, thanks to the unprecedented advancement in digitalization and energy storage technologies, which were unimaginable even a decade ago (IRENA, 2019).

The triumph of renewables is evident in Fig. 9.1 which shows that since 2011 power addition from renewables has been higher than fossil fuel. Renewables' share in global power addition reached to 90% in 2022 (International Energy Agency, 2023). Fig. 9.2, on the other hand, reveals the main driver of this transition. As can be seen from the figure, the cost of producing electricity is increasingly becoming lower for renewable energy compared to fossil fuel.

Energy transition will not only entail a profound shift in global geopolitics, it is also going to impact deeply the global trade regime and hence economic architecture. Irrespective of their approach toward energy transition – proactive, reactive or reluctant, no countries can avoid the impact of energy transition in the coming future be it energy rich or energy poor in the existing energy architecture. This is why, so far, as many as 166 have come up with specific renewable energy targets (REN21, 2023) and the issue is increasingly being taken up with utmost importance in various regional and international organizations and platforms.

The Economic Potential of Islamic Countries, Part A: Economics, Demographics and Financial Services, 205–241

Published under exclusive licence by Emerald Publishing Limited
doi:10.1108/978-1-83708-000-720251011

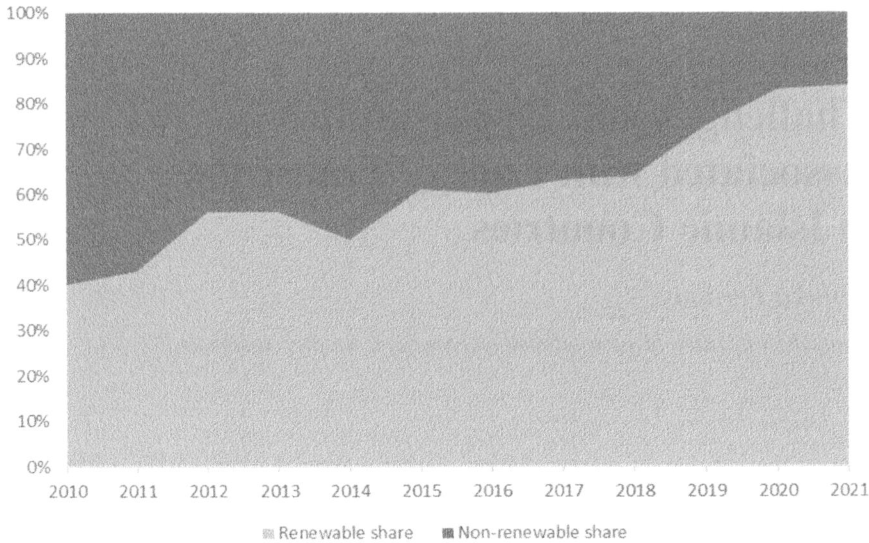

Fig. 9.1. Share of Renewable Energy in Net Annual Additions in Power Generating Capacity, 2010–2020. *Source*: REN21 (Global Status Report various issues).

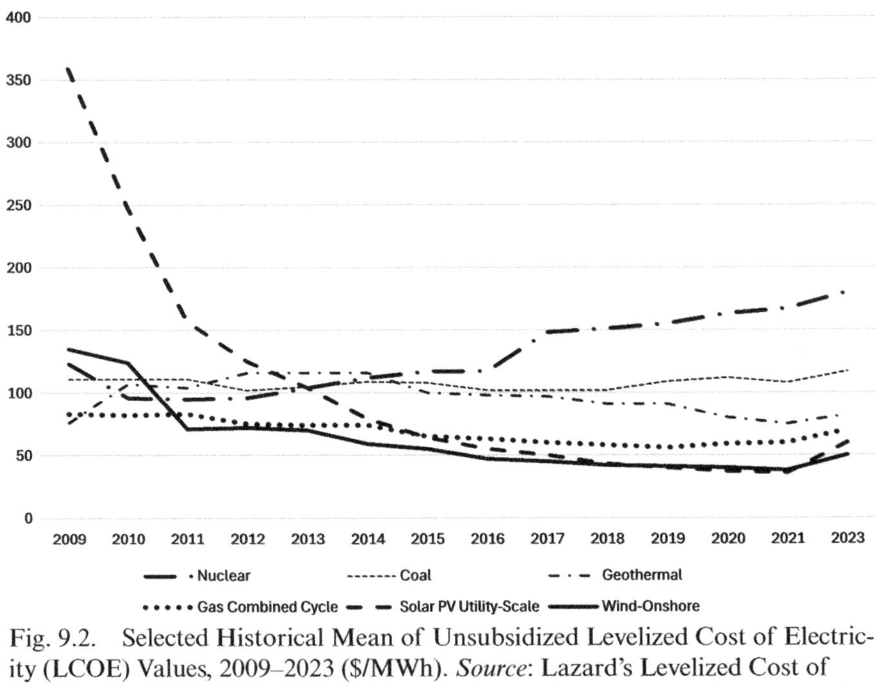

Fig. 9.2. Selected Historical Mean of Unsubsidized Levelized Cost of Electricity (LCOE) Values, 2009–2023 ($/MWh). *Source*: Lazard's Levelized Cost of Energy Analysis – Version 16.0 (APRIL 2023), available at https://www.lazard.com/media/typdgxmm/lazards-lcoeplus-april-2023.pdf.

The OIC is an international intergovernmental organization consisting a diverse set of countries in terms of geography, climatic conditions, resource endowment, social and political settings, and economic and human development. Notwithstanding the diversity, most of its member countries are now going through a phase of socio-economic transition in which energy is supposed to play a vital role. Therefore, to thrive as an international organization for cooperation among Muslims, the OIC needs to assess the impact and level of preparedness of its member countries with a view to making them more equipped for the inevitable energy transition. The fact that OIC consists of the fossil fuel-rich MENA countries which, with their 75% and 50% share of global crude oil and natural gas reserve, are going to face the most profound impact of energy transition, adds to the importance of the issue. It is in this context that the present chapter will examine the situation of OIC member countries in terms of their preparedness for the upcoming energy transition with a view to identify the challenges and the scopes for cooperation.

Taking the diverse nature of OIC member countries into consideration, the chapter will discuss the issue by dividing the member countries into six geographical group – MENA region, Europe, Central Asia, Sub-Saharan Africa, South Asia, Southeast Asia, and Latin America. The reason for such categorizing is that the member countries in the mentioned geographical groups show a good extent of similarity in socio-economic and political architecture.

The study uses qualitative research method and is based on secondary data which have been collected from relevant books, journals, reports, and documents. It is organized as follows. Following introduction, section two provides the energy profile of the OIC. Section three examines the potentials and drivers of renewable energy in the OIC. Section four presents the commitments and achievements of the OIC countries in terms of renewable energy. Section five identifies the challenges and section six finds out the scopes for cooperation. Section seven concludes the chapter.

2. Energy Profile of the OIC

This section will set the background for the discussion on energy transition in the OIC by examining the energy profile of the OIC member countries. It will look into the energy resource endowment, energy production and energy sector composition of the OIC member states.

2.1. Distribution of Energy Resources

With two third of the world's supergiant oil fields and some of the largest gas fields located in the Arabian-Iranian sedimentary basin, the OIC accounts for three fourth of world's proven crude oil reserve and half of world's proven gas reserve. Yet, OIC is not a club of hydrocarbon-rich countries. As can be seen from Figs. 9.3 and 9.4, there is considerable disparity among OIC members with regard to energy resource endowment. OIC's hydrocarbon resources are mainly concentrated in the MENA region which accounts for about 90% of OIC's proven crude

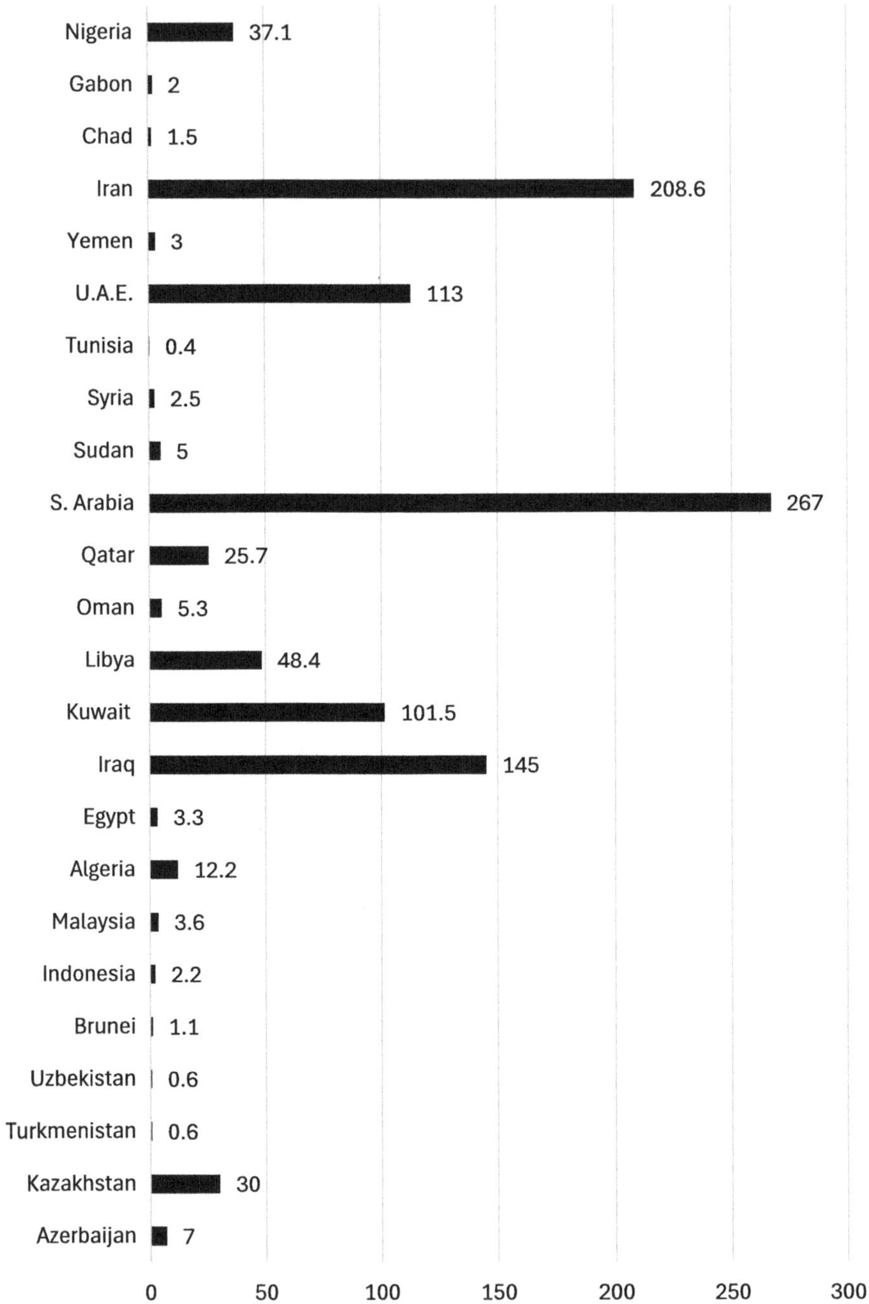

Fig. 9.3. Proven Oil Reserve in OIC Countries, 2022 (Billion Barrels).
Source: OPEC (2023, OPEC Annual Statistical Bulletin, p. 22).

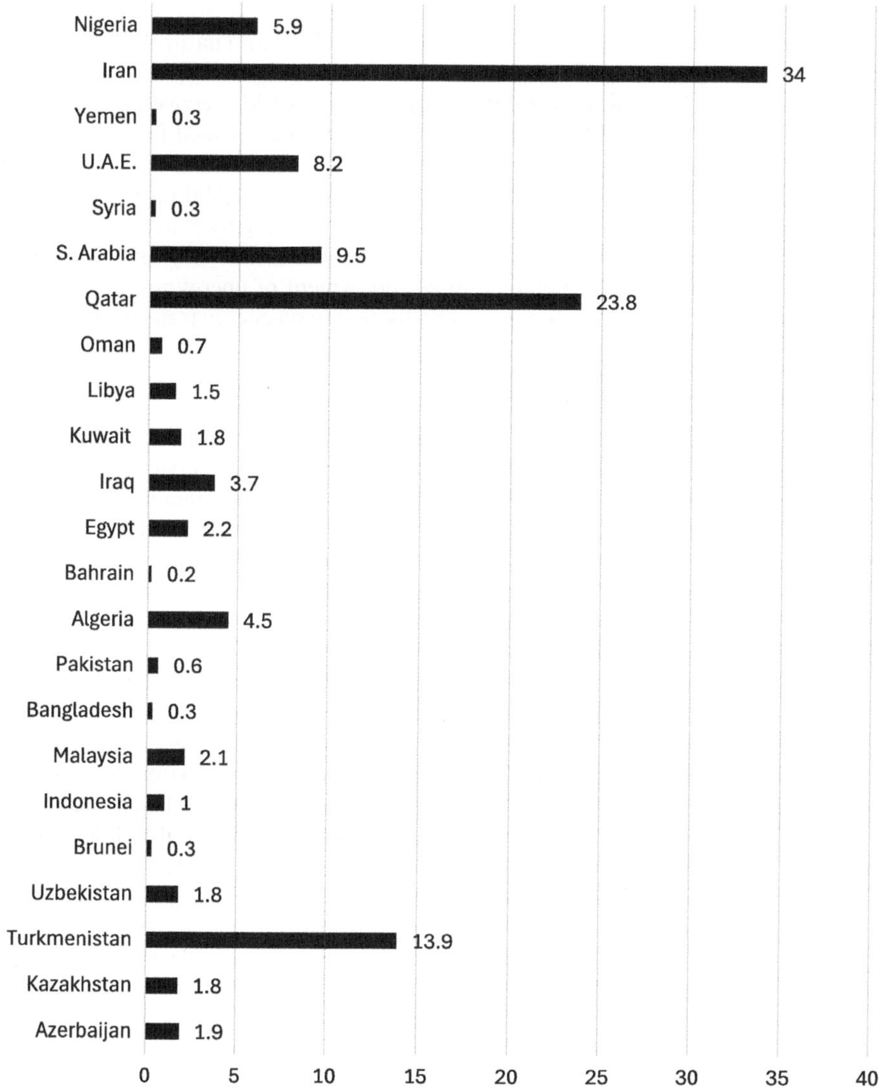

Fig. 9.4. Proven Natural Gas Reserve in OIC Countries, 2022 (Trillion Cubic Meter). *Source*: OPEC (2023 OPEC Annual Statistical Bulletin, p. 76).

oil reserve and about three-fourth of OIC's proven gas reserve. Even within the MENA region, five countries – Saudi Arabia, Iraq, Iran, Kuwait, and the UAE – have 85% of OIC crude oil reserve while Iran, Qatar, Saudi Arabia, and the UAE jointly account for 61% of OIC gas reserve.

Among the other geographical groups of OIC, Turkmenistan of Central Asia has significant gas reserve while Kazakhstan has a good amount of oil. Among the Sub-Saharan member countries, the only country that is endowed with energy resources is Nigeria which has a good amount of oil reserve and some gas also. In Southeast Asia, Indonesia and Malaysia have both oil and natural gas while in South Asia, Bangladesh and Pakistan have some natural gas reserve.

OIC is not rich in coal. It accounts for only 5% of world's recoverable reserve. However, like crude oil and gas, coal of OIC is also concentrated in a few countries with Kazakhstan accounting for 64.8% of the OIC total while Indonesia, Uzbekistan, Turkey, Pakistan, and Iran account for the rest (Haktanir, 2004).

The distribution of OIC's fossil fuel resources are thus highly concentrated leaving the vast majority of OIC member countries in a situation very different from some MENA countries which enjoy a huge endowment of energy resources. This reality needs to be taken into account in any discussion on energy transition in OIC.

2.2. Energy Production in the OIC

The differences in energy resource endowment of various geographical groups of the OIC member states is reflected in their energy production capacity measured by per capita electricity consumption (see Fig. 9.5). In MENA region, in the four fossil fuel-rich countries – Saudi Arabia, Kuwait, Qatar, and the UAE, per capita electricity consumption is three to five times of world average. However, some countries in the MENA region lags behind in electricity consumption despite having energy resources which is mainly due to political instability. They include Iraq, Syria, Sudan, and Libya.

On the other extreme, in electricity consumption, the OIC member countries in South Asia and Sub-Saharan Africa lag far behind the word average which mostly reflects their poor energy resource endowment. The geographical cluster of Southeast Asia and EU-Central Asia lies in between the two extremes consuming electricity close to the world average level while the fossil fuel-rich countries consume at a level higher than the world average, for example, coal-rich Kazakhstan and oil-rich Brunei and Malaysia. One interesting thing about the EU-Central Asia cluster is that many member states of this group enjoy a higher level of electricity consumption than is suggested by their fossil fuel endowment. This has been possible due to their success in harnessing various renewable energy sources such as hydro, geothermal, wind, etc.

2.3. Energy Mix in OIC

The energy mix of the OIC member countries reflects their fossil fuel endowment and the level of socio-economic development. Table 9.1 presents the energy mix and the electricity generation mix of the OIC member states while Fig. 9.6 provides the region-wise energy mix within the OIC. As expected, being endowed with huge hydrocarbon resources, Middle East depends more on fossil fuels, particularly natural gas and oil. Due to the presence of coal-rich countries, Southeast Asia and EU-Central Asia cluster have higher share of coal in their energy mix. South Asia is mainly endowed with natural gas and hence more of its electricity is produced from gas. On the other hand, the energy-poor OIC members of Sub-Saharan Africa and other regions largely depend on biomass for energy supply.

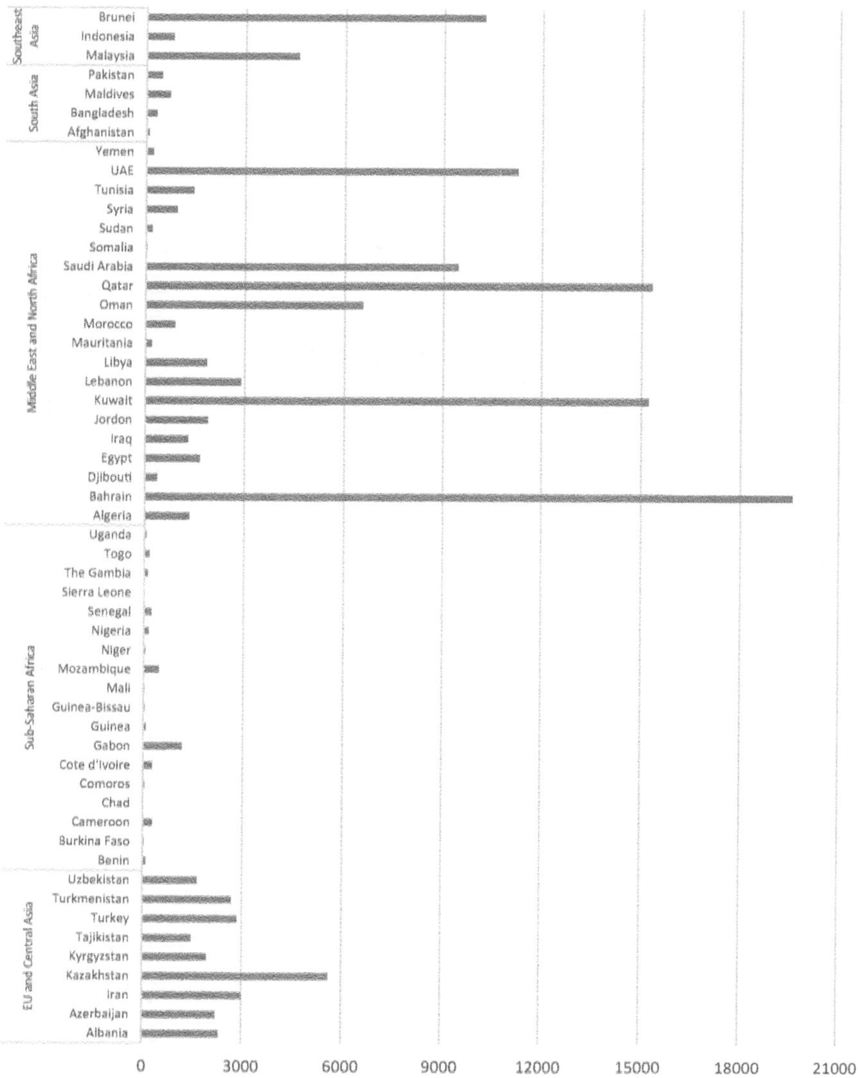

Fig. 9.5. Per Capita Electricity Consumption in OIC (kWh). *Source*: Khan and Akram (2018).

One can see from Table 9.1 that though MENA region is the largest exporter of crude oil, in their domestic electricity production, they use more natural gas than crude oil. This is due to their concern over domestic environment on one hand and the difficulties of exporting gas on the other hand (Hafner et al., 2023). On the other hand, countries less endowed with fossil fuel make more use of renewable energy sources for electricity generation. Some of the energy-poor countries such as Benin, Burkina Faso, Djibouti and Afghanistan depend mainly on electricity import for domestic consumption.

Table 9.1. Energy Mix in the OIC Member States, 2021.

Region	Country	Energy Mix	Electricity Generation Mix
EU and Central Asia	Albania	Oil 44%, hydro 33%, coal 10%, wind, biofuel, and waste 11%	Hydro 100%
	Azerbaijan	Gas 66%, oil 32.5%	Gas 95%, hydro and other renewable 5%
	Kazakhstan	Coal 49%, gas 25%, oil 25%, hydro 1%	Fossil fuel 88%, hydro 12%
	Kyrgyzstan	Hydro 53%, coal 37%	Hydro 90%
	Tajikistan	Hydro 41%, oil 28%, coal 25%, gas 25%	Hydro 90%, coal 6%
	Turkey	Oil 29%, coal 25%, gas 27.4%, solar and wind 11.6%, hydro 3.7%	Coal 35%, gas 23%, hydro 20.5%, wind 10.8%, solar 4.7%
	Turkmenistan	Gas 75%, oil 25%	Gas 100%
Southeast Asia	Brunei	Gas 57.5%, oil 25%, coal 18%	Gas 77.5%, coal 22%
	Indonesia	Coal 30%, oil 30%, gas 15%, renewable (wind, solar, geothermal) 12%, biofuel and waste 14%	Coal 61%, gas 16.5%, hydro 8%, biofuel 6%
	Malaysia	Gas 45%, oil 27%, coal 24%, hydro 3%	Coal and gas 83%, hydro 16%, solar 1%
Middle East and North Africa	Algeria	Gas 66%, oil 33%	Gas 99%
	Bahrain		Gas 99%
	Egypt	Gas 55%, 37% oil, biofuel and waste 2.5%, coal 1.5%	Fossil fuel 92%, hydro 7%, wind 1%
	Iraq	Oil 63%, gas 36%, hydro 1%	Gas 57%, oil 37%, hydro 6%
	Iran	Gas 71%, oil 28%, hydro 0.5%	Fossil fuel 92%, hydro 6%, nuclear 2%

	Jordan	Oil 51%, gas 38%, wind-solar 8%, coal 2.5%	Renewable 13%, 2019,
	Kuwait	Oil 66%, gas 34%	Gas 58%, other fossil fuel 42%
	Lebanon	Oil 93%, coal 2%, biomass 5%	Oil 91%, hydro 6%, solar 3%
	Libya	Oil 62%, gas 34%, biofuel and waste 4%	Gas 74%, oil 26%
	Morocco	Oil 56%, coal 31%, gas 2.5%, renewable 3%, biomass 7%	Fossil fuel 81%, wind 12%, solar 4%, hydro 2%
	Oman	Gas 90.5%, oil 9.5%	Gas 96.5%, solar 3.5%
	Qatar	Natural gas 92%, oil 8%	Gas 100%
	Saudi Arabia	Oil 64.5%, gas 35.5%	Gas 60%, oil 40%
	Sudan	Biomass 63%, oil 32.5%, hydro 4.5%	Hydro 62%, oil 38%
	Syria	Oil 68%, natural gas 31%, hydro 0.7%	Natural gas 56%, oil 40%, hydro 4.5%
	Tunisia	Gas 50%, oil 40%, biomass 10%	Gas 95%, wind 2%, solar 2%
	UAE	Gas 63.5%, oil 30%, coal 3%, nuclear 3%	Gas 89%, nuclear 7%, solar 4.5%
South Asia	Afghanistan		Electricity imported 80%, 20% from hydro and diesel
	Maldives	Oil 99%, solar 0.5%, biomass 0.5%	Oil 94%, solar 6%
	Bangladesh	Gas 55%, oil 22%, coal 7%, biomass 16%	Fossil fuel 96%, renewable 4%
	Pakistan	Biomass 31%, gas 29%, oil 20%, coal 13.5%, nuclear 3.5%, hydro 1.5%	Gas 35%, coal 9.5%, other fossil fuel 12%, hydro 24%, wind 2.7%, solar 1%, nuclear 14%
Sub-Saharan Africa	Benin	Biomass 60.5%, oil 35%, gas 3%, coal 1.5%	Import significant part of electricity Domestic production: gas 80%, oil 19.5%, solar 1.5%

(Continued)

Table 9.1. (*Continued*)

Region	Country	Energy Mix	Electricity Generation Mix
	Burkina Faso	Biofuel (66%?), oil 33%	Import 41%, oil 53%, renewable (hydro) 10%
	Cameroon	Renewable 20%, gas 21%, oil 23%	Renewable (hydro) 62%
	Comoros	Imported heavy oil and biomass	
	Djibouti	Biomass 39%, 43% gas, 18% coal and others	Import 65% electricity from Ethiopia Domestic production of electricity: wind 35%, fossil fuel 65%
	Gabon	Biomass 77%, oil 14%, gas 7%	Gas 47%, hydro 42%, oil 10%
	Ivory Coast	Biomass 56%, oil 24%, gas 17%	Gas 76%, hydro 23%
	Gambia	Oil 57%, biomass 43%	Fossil fuel 98%, Renewable 2%
	Mali	Biofuels and wastes (65%), oil (32%), with coal and hydro 3%	Hydro 57%, solar 3%, bioenergy 3%, fossil fuel 38%
	Mozambique	Biomass 65%, oil 16%, hydro 12%, gas 7%	Hydro 82%, gas 16%
	Niger	Biomass 80%, oil 17%, coal 2%, gas 1%	Oil 63%, coal 26%, gas 7%, solar 3.5%
	Nigeria	Biomass 74%, oil 14%, gas 10%, coal 1%	Gas 80%, oil 20%
	Senegal	Oil 49%, biomass 39%, coal 10.5%, renewable 1.5%	Oil 76.5%, solar 8.5%, wind 6.3%, coal 6.3%
	Sierra Leone	Biomass 79%, oil 21%	Hydro 70%, fossil fuel 25%, solar 2%, biomass 3%
	Somalia	Oil 95%, biomass 5%	Fossil fuel 89%, solar 10%, wind 1%
	Togo	Biomass 83%, oil 13%, gas 3%	Gas 65%, hydro 20%, solar 7%, oil 8%
	Uganda	Biomass 90%, oil 8%, hydro 2%	Hydro 90%, biofuel 7%, oil 2%

Source: Compiled by the author from IEA and IRENA.

Fig. 9.6. Energy Mix of Different Geographical Regions Within the OIC, 2017. *Source*: Khan and Akram (2018, p. 14).

The energy sector of OIC, thus, shows a great diversity in terms of reserve, energy production and composition reflecting their diverse resource endowment and socio-economic condition. This diversity is expected to affect the energy transition scenario of the OIC in terms of commitment, achievement, drivers and challenges of renewable energy which will be discussed in subsequent sections.

3. Renewables in the OIC: Potentials and Drivers

It is widely argued that compared to fossil fuel, renewable energy is more evenly distributed which contributes in ensuring energy security of countries as well as in reducing conflict among them (O'Sullivan et al., 2017). This section will try to see whether this is the case for the OIC. It will also endeavor to identify the drivers of energy transition in the OIC.

3.1. Renewable Energy Potential in the OIC

For their geographic location, the MENA and Sub-Saharan Africa have tremendous potential of solar energy. Most of the MENA countries lie in the so-called Sunbelt, with global horizontal irradiance values ranging from 1,600 to 2,600 $kWh/m^2/y$, and direct normal irradiance of 1,800 to more than 2,800 $kWh/m^2/y$ (Al-Shalabi et al., 2014, p. 190). According to an estimate, the MENA region is the most potential area for solar energy which receives one-fourth of world's solar energy making (World Economic Forum, 2023). The rest of the regions – South East Asia, South Asia, EU-Central Asia, and Latin America also have moderate potential of solar energy. For wind energy also, MENA region has good potential with 75% of its area receiving winds strong enough for utility-scale wind farms (World Economic Forum, 2023). The potential for wind is particularly high in Mediterranean countries like Morocco, Egypt, and Turkey while Iran has moderate potential. Central Asia and some pockets of Sub-Saharan Africa also have moderate to good potential. The rest of the OIC has low to moderate potential for wind energy.

In terms of hydro energy, Central Asia enjoys to have some of the greatest potential in the world. With a vast network of river which are formed from glacier meltwater of the Pamir and Tien Shan mountain ranges, the region has numerous suitable locations for hydroelectric dams and countries of this region are already harnessing their hydro potential (Zandi, 2023). Some of the Southeast Asian members of the OIC also have good potential for hydro energy. Being a water-scarce region, MENA and Sub-Saharan Africa naturally lacks in hydro potential. Geothermal is a rare source of renewable energy which, so far, has been found to be distributed in a limited area of the world. Fortunately, some of the geographical clusters of the OIC, namely the Southeast Asia and EU-Central Asia has a good potential of geothermal and some countries in these regions – namely Indonesia, Iran, and Turkey have already started utilizing this resource.

3.2. Drivers of Renewable Energy in the OIC

Within the OIC, the drivers of energy transition vary with the member state's existing energy resource endowment, socio-economic and political architecture, and potential of renewable energy sources. Motivation behind energy transition for a fossil fuel-rich country is bound to be different from that for a energy-poor country.

3.2.1. Concern over Stranded Asset

For the fossil fuel-rich OIC members, the foremost concern is stranded asset is expected to act as the strongest motivation for energy transition. Materializing the avowed commitment of COP 21 to keep the global temperature rise below 2°C, a commitment being facilitated by the declining cost of renewables, would require the world to keep a substantial part of the existing fossil fuel reserve as stranded. It is estimated that globally 33% of oil, 49% of gas, and 82% of coal would become unburnable. The extent of stranded asset will be even higher if global temperature rise is targeted at 1.5°C (McGlade & Ekins, 2015; Welsby et al., 2021). Not only the fossil fuel reserves will be stranded, the structures and capital engaged in their extraction will also be abandoned. Globally, the accruing loss is estimated to be USD 1.4 trillion (Mercure et al., 2018). The Middle East stands to be the largest looser in the world with stranded fossil fuel. The region will account for 61% of the world's total stranded oil reserve. For gas, Middle East's share in total stranded reserve will be 48% (McGlade & Ekins. 2015).

There is, however, debate on the role of fear of stranded asset on energy transition. Some scholars believe that in the short run, the fear of stranded asset might give rise to "green paradox" where the fossil fuel-rich countries will rush to increase the production of fossil fuel before it is abandoned resulting in delay of energy transition (Arezki & Obstfeld, 2015; van der Ploeg, 2011). Others point out that the delay will not be long since countries would rather prefer to achieve resilience for the long run (World Bank, 2020). The energy scenario depicted in Table 9.1, which shows the reluctance of the fossil fuel-rich OIC countries in general and MENA countries in particular, supports the argument that at least in the short run, abundance of fossil fuel may slow down the growth of renewable energy in the OIC. However, the recent developments in the energy-rich MENA countries, in terms of their response to the global call of decarbonization indicates that they are aware of the evolving global energy sector and are being prepared in that direction.

3.2.2. Economic Drivers

For OIC member countries which are comparatively less endowed with fossil fuels, reducing import dependence for energy acts as the main driver for energy transition which not only drains out their valuable foreign exchanges but also expose them to the volatility of energy market and thus affecting their energy security. For them, further economic incentive comes from the falling cost of renewables compared to other fossil fuels. As was shown in Fig. 9.2, over the last decade, production of electricity from modern renewable energy like solar or wind has become several times cheaper than that from fossil fuel.

To see how fossil fuel abundance/scarcity influences OIC countries' adoption of renewable energy, Table 9.2 contrasts the share of renewable energy in these countries with their fossil fuel reserve. In Table 9.2, an inverse relation between fossil fuel reserve and adoption of renewable energy is evident. For example, Kyrgyzstan, Tajikistan and Turkey – three fossil fuel deprived countries

Table 9.2. Oil and Gas Reserves and Share of Renewable Energy in Electricity Generation in the OIC, 2021.

Region	Country	Proven Oil Reserve (1,000 Million Barrels)	Proven Natural Gas Reserve (Trillion Cubic Meter)	Share of Renewable in Electricity Generation (%)
Europe and Central Asia	Albania			100
	Azerbaijan	7	1.2	5
	Kazakhstan	30	1.5	12
	Kyrgyzstan			90
	Tajikistan			90
	Turkey			26
	Turkmenistan	0.6	17.5	0
	Uzbekistan	0.6	1.1	
South East Asia	Brunei	1.1	0.3	0
	Indonesia	3.7	2.9	8
	Malaysia	3.8	1.1	17
South Asia	Afghanisthan			82
	Bangladesh		0.3	4
	Maldives			6
	Pakistan		0.6	28
Middle East & North Africa	Algeria	12.2	4.5	0
	Bahrain		0.2	1
	Egypt	3.6	1.8	8
	Iraq	150	3.6	6
	Jordan			13
	Kuwait	101.5	1.8	0
	Lebanon			9
	Libya	48.4	1.5	0
	Morocco			18
	Oman	5.2	0.7	3.5
	Qatar	25.7	24.5	0
	Saudi Arabia	267	8.2	0
	Sudan	1.5		62
	Syria	2.5	0.3	4.5

Table 9.2. (*Continued*)

Region	Country	Proven Oil Reserve (1,000 Million Barrels)	Proven Natural Gas Reserve (Trillion Cubic Meter)	Share of Renewable in Electricity Generation (%)
	Tunisia	0.4		4
	UAE.	97.8	6.1	4.5
	Yemen	3	0.3	
	Iran	157.8	34	6
Sub-Saharan Africa	Benin			1.5
	Burkina Faso			
	Cameroon			62
	Chad	1.5		
	Comoros			
	Djibouti			35
	Gambia			2
	Guinea			
	Guinea- Bissau			
	Gabon	2		60
	Mali			60
	Mauritania			
	Mozambique			82
	Niger			3.5
	Nigeria	37.1	5.1	0
	Senegal			14.8
	Sierra Leone			73
	Somalia			10
	Togo			
	Uganda			

Source: Compiled by the Author from OPEC, IEA and IRENA.

of EU-Central Asia region produces 26–90% of their electricity from renewables. Similar are the cases with Jordan and Morocco, the two fossil fuel deprived countries of the MENA who produce 13–18% electricity from renewables. Such tendency is even more evident in Sub-Saharan Africa where energy-poor countries such as Djibouti, Mali, and Mozambique produce 35–82% electricity from renewables. In contrast, the share of renewables in electricity generation in fossil fuel-rich countries such as Brunei in Southeast Asia and Saudi Arabia, Qatar, and Kuwait in MENA, use of renewable energy is virtually absent. This finding matches with that of Gallagher and Winter (2013) which showed that in the western developed world, countries or areas lacking in fossil fuel were more advanced in adopting renewable energy.

For hydrocarbon-rich countries, however, there are other economic factors which may encourage them in renewable energy. For them, the first economic incentive of renewable energy is that it offers a substitution for their domestic consumption which makes more fossil fuel available for export. According to an estimate, pursuing their renewable energy objectives, MENA countries can save 90 Mtoe of energy over the period 2017–2030 which is equivalent to the total primary energy supply of the region in 2014 (Menichetti & Gharras, 2017). Another economic factor that may encourage the hydrocarbon-rich countries, particularly in the MENA region is the possible job opportunity that will be created by the emerging renewable energy sector which will benefit them greatly in diversifying their economies. Achieving the renewable energy targets of the MENA countries are estimated to create 430,000 jobs by 2030 (Menichetti & Gharras, 2017).

3.2.3. Climate Change Regime as External Driver

Among the external drivers of energy transition in the OIC, the most important is the pressure coming from emerging global climate change regime characterized by the Paris Agreement. Some of the OIC members who are in the list of top fossil fuel reserves are also in the list of top CO_2 emitters. As can be seen from Table 9.3, in 2022, three OIC members – Indonesia, Iran and Saudi Arabia were the 6th, 7th, and 10th largest emitter of CO_2. The reason that Indonesia and Iran

Table 9.3. Top 10 Country in CO_2 Emissions in the World, 2022 (Million Tons).

Rank	**Country**	**CO_2 Emissions 2022 (Million Tons)**
1	China	12,667.43
2	USA	4,853.78
3	India	2,693.03
4	Russia	1,909.04
5	Japan	1,082.65
6	Indonesia	692.24
7	Iran	686.42
8	Germany	673.6
9	South Korea	635.5
10	Saudi Arabia	607.91

Source: World Population Review (2024).

emits more CO_2 than Saudi Arabia despite their lower per capita electricity consumption compared to the latter (which is one-third and one-eleventh of Saudi Arabia, respectively) is because these two countries use significant amount of coal for energy generation.

If per capita CO_2 emission is considered instead of total emission, the scenario become worse for the OIC since 6 out of 10 top emitters are from the OIC. The top emitters include Qatar, Kuwait, the UAE, Bahrain, Brunei, and Oman (see Table 9.4). Too high consumption of electricity in these countries, which falls in the range of 10,000–20,000 kWh/capita compared to the world average of 3,144 kWh/capita, can be attributed for their position as top emitters (per capita).

The contribution of the OIC's fossil fuel-rich members in global warming is coming under increasing scrutiny and criticism as was evident in the recent COP summits. It can be mentioned here that all MENA countries are parties to the UNFCCC and its legally binding instruments – the Kyoto Protocol and the Paris Agreement. They also submitted their NDCs following the 2015 Agreement. These commitments at international level act as a driver of energy transition, particularly in the fossil fuel-rich member states irrespective of their approach toward the energy transition.

3.2.4. Climate Change as Internal Driver

Though climate change regime acts as an external driver for the energy-rich member states of OIC, in all member states – energy-rich and energy-poor – climate change itself act as an internal driver. Interestingly, the climate change driver is stronger in the fossil fuel-rich MENA region, particularly in the oil- and gas-rich countries. This is because these countries themselves are experiencing the negative effects of climate

Table 9.4. Top 10 Country in Per Capita CO_2 Emissions in the World, 2022 (Million Tons).

Rank	**Country**	**CO_2 Emissions 2022 (Million Tons)**
1	Palau	59
2	Qatar	35.52
3	Kuwait	24.9
4	UAE	21.75
5	Bahrain	21.31
6	Trinidad and Tobago	21.17
7	Brunei	20.65
8	Gibraltar	18.96
9	New Caledonia	18.24
10	Oman	17.09

Source: World Population Review (2024).

change such as rising air and water temperature, water scarcity, desertification, and so on. These climate change effects increase perpetuates the increasing trend of their energy consumption which is already much higher than world average.

It can be noted here that residential use is one of the main drivers of increasing consumption of energy-rich MENA countries with air cooling accounting for about 70% of residential and commercial electricity demand (Hafner et al., 2023). A vicious circle is thus created where climate change increases energy consumption and vice versa. Similar is the case with water. Though the MENA region is endowed with half of world's crude oil and natural gas, the region has as little as 1% share in global freshwater resources resulting in demand for water desalinization projects which is energy intensive. Climate change reduces water supply, increases demand for desalinization and thus another vicious circle is created. A World Bank (2022) study found that increasing water scarcity owing to climate change may reduce MENA region's GDP by 6–14%.

Outside MENA, coal-rich countries of the OIC, for example, Indonesia in the Southeast Asia and Kazakhstan in Central Asia suffer from dilemma similar to the MENA region. They need to extract and use coal but at the same time coal is negatively affecting them through climate change impacts.

4. Renewable Energy in the OIC: Targets and Achievements

With growing social awareness about climate change and amidst constant calls for decarbonization, the past decade saw an increasing number of countries having formulated their renewable energy policies and announcing their targets regarding renewable energy while revising it time to time. This section will discuss the renewable energy commitments of the OIC members and will try to evaluate their implementation.

Out of 57 OIC member countries, 47 have specific targets for renewable energy either in terms of energy or power or both, though only 24, mostly countries with low fossil fuel endowments, have net zero target. The OIC lags behind in terms of legislations regarding renewable energy. Only 17 OIC countries have feed in tariff policy and 15 have net metering policy. Eighteen countries have declared financial incentives for renewables in the form of public investment, loans, grants, capital subsidies, or rebates (REN21, 2023).

Table 9.5 presents the renewable energy targets of the OIC countries along with their achievements. The renewable energy targets largely resemble the difference which is observed among OIC member states in terms of energy mix. The renewable energy target of the hydrocarbon-rich countries in MENA and other regions, for example, Qatar, Bahrain, Brunei and Kazakhstan is suggestive of their hesitant approach toward energy transition which is also reflected in their mix. In comparison, countries with modest to poor endowment of traditional energy resources are more assertive in their renewable energy targets. The Sub-Saharan countries, the most energy poor ones in the OIC, have set the most ambitious renewable energy targets.

Among all the geographical groups within the OIC, the Central Asian countries are ahead of others in producing renewable energy. As mentioned in the

Table 9.5. Renewable Energy Targets and Achievements of the OIC Countries.

Region	Country	Renewable Energy Target	Share of Renewables in Energy Mix, 2021	Share of Renewables in Electricity Generation, 2021	Electricity Consumption (kWh/capita), 2017
EU and Central Asia	Albania	N/A	43%	100%	2,309
	Azerbaijan	20% by 2020	0%	5%	2,202
	Kazakhstan	3% by 2020	1%	12%	5,600
	Kyrgyzstan	N/A	53%	90%	1,941
	Tajikistan	N/A	41%	90%	1,480
	Turkey	30% by 2023	15.3%	36%	2,855
	Turkmenistan	N/A	0%		2,679
Southeast Asia	Brunei	10% by 2035	0%	0.1%	10,243
	Indonesia	26% by 2025	12%	8%	812
	Malaysia	9% by 2020	3%	17%	4,596
Middle East and North Africa	Algeria	27% by 2023	0%		1,356
	Bahrain	5% by 2030	0%		19,592
	Egypt	20% by 2022	Less than 1%	8%	1,658
	Iraq	10% by 2025	1%	6%	1,306
	Iran	N/A	0.5%	6%	2,986
	Jordan	N/A	8%	23%	1,888

(*Continued*)

Table 9.5. (*Continued*)

Region	Country	Renewable Energy Target	Share of Renewables in Energy Mix, 2021	Share of Renewables in Electricity Generation, 2021	Electricity Consumption (kWh/capita), 2017
	Kuwait	N/A	0%	0%	15,213
	Lebanon	12% by 2020	Less than 1%	9%	2,893
	Libya	10% by 2025	0%	0%	1,857
	Morocco	52% by 2039	3%	18%	901
	Oman	N/A	Less than 1%	3.5%	6,554
	Qatar	2% by 2020	0%	0%	15,309
	Saudi Arabia	59 GW by 2030	0%	0%	9,444
	Sudan	20% by 2030	4.5%	62%	190
	Syria	N/A	0.7%	4.5%	950
	Tunisia	30% by 2030	Less than 1%	6%	1,444
	UAE	7% by 2020	Less than 1%	4.5%	11,264
South Asia	Afghanistan	100% by 2050	Less than 1%	20%	78
	Maldives	16% by 2017	0.5%	6%	711
	Bangladesh	10% by 2020	Less than 1%	4%	310
	Pakistan	N/A	1.5%	27.7%	471
Sub-Saharan Africa	Benin	N/A	Less than 1%	1.5%	100
	Burkina Faso	100% by 2050	Less than 1%	10%	42
	Cameroon	N/A	20%	62%	281

Comoros	N/A	Imported heavy oil and biomass		49
Djibouti	35% by 2035	Less than 1%	35%	373
Gambia	35% by	Less than 1%	2%	111
Gabon	80% by 2025	Less than 1%	42%	1,173
Ivory Coast	42% by 2020	Less than 1%	23%	276
Mali	25% by 2033	3%	60%	29
Mozambique	N/A	12%	82%	463
Niger	100% by 2050	Less than 1%	3.5%	51
Nigeria	10% by 2020	0%	0%	144
Senegal	20% by 2017	1.5%	14.8%	223
Sierra Leone	33% by 2020	Less than 1%	72%	24
Somalia	N/A	Less than 1%	11%	
Togo	15% by 2020	Less than 1%	27%	153
Uganda	61% by 2017	2%	90%	61

Source: Compiled by the authors from IRENA, IEA, & REN21 (2018).

previous section, Central Asia has immense hydro potential and the countries of this region are already utilizing their hydro potential, as is evident from Table 9.5. Upstream Central Asian countries such as Kyrgyzstan, Tajikistan, and Albania already produce 90–100% of their electricity from hydro power and renewables contribute 40–50% of their energy mix. Their hydropower facilities, however, are built long ago and hence face difficulties to address modern day challenges. Climate change is also affecting the hydropower generation through reducing water flows. The hydro potential of the two hydrocarbon-rich countries of this region – Azerbaijan and Kazakhstan remain mostly untapped. Turkey, with its modest energy endowment has shown success in diversifying its energy mix which includes coal, gas, and oil on one hand and a variety of renewable technologies such as wind, solar, and geothermal on the other hand.

Among the Southeast Asian countries of the OIC, Indonesia leads in renewable energy achievement though it is also the largest user of coal in this group. Among the OIC countries, Indonesia has the largest capacity for geothermal energy which amounts to 1,640 MW. Malaysia, on the other hand, is the third largest assembler of solar modules in the world after China and Taiwan though the country itself lag behinds in harnessing its solar potential (Khan, 2018).

Despite their promising potential for renewable energy in general and solar energy in particular, initially MENA region has been quite slow in development of renewable energy. For example, in 2013 more solar power plants were built in Slovenia than in all the countries of the Middle East combined (Middle East Solar Industry Association, 2015). From 2006 to 2013, only 70 MW of solar PV projects were awarded in the MENA region compared with the global installed capacity of 139 GW (REN21, 2014). The scenario, however, improved to some extent in the last decade with the region's installed capacity of 32 GW by 2023 (Middle East Solar Industry Association, 2024).

Within MENA, the three hydrocarbon poor countries of MENA, namely Jordan, Lebanon, and Morocco have shown greater success in overcoming the barrier of low resource endowment using renewable energy sources. Morocco is a pioneer of wind energy in this region while Jordan and Lebanon focus on solar energy. Egypt also harness wind energy. On the other hand, the hydrocarbon-rich countries of this region clearly lag behind in terms of motivation, commitment, and implementation regarding renewable energy. Among the hydrocarbon-rich countries, at one end of the spectrum stand Qatar, Kuwait, Oman and Bahrain who have so far shown reluctance to energy transition. On the other end, there is the UAE which has shown its enthusiasm toward renewable energy by hosting the headquarter of IRENA and by making considerable investment in R&D for renewable technology. Algeria, Tunisia, and Saudi Arabia stand in the middle with lukewarm motivation for energy transition.

Despite sluggish progress of the hydrocarbon-rich MENA countries, the rapidly evolving regulatory framework of those countries are expected to create a more favorable environment for renewable energy investments (Keulertz et al., 2016). In recent years, government-backed tenders have resulted in some of the world's most cost-effective projects in the MENA region for solar and wind with record low prices in Morocco and the UAE. Saudi Arabia saw a 1.5 GW solar project operational in 2024 while the UAE is expecting a total of 1 GW solar projects to be operationalized soon.

The South Asian members of the OIC lag behind in terms of both energy production and utilization of renewable energy sources. Afghanistan and Pakistan have untapped hydro potential. While Pakistan is already using hydro energy and is trying to yield more, being devastated by war, Afghanistan remains to be energy poor with its vast potential of hydro energy. Bangladesh is increasing its production of solar power and is taking endeavors to utilize its wind potential overcoming the problem of land scarcity.

The Sub-Saharan countries are the most energy poor countries of the world. Some Sub-Saharan members of the OIC, namely Sierra Leon, Niger, Mali, Comoros, and Burkina Faso consume as less as 25–50 kWh of electricity per person where the world average in 3,144 kWh/capita. Though the electricity generation mix of many Sub-Saharan countries, for example, Uganda, Sierra Lion, Mali, Cameroon, and Mozambique shows renewable share to an extent as high as 60–90%, most of which are hydroelectricity; the picture would not be encouraging if one takes into account the level of electricity consumption in these countries which are below 100 kWh/capita. The vast solar potential of the Sub-Saharan region thus has remained untapped.

To summarize, there is great diversity among the OIC members both at regional and individual state level in terms of motivation, commitment and implementation of renewable energy development. Despite their moderate to huge potential for renewable energy, very few could make progress toward fulfilling their renewable energy targets. Like in other parts of the world, hydro has been the main source of renewable energy in the OIC though in recent years, modern renewable technologies such as solar PV, solar CSP, wind, and geothermal have penetrated in the OIC countries.

5. Energy Transition in the OIC: Challenges and Concerns

The set of challenges involved in the process of energy transition is bound to be different for energy-rich and -poor countries. As Ansari and Holz (2020) observes: "It is crucial to accept that the transformation of resource-rich economies is entirely different from greening a resource importer." This section attempts to identify the barriers of energy transition in the OIC taking into account the differences between the resource-rich and -poor countries in this regard.

5.1. Economic Dependence on Fossil Fuel Rent

Economic dependence of countries on fossil fuel acts as the largest challenge for energy transition in MENA region and beyond. Historically, in these countries, hydrocarbon endowment played a crucial role in ensuring socio-economic growth, shaping the political economy and sometimes consolidating their governance. For MENA countries, studies have found causal relationship between energy consumption and economic growth (Sopian et al., 2011; Taşdemiroğlu, 1989; Usama, 2011). Usama (2011), for example, found a bi-directional Granger causality between oil consumption, CO_2 emission, and economic growth in the MENA region over the period.

The impact of resource dependency in resource-rich countries has been widely discussed by scholars. The negative consequences of resource dependency such as de-industrialization, real exchange rate overvaluations, volatile macroeconomic indicators, and institutional have been summarized under the term "resource curse" (Collier & Hoeffler, 2005; Ross, 1999; van der Ploeg, 2011). To avoid resource curse, the energy-rich countries of MENA have long been putting the diversification agenda as a policy priority, though with little success so far (Alsharif et al., 2017). Saudi Arabia, for example, has issued 10 development plans since 1970 with economic diversification as a key objective (Albassam, 2015). Even in recent years, in the wake of the Arab Spring, most of the energy-rich MENA countries – Saudi Arabia, Kuwait, Oman, Qatar, Bahrain, and the UAE – further adopted long-term plans termed as "National Visions" with special focus on diversification of economy (Ferdousi, 2019). However, as Figs. 9.7 and 9.8 show, with the exception of the UAE and Qatar, the energy-rich MENA countries are far away from economic diversification.

The economies of the hydrocarbon-rich countries of the OIC, both in and outside MENA region, for example, Azerbaijan and Kazakhstan from Central Asia, Nigeria and Mozambique from Sub-Saharan Africa, and Brunei from Southeast Asia can be characterized by heavy resource dependence. From Fig. 9.7, one can see that for many hydrocarbon-rich MENA countries, oil and gas rent still constitute 20–40% of GDP. Fig. 9.8 shows that out of top 10 countries most dependent on fossil fuel for export, six are from the OIC for all of whom fossil fuel constitutes more than 85% of their merchandise export.

In many of the MENA energy-rich countries, established industries such as petrochemicals, steel, and aluminum are energy intensive in nature, which add to these countries' dependence on fossil fuel. Also, in these countries, government spending acts as an engine of growth (El-Katiri, 2016). Given that their

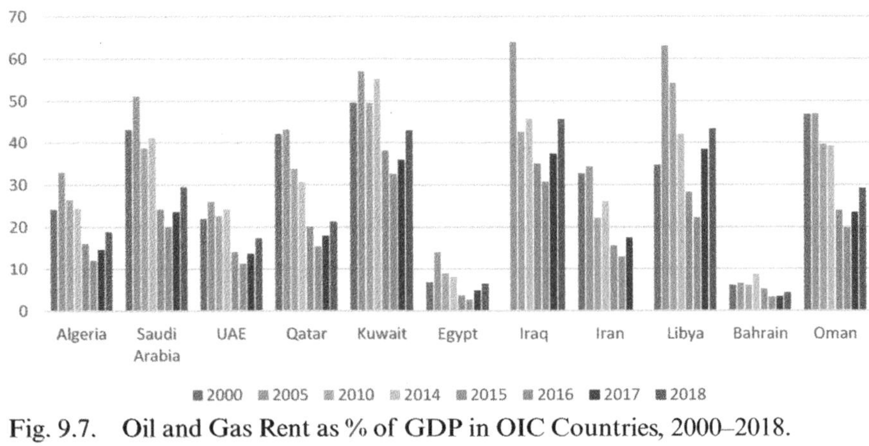

Fig. 9.7. Oil and Gas Rent as % of GDP in OIC Countries, 2000–2018.
Source: Hafner et al. (2023).

governments' income depends heavily on fossil fuel rent, the whole growth process of these countries is thus tied to the fossil fuel industry. Energy transition thus imply loss to the countries currently enjoying resource rent, the extent of loss being determined by the level of dependence of the economy on fossil fuel.

Even countries with modest endowment of fossil fuel are at the risk of losing since resource rents finance a range of their essential expenditure. The development plans of such middle- and low-income countries for example, Angola, Cameroon, Kazakhstan, Mozambique, and Uganda – often rely on resource rent for investment in health, education, and infrastructure development. Energy transition would incur loss to these countries also.

From the previous discussion, it is clear that the hydrocarbon-rich countries of the OIC, in MENA region and beyond, stand to lose a significant share of their revenue directly impacting their GDP. While stranded asset is their major concern in the process of energy transition, the heavy dependence of their economies on fossil fuel revenue resulting from lack of economic diversification makes them more vulnerable. This sense of vulnerability make the major hydrocarbon-rich countries of the OIC reluctant toward energy transition which acts as the most formidable barrier of energy transition in the OIC.

5.2. Distribution of Fossil Fuel Rent and Socio-political Compulsions

Hydrocarbon-rich countries often use public job as a means of distributing a part of resource rent with a view to maintaining stability of the regime. Particularly MENA region is the home to some of the largest public sectors in the world. As can be seen from Fig. 9.9, public sector accounts for 25% of the total employment

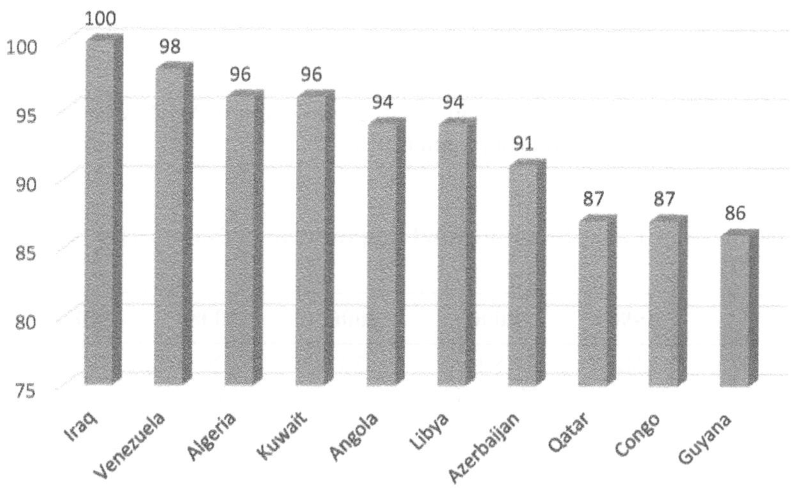

Fig. 9.8. Share of Fossil Fuel in Total Merchandise Export, Top 10 Countries in the World. *Source*: World Bank, available at https://data.worldbank.org/indicator/TX.VAL.FUEL.ZS.UN.

in Egypt while the share in Algeria, Saudi Arabia, and Jordan are 30%, 38%, and 40%, respectively. Share of public sector is even higher if only nationals are considered (see Table 9.6). As Table 9.6 shows, the government is the largest employer of nationals in a number of MENA energy-rich countries. Despite a declining trend, 62–78% of the nationals of Saudi Arabia, Kuwait, and Qatar are still employed by the government.

Economic dependence of resource-rich countries on resource rents (fossil fuel in this case) are often intertwined with their political dependence on it. Existing literature suggests that the provision of public sector employment in resource-rich countries is a central component of social contract between the rulers and the ruled. In the case of MENA region, regimes in power provide jobs and subsidized services and commodities to the nationals in return for their consent or sometimes, political quiescence (Amin et al., 2012; Assaad, 2014; Desai et al., 2009).

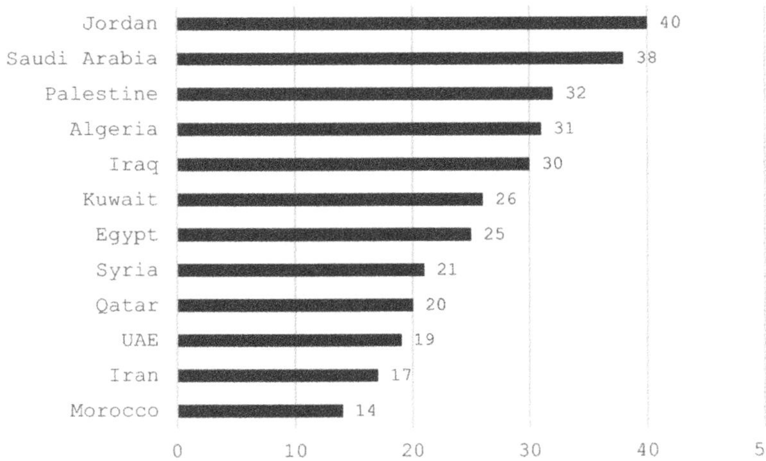

Fig. 9.9. Share of Public Sector (%) in Total Employment in MENA Countries in the 2000s. *Source*: Assaad and Barsoum (2019).

Table 9.6. Share of Public Sector in Total Employment of Nationals in OIC Countries, 2017.

Country	1990	2000	2006	2008	2017
Bahrain	68	80	38	29	
Kuwait	42	75	87	86	78
Oman	76		50	47	
Saudi Arabia	70	82	73	72	63
Qatar			89	88	62

Sources: Baldwin-Edwards (2011) and Tagliapietra (2017).

Such provision of public sectors jobs have resulted in labor market segmentation in the hydrocarbon-rich MENA countries, where the public sector jobs are characterized by higher wages often not complying with the level of productivity (World Economic Forum, 2014). By distorting the incentive structure of labor market, the segmented labor market leads to low labor productivity and inhibits economic diversification (Hertog, 2013, 2014). Furthermore, the large public sector creates pressure on fiscal stability and budgetary sustainability (World Bank, 2016). The fact that despite the productivity loss and fiscal burden, hydrocarbon-rich MENA countries are continuing the path of provision of protected public sector jobs, is reflective of the socio-political compulsions over these countries which is further intensified by the bargaining youth unemployment with which they are struggling particularly since the Arab Spring. This socio-political compulsions further tie these countries to fossil fuel rent since it remains to be the main source of income for them.

It can be mentioned here that though the issue of public jobs in more debated and intricate in MENA region, hydrocarbon-rich member countries of the OIC in other regions also suffer from the problem of outsized public sector. Examples include Kazakhstan in Central Asia and Brunei in Southeast Asia and Nigeria in Sub-Saharan Africa. In Kazakhstan and Brunei, the share of public sector in total employment is 37% and 47%, respectively while in Nigeria, the government is the biggest employer of wage labor. In all three countries, the huge public sector employment is backed up by the fossil fuel revenue (Federal Republic of Nigeria, 2017; OECD, 2018; Our World in Data, 2020). Though their political stake in maintaining the large public sector is not as high as their MENA counterparts, the issue still bears economic and political significance for them given the sheer size of employment share of public sector.

5.3. The Economics and Politics of Energy Subsidy

The second most used way of distribution of resource rent by resource-rich countries is energy subsidy. It is also the second most important component of social contract in these countries. Nowhere in the world the energy subsidy is as pervasive as it is in the MENA region, the GCC countries in particular (see Fig. 9.10). In five GCC countries – Saudia Arabia, Kuwait, Qatar, the UAE, and Bahrain – per capita fossil fuel subsidy falls in the range of USD 1,138 to USD 2,535. The amount is several times higher if compared to other OIC countries (USD 250–650) as well as to other fossil fuel countries outside the OIC, for example, Russia (USD 200), the US (USD 28), Australia (USD 359), and even Venezuella (USD 744).

Like large public sector, pervasive energy subsidy has long been an issue of policy debate in the MENA region. There has been growing realization that spending 5–10% or more of GDP for fossil fuel subsidy is neither viable nor sustainable. The realization was further strengthened by the fall in oil prices in 2014 whereafter countries undertook various energy reform measures including cutting fossil fuel subsidies. Some subsidy reform targeted specific energy sources for example, petroleum in the UAE. Egypt reduced level of energy subsidy and substituted energy subsidy with food subsidies and cash transfer (Breisinger et al., 2019). The

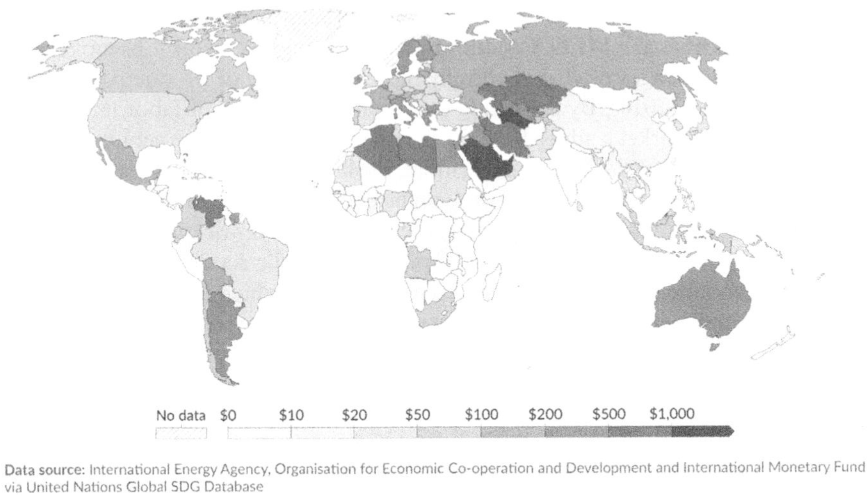

Fig. 9.10. Per Capita Fossil Fuel Subsidy by Country (USD). *Source*: Our World in Data, based on IEA, OECD.

most comprehensive energy reform was undertaken by Iran who replaced energy subsidy with universal cash transfer (EL Katiri & Fattouh, 2015). Nevertheless, the fossil fuel-rich MENA countries still have a long way to go as is evident from Fig. 9.11. They have been taking a cautious approach toward curtail of energy subsidy due to its probable political implications.

However, in the OIC, energy subsidy is not practiced in the MENA region alone. Rather, as Fig. 9.11 shows, as a whole the OIC countries are disproportionately ahead of others in terms of fossil fuel subsidy. Out of top 25 countries in terms of amount of fossil fuel subsidies, 18 are from the OIC. Of the 18 OIC countries in the list, 9 are from MENA region, 4 from Central Asia, 2 from Southeast Asia, 2 from South Asia, and 1 is from Sub-Saharan Africa. It is interesting to note that besides the fossil fuel-rich countries, some countries with modest (Uzbekistan, Indonesia, Malaysia, and Egypt) or even low fossil fuel endowment (Bangladesh and Pakistan) have also been included in the list which suggests that energy subsidy is not a function of resource endowment only, it is also a matter of policy choice.

For fossil fuel exporting countries, energy subsidy has several significant drawbacks. Subsidized domestic price implies less revenue for the government. Moreover, subsidized price leads to wasteful domestic demand for energy, create stress on export quantity and causes harmful effect on environment (Coady et al., 2019). For energy net importers, on the other hand, energy subsidy means fiscal pressure. Some effects of energy subsidy, however, is common for both net energy importer and exporter. Energy subsidy creates distortion in the energy market by interfering with price signal of energy resources leading to inefficient allocation of resources and holding back the competitiveness of renewable energy superficially. The widespread practice of energy subsidy among the OIC member states acts as an obstacle to energy transition. Governments often find reforming or abolishing subsidies challenging since it involves significant economic and political stakes.

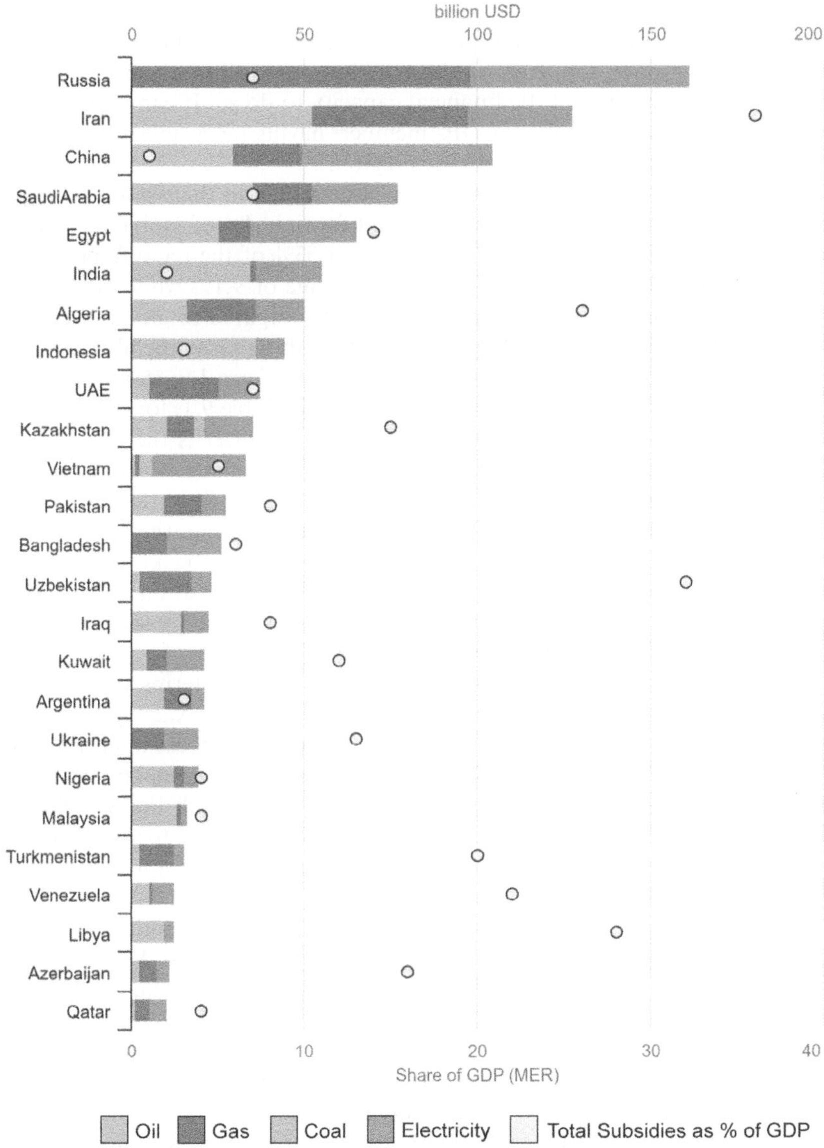

Fig. 9.11. Value of Fossil Fuel Subsidies by Fuel in the Top 25 Countries, 2022. *Source*: IEA, available at https://www.iea.org/data-and-statistics/charts/value-of-fossil-fuel-subsidies-by-fuel-in-the-top-25-countries-2022.

5.4. Investment Gap

Being the energy poor region of the OIC, the Sub-Saharan member states face a different set of challenges in energy transition as compared to their energy-rich counterparts. In fact, the challenges of the former mirror that of the latter. While the energy-rich countries, with no significant financial barrier, lack in motivation for renewable energy out of multiple economic, social, and political considerations, the energy-poor countries of the OIC have the full motivation to deploy renewable energy but have little financial capacity to do so. It can be mentioned here that of the limited number of OIC members having renewable related regulations, most are from Sub-Saharan Africa region.

Sub-Saharan Africa is the most energy-poor region in the world. With their 13% share in global population, they account for only 4% of global energy consumption (World Energy Council, 2017). About 53% of the region's population lacks access to electricity against the global average of 9.1% while only 82% of its population lacks access to clean cooking fuel compared to global average of 4% (World Bank, 2020; UNCTAD, 2023). Some Sub-Saharan member countries of OIC, for example, Burkina Faso, Mali, Uganda, Sierra Lione, and Comoros consume less than 100 kWh per capita. As shown in Table 9.1, for most of these energy-poor countries of Sub-Saharan Africa, hydropower is the major source of electricity production. For some countries such as Uganda, Sierra Lione, and Mozambique, share of hydroelectricity is as high as 70–90%. Due to climate change induced reduction in water flow, these countries are at the risk of reduction of their hydropower production capacity. Amidst this background, for the energy-poor Sub-Saharan members of the OIC, energy transition is more about supplying adequate energy for the people and ensuring energy security for the country; instead of replacing one energy source with another.

Though the Sub-Saharan countries are energy poor in terms of traditional energy resources, for renewable energy sources, the scenario is exact opposite. With 60% of the world's most suitable locations for solar energy, these countries boost in energy potential. The region is also rich in wind and geothermal potential. But harnessing this vast potential requires huge investment which the Sub-Saharan countries seriously lack in. According to an UNFCCC estimate, to avoid the worst impacts of climate change about USD 125 trillion of direct capital investments will be needed globally of which USD 1.7 trillion (5.3%) will be needed in Sub-Saharan Africa. This implies an annual investment of USD 170 billion per year, an amount equal to the total GDP of the region in 2020 (Bourne & Wallace, 2022).

Realizing this huge amount will require increasing concessional funding from both government and development partners as well as mobilizing private capital. Moreover, to create a sustainable long-term source of finance, domestic financial systems also needs to be strengthened. However, in reality energy investment has been declining in Africa and in 2022 energy investment in the continent stood at USD 90 billion, less than half of what is required for ensuring sustainable energy for Africa. Clean energy investment was even lower – 25 billion which comprises only 2% of global investment in clean energy.

An examination of recent trends in energy financing in Africa reveals significant challenges for the sector in terms of external funding (International Energy Agency, 2022). The amount of concessional funds is not increasing in Africa and whatever fund is being provided, the share of energy in such funding continues to be low at 6% of the total flow. This is true for the international climate change finance under UNFCCC too. The picture is not encouraging in the case of foreign direct investment (FDI) either. FDI flow to Africa has been volatile over recent years and the during the Covid-19 pandemic it fell to a 15-year low level of USD 40 billion. Though the flow rebounded later, excluding South Africa, inflows are still nearly 20% lower than the level of 2015.

Though Sub-Saharan Africa receives most attention in the discussion on energy investment, investment gap is a major hurdle for OIC members in all regions – South Asia, Southeast Asia, and even in MENA. For example, the comparatively energy-rich MENA region will require a 10-fold investment in energy sector than today to meet the clean energy target which amounts to USD 70 billion annually (Yilmaz et al., 2022). This is because though the operation cost of renewable energy has become lower than fossil fuel due to technological advancement, its upfront cost is higher than the latter.

Besides insufficient flow of external funds, the energy-poor countries of the OIC suffer from some common internal bottlenecks which prevent them from harnessing the existing available fund. These include lack of capacity in project development, lack of appropriate legislations and infrastructure and undevelopment domestic financial market. For some countries higher cost of capital for utility-scale projects and macroeconomic instability owing to increasing indebtness created further hurdles which discourage investment.

6. Scopes for Cooperation

The OIC, as discussed above, is a set of heterogenous countries not only in terms of geography, fossil fuel and renewable energy endowment, level of economic development, and socio-economic and political structure, but also in terms of motivation toward and preparedness for renewable energy too. At one end, there are countries who are poor in terms of fossil fuel endowment, are eager for deploying renewable energy but lack in financial and other capacity. At the other end, there are countries rich in fossil fuel and have the financial capacity for energy transition but lacks in motivation. These differences among countries imply that there are good chance for cooperation for energy transition among the OIC members themselves.

Particularly, the hydrocarbon-rich MENA countries, the most reluctant cohort of the OIC toward energy transition, have the potential for becoming the drivers of energy transition. Having some of the world's largest sovereign wealth funds, they can play a role to meet the investment gap. In terms of financing renewable energy projects, sovereign wealth funds have an advantage over private equity firms or corporate investors in the sense that unlike private finance these funds are not under pressure to deliver fast returns (World Economic Forum, 2023). In fact, some sovereign wealth funds are already engaged in low-carbon technologies. Also, the hydrocarbon-rich countries already have energy trade-related soft and hard infrastructures which might be utilized.

Some of the OIC countries, particularly those with modest endowment of fossil fuel, have already made some progress in harnessing renewable energy. The UAE and Malaysia, for example, enjoy some technological edge in renewable energy while Morocco has gained expertise in attracting FDI in renewable energy sector. Thus there exits some room for exchange of technology and expertise within the OIC.

The best technology exchange options, however, involves trans-regional cooperation, for example between the OIC countries and Europe who mirror each other in terms of technology and renewable resource endowment. Back in 2008, an initiative called the Mediterranean Solar Plan was taken by MENA countries and Europe which aimed at addressing the technology and investment gap in the MENA region where, in exchange, the European counterparts were hoping for renewable electricity import from MENA region. However, the Plan could not be materialized due to lack of political endorsement (Elfving, 2016). Later, in the wake of the Russia–Ukraine war, which exposed the vulnerability of Europe stemming from overdependence on Russia for energy supply, there was a renewed attempt by the EU to partnering with the MENA countries for deploying renewable energy which has been reflected in their new agenda "Renewed partnership with the Southern Neighbourhood" adopted in 2021. The renewed cooperation with MENA in renewable energy is expected to be included in the EU's Global Gateway initiative (Hafner, 2022). The EU has also expressed interest to invest in renewable energy sector of South and Southeast Asia under its Global Gateway initiative.

Multilateral institutions like the World Bank, the International Monetary Fund (IMF), the Arab Fund for Economic and Social Development, the African Development Bank, and the Islamic Development Bank can play an active role in supporting the energy transition of the OIC countries not only by increasing financing of renewable energy projects and helping countries to mobilize private sector investment but also by helping countries to formulate strategies so as to enabling them balance between energy transition and development priorities and supporting them in their initiatives for reforming energy sector including market structure and regulations (Arezki & Mazarei, 2023).

7. Conclusion

Energy transition is going to have a deep impact on global trade regime, economic architecture as well on geopolitics. No countries can avoid the impact of energy transition in the coming future be it energy rich or energy poor in the existing energy architecture. It is in this context that the present chapter examines the situation of OIC member countries in terms of their potentials and achievements, with a view to identify the challenges and the scopes for cooperation.

Though the OIC is home to some of the largest oil and gas reserves, it is not a club of hydrocarbon-rich countries. Rather, there is considerable disparity among OIC members with regard to energy resource endowment. The differences in energy resource endowment of various geographical groups of the OIC member states are reflected in their energy production capacity and energy mix. Middle East depends more on natural gas and oil and Southeast Asia and EU-Central Asia cluster have higher share of coal while the energy-poor OIC members of Sub-Saharan Africa and other regions largely depend on biomass for energy supply. On the other hand, countries less endowed with fossil fuel make more use of renewable energy sources for electricity generation.

For their geographic location, the MENA and Sub-Saharan Africa have tremendous potential of solar energy. The potential for wind is particularly high in Mediterranean countries. In terms of hydro energy, Central Asia enjoys to have some of the greatest potential in the world. Some of the geographical clusters of the OIC, namely the Southeast Asia and EU-Central Asia has a good potential of geothermal and some countries in these regions have already started utilizing this resource.

For the fossil fuel-rich OIC members, the foremost concern is stranded asset is expected to act as the strongest motivation for energy transition, though there is debate on the role of fear of stranded asset on energy transition. The reluctance of the fossil fuel-rich OIC countries in general and MENA countries in particular, supports the argument that at least in the short run, abundance of fossil fuel may slow down the growth of renewable energy in the OIC.

For OIC member countries which are comparatively less endowed with fossil fuels, reducing import dependence for energy acts as the main driver for energy transition which not only drains out their valuable foreign exchanges but also expose them to the volatility of energy market.

Among the external drivers of energy transition in the OIC, the most important is the pressure coming from emerging global climate change regime characterized by the Paris Agreement. Some of the OIC members are in the list of top CO_2 emitters. On the other hand, in all member states – energy-rich and energy-poor – climate change itself act as an internal driver.

The renewable energy targets of the OIC countries largely resemble the difference which is observed among OIC member states in terms of energy mix. Hydrocarbon rich countries show a hesitant approach toward energy transition. In comparison, countries with modest to poor endowment of traditional energy resources are more assertive in their renewable energy targets.

Despite their promising potential for renewable energy in general and solar energy in particular, MENA region has been slow in development of renewable energy. Within MENA, the three hydrocarbon-poor countries of MENA, namely Jordan, Lebanon, and Morocco, have shown greater success. There is great diversity among the OIC members both at regional and individual state level in terms of motivation, commitment, and implementation of renewable energy development.

Hydrocarbon-rich countries of the OIC, in MENA region and beyond, stand to lose a significant share of their revenue directly impacting their GDP. Heavy dependence of their economies on fossil fuel revenue resulting from lack of economic diversification, make them more vulnerable. Economic dependence of resource-rich countries on resource rents (fossil fuel in this case) are often intertwined with their political dependence on it. In the case of MENA region, regimes in power provide jobs and subsidized services and commodities to the nationals in return for their consent. Such provision of public sectors jobs have resulted in labor market segmentation which in turn leads to low labor productivity and inhibits economic diversification

The second most used way of distribution of resource rent by resource-rich countries is energy subsidy. It is also the second most important component of social contract in these countries. However, in the OIC, energy subsidy is widely practiced in the MENA region and beyond. Some countries with modest or even low fossil fuel endowment provide significant amount of energy subsidy. The widespread practice of energy subsidy among the OIC member states acts as an obstacle to energy transition. Governments often find reforming or abolishing subsidies challenging since it involves significant economic and political stakes.

Though the Sub-Saharan countries are energy poor in terms of traditional energy resources, the region is rich in solar, wind, and geothermal potential. But to harness this vast potential, the region will require USD 170 billion annually. Realizing this huge amount will require increasing concessional funding from both government and development partners as well as mobilizing private capital. Moreover, to create a sustainable long-term source of finance, domestic financial systems also needs to be strengthened.

There are good chances for cooperation for energy transition among the OIC members themselves. Particularly, the hydrocarbon-rich MENA countries, the most reluctant cohort of the OIC toward energy transition, have the potential for becoming the drivers of energy transition. Having some of the world's largest sovereign wealth funds, they can play a role to meet the investment gap.

The best technology exchange options, however, involve trans-regional cooperation, for example, between the OIC countries and Europe who mirror each other in terms of technology and renewable resource endowment. Finally, multilateral institutions like the World Bank, the IMF, and the African Development Bank can play an active role in supporting the energy transition of the OIC countries not only by increasing financing of renewable energy projects and helping countries to overcome the existing challenge.

References

Albassam, B. A. (2015). Economic diversification in Saudi Arabia: Myth or reality?. *Resources Policy*, *44*, 112–117.

Al-Shalabi, A., Cottret, N., & Menichetti, E. (2014). EU-GCC cooperation on energy. In S. Colombo (Ed.), *Bridging the Gulf: EU-GCC relations at a crossroads*. IAI Research Papers. https://www.files.ethz.ch/isn/182093/iairp_14.pdf

Alsharif, N., Bhattacharyya, S., & Intartaglia, M. (2017). Economic diversification in resource rich countries: History, state of knowledge and research agenda. *Resources Policy*, *52*, 154–164.

Amin, M., Assaad, R., Al-Baharna, N., Dervis, K., Desai, R. M., Dhillon, N. S., Galal, A., Ghanem, H., & Graham, C. (2012). *After the spring: Economic transitions in the Arab world*. Oxford University Press.

Ansari, D., & Holz, F. (2020). Between stranded assets and green transformation: Fossil-fuel-producing developing countries towards 2055. *World Development*, *130*, 1–17.

Arezki, R., & Mazarei, A. (2023). *MENA and the global energy conundrum* [Policy Paper 283]. Center for Global Development. https://www.cgdev.org/sites/default/files/mena-and-global-energy-conundrum.pdf

Arezki, R., & Obstfeld, M. (2015, December 3). *The price of oil and the price of carbon*. iMFdirect, December 2 and VoxEU.org. https://www.imf.org/en/Blogs/Articles/2015/12/02/the-price-of-oil-and-the-price-of-carbon.

Assaad, R. (2014). Making sense of Arab labor markets: The enduring legacy of dualism. *IZA Journal of Labor and Development*, *3*, 6.

Assaad, R., & Barsoum, G. (2019). *Public employment in the Middle East and North Africa: Does a changing public sector workforce in the MENA region provide an opportunity for efficient restructuring?* IZA World of Labor. https://wol.iza.org/uploads/articles/500/pdfs/public-employment-in-the-middle-east-and-north-africa.pdf?v=1

Baldwin-Edwards, M. (2011). *Labour immigration and labour markets in the GCC countries: National patterns and trends* (Number 15). The London School of Economics and Political Science, Global Governance, London, UK.

Bourne, K., & Wallace, G. (2022, June). Financing Sub-Saharan Africa's energy transition. *ESG and Climate Research*. Issue 38. https://www.spglobal.com/esg/insights/topics/financing-sub-saharan-africa-s-energy-transition

Breisinger, C., Mukashov, A., Raouf, M., & Wiebelt, M. (2019, June). Energy subsidy reform for growth and equity in Egypt: The approach matters. *Energy Policy*, *129*, 661–671.

Coady, D., Parry, I., Le, N-P., & Shang, B. (2019, May). *Global fossil fuel subsidies remain large: An update based on country-level estimates* [IMF Working Paper, Vol. 2019(089)]. https://www.imf.org/en/Publications/WP/Issues/2019/05/02/Global-Fossil-Fuel-Subsidies-Remain-Large-An-Update-Based-on-Country-Level-Estimates-46509

Collier, P., & Hoeffler, A. (2005). Resource rents, governance, and conflict. *Journal of Conflict Resolution*, *49*(4), 625–633.

Desai, R. M., Olofsgard, A., & Yousef, T. M. (2009). The logic of authoritarian bargains. *Economics & Politics*, *21*(1), 93–125.

El-Katiri, L. (2016, December). *Vulnerability, resilience and reform: The GCC and the oil price crisis 2014–2016*. Center on Global Energy Policy, Columbia University.

El Katiri, L., & Fattouh, B. (2015). A brief political economy of energy subsidies in the Middle East and North Africa Oxford Institute of Energy Studies. *OIES Paper MEP*, *11*, 1–21.

Elfving, S. (2016). Prospective governance and legal framework between the EU and MENA in renewable energy cooperation. *Renewable Energy Law and Policy Review*, *7*(2), 157–171.

Federal Republic of Nigeria. (2017). *National employment policy*. https://webapps.ilo.org/static/english/emplab/download/nep/nigeria/nigeria_national_employment_policy_2017.pdf

Ferdousi, B. (2019). Localization of jobs in the GCC region: Implications for Bangladesh. *BIISS Journal*, *40*(1), 41–66.

Gallagher, K. S., & Winter, D. (2013). Why and how governments support renewable energy. *The Alternative Energy Future*, *142*(1), 59–77.

Hafner, M. (2022). EU energy policy and the MENA region in the wake of Russia's invasion of Ukraine. In V. Talbot (Ed.), *Energy politics in the MENA region from hydrocarbons to renewables?* (pp. 13–34). ISPI.

Hafner, M., Raimondi, P. P., & Bonometti, B. (2023). *The energy sector and energy geopolitics in the MENA region at a crossroad towards a great transformation?* Spriner Nature Switzerland.

Haktanır, H. (2004). The state of energy in the OIC member countries. *Journal of Economic Cooperation*, *25*(2), 1–74.

Hertog, S. (2013). *The private sector and reform in the Gulf Cooperation Council, LSE Kuwait Programme on development, governance and globalisation in the Gulf States*. The London School of Economics and Political Science.

Hertog, S. (2014). *Arab Gulf states: An assessment of nationalisation policies* [Gulf Labour Markets and Migration programme (GLMM) Research Paper 1]. https://eprints.lse.ac.uk/57578/1/__lse.ac.uk_storage_LIBRARY_Secondary_libfile_shared_repository_Content_Hertog%2C%20S_Hertog_Arab_Gulf_States_Hertog_Arab_Gulf_States_2014.pdf

International Energy Agency (IEA). (2022). *Africa energy outlook*. International Energy Agency. https://iea.blob.core.windows.net/assets/220b2862-33a6-47bd-81e9-00e586f4d384/AfricaEnergyOutlook2022.pdf

International Energy Agency (IEA). (2023). *CO2 emissions in 2022*. https://iea.blob.core.windows.net/assets/3c8fa115-35c4-4474-b237-1b00424c8844/CO2Emissionsin2022.pdf

International Energy Agency (IEA), & International Renewable Energy Agency (IRENA). (2017). *Perspectives for the energy transition: Investment needs for a low-carbon energy system*. International Energy Agency (IEA), & International Renewable Energy Agency (IRENA). https://www.irena.org/-/media/Files/IRENA/Agency/Publication/2017/Mar/Perspectives_for_the_Energy_Transition_2017.pdf

International Renewable Energy Agency (IRENA). (2019). *A new world: The geopolitics of the energy transformation*. https://www.irena.org/-/media/files/irena/agency/publication/2019/jan/global_commission_geopolitics_new_world_2019.pdf

IRENA, IEA, & REN21. (2018). *Renewable energy policies in a time of transition*. IRENA, OECD/IEA and REN21, 1–112. https://www.irena.org/-/media/Files/IRENA/Agency/Publication/2018/Apr/IRENA_IEA_REN21_Policies_2018.pdf?rev=72587b606dc442bd8c8b4f74e0f4a574

Khan, S. H., & Akram, M. H. (2018). *Renewable energy profile of OIC countries*. OIC and COMSTECH.

Keulertz, M., Mulligan, M., Woertz, E., Menichetti, E., & Biscop, S. (2016, December). *Material factors for the Mena region: Data sources, trends and drivers*. Middle East and North Africa Regional Architecture (MENARA).

McGlade, C.E., & Ekins, P. (2015). The geographical distribution of fossil fuel unused when limiting global warming to 2°C. *Nature*, *517*, 187–190.

Menichetti, E., & Gharras, A. E. (2017). *How can renewable energy help contribute to the development of the Mena countries?* Middle East and North Africa Regional Architecture.

Mercure, J.-F., Pollitt, H., Viñuales, J. E., Edwards, J. R., Holden, P. B., Chewpreecha, U., Salas, P., Sognnaes, I., Lam, A., & Knobloch, F. (2018). Macroeconomic impact of stranded fossil fuel assets. *Nature Climate Change*, *8*, 588–593. https://doi.org/10.1038/s41558-018-0182-1

Middle East Solar Industry Association (MESIA). (2015, January). *MENA solar outlook 2015, Dubai*. http://www.mesia.com/wp-content/uploads/Mesia-Rev3-5.pdf

Middle East Solar Industry Association (MESIA). (2024). *MENA solar outlook 2024, Dubai*. https://files.constantcontact.com/23ca2798201/a6c2c264-73e6-4202-a3ee-9d08de8b9a82.pdf

OECD. (2018). *SME policy index: ASEAN 2018*. https://www.oecd-ilibrary.org/sites/9789264305328-16-en/index.html?itemId=/content/component/9789264305328-16-en#:~:text=A%20substantial%20share%20of%20the,IMF%2C%202016%5B4%5D.

O'Sullivan, M., Overland, I., & Sandalow, D. (2017). *The geopolitics of renewable energy* [Working Paper Rwp17-027]. Center on Global Energy Policy, Columbia University. https://www.hks.harvard.edu/publications/geopolitics-renewable-energy

Our World in Data. (2020). *Public sector employment as a share of total employment*. https://ourworldindata.org/grapher/public-sector-employment-as-a-share-of-total-employment

REN21. (2014). *Renewables 2014 global status report*. REN21 Secretariat. http://www.ren21.net/GSR-2014-Report-Full-report-EN

REN21. (2023). *Renewables 2023 global status report*. https://www.ren21.net/wp-content/uploads/2019/05/GSR2023_GlobalOverview_Full_Report_with_endnotes_web.pdf

Ross, M. L. (1999). The political economy of the resource curse. *World Politics*, *51*(2), 297–322.

Sopian, K., Ali, B., & Asim, N. (2011). Strategies for renewable energy applications in the organization of Islamic conference (OIC) countries. *Renewable and Sustainable Energy Reviews*, *15*, 4706–4725.

Taşdemiroğlu, T. (1989). The energy situation in OIC countries: The possible contribution of renewable energy resources. *Energy Policy*, *17*(6), 577–590.

Tagliapietra, S. (2017). *The political economy of Middle East and North Africa oil exporters in times of global decarbonization* [Bruegel Working Paper, Issue 05]. https://www.bruegel.org/system/files/wp_attachments/WP-2017_05.pdf

United Nations Conference on Trade and Development (UNCTAD). (2023). *Commodities at a glance*. Special issue on access to energy in sub-Saharan Africa. United Nations. https://unctad.org/system/files/official-document/ditccom2023d1_en.pdf

Usama, A. (2011). Oil consumption, CO_2 emission and economic growth in MENA countries. *Energy*, *36*(10), 6165–6171.

van der Ploeg, F. (2011, June). Natural resources: Curse or blessing? *Journal of Economic Literature, American Economic Association*, *49*(2), 366–420.

Welsby, D., Price, J., Pye, S., & Ekins, P. (2021, September). Unextractable fossil fuels in a 1.5°C world. *Nature*, *597*, 230–240.

World Bank. (2016). *Middle East and North Africa public employment and governance in MENA*. World Bank.

World Bank. (2020). *Diversification and cooperation in a decarbonizing world. Climate-strategies for fossil-fuel dependent countries*. World Bank Group. https://documents1.worldbank.org/curated/en/469241593746087038/pdf/Diversification-and-Cooperation-in-a-Decarbonizing-World-Climate-Strategies-of-Fossil-Fuel-Dependent-Countries.pdf

World Bank. (2022, January 25). *Middle East & North Africa climate roadmap (2021–2025). Driving transformational climate action and green recovery in MENA*. The World Bank. https://thedocs.worldbank.org/en/doc/6f868d4a875db3ef23ef1dc747fcf2ca-0280012022/original/MENA-Roadmap-Final-01-20.pdf

World Economic Forum. (2014). *Rethinking Arab employment – A systemic approach for resource-endowed economies*. World Economic Forum. https://www3.weforum.org/docs/WEF_MENA14_RethinkingArabEmployment.pdf.

World Economic Forum. (2023). *How MENA can play a pivotal role in the global energy transition*. https://www.weforum.org/agenda/2023/11/mena-energy-transition-solar-renewables/

World Energy Council. (2017). *World energy scenario 2017: Regional perspective for Sub-Saharan Africa*. World Energy Council. https://www.worldenergy.org/assets/downloads/Scenarios_Regional-Perspective-for-Sub-Saharan-Africa-1.pdf

World Population Review. (2024). *CO_2 emissions by country 2024*. https://worldpopulationreview.com/country-rankings/co2-emissions-by-country

Yilmaz, F., Alswaina, F., Belaid, F., Hejazi, M., Luomi, M., & Soummane, S. (2022). *Closing the investment gap to close Paris agreement goals*. King Abdullah Petroleum Studies and Research Center.

Zandi, M. (2023). *Central Asia's clean energy opportunity: Hydropower energy source*. Atlantic Council.

Chapter 10

Renewable Energy Investments: Azerbaijan's Cooperation with the Islamic World

Vusala Jafarova

Center for Analysis of Economic Reforms and Communication of Azerbaijan, Azerbaijan

1. Introduction

Azerbaijan's strategic position as a crossroads between East and West has made it a focal point of energy development. While traditionally known for its oil and gas reserves, Azerbaijan has been increasingly focusing on renewable energy, aligning with global trends toward sustainability. The country's cooperation with the Islamic world has played a critical role in advancing its renewable energy sector. This chapter explores Azerbaijan's renewable energy investments in partnership with Islamic countries, focusing on data-driven insights to showcase the extent of these collaborations.

Azerbaijan has set ambitious goals to increase the share of renewable energy in its energy mix. Renewable energy sources accounted for around 17% of the country's total energy generation in 2022, with significant contributions from hydropower, wind, and solar energy (Ministry of Energy of Azerbaijan, 2023). The government aims to increase this to 30% by 2030, reflecting the national commitment to the Paris Agreement and the Sustainable Development Goals (SDGs). The overall installed capacity for renewable energy sources in Azerbaijan is about 1,280 MW, primarily from hydropower plants, with a strategic focus on expanding wind and solar energy generation.

Azerbaijan, rich in petroleum, aims to harness the Caspian Sea's renewable energy to meet domestic needs and become a green energy exporter. Over the next decades, the country plans to develop renewable energy sources to serve both domestic demand and the European market. As part of this, Azerbaijan will partner internationally to install a 4-GW power cable across the Black Sea. These initiatives would support economic sustainability, reduce carbon emissions, and offer regional and global benefits. This manuscript explores the political,

The Economic Potential of Islamic Countries, Part A:
Economics, Demographics and Financial Services, 243–259

doi:10.1108/978-1-83708-000-720251012

economic, sociocultural, and environmental impacts of Azerbaijan's shift to wind energy, including its effects on neighboring countries (Gasimli et al., 2024a).

2. Key Partners in the Islamic World

Azerbaijan's cooperation with various Islamic countries has been essential in accelerating its renewable energy development. Countries such as the United Arab Emirates (UAE), Saudi Arabia, and Turkiye have emerged as key investors in Azerbaijan's renewable energy projects. Notably, the UAE-based *Masdar* and Saudi *ACWA Power* are leading players in Azerbaijan's renewable energy landscape.

In 2020, *Masdar*, one of the largest renewable energy companies in the Middle East, signed a framework agreement with the Azerbaijani government to develop solar and wind energy projects with a total capacity of 400 MW. This includes a significant 230 MW solar project and a 240 MW wind energy project in the Gobustan region. The projects are expected to generate 1 billion kWh of electricity annually, contributing to the reduction of approximately 400,000 tons of CO_2 emissions annually (Masdar, 2020).

Saudi Arabia's *ACWA Power* signed an agreement with Azerbaijan in 2021 to develop a 240-MW wind farm, one of the largest wind energy projects in the Caspian region. This project is expected to produce around 1 billion kWh of electricity annually and reduce CO_2 emissions by 400,000 tons, aligning with Azerbaijan's green energy transition goals. The project also highlights Saudi Arabia's commitment to diversifying its investments beyond oil and gas, focusing on sustainability and clean energy (ACWA Power, 2021).

3. Benefits of Islamic World Cooperation

The cooperation between Azerbaijan and Islamic countries in renewable energy brings several benefits:

Technological transfer and expertise: Azerbaijan has benefited from the technological expertise and advanced renewable energy solutions provided by companies like *Masdar* and *ACWA Power*. This has enabled the country to fast-track its renewable energy projects.

Economic diversification: Azerbaijan's reliance on oil and gas has been a concern for long-term economic sustainability. Investment from Islamic countries is helping Azerbaijan diversify its economy by focusing on clean energy.

Climate goals alignment: The renewable energy investments align with Azerbaijan's commitment to reducing its carbon footprint in accordance with the Paris Agreement. The reduction of CO_2 emissions from wind and solar projects is crucial to achieving these targets (UNFCCC, 2022).

Energy security: The expansion of renewable energy contributes to Azerbaijan's energy security, reducing its reliance on hydrocarbon exports and improving resilience against global oil price volatility.

Looking ahead, Azerbaijan plans to further strengthen its renewable energy partnerships with Islamic countries. The Ministry of Energy has set a target to attract $2 billion in investments by 2030 for renewable projects. This will include offshore wind energy development, where the Caspian Sea's wind potential is estimated to be around 157 GW (World Bank, 2022).

Additionally, Azerbaijan is exploring opportunities to export green electricity to neighboring Islamic countries through interconnected grids, potentially becoming a regional energy hub for clean energy in the South Caucasus.

Azerbaijan's collaboration with the Islamic world in the renewable energy sector has proven to be a pivotal driver of its transition toward sustainability. Strategic partnerships with countries like the UAE, Saudi Arabia, and Turkiye have facilitated significant investments in wind, solar, and hydropower projects, contributing to both Azerbaijan's energy security and its climate goals. The future looks promising, with further investments expected to solidify Azerbaijan's position as a leader in renewable energy in the region.

Azerbaijan, a country rich in fossil fuel resources, has been progressively shifting its focus toward renewable energy in response to global sustainability trends and the need for diversified economic growth. This shift is significantly bolstered by Azerbaijan's strategic partnerships with countries within the Islamic world, fostering collaborative efforts in renewable energy investments.

Azerbaijan's geographical location offers substantial potential for renewable energy sources, particularly solar, wind, and hydroelectric power. The government has outlined ambitious plans to increase the share of renewable energy in its energy mix, aiming to reduce dependence on oil and gas. This transition aligns with Azerbaijan's commitments to international environmental agreements and the broader goals of sustainable development.

Azerbaijan's cooperation with Islamic countries in renewable energy is facilitated through bilateral and multilateral platforms, including the Organization of Islamic Cooperation (OIC) and the Islamic Development Bank (IDB). These collaborations are crucial in leveraging financial, technical, and knowledge-sharing resources to advance renewable energy projects.

Islamic countries, many of which are part of regions particularly vulnerable to the impacts of climate change, have been increasingly active in addressing global climate challenges. These nations have committed to climate action through various international agreements, most notably the Paris Agreement, aiming to mitigate their carbon emissions and adapt to the changing climate. This chapter examines the specific climate change commitments of key Islamic countries, their strategies to reduce greenhouse gas emissions, and their progress toward a sustainable future.

4. Climate Commitments in Islamic Countries

Saudi Arabia, the largest oil producer in the world, has recognized the need to transition toward more sustainable energy sources. Under its *Vision 2030* plan, Saudi Arabia aims to diversify its economy and reduce its dependence on oil.

The country's *Saudi Green Initiative* sets ambitious targets (Saudi Green Initiative, 2021). These include:

- Achieving *net-zero carbon emissions by 2060*.
- Planting *10 billion trees* domestically and contributing to the planting of 50 billion trees across the Middle East, in collaboration with neighboring countries.
- Generating *50% of its electricity from renewable energy sources* by 2030, with major investments in solar and wind energy projects. One of the flagship projects is *NEOM*, a futuristic city powered entirely by renewable energy.

The UAE has been a leader in the region's clean energy transition and climate commitments. It is the first country in the Gulf to set a net-zero target (UAE Ministry of Climate Change and Environment, 2022). The UAE has pledged to achieve *net-zero emissions by 2050*. Key actions include:

- The UAE's energy mix is projected to include *44% clean energy* by 2050.
- The country is investing heavily in solar energy, including the development of the world's largest single-site solar park, *Mohammed bin Rashid Al Maktoum Solar Park*, with a planned capacity of 5,000 MW by 2030.
- Hosting the *COP28* in 2023 further highlights the UAE's leadership role in climate diplomacy.

Turkiye has ramped up its climate action in recent years, ratifying the Paris Agreement in 2021. As part of its Nationally Determined Contributions (NDCs) (Ministry of Environment and Urbanization of Turkiye, 2021), Turkiye has committed to:

- Reducing *up to 21%* of its greenhouse gas emissions from business-as-usual levels by 2030.
- Increasing the share of renewable energy in its electricity production to *38% by 2030*, with a focus on solar and wind power.
- Expanding its *afforestation projects* to absorb carbon and counteract land degradation.

Indonesia, the largest economy in Southeast Asia, is one of the most vulnerable countries to the impacts of climate change due to its large population and extensive coastlines. Indonesia's climate commitments include:

- Achieving *net-zero emissions by 2060* or sooner, contingent on international support.
- Aiming to reduce greenhouse gas emissions by *29% by 2030*, and up to 41% with international aid.
- Halting deforestation and increasing the use of renewable energy, with a target of *23% renewables* in its energy mix by 2025.
- Indonesia has also launched a carbon trading scheme to incentivize emission reductions.

Morocco has been a pioneer in renewable energy in the Islamic world and is considered one of the most proactive countries in climate action (Moroccan Agency for Sustainable Energy (MASEN), 2022).

The country's climate commitments include:

- Aiming for *52% of its electricity generation to come from renewable sources* by 2030, a target it is on track to achieve.
- Developing the world's largest concentrated solar power plant, the *Noor Ouarzazate Solar Complex*, with a total installed capacity of 580 MW.
- Morocco's NDCs aim to reduce greenhouse gas emissions by *45.5% by 2030*, conditional on receiving international financial and technical support.

Qatar, a leading natural gas exporter, is also moving toward a more sustainable energy future while managing its carbon footprint. The country's key climate actions include:

- Committing to reduce greenhouse gas emissions by *25% by 2030* (Government of Qatar, 2023).
- Investing in *carbon capture and storage (CCS)* technologies to mitigate emissions from its gas operations.
- Expanding its renewable energy capacity, with a focus on solar power, including the development of the *800 MW Al Kharsaah Solar Plant.*

Egypt's updated NDCs aim to reduce greenhouse gas emissions by 33% in the electricity sector, 65% in the oil and gas sector, and 7% in the transport sector by 2030 compared to the business-as-usual scenario. Egypt is heavily investing in renewable energy projects, such as the Benban Solar Park, one of the largest solar installations in the world (United Nations Framework Convention on Climate Change [UNFCCC], 2023).

Malaysia's Renewable Energy Targets aim to increase the share of renewable energy in its installed capacity to 31% by 2025 and 40% by 2035. Malaysia has pledged to reduce its greenhouse gas emissions intensity of GDP by 45% by 2030 relative to the 2005 level (Sustainable Energy Development Authority (SEDA) Malaysia, 2021).

Pakistan's Clean Green Pakistan initiative aims to plant 10 billion trees by 2023 and promotes renewable energy projects. Pakistan has committed to reducing its projected greenhouse gas emissions by 20% by 2030, subject to the availability of international financial support (IDB, 2023).

Uzbekistan has made history by becoming the first country in the world to receive a payment for reducing carbon emissions as a result of policy change pursuant to Article 6 of the Paris Accord, under the iCRAFT Project. Uzbekistan is the first country to receive The World Bank carbon funds after cutting emissions through a policy crediting program. Pioneer iCRAFT Project is supporting the Government to improve Energy Efficiency, phase out subsidies, and access carbon markets (World Bank, 2023).

The World Bank's Transformative Carbon Asset Facility rewarded Uzbekistan with a $7.5 million grant for successfully cutting 500,000 tons of carbon emissions under the iCRAFT Project. These emission reductions were independently verified. The above-mentioned payment is the first of several anticipated payments under the iCRAFT Project. Uzbekistan could receive up to $20 million in grants for verified emission reductions or carbon credits generated through its energy subsidy reforms. The country aims to reduce 60 million tons of CO_2 through the Project, with the iCRAFT set to purchase approximately 2.5 million tons of CO_2. It will have the opportunity to sell the remaining carbon credits on international carbon markets, using the systems and processes established by the iCRAFT Project (World Bank, 2024, June 21).

Islamic countries are making significant strides in addressing climate change through various commitments and initiatives. These efforts include ambitious targets for reducing greenhouse gas emissions, increasing the share of renewable energy, and achieving net-zero emissions by specific target years. By implementing these strategies, these countries are contributing to global efforts to combat climate change and transition to sustainable energy systems.

5. Islamic Countries' Role in Global Climate Agreements

Islamic countries, many of which are members of the *OIC*, have collectively emphasized the importance of global climate cooperation. The OIC has established a framework to encourage member states to integrate climate resilience into their development agendas. Key milestones include the following:

Almost all Islamic countries are signatories to the Paris Agreement, committing to keep global warming below 2°C and to pursue efforts to limit it to 1.5°C. The agreement also underscores the principle of "common but differentiated responsibilities," acknowledging that while all nations must act, developed countries bear a greater responsibility for historical emissions.

Islamic countries have developed *NDCs* outlining their plans to reduce emissions and adapt to climate impacts. These NDCs vary widely based on each country's level of economic development, energy dependence, and vulnerability to climate change.

Islamic countries have adopted various adaptation and mitigation strategies to cope with the effects of climate change. These include renewable energy investments, afforestation and reforestation, water conservation, and carbon markets.

Many Islamic countries are investing in renewable energy to diversify their energy sources. Solar, wind, and hydropower projects have received significant attention in Saudi Arabia, the UAE, and Morocco. Afforestation projects, such as Saudi Arabia's ambitious tree-planting initiative, are helping to combat desertification and absorb CO_2 from the atmosphere. Countries in the Middle East and North Africa (MENA) region, such as Egypt and Jordan, are focusing on improving water management systems, particularly as water scarcity becomes an increasingly severe issue due to climate change. Countries like Indonesia are exploring carbon trading schemes to reduce emissions and attract investment for green projects. Carbon pricing mechanisms are seen as a way to incentivize emission reductions in sectors such as energy, manufacturing, and forestry (Government of Indonesia, 2022).

Islamic countries face unique challenges in addressing climate change. These include:

- *Economic diversification*: For fossil fuel-dependent economies such as Saudi Arabia, the UAE, and Qatar, transitioning away from hydrocarbons presents both a challenge and an opportunity. The shift to renewable energy is essential for long-term economic sustainability.
- *Vulnerability to climate impacts*: Many Islamic countries are highly vulnerable to climate-related disasters such as droughts, floods, and rising sea levels. Countries like Bangladesh, Indonesia, and Pakistan are already experiencing the severe consequences of climate change, including displacement and loss of livelihoods.
- *Financing*: Achieving climate goals requires substantial financial resources. Many Islamic countries have called for increased financial support from developed nations to assist with their adaptation and mitigation efforts, in line with the commitments made under the Paris Agreement.

Islamic countries are increasingly taking significant steps to address climate change, reflecting their growing recognition of the existential threat it poses. Through ambitious renewable energy projects, afforestation initiatives, and international cooperation, countries like Saudi Arabia, the UAE, and Morocco are setting an example of how nations can transition to sustainable development pathways. However, the path ahead is complex, and substantial investment, technology transfer, and global cooperation will be critical to ensuring that these countries meet their climate targets.

In addition to large-scale solar parks, Masdar is involved in smaller, distributed solar projects across Azerbaijan. These initiatives aim to add a combined capacity of 100 MW, generating approximately 150 GWh of electricity annually, and reducing CO_2 emissions by 75,000 tons per year.

Masdar and Azerbaijani institutions have established joint innovation centers focused on developing cutting-edge renewable energy technologies. These centers aim to advance research in areas such as photovoltaic efficiency, solar panel durability, and energy storage solutions. The collaboration between Masdar and Azerbaijan includes significant technology transfer initiatives. These involve sharing expertise in solar technology design, installation, and maintenance, which helps build local capacity and expertise. Azerbaijani engineers and technicians have access to advanced training programs and workshops conducted by Masdar's experts.

Capacity building is a crucial component of the partnership. Masdar has initiated several training programs aimed at enhancing the skills of Azerbaijani professionals in the renewable energy sector. Over 400 local engineers and technicians have participated in these programs, gaining valuable knowledge and experience in the latest renewable energy technologies and practices.

The strategic partnership between Azerbaijan and the UAE, particularly through Masdar, has a profound impact on the renewable energy landscape in

Azerbaijan. These collaborations are essential for achieving Azerbaijan's renewable energy targets, which include increasing the share of renewables in the energy mix to 30% by 2030. The projects facilitated by Masdar are expected to reduce Azerbaijan's carbon emissions by millions of tons over the coming decades.

The future prospects of this partnership are highly promising. Continuous investments in renewable energy infrastructure, combined with ongoing research and development efforts, will play a vital role in advancing the energy transition in Azerbaijan. The partnership also serves as a model for international cooperation in renewable energy, demonstrating how collaborative efforts can drive significant progress toward a sustainable energy future.

By leveraging the expertise and resources of Masdar, Azerbaijan is well-positioned to accelerate its adoption of renewable energy, enhance energy security, and contribute to global efforts to combat climate change. This partnership highlights the potential for mutually beneficial collaborations between countries in the pursuit of SDGs.

Investments in renewable energy are transforming Azerbaijan's economic landscape. The development of green energy infrastructure generates employment opportunities, stimulates technological advancements, and attracts foreign direct investment. Moreover, the environmental benefits contribute to improved public health and a reduction in carbon emissions, aligning with global sustainability goals.

Despite the progress, challenges such as regulatory hurdles, limited local expertise, and the need for substantial capital investment persist. However, the strong foundation of cooperation with Islamic countries provides a robust framework to overcome these challenges. Future prospects include expanding renewable energy capacity, enhancing grid infrastructure, and fostering regional energy integration.

6. Renewable Energy Potential for Azerbaijan

Azerbaijan possesses significant potential for renewable energy development, particularly in solar, wind, and hydroelectric power. The country's diverse geography offers ample opportunities for harnessing these resources:

Solar energy: With an average of over 2,400 hours of sunshine annually, Azerbaijan has substantial potential for solar energy generation. The Absheron Peninsula, in particular, is well-suited for large-scale solar power projects.

Wind energy: The coastal areas along the Caspian Sea and the mountainous regions of Azerbaijan experience strong and consistent winds, making them ideal for wind energy production. The government has identified several key sites for wind farm development.

Hydroelectric power: Azerbaijan has a number of rivers and water bodies that are suitable for hydroelectric power generation. Small and medium-sized hydropower plants are being developed to tap into this renewable resource, contributing to the country's energy mix.

Government Initiatives and Policies: The Azerbaijani government has implemented various initiatives and policies to promote renewable energy development. Key measures include:

Legislative framework: The government has established a supportive legislative and regulatory framework to attract investment in the renewable energy sector. This includes laws and regulations that provide incentives for renewable energy projects, such as tax exemptions, feed-in tariffs, and streamlined permitting processes.

In 2016, Azerbaijan has developed strategic roadmaps outlining its vision for renewable energy development. The "Strategic Roadmap for the Development of Utilities (Electricity and Thermal Energy, Water and Gas Supply)" sets specific targets for increasing the share of renewables in the energy mix and identifies priority projects and investment opportunities. Azerbaijan actively engages in international cooperation to advance its renewable energy goals. This includes partnerships with international organizations, financial institutions, and other countries to access funding, technology, and expertise.

Azerbaijan's 2022–2026 socio-economic development strategy emphasizes a robust commitment to addressing climate change through a comprehensive set of targets and initiatives. The strategy outlines ambitious goals to reduce greenhouse gas emissions, enhance energy efficiency, and increase the use of renewable energy sources. Key measures include the development of sustainable infrastructure, the promotion of green technologies, and the implementation of policies that foster environmental resilience. Azerbaijan aims to integrate climate action into its broader economic planning, ensuring that economic growth is aligned with environmental sustainability. This holistic approach not only supports the country's international climate commitments but also promotes long-term socio-economic development by reducing vulnerability to climate-related risks and enhancing the overall quality of life for its citizens. The strategy reflects Azerbaijan's proactive stance in contributing to global climate change mitigation efforts while pursuing a sustainable and resilient economic future.

7. Baku Energy Week: Important Event in Region's Energy Sector

Baku, which has become one of the main cities where international level forums are held, has traditionally hosted the Baku Energy Week for several years. Baku Energy Week, which is an important event in the region's energy field, is held every year on June 4–6. The last Baku Energy Week held in 2024 combined three prestigious events: the 29th International Caspian Oil and Gas Exhibition – "Caspian Oil & Gas," the 12th Caspian International Energy and Green Energy Exhibition – "Caspian Power" and the 29th Baku Energy Forum.

The main topic of discussion is that Azerbaijan, the initiator and participant of large-scale energy projects, has an important role in this field. About 300 companies from 37 countries participated in the Baku Energy Week, a platform where global issues in the field of energy are discussed. In addition to Azerbaijan, the United States, Germany, Australia, Austria, Belarus, Belgium, Bahrain, UAE, Bulgaria, Great Britain, Czech Republic, China, Algeria, Finland, France, Georgia, India, Iraq, Israel, Sweden, Italy, Latvia participated in the event. Kazakhstan,

Qatar, Hungary, Monaco, Netherlands, Norway, Uzbekistan, Romania, Russian Federation, Saudi Arabia, Slovenia, Turkiye, Ukraine, Sweden, India, Slovenia, and Japan participated.

The event is traditionally attended by heads of related state structures, companies operating in the energy field, and heads of diplomatic missions of foreign countries in Azerbaijan.

The main oil and gas projects of the Caspian region and energy security in the region were discussed at the "Caspian Oil & Gas" exhibition, and the important sections covered by the exhibition include development of oil and gas deposits, oil and gas transportation and production, telecommunications and IT, oil and gas processing, construction in the energy sector, installation work, innovative technologies, etc. Innovations related to artificial intelligence, drilling field, as well as production and storage of oil and non-gas products were also presented at the exhibition.

At the Caspian International Energy and Green Energy "Caspian Power" exhibition, innovations in the field of development and use of energy and renewable energy sources of international and local companies and related proposals were on the agenda. Products and services in solar energy, wind energy, geothermal energy, thermal energy, nuclear energy, engineering and energy equipment, electric vehicles and electric cars, energy and resource-saving technologies and other sectors, as well as new projects were displayed at the exhibition.

Energy issues important to both Azerbaijan and the Caspian region were discussed at the Baku Energy Forum, and more than 600 participants (including local participants) participated in the Forum. At the event, international cooperation on energy security and sustainability, green energy potential in the Caspian region.

8. Role of Azerbaijan in Energy Security as Tradition Energy Supplier

8.1. Southern Gas Corridor

Carried out under the initiative and leadership of Azerbaijan, it contributes to the strengthening of Europe's energy security by delivering Azerbaijani gas to European markets. With the "Southern Gas Corridor" project, Azerbaijan exports the gas it produces to neighboring countries, and new pipelines have been built to start exporting to the European market. Today, by supplying oil and gas resources, Azerbaijan plays a decisive role not only in the region, but also in ensuring the energy security of the European Union (EU). The importance of the "Shah Deniz" field in the implementation of these projects is very great. "Shahdeniz" field has been making important contributions to ensuring the energy security of Azerbaijan and Europe for many years. The "Shahdeniz" field, located in the Azerbaijani sector of the Caspian Sea, was discovered in 1999. Located 70 kilometers southeast of Baku, on the shelf of the Caspian Sea, where the water depth varies between 50 and 500 meters, this field is one of the largest gas-condensate fields in the world. The discovery of the "Shah Deniz" field and the successful implementation of the "Shah Deniz" gas project have recognized Azerbaijan as a country that exports gas to the world.

8.2. Heydar Aliyev, the Visionary Architect Behind the Integration of Caspian Energy Resources into the Global Market

Back in July 1999, during his speech at the presentation ceremony of the results achieved in the field, Great Leader Heydar Aliyev called the "Shah Deniz" field a world important field and declared how important it is for Azerbaijan:

> We knew the potential of the "Shah Deniz" field. Therefore, we signed a contract based on this field and we knew that we would get good results from it (Aliev, (2005). They were all predictions. But now it seems that these predictions were reasonable and correct. This shows how high-level knowledge Azerbaijani oil-men, scientists, and geologists have, that they make predictions in such conditions, and this prediction is confirmed in excess. I once again thank our scientists, oil workers, geologists who discovered the "Shah Deniz" field and all other fields in the Caspian Sea, both those who passed away and those who are alive today, all Azerbaijani oil workers. "Shah Deniz" field has a long history. The information given by the president of the "Shahdeniz" consortium and other speakers makes us very happy and I believe that this will become a big event on a world scale. If the president of the "Shahdeniz" consortium raises the issue of exporting the produced gas to the world markets and shows the appropriate route for this, it means that the achieved achievement is so fundamental that this achievement is not only counted in numbers, but probably more than that, because the world in order to export gas, there should be enough gas, that is, there is as much gas in the "Shahdeniz" field as it is said, and maybe more than it is said. This is the most gratifying thing.

8.3. Shahdeniz Gas Reserve

The confirmed reserve of the Shah Deniz field consists of 1 trillion cubic meters of gas and 240 million tons of condensate. This is about 50% of Azerbaijan's gas potential. With the commissioning of the "Shahdeniz" field, Azerbaijan became a potential gas exporter in the world, and an opportunity was created for the gasification of the country's industry. In the past, Azerbaijan has acquired areas that create added value in the industry, such as methanol, carbamide, as well as a number of gas-chemical plants. Today, Azerbaijan has the world's longest energy corridor for the export of Shah Deniz gas. Currently, the 3,500-km Southern Gas Corridor stretches from Baku to Italy and connects Azerbaijan directly with the EU. This has greatly strengthened the position of our country as a reliable energy partner. The "Shah Deniz" project has greatly accelerated the flow of foreign capital to our country.

8.4. Oil and Gas Pipelines from the Caspian to the EU

In order to create the infrastructure for the export of Azerbaijani gas to the EU market, several main projects have been implemented. In 2007, the "Baku-Tbilisi-Erzurum" gas pipeline (South Caucasus gas pipeline) was put into operation, and the gas produced within the first stage of the "Shah Deniz" field began to be exported to Georgia, Turkiye, and Greece. In 2012, the TANAP (Trans-Anatolian natural gas pipeline) project was signed between Azerbaijan and Turkiye in Istanbul at the initiative of the President of Azerbaijan Ilham Aliyev and the (then) Prime Minister of Turkiye Recep Tayyip Erdogan. In 2013, the "Shahdeniz" consortium agreed on the TAP (Trans-Adriatic natural gas pipeline) project connecting the border of Turkiye with the south of Italy to deliver Azerbaijani gas to the European market through the TANAP pipeline, and the construction of the pipeline was completed in 2020. These projects enabled the realization of the "Southern Gas Corridor" project by connecting the "Shahdeniz" field to the south of Italy. The Southern Gas Corridor, which is already operating at full capacity, is an important and large energy infrastructure that became a reality as a result of the initiative of Azerbaijan, the political will and determination of the President of Azerbaijan and made serious changes to the energy map of Europe.

Azerbaijan currently exports its natural gas to nine countries. If in 2021, Azerbaijan exported 8 billion cubic meters of gas to Europe, this year this figure is expected to increase to 12 billion. By the end of 2027, it is planned to transport 20 billion cubic meters of gas to the EU alone. The existence of this plan is a manifestation of the positive prospects of Azerbaijan's gas export. Azerbaijan is also strengthening its positions in the field of alternative energy resources.

In general, Azerbaijan is one of the countries with high potential for renewable energy sources. Thus, the technical potential of renewable energy sources of our country is 135 GW on land and 157 GW at sea (Gasimli et al., 2024b).

The foundation of a 240 MW solar power plant will be laid by BP this year in Jabrayl. Negotiations were also held for the construction of solar power plants with "Nobel Energy" in Jabrayl, and with a Chinese company in Fuzuli. The first floating solar plant in the country was installed on the 100 kW pilot project in Buyukshor Lake.

9. Green Energy Projects of Azerbaijan in Liberated Territories

Last year, substations and hydropower plants built in 12 regions in the territories freed from occupation were inaugurated. With the participation of President Ilham Aliyev, the 330-kilovolt "Jabrayil" junction substation, built within the framework of the Azerbaijan–Turkiye–Europe international energy corridor project, was put into operation. Also, in accordance with the green energy strategy, in 2023, in Kalbajar region, 8.33 MW Chirag-1, 3.6 MW Chirag-2, 6.33 MW Qamishli, 5.3 MW Soyugbulag" and 3.4 MW "Meydan" small hydropower plants were opened after reconstruction. In parallel, the 110 kilovolt "Gorchu" substation and the "Lachin" city junction substation, which were newly built in Lachin by "AzerEnergy," were inaugurated last year. Besides, the 8.25 MW "Mishni" and 6 MW "Alkhasli" small hydroelectric power stations reconstructed in Lachin district were reconstructed and put into operation. President Ilham Aliyev also participated in the opening of the newly built 10.5 MW "Jahangirbeyli" Hydropower Station of "AzerEnergy." Also, in December of last year, the 110 kilovolt "Aghdam" junction substation was inaugurated. The construction of nine power plants of "AzerEnergy" has started in the territories freed from occupation last year, and currently, including those nine plants, the construction of hydroelectric power plants that will produce ecologically clean green energy in 12 places in Karabakh and Eastern Zangezur continues, and work has been completed on several of them.

In addition, by the end of 2027, it is planned to prepare the State Program for strengthening the electricity network to ensure the integration of 1,862 MW of "green power" into the country's energy system. At the same time, intensive work is being done to create the "Caspian-EU green energy corridor" and Azerbaijan–Turkiye–Europe corridor and to export about 5 GW of green electricity through diversified routes by 2030. Corresponding steps are being taken in the direction of the technical and economic justification of the corridor starting from the Caspian Sea, passing through the Black Sea, Romania, Hungary and Bulgaria, and establishing a Joint Enterprise. Also, the initiative to export electricity from Central Asia to our country and from here to Europe is being evaluated between Azerbaijan, Uzbekistan, Kazakhstan and Turkmenistan. Here we witness another wise approach of Ilham Aliyev. This means that the development of energy resources and their export to world markets should be carried out together. Thanks to this kind of approach, the energy map in Eurasia is continuously being drawn up through Azerbaijan. In general, it is planned to gradually create 7 GW of production capacity by 2030. Depending on export requirements, this volume may increase significantly by 2037.

Additionally, the 9th meeting of ministers within the framework of the Southern Gas Corridor Consultative Council took place in Baku on February 3 last year. For the first time, the 1st meeting of ministers was also held under the newly established Green Energy Consultative Council. This highlights Azerbaijan's commitment to expanding its role in the global energy transition. Furthermore, the President of Azerbaijan declared the country's liberated territories as a designated green energy zone, with an action plan for 2022–2026 already approved. The ultimate goal is to transform these areas into "Net Zero Emission" zones by 2050 (President of the Republic of Azerbaijan, 2024).

10. Future of Renewable Energy

The economic implications of climate change are broad and far-reaching. Climate-related shocks, including extreme weather events like floods, droughts, and heatwaves threaten the stability of both developed and developing economies. According to the World Bank (2020), climate-related disruptions could push up to 100 million people into extreme poverty by 2030, predominantly affecting low- and middle-income countries, which often lack the infrastructure or financial capacity to cope with the devastating effects of climate change.

The most vulnerable sectors of the global economy include agriculture, infrastructure, and energy. The Food and Agriculture Organization (FAO) warns that climate change could reduce global crop yields by up to 30% by 2050, especially in regions that are already facing water scarcity or extreme weather patterns. This reduction in crop yields would exacerbate global food insecurity and drive up food prices, which could affect millions of people across the world, particularly in developing countries. Agriculture plays a central role in the economies of many OIC countries, particularly in countries such as *Pakistan*, *Bangladesh*, *Indonesia*, *Egypt*, and *Nigeria*, where a significant proportion of the population depends on farming for their livelihood. Climate change poses a direct threat to agricultural productivity, through rising temperatures, changing rainfall patterns, and more frequent extreme weather events (FAO, 2021). *Sub-Saharan Africa*: Countries such as *Sudan*, *Mali*, *Somalia*, and *Chad* are experiencing desertification and droughts, which have led to widespread crop failures and food shortages. The *FAO* warns that crop production in some African regions could decline by up to 50% by 2050 due to climate variability (FAO, 2021).

Many OIC countries are water-stressed, facing challenges in accessing and managing water resources. *Saudi Arabia*, *Jordan*, *Kuwait*, and *Yemen* are already among the most water-scarce countries globally, and climate change is expected to exacerbate these conditions (United Nations Development Programme [UNDP], 2021). *Saudi Arabia* and *Kuwait* are highly reliant on desalination for their water needs. However, rising temperatures and increased evaporation rates could strain water resources, threatening both human populations and agriculture (UNDP, 2021). *Pakistan* and *India* share the critical *Indus River Basin*, and changes in glacier melt, precipitation patterns, and water runoff are expected to reduce water availability, affecting millions of people and agricultural productivity (World Bank, 2020).

Hence, the energy sector in OIC countries is highly vulnerable to climate change, particularly in *oil and gas* dependent economies like those in the *MENA*. As the world shifts toward renewable energy, these countries must navigate both the *economic consequences of reduced fossil fuel demand* and the need to *adapt energy infrastructure* to more extreme weather conditions.

10.1. Fossil Fuel Dependency

Saudi Arabia, one of the largest oil exporters in the world, is highly vulnerable to the global transition away from fossil fuels. By 2030, the country's energy exports could drop by *25–30%* as global demand for oil decreases, particularly due to the decarbonization efforts of major economies (International Energy Agency [IEA], 2021). Saudi Arabia's economic diversification efforts, notably through *Vision 2030*, aim to reduce its dependence on oil by investing in *renewable energy*. This includes a goal to produce *50% of energy from renewable sources* by 2030.

Climate risks to energy infrastructure: Extreme temperatures and frequent dust storms are expected to damage energy infrastructure in the *Gulf region*, affecting both oil production and solar energy projects. The **IEA** report warns that failure to adapt could lead to a *loss of up to $10 billion annually* in energy-related economic activities in the region.

11. Azerbaijan's Role as a Global Leader, Player, and Enabler in Climate Action Through Hosting COP29

Azerbaijan's hosting of COP29 in November 2024 positioned the country as a key player in global climate action. The conference highlighted Azerbaijan's growing leadership in the renewable energy sector and its commitment to reducing greenhouse gas emissions by 35% by 2030, relative to 1990 levels. Azerbaijan's National Renewable Energy Action Plan envisions solar energy contributing 20% of its energy mix by 2030, with plans to expand its installed solar capacity from 7 MW in 2022 to 500 MW by 2030. The country also focuses on energy efficiency, water management, and agricultural adaptation to climate change, showcasing its proactive approach to sustainability. (King's College London, 2024).

Key announcements at COP29 included the New Collective Quantified Goal on climate finance, which commits to $1.3 trillion annually by 2035, with $300 billion allocated for developing countries. Additionally, agreements were made on Articles 6.2 and 6.4 of the Paris Rulebook. Azerbaijan's hosting of the conference provided an opportunity for it to foster regional cooperation, especially through its memberships in the OIC and Caspian Sea cooperation, enabling the exchange of best practices and the development of sustainable solutions for neighboring countries.

Azerbaijan's strategic location and energy ambitions solidified its role in shaping the global climate agenda. Hosting COP29 underscored its importance in driving multilateral climate diplomacy and advancing green economy initiatives. This event reinforced Azerbaijan's position as a leader in climate action, both regionally and globally.

12. Conclusion

Azerbaijan's collaboration with the Islamic world in renewable energy investments exemplifies a successful model of regional cooperation. By leveraging the financial, technical, and knowledge resources of its partners, Azerbaijan is making significant strides toward a sustainable and diversified energy future. These efforts not only contribute to the country's economic growth but also reinforce its commitment to global environmental sustainability.

References

ACWA Power. (2021). *Wind energy agreement with Azerbaijan*. ACWA Power. https://www.acwapower.com/news/acwa-power-signs-wind-energy-agreement-with-azerbaijan/

Aliev, H. (2005). *Heydar Aliyev and the Caspian energy policy*. Azerbaijan National Academy of Sciences.

Islamic Development Bank. (2023). *Pakistan: Climate change and green growth—Transitioning to a low-carbon economy*. https://www.isdb.org/publications/pakistan-climate-change-and-green-growth-transitioning-to-a-low-carbon-economy

Food and Agriculture Organization of the United Nations. (2021). *The state of food and agriculture 2021: Making agrifood systems more resilient to shocks and stresses*. Food and Agriculture Organization of the United Nations. https://www.fao.org/documents/card/en/c/cb4476en

Gasimli, V., Huseyn, R., & Huseynov, R. (2024a). What advantages arise from the shift towards sustainable energy sources in resource-rich economies? Empirical insights from Azerbaijan. *International Journal of Energy Economics and Policy*, *14*(1), 12–20. https://doi.org/10.32479/ijeep.15016

Gasimli, V., Huseyn, R., & Huseynov, R. (2024b). Economy-wide and environmental benefits of green energy development in oil-rich countries: Evidence from Azerbaijan. *Economic Annals, Faculty of Economics and Business, University of Belgrade*, *69*(241), 41–64. https://doi.org/10.2298/EKA2441041G

Government of Indonesia. (2022). *Indonesia's updated nationally determined contribution (NDC)*. Ministry of Environment and Forestry. https://www4.unfccc.int/sites/ndcstaging/PublishedDocuments/Indonesia%20First/Updated%20NDC%20Indonesia%202022.pdf

Government of Qatar. (2023). *Qatar's climate change strategy*. Ministry of Environment and Climate Change. https://www.mme.gov.qa/static/media/f9ab4087-7538-4662-a0b3-5d5532f91850

International Energy Agency. (2021). *World energy outlook 2021*. https://www.iea.org/reports/world-energy-outlook-2021

King's College London. (2024). *COP29 outcomes and implications and public perceptions of the climate threat*. King's Policy Institute. https://www.kcl.ac.uk/cop29-outcomes

Masdar. (2020). *Renewable energy projects in Azerbaijan*. Masdar Clean Energy. https://news.masdar.ae/en/news/2020/01/09/12/01/masdar-signs-deals-to-develop-solar-wind-projects-in-azerbaijan

Ministry of Energy of Azerbaijan. (2023). *Renewable energy overview*. Government of Azerbaijan. https://minenergy.gov.az/en/article/energetika-sahesi

Ministry of Environment and Urbanization of Turkiye. (2021). *Turkiye's national climate change strategy*. Government of Turkiye. https://webdosya.csb.gov.tr/db/iklim/editordosya/file/strateji2021.pdf

Moroccan Agency for Sustainable Energy (MASEN). (2022). *Morocco's renewable energy plan*. https://www.masen.ma/en/renewable-energies

President of the Republic of Azerbaijan. (2024, March 1). *Speech by Ilham Aliyev at the 10th Southern Gas Corridor Advisory Council Ministerial Meeting and 2nd Green Energy Advisory Council Ministerial Meeting*. https://president.az/en/articles/view/65151

Saudi Green Initiative. (2021). *Vision 2030 and climate action*. Ministry of Energy, Saudi Arabia. https://www.saudigreeninitiative.org

Sustainable Energy Development Authority (SEDA) Malaysia. (2021). *Malaysia renewable energy roadmap (MyRER) 2021–2035*. SEDA Malaysia. https://www.seda.gov.my/reportal/myrer/

UAE Ministry of Climate Change and Environment. (2022). *Net zero by 2050 roadmap*. Government of the UAE. https://www.moec.gov.ae/en/-/uae-net-zero-by-2050

United Nations Framework Convention on Climate Change (UNFCCC). (2022). *Nationally determined contributions reports*. UNFCCC. https://unfccc.int/NDCs

United Nations Development Programme. (2021). *Water governance in the Arab Region: Managing scarcity and securing the future*. https://www.undp.org/sites/g/files/zskgke326/files/migration/arabstates/ARAB_WATER_REPORT_December_Final_Eng.pdf

United Nations Framework Convention on Climate Change. (2023). *Egypt's updated first nationally determined contribution 2030 (Second Update)*. https://unfccc.int/documents/631506

World Bank. (2020). *Revised estimates of the impact of climate change on extreme poverty by 2030*. https://documents1.worldbank.org/curated/en/706751601388457990/pdf/Revised-Estimates-of-the-Impact-of-Climate-Change-on-Extreme-Poverty-by-2030.pdf

World Bank. (2022). *Caspian Sea wind energy potential report*. World Bank Group. https://documents.worldbank.org/en/publication/documents-reports/documentdetail/098241407142232655/IDU032002f8705c4404fda08acb0bd5e0d4b3d80

World Bank. (2023). *Uzbekistan to cut fossil fuel subsidies and reduce emissions with support from the World Bank*. World Bank Group. https://www.worldbank.org/en/news/press-release/2023/09/06/uzbekistan-to-cut-fossil-fuel-subsidies-and-reduce-emissions

World Bank. (2024, June 21). *Uzbekistan receives $7.5 million in carbon credits for enabling half a million tons of emissions reduction*. World Bank Group. https://www.worldbank.org/en/news/press-release/2024/06/21/uzbekistan-receives-7-5-million-in-carbon-credits-for-enabling-half-a-million-tons-of-emissions-reduction

Chapter 11

Egypt and Carbon Reduction: Transitioning to Renewable and Clean Energy

Alshaymaa Alsadek and Hager Elsayed

The Egyptian Cabinet's Information and Decision Support Center (IDSC), Egypt

1. Introduction

Energy serves as the cornerstone for comprehensive development in all societies. Countries strive to secure their energy needs from various sources. Amid current global challenges and their economic, social, and environmental repercussions, along with the global economic slowdown, renewable energy markets have maintained their dynamism and vitality. Their resilience has been bolstered by flexible legislative frameworks and diverse financing mechanisms that have sustained their competitiveness against traditional energy markets. Forecasts by the International Energy Agency (IEA) indicate that renewable energy sources will constitute more than a third of the total electricity generation worldwide by early 2025 (IEA, 2024). Global investment in clean energy sources also reached around USD 1,740 billion in 2023, compared to USD 1,050 billion in traditional energy sources for the same year (IEA, 2023).

Recently, there has been a call for reliance on more sustainable energy sources as part of countries' efforts to reduce greenhouse gas emissions in compliance with the Paris Agreement and the United Nations Framework Convention on Climate Change (UNFCCC). Consequently, several strategies have been launched by most governments to transition to renewable and clean energy to meet the needs of various economic sectors.

Given Egypt's vast and diverse potential in renewable energy sources, the Egyptian Government has outlined a roadmap for parallel developmental pathways, especially concerning expanding green economy projects, developing and diversifying renewable energy sources, and maximizing their value as a means to mitigate climate change and alleviate the economic burden associated with the use of traditional energy sources. Additionally, Egypt targets expanding partnerships

The Economic Potential of Islamic Countries, Part A:
Economics, Demographics and Financial Services, 261–267

doi:10.1108/978-1-83708-000-720251013

with the private sector and international partners in clean and renewable energy and providing the necessary technology, qualifying it to become one of the largest producers of clean energy in Africa and the world.

2. The Egyptian Government Efforts Toward Transitioning to Renewable Energy

Egypt possesses a vast wealth of renewable energy sources, including hydropower, wind energy, solar energy, and biomass energy. Since 2014, the Government has intensified its efforts to generate and utilize more renewable energy to overcome the increasing difficulties associated with energy. It targeted generating 20% of electricity from renewable sources by 2022 (SIS, 2021). Moreover, Egypt plans to integrate green hydrogen into its comprehensive energy system by 2035, with plans to launch it at a value of USD 40 billion (Sultan, 2023). The renewable energy mix for 2023 is given in Fig 11.1 below:

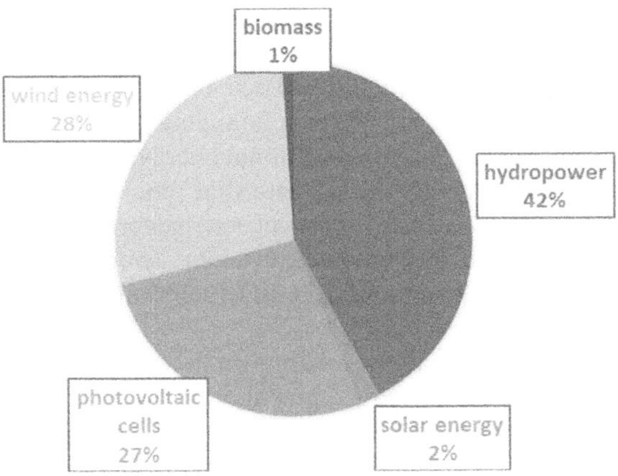

Fig. 11.1. Indicators of the Renewable Energy Sector in Egypt for 2022/2023. *Source*: The New and Renewable Energy Authority, Egypt (NREA, 2023).

In other words, renewable energy projects are the top priority of the Egyptian State. Many important projects based on both wind and solar energy are planned to be executed. One of these projects is the Benban Solar Park, which has revolutionized energy supplies. The Egyptian State has placed itself on the map of clean energy due to the project comprising approximately 31 solar power stations with a capacity of around 1,465 megawatts, equivalent to about 90% of the energy produced from the High Dam. It has provided approximately 10,000 direct and indirect job opportunities, with total investments reaching USD 2 billion. Planned energy mix for 2030 is given in Fig 11.2 below:

The Benban project was not the only breakthrough witnessed by Egypt in the clean and renewable energy sector. Egypt was among the first countries to

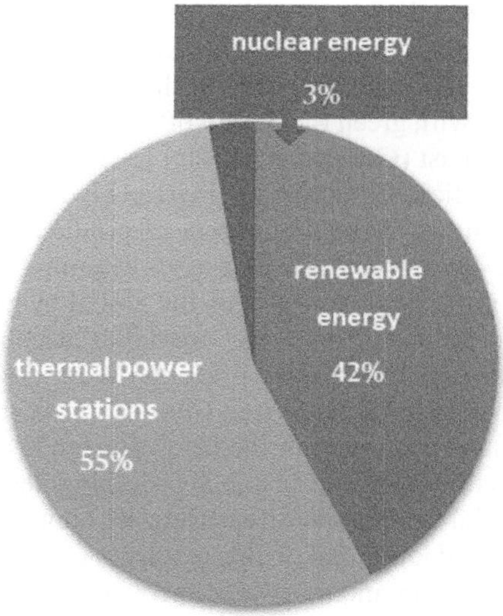

Fig. 11.2. Planned Mix for 2030. *Source*: The New and Renewable Energy Authority, Egypt (NREA, 2023).

establish wind power stations in 2000 and ranks at the forefront of Arab countries in the field of renewable energy. The European Union, in collaboration with the Ministry of Electricity and Renewable Energy, inaugurated the largest wind farm in Africa at the Zafarana, Gabal El Zeit, and Gulf of Suez stations. Wind farms are an important part of Egypt's long-term energy strategy to harness the abundant renewable energy sources available in Egypt.

As a result, Egypt ranks first in the Arab region in electricity production from solar and wind energy, with production rates reaching about 3.5 gigawatts. In Africa, Egypt ranks second in terms of its contribution to solar energy production, accounting for approximately 16%, and third in wind energy production, with a percentage of about 21% (NREA, 2023).

2.1. Green Hydrogen

Green hydrogen is considered the fuel of the future for many countries worldwide. Several countries have adopted legislative frameworks aimed at promoting investment in green hydrogen projects. The Egyptian Government has shown great interest in enhancing the competitiveness of the Egyptian market to attract more foreign direct investment in green hydrogen production. As a result, Egypt ranked fifth in the Arab world and North Africa and 53rd globally in the Green Hydrogen Index by Fitch Solutions 2022 (Fawzy, 2023).

In terms of projects, Egypt tops the list of Arab countries in terms of the number of projects targeting localizing the green hydrogen industry, with approximately 23 projects out of a total of 73 projects in the Arab world (SIS, 2024).

Notably, the first operation to supply a container ship, owned by the global shipping company Maersk, with green fuel (methanol) at the East Port Said port was successful. It is the first container ship in the world to operate on green fuel, and supplying this ship with green fuel in Egypt is the first operation of its kind in Africa and the Middle East (General Authority for Information, 2024).

In addition, the adoption of the National Green Hydrogen Strategy reflects the Egyptian State's recognition of the importance of producing, storing, and trading green hydrogen and green ammonia as part of its economic development strategy. The strategy aims at attracting about 8% of the global hydrogen market (Sultan, 2024). Egypt has also been drafting a law providing incentives for projects concerned with green hydrogen and its derivatives and water desalination plants (SIS, 2023). In addition, the National Hydrogen Council has been established to unify State efforts to stimulate investment in the field of green hydrogen and its derivatives, in line with the requirements of sustainable development and the State's plans for economic and social development, ensuring its competitiveness at both the international and regional levels. All of this reaffirms Egypt's serious commitment to the transition toward clean and renewable energy (Cabinet, 2023).

2.2. Increased Reliance on Natural Gas

Egypt has been diligently working in the previous period to launch projects to replace traditional energy sources with natural gas for environmental, economic, and social reasons. Egypt is one of the leading countries in this field in the Arab and African regions, as evidenced by the following projects adopted by Egypt in the past few decades.

The Natural Gas for Vehicles Project: This project targets converting vehicles from running on gasoline to natural gas to reduce environmental pollution and fuel costs. It has achieved an annual reduction of over two million tons of carbon dioxide equivalent by converting around 534,000 cars to run on compressed natural gas (CNG) since the project's inception.

Expansion in the Use of CNG as a Fuel for Vehicle Supply Project: As part of the presidential initiative to expand the use of natural gas as a fuel for vehicles, the number of stations has significantly increased, reaching nearly 1,000 stations serving about 534,000 gas-operating cars nationwide. Additionally, the first mobile center for converting and maintaining cars to run on natural gas was launched in March 2023, the first of its kind in Egypt and the Middle East. The State plans to expand the use of natural gas in vehicles by providing non-traditional applications and solutions. The center features all the components and equipment used in the conversion process in a single mobile unit, encouraging citizens to convert their cars to run on natural gas. Measures have been taken to facilitate the installment of the conversion cost without interest, in addition to providing incentives to customers.

The Natural Gas for Homes Project: In line with the State's policy to achieve a form of social justice, especially for the neediest areas, the use of natural gas in homes as an alternative to butane gas has been promoted. The number of beneficiaries from natural gas services has exceeded 62 million citizens, and approximately 14.5 million housing units have been connected to the natural gas network. The project has resulted in an annual reduction estimated at about 900,000 tons of carbon dioxide (Cabinet Office, 2023).

3. Multifaceted Challenges Hindering the Transition Toward Clean and Renewable Energy

High cost: The primary challenge facing renewable and clean energy projects is the high cost of restructuring the energy infrastructure and the lack of information about the costs associated with grid connection. This obstacle continues to hamper the competitiveness of Egyptian energy sources in global markets.

Limited demand: There is limited demand for renewable and clean energies, further complicating the situation. Securing the necessary raw materials for renewable energy technologies is also problematic.

Supply chain constraints: Expanding the supply of vital components and raw materials, such as metals needed for wind turbines and electric cars, poses a significant challenge. The rare earth minerals needed to produce wind turbines and electric vehicle batteries are clear examples.

Global fossil fuel support: Worldwide support for fossil fuels remains one of the major obstacles hindering the world's transition to renewable energy. The continued backing of fossil fuels by many governments and industries undermines efforts to promote clean and renewable energy sources.

Energy storage: There is a significant challenge associated with how to store renewable energy sources such as wind and solar power. However, advancements in energy storage technologies may allow consumers to generate and store energy without relying on traditional electric utilities in the future.

4. Requirements for Enhancing the Transition to Clean and Renewable Energy in Egypt

Increased investment: Both the public and private sectors need to boost investments in clean energy projects. A suitable infrastructure is required for transmitting and distributing clean energy, such as building more solar and wind farms and enhancing efficient energy storage systems.

Effective regulatory framework: Developing an effective and supportive regulatory framework for clean energy projects is crucial. For instance, financial incentives need to be provided, and administrative procedures need to be streamlined to encourage investment in clean energy.

Capacity building: Building the capacity of human resources in the field of clean energy is essential. Training and education must be offered to individuals involved in the clean energy sector to enhance their skills and expertise.

Support for research and development: Supporting research and development in the field of clean energy is necessary to foster innovation and technological advancement. It can lead to the development of more efficient and cost-effective clean energy solutions.

International cooperation: Enhancing cooperation with international partners and organizations to transfer technology and exchange experiences in the field of renewable energy is essential to strengthen Egypt's ability to benefit from these technologies and accelerate its transition to clean energy.

5. Opportunities for Partnership with Member States of the Organization of Islamic Cooperation (OIC)

Egypt enjoys a strategic location that makes it a gateway to OIC countries, opening up broad prospects for cooperation in the field of clean and renewable energy. Egypt is also considered a leader in solar and wind energy due to its extensive experience in these fields, making Egyptian expertise and participation with OIC countries a promising opportunity to assist those countries in developing their experiences in these areas.

Furthermore, Egypt can benefit from the experiences of leading countries in the field of clean and renewable energy, such as Saudi Arabia, the United Arab Emirates, and Turkey. Cooperation can be boosted among OIC countries in capacity building and human resource training in the field of clean and renewable energy. Egypt could benefit from training and education programs offered by OIC countries, especially since some member states, such as Bahrain, the United Arab Emirates, Iraq, Iran, Qatar, and Kuwait, are among the largest energy producers and suppliers in the world.

6. Conclusion

The transition to renewable energy is a dynamic issue, the more carbon emissions rise the more the need to renewable energy projects. The declaration of transitioning away from fossil fuel to renewable energy in COP 29th climate summit in Azerbaijan was one of the bravest results of the conference. Countries pledged to triple renewable energy capacity globally by 2030, and they would think again about their economic objectives in light of the environmental emissions. It is a promising opportunity to build common frameworks regarding the transition to clean energy to enhance cooperation among OIC countries that are members in the UNFCCC. Efforts can be made to establish facilitations and incentives to enhance trade and investment exchanges in this sector, conclude agreements for technology and knowledge exchange, provide joint financing for renewable energy projects, leverage the diplomatic network of the organization to facilitate bilateral cooperation between Egypt and member states in the field of renewable energy, and strengthen economic and technical relations in this regard.

References

Cabinet. (2023). *The Prime Minister chairs the meeting of the National Green Hydrogen Council*. https://www.cabinet.gov.eg/News/Details/74327

Cabinet Office. (2023). *2023 Harvest of the Ministry of Petroleum and Mineral Resources*. https://www.cabinet.gov.eg/News/Details/74700

Fawzy, M. (2023). *Policy compass* (Issue 4, p. 23). Information and Decision Support Center. Retrieved from https://idsc.gov.eg/upload/DocumentLibraryIssues/AttachmentE/8444/Egyptian%20Path%20of%20Investments%20in%20Green%20Hydrogen.pdf

General Authority for Information. (2024). *Success of the first operation to supply a container ship with green fuel at East Port Said Port*. https://rb.gy/5h3183

IEA. (2023). *World energy investment 2023*. https://www.iea.org/reports/world-energy-investment-2023/overview-and-key-findings#

IEA. (2024). *Clean sources of generation are set to cover all of the world's additional electricity demand over the next three years*. International Energy Agency. https://www.iea.org/news/clean-sources-of-generation-are-set-to-cover-all-of-the-world-s-additional-electricity-demand-over-the-next-three-years

NREA. (2023). *Annual report 2023*. New and Renewable Energy Authority. http://nrea.gov.eg/Content/reports/Annual%20Report%202023%20Ar.pdf

SIS. (2021). *Benban Solar Power Plant*. General Authority for Information. https://rb.gy/p2im51

SIS. (2023). *Parliament finally approves draft law on incentives for green hydrogen production*. General Authority for Information. https://2u.pw/c6Cu22Yw

SIS. (2024). *Economic development*. General Authority for Information. https://rb.gy/sz7h7m

Sultan, A. (2023). *The Egyptian national hydrogen strategy: Determinants and objectives*. Egyptian Center for Thought and Strategic Studies. Retrieved February 21, 2024, from https://rb.gy/b478gx

Sultan, A. (2024). *A new vision for the Egyptian economy: How does the hydrogen industry contribute to economic growth?* Egyptian Center for Thought and Strategic Studies. https://ecss.com.eg/44456/

Chapter 12

Investments in Green Infrastructure: Challenges and Opportunities

Gehad Omar Elkhateeb

The Egyptian Cabinet's Information and Decision Support Center (IDSC), Egypt

1. Introduction

In light of the momentum surrounding the concept of green transformation, closely related concepts, the increasing interest in environmental and climate issues, and the integration of environmental sustainability dimensions into countries' developmental plans and strategies, the concept of "green" infrastructure has emerged as an alternative to traditional or "gray" infrastructure. The concept of "green" infrastructure refers to any infrastructure system that aims at enhancing and protecting the natural environment directly or indirectly to achieve multiple environmental, economic, and social gains (World Green Infrastructure Network, 2021).

The most prominent of these are supporting the individuals' physical and psychological health, alleviating heat waves, reducing the amount of wastewater and carbon emissions rates, and enhancing climate change mitigation and adaptation measures. In fact, green infrastructure projects represent promising opportunities to attract local and foreign investments (European Commission, 2024).

Greening public investments is a current trend in the Egyptian government. It announced that it aims at raising the percentage of green public investments to 50% in the plan for the current financial year 2024/2025 (Ministry of Planning and Economic Development, 2023), from only 15% of the total public investments when this trend was issued in 2021. It is the first of its kind in raising awareness of sectors and interventions that positively impact the environment, directing the public and private sectors to invest in it, and presenting the performance indicators that measure progress in achieving that goal (Ministry of Planning and Economic Development, Environment, 2021).

These green projects are mainly concentrated in the infrastructure sectors, most notably smart transportation, housing, and new and renewable energy

The Economic Potential of Islamic Countries, Part A:
Economics, Demographics and Financial Services, 269–278

doi:10.1108/978-1-83708-000-720251014

projects in several Egyptian governorates. Cairo, Giza, and Alexandria account for the largest percentage of these projects (Ministry of Planning and Economic Development, 2023).

Despite the still recent concept of green investments, Egypt has taken important steps in the past few years to promote this type of investment. It has developed strategic frameworks and reference guides regulating green investment projects in terms of defining regulatory and legislative procedures and frameworks. Such procedures aim at integrating the environmental dimension into all development sectors while identifying priority work sectors and environmental sustainability standards for each sector.

Based on the above, this section seeks to illuminate the most prominent Egyptian movements to develop regulatory and legislative frameworks for green infrastructure investments and the most important national initiatives for green investment projects in Egypt.

2. Current Egyptian Moves to Enhance Green Infrastructure Investment

2.1. Launching Strategic Frameworks to Enhance Green Infrastructure

Over the past few years, the Egyptian government has paid great attention to spreading the culture of sustainable development and expanding the integration of its economic, social, and environmental dimensions into the planning system. The aim is to achieve an integrated and fair planning system to promote green investments in economic sectors in general and the infrastructure sector in particular. The most prominent Egyptian strategic directions in this regard are:

2.1.1. Launching Egypt Vision 2030

Egypt Vision 2030 is a national agenda whose "first" version was launched in February 2016. It represents the State's long-term strategic plan to achieve the principles and goals of sustainable development in all fields and localize them in various state agencies. Egypt Vision 2030 is based on comprehensive sustainable development and balanced regional development. It reflects the three dimensions of sustainable development: the economic, social, and environmental (Egypt Vision 2030).

In its updated version of 2022, the vision adopted several goals, mainly the fifth goal, related to "advanced infrastructure," which reflects Egypt's awareness of the importance of enhancing investments in green infrastructure. This goal includes a set of basic programs, the most prominent of which are (Ministry of Planning and Economic Development, 2022):

- *Providing safe and sustainable transportation systems*: Egypt Vision 2030 aims at providing safe and sustainable transportation systems to improve individuals' living standards, raise the efficiency of transportation services provided to all users, maximize the benefit of Egypt's geographical position in the heart of the world, and exploit the economic advantage of the two means of river transportation and railway transportation and increasing their competitiveness. They are considered one of the least fuel-consuming means of transportation, which reduces polluting emissions and improves the surrounding environment and the health of citizens. The most important ways to achieve the goal are:

- Gradual shift toward "clean" means of transportation (electric and hydrogen) that do not use fossil fuels to reduce pollution and spread a culture of saving fuel.
- Expanding "smart" transportation applications that use modern technology applications to manage means of transportation and link them to users and the road network.
- Expanding passenger transportation services with distinguished service (safe, easy to access, smart, air-conditioned, Internet service available, and time-saving) to motivate private car owners to switch to using public transportation in their daily trips.
- Accelerating the implementation of sustainable infrastructure projects for rapid mass transportation, such as electric trains, subways, and monorails, and integrating with other means of passenger transportation.
- Integrating sustainable transport concepts into urban planning of cities and encouraging non-motorized transport, including walking and cycling, within small towns and large city neighborhoods.

- *Strengthening sustainable energy systems and resources*: Egypt Vision 2030 aims for the energy sector to meet all development needs for energy resources and maximize the efficient use of its various sources (traditional and renewable), contributing effectively to advancing the economy and preserving the environment. It seeks to reduce the negative effects of the depletion of traditional energy sources, which are depleted by nature, and to increase reliance on renewable energy sources while achieving leadership. The most important ways to achieve the goal are (Egypt Vision, 2030):

  - Increasing the capacity of the electrical network to absorb electricity from renewable sources and the resulting disparity in the energy discharged into it.
  - Creating an attractive climate for investment in new and renewable energy and cooperating with research centers to solve the problem of the high cost of energy storage.
  - Following up on developments in electrical energy storage technology related to renewable energy systems such as lithium batteries, green hydrogen production, and thermal energy storage systems, and studying their benefit in maintaining the stability of the electricity network.
  - Encouraging the uses of decentralized, small-scale renewable energies in industrial, tourism, residential, and service facilities, such as solar heaters and rooftop photovoltaic stations, the use of biogas in rural homes as an alternative to butane cylinders, and providing appropriate finance

mechanisms to achieve the gradual transformation of energy consumers into producers to meet their energy needs.

- o Stimulating the private sector's participation in implementing projects to produce electricity from renewable energy by creating a competitive market for electricity, issuing and updating the feed-in tariff, and implementing the net metering system.
- o Disseminating technology to improve energy efficiency to reduce electricity and fuel consumption in various sectors, such as energy management programs in facilities and the Egyptian market's shift to energy-saving electrical and mechanical devices, activating codes for energy-efficient buildings, and converting cars to run on gas.

2.1.2. Environmental Sustainability Standards Guide

The Ministry of Planning and Economic Development launched the *Environmental Sustainability Standards Guide: Strategic Framework for Green Recovery* in cooperation with the Ministry of Environment and coordination with relevant government agencies. It is the first guide of its kind that aims at raising awareness of sectors and interventions that positively affect the environment, guiding public and private sectors to invest in, and presenting key performance indicators that measure progress in achieving that goal. The aim is to pave the way for serious and ambitious steps toward achieving sustainable development, of which the green economy is one of its basic foundations (Ministry of Planning and Economic Development, 2021).

Therefore, the methodology for preparing this guide sets out general indicative standards to integrate sustainable and equitable development standards into development plans. It is prepared in a way that maximizes the return on public investment and development returns, improves the quality of life of citizens, and ensures achieving a specific development goal of doubling the proportion of public green investments that take the dimensions of sustainability into account. On this basis, the guide included many codes aimed at greening investments in various sectors (transport, water resources and irrigation, energy, health, etc.), the most prominent of which are (Environmental Sustainability Standards Guide):

- *Water resources and irrigation sector*: The Egyptian Code for Water Resources and Irrigation for the year 2003, issued by Minister of Housing, Utilities, and Urban Communities Resolution No. 350 of 2003, includes unified systems for managing irrigation and drainage networks and implementing their projects, including work to protect and develop marine coasts. It also includes testing methods and designing and implementing standards, testing construction materials, tightening control over all construction works, irrigation and drainage network management, and mechanical and electrical works.

    - *Energy sector*: Code for connecting wind plants to the electrical grid, code for connecting solar plants to the electrical grid

(March 2017), and an energy efficiency code (Environmental Sustainability Standards Guide).

- *Transport sector*: The Egyptian code for river transport, the Egyptian code for urban and cellular road works (road code), and road project evaluations should include an accurate assessment of the effects of ambient noise so that it does not exceed 3 decibels (Environmental Sustainability Standards Guide).

Sustainability Codes in Housing Sector, the most important of which are (Environmental Sustainability Standards Guide):

- *The Egyptian Code for the Reuse of Treated Wastewater in Agriculture No. (501)* specifies the requirements and standards for using treated wastewater within and around cities for agricultural purposes.
- *The Code of Wastewater Collection and Treatment Systems Design and Implementation Conditions for Egyptian Villages*: It is concerned with possible applications for sanitation projects in Egyptian villages, whether for the work of assembling networks, lifting stations, and expulsion lines or treatment works to reach the required standards in accordance with the regulating laws and decisions.
- *The Egyptian Code for Improving Energy Efficiency in Buildings No. (306)*, which includes requirements for improving energy efficiency in air-conditioned or non-air-conditioned commercial buildings.
- *The Egyptian Code for Designing Water Desalination Plants Standards,* which is related to producing new units or materials suitable for further use.
- *The Egyptian Code for Housing and Residential Group Design, Code No. (602)* aims at establishing the foundations, standards, environmental controls, and technical requirements that must be met as a minimum in the design of the dwelling and its components and the planning, design, and development of the residential group.

Health sector and green health facilities: This is a guide for designing green hospitals and health facilities. The guide adheres to the design standards for hospitals and health facilities and codes related to the safety of building and facility design. The first stage of the guide deals with the green hospital evaluation system, and the second stage deals with how to apply sustainable design during the various stages of construction and operation of the buildings (Environmental Sustainability Standards Guide).

2.2. The National Initiative for Smart Green Projects

The initiative was launched within the framework of efforts aimed at achieving sustainable development and in the context of implementing Egypt Vision 2030 by preserving the environment, improving the quality of life, taking the rights of future generations into account, and implementing the National Climate Change Strategy 2050. The initiative is being implemented in the Republic's governorates in cooperation with national and international partners by developing a map at the governorate level for green and smart projects, linking them to financing agencies, and attracting the necessary investments from inside or outside the country (Egyptian National Competitiveness Council).

The initiative targets smart green projects, which fall into the following categories: the large-sized projects category, the medium-sized projects category, the small local projects category (Decent Life Initiative), the projects submitted by startups, development projects related to women, climate change and sustainability, and community initiatives and participations, non-profit initiatives, and participations (State Information Service, 2023).

The evaluation and selection process among the projects submitted for the initiative takes the availability of several criteria into account, the most important of which are ensuring the presence of the green component and the technological/smart component in the project, achieving empowerment and equal opportunities to enhance the participation of women and youth in economic activity, and supporting the State's direction in transitioning toward a green economy. In addition, there are criteria of replicability, expansion of application, and sustainability of development impact supported by realistic results and reliable data (El-Saeed, 2023).

In the context of ensuring the implementation of governance principles and sustainability in achieving this initiative's desired goals, the initiative included a main component aimed at capacity building. Many training programs were organized for the executive committees to explain the tasks assigned to them, introduce what green and smart projects are, and the mechanisms for using the electronic platform and how to submit projects on it. In addition, programs were implemented to prepare specialized evaluators to join the membership of the governorate teams.

2.3. The Green Village Initiative

It aims at qualifying the villages under the Decent Life Initiative to comply with global environmental standards and enable them to manage their land and water resources sustainably in the long term through an independent verification body, the Egyptian Green Building Association. The initiative has already rehabilitated the village of Fares and, then, recently, the village of Nahtay in Gharbia. The goal is to have a successful model in every governorate, that is, 20 villages in 20 governorates. Therefore, the governors are informed to disseminate these experiences at the internal level of each governorate, which encourages the localization of the sustainable development goals, taking the environmental dimension into account (Ministry of Planning and Economic Development, 2021).

2.4. Sustainable/Integrated Cities (Fourth-Generation Cities)

The State has recently expanded the launching of the fourth-generation cities (37 cities with an area of about 380,000 feddans) (El-Menshawy, 2023). The fourth-generation cities are characterized by increasing the green areas, exploiting renewable energy resources, providing a healthy life, and providing everyone with access to safe, sustainable, low-cost transportation systems. Meanwhile, they apply all sustainability standards, including waste recycling, ensuring the implementation of green building standards, and providing all services electronically. Moreover, some projects that contribute to providing job opportunities for young people and achieving economic growth have been completed (El-Menshawy, 2023).

2.5. The Green Pyramid Code for Sustainability of Government Buildings

The Green Pyramid Rating System code aims at evaluating green buildings and encouraging the application of its principles. It passed in multiple stages, which aimed at disseminating and introducing this system, training on it, and applying it in evaluating the buildings' sustainability. It is to be updated according to future requirements since it was presented to scientists, researchers, and sustainability partners at several levels until decision No. 294 of 2017 was issued by His Excellency Minister of Housing at the time, Mostafa Madbouly, to implement the Green Pyramid system to evaluate the sustainability of buildings attached to this decision (Egyptian Gazette, 2019).

3. The Future of Investment in Green Infrastructure in Egypt

Despite positive Egyptian moves to promote green investments in development sectors in general and the infrastructure sector in particular, major challenges limit the State's ability to expand such investments. However, there are still promising opportunities that can be considered cornerstones in overcoming these challenges and strengthening regional and international partnerships in green infrastructure, as follows:

3.1. Challenges

- The high cost of implementing environmental policies to obtain renewable energy compared to traditional energy.
- High cost of research and development in green environmental technologies.
- Population increases at significant rates, which poses a burden on the infrastructure and traditional energy sectors.
- Weak sources of green financing (mitigation and adaptation projects) by developed countries (causing climate crises) for developing countries.
- Limited role of the private sector in financing mitigation and adaptation projects, including green infrastructure projects, as a result of low investor awareness of the high returns on green investment projects.
- The concept of investments in green infrastructure isstill new, and the lack of local experiences and practices in this regard, which limits the possibility of launching new initiatives and projects in this field.

3.2. Opportunities for Partnerships and Investments

- Providing a framework that integrates the environmental dimension into the country's strategies and investment plans and ensuring the application of environmental sustainability standards and codes in various economic sectors.
- The Egyptian Government's current approach is to green public investments to reach 50% in next year's plan 2024/2025. Such investments focus mainly on smart transportation projects, the housing sector, and renewable energy projects.
- Egypt was the first country in the Middle East and North Africa to issue green sovereign bonds in 2020 (23), and the proceeds from the sale of the bonds were allocated to finance clean transportation, renewable energy, sustainable management of drinking water, and sanitation, energy efficiency, and other projects (World Bank, 2022).
- Egypt grants tax incentives for investment projects in the electricity and renewable energy sector, as well as other green infrastructure projects.
- The infrastructure sector in Egypt is developing rapidly. Egypt's ranking has improved by 12 places in the Market Access and Infrastructure Index of the Global Index of Economic Openness, reaching 88th globally out of 157 countries in 2020. In addition, its ranking has been advanced in the Infrastructure Index in the Global Competitiveness Report, from 56th out of 140 countries in 2018 to 52nd out of 141 countries in 2019 (Egypt Vision, 2030).
- The remarkable expansion of the fourth-generation cities (37 new sustainable cities) nationwide, which provide promising opportunities for investments in green infrastructure.

4. Conclusion

At the end of this chapter, it is important to emphasize the main determinants of the sustainable development process, which can be extracted from all the topics discussed above. The first of which is technology: the new outside-the-box ideas it entails, the different methods to enhance the uses of current resources, and the use of modern technical tools, artificial intelligence, science, and new research in the field of adaptation and mitigation techniques of the effects of climate change and renewable energy transition technology. The second is finance: decision-makers in any country will not be able to exploit ideas and implement them with the help of modern technologies except by developing the necessary financial resources, inventing new ones, and establishing green investment cooperation funds among OIC countries to achieve sustainable development goals. The third is capacity building: the human element is one of the most important determinants, and without it, countries cannot take successful steps toward sustainable development. Cooperation among OIC countries in the field of building human capabilities, transferring expertise, and benefiting from the experiences of successful countries in any of the areas of sustainable development is considered the basic foundation for the sound transition from traditional economic development to sustainable development provided the use of innovative scientific and methodological instruments. This could be achieved by participating in scientific conferences, research missions, educational workshops and seminars, and international cooperation among universities and scientific research centers. The fourth is national, regional, and international regulatory frameworks: most countries have already taken great strides in building strategies and frameworks, such as signing international agreements on environment, climate change, and sustainable development, building national strategies for sustainable development, and integrating the environmental dimension into all strategic plans for state development. However, most countries still lack governance principles in their regulatory frameworks and monitoring and evaluation tools to more effectively and accurately implement the objectives of strategies concerned with the environment and sustainable development. OIC member states must pay attention to these determinants in the near future to better exploit current countries' resources and preserve future generations' rights.

References

Egyptian Gazette. (2019, April 11). *Ministry of housing, utilities, and urban communities* [Decision No. 294 of 2017, Issue No. 85]. Retrieved from https://www.egypt-gbc.org/ratings.html

Egyptian National Competitiveness Council. (2022, August 7). *What is the national initiative for smart green projects?* https://rb.gy/42taw5

Egypt Vision. (2030). *Presidency of the Arab Republic of Egypt*. Egypt Vision 2030. https://www.presidency.eg/ar/%D9%85%D8%B5%D8%B1/%D8%B1%D8%A4%D9%8A%D8%A9-%D9%85%D8%B5%D8%B1-2030

El-Menshawy, R. (2023, January 29). *Fourth generation cities and the future of sustainable urban development in Egypt*. Information and Decision Support Center. https://www.idsc.gov.eg/Article/details/7864

El-Saeed, H. (2023, March 19). *The national initiative for smart green projects "A new step on the road to green transformation"*. Information and Decision Support Center. https://www.idsc.gov.eg/Article/details/8273

Environmental sustainability standards guide: Strategic framework for green recovery. (2021). Ministry of Planning and Economic Development, & Ministry of Environment. Retrieved from https://mped.gov.eg/adminpanel/sharedFiles/EN-Final_Environmental_Sustainability_Standards_Guide_b75.pdf

European Commission. (2024). Green infrastructure. Retrieved from https://environment.ec.europa.eu/topics/nature-and-biodiversity/green-infrastructure_en

Ministry of Planning and Economic Development. (2021). *Environmental sustainability standards guide: Strategic framework for green recovery*. https://mped.gov.eg/DynamicPage?id=95

Ministry of Planning and Economic Development. (2022). *Sustainable development strategy*. Egypt Vision 2030 (pp. 147–150). https://mped.gov.eg/Files/Egypt_Vision_2030_EnglishDigitalUse.pdf

Ministry of Planning and Economic Development. (2023, October 1). *Deputy minister of planning and economic development inaugurates the "Be an Ambassador" initiative workshop "Greening Public Investments"*. https://mped.gov.eg/singlenews?id=5125&lang=ar

Ministry of Planning and Economic Development. (2021). *Before the Planning and Budget Committee of the House of Representatives, in the presence of Dr. Hala El-Said, Minister of Planning and Economic Development: Dr. Gamil Helmy, Assistant Minister for Sustainable Development Plan Follow-up, reviews the most prominent indicators of the first phase of the National Project for Developing the Egyptian Countryside "Decent Life"*. https://rb.gy/n3qrsn

Ministry of Planning and Economic Development, Ministry of Environment. (2021). *Environmental sustainability standards guide. Strategic framework for green recovery* (1st ed., pp. 10, 11). Retrieved from https://mped.gov.eg/adminpanel/sharedFiles/EN-Final_Environmental_Sustainability_Standards_Guide_b75.pdf

State Information Service. (2023, November 10). *The national initiative for smart green projects*. https://rb.gy/b6sf34

World Bank. (2022, March 15). *Supporting Egypt's inaugural green bond issuance*. https://rb.gy/nd3qqj

World Green Infrastructure Network. (2021, April 12). *Key definition: Green infrastructure*. https://worldgreeninfrastructurenetwork.org/key-definition-green-infrastructure/